D0016613

No Intermissions

Also by Carol Easton

Jacqueline du Pré
The Search for Sam Goldwyn
Straight Ahead: The Story of Stan Kenton

No Intermissions

The Life of Agnes de Mille

CAROL EASTON

Little, Brown and Company Boston New York Toronto London

First Edition

Library of Congress Cataloging-in-Publication Data

Easton, Carol.
No intermissions : the life of Agnes de Mille / Carol Easton. — 1st ed.
p. cm.
Includes bibliographical references and index.
ISBN 0-316-19970-2
1. De Mille, Agnes. 2. Dancers — United States — Biography. 3. Choreographers — United States — Biography. I. Title.
GV1785.D36E27 1996
792.8′028′092 — dc20
[B] 95-8599

10 9 8 7 6 5 4 3 2 1

MV-NY

Published simultaneously in Canada by Little, Brown & Company (Canada) Limited

Printed in the United States of America

For Marguerite Courtney

Contents

Pay attention to the phrasing of every step, even of the exercises you practice daily. Each has a beginning, a development, climax, and decrescendo — the release is as important as the start or the highest point of effort. Finish through. Don't just let go when the hardest part has been achieved. Try to consider the step as a whole, a long curve, and sustain throughout.

To a Young Dancer

No Intermissions

Introduction

In 1942, every moviegoer in the world knew that "De Mille" meant power and wealth. Agnes de Mille, however, had neither.

Born into a family of driven overachievers who viewed the world from high moral ground, Agnes grew up with all the advantages of the intellectual and artistic upper class. What she wanted most, however, was forbidden: to dance. When she did start, it was with two enormous handicaps: her body and her age.

As a dancer and choreographer, she had struggled through fourteen years of dead ends and wild-goose chases on two continents, acquiring limited artistic recognition and a mountain of debt. Romantically, her luck was poor and her judgment worse. Lovers had rejected or betrayed her; one of them died. At the age of thirty-six, spinsterhood, her greatest fear, had come upon her. As an artist and a woman, she considered herself a failure. But in the de Mille family, failure was not allowed.

Dancers in the classes she attended were mystified by the tiny woman with child-sized feet, older than most of them, heavy in bust and beam, always in disarray with holes in her tights, masses of uncontrollable red hair — an ugly duckling who would never become a swan queen. Her dances were uncategorizable, neither classical nor modern, making her an easy target for purists in both camps. Her occasional work in films and on Broadway had ended disastrously. Her most ambitious venture — a touring company that performed her own work — had disintegrated. The most crushing disappointment had come the previous year, when the newly formed Ballet Theatre, seemingly the ideal home for her work, pointedly did not invite her to join them. As a guest artist, she had choreographed ballets for their first two seasons, but they had rejected her latest offering. The only job available to her was dancing in a nightclub — a lateral, if not backward, move.

The future of the world was uncertain; a war was under way, and the United States had entered it. Agnes's personal future looked grim. Not even she could have believed that she was about to make history in the ballet world, become the Queen of Broadway, and marry the love of her life.

Agnes said "one cannot be more than a dancer," but no other dancer has approached the breadth of her achievements.[1] By synthesizing the brilliance of classical ballet technique, the freedom of modern dance, and the familiarity of folk dances, she created an original kind of movement that told a story in a theatrically striking way, thus becoming the first

American-born choreographer to reach a mass public. Her twenty-one ballets include two classics that are performed all over the world. Her dances for *Oklahoma!* permanently changed the look of the American musical. In the winter of 1944–45, with three hit musicals — *Oklahoma!, One Touch of Venus,* and *Bloomer Girl* — running simultaneously on Broadway, she became the first woman to equal the accomplishments of Berlin, Gershwin, and Porter; eleven more Broadway musicals, including *Carousel, Brigadoon,* and *Gentlemen Prefer Blondes,* were yet to come. She was the first woman to choreograph *and* direct a large-scale Broadway musical, and the first woman president of a national labor union. Her books on dance are arguably the finest, and certainly the most readable, on the subject. As a spokesperson for the arts in this country, she brought tears to the stony eyes of bureaucrats. Concurrent with all these activities, she maintained a marriage and raised a child. "If you had been active in the court of Louis XIV," designer Oliver Smith wrote after her famous demolition of McCarthyite Hedda Hopper on national television, "you probably would have changed the history of the world."[2]

She has been called a national treasure, as American as a cowboy, or the Gold Rush — or Lizzie Borden. To her detractors she was an arrogant, stubborn, cantankerous, ruthless, self-dramatizing, full-of-herself virago. To her admirers she was a class act, in a class by herself — an exciting, courageous, warm, understanding, and endlessly entertaining friend. Examples of her loyalty, her generosity, and her monumental ego are legion. So are examples of her wit: Sylvia Fine "talks like a lawn sprinkler"; Leonard Bernstein had "a sliver of mirror for a heart"; Joan Crawford's apartment was "the dazzling white of cheap dentures"; and the Lennon sisters "had voices like trapped flies."

"The vile particulars of my life are all in my books,"[3] Agnes said, but we cannot see ourselves from every angle, and certainly not from the Busby Berkeley perspective that reveals patterns not visible to the dancers. Her memoirs are colorful and candid, accurate in spirit but not in every detail (she also said, "I don't think facts matter except in a dictionary or an encyclopedia"[4] — an exaggeration, but not entirely untrue), and skewed by her admittedly opinionated point of view. In her books, as in her choreography, she danced to the brink of her deepest feelings, then skipped away with a joke. In her real life, nothing was ever that simple.

o n e

Genes

Agnes de Mille's genetic cards were dealt from a deck stacked with the qualities of women born to prevail. Her mother and grandmothers had the strength and the stamina of pioneers; one can imagine any of them reining in a team of runaway horses with one hand, meticulously stitching a quilt with another, and removing her own appendix with a third, all the while planning what to serve for supper. History neglects them, for the history of their time was made by men, and extramarital ambition for a woman was unthinkable. They planned, pushed, and applauded not for their own dreams, but for those of their husbands and children. Even when one of Agnes's remarkable grandmothers managed, after being prematurely widowed, to create her own history, it was as Mrs. H. C. De Mille.

The enterprising widow, born Matilda Beatrice Samuel (known as Beatrice, or "Bebe"), provided the Jewish thread in Agnes's hereditary tapestry. Beatrice was eighteen when her parents (the German-Jewish Sylvester Samuel, a businessman, and his Ashkenazy wife, Cecilia) emigrated from England in 1871. They settled in Brooklyn, and there, at a meeting of the local music and literary society, Bebe met a tall, redheaded student who shared her love of the theater. He was Henry Churchill De

Mille, descended from the Dutch Episcopalian DeMils who had emigrated to America in 1658. Like Beatrice, Henry was born in 1853, but in vastly different circumstances. While she was growing up in a middle-class English household, Henry's father, a North Carolinian, was fighting on the losing side in the Civil War.* As a boy in those difficult times, Henry dreamed of a career as a playwright — he wrote his first play at fifteen — but his parents sent him to New York to pursue not his dream but theirs, and he entered Columbia College as a theology student. He changed his major, however, to education, a field with broader possibilities.

Henry was tall, slender, and mild-mannered; it's unlikely that he had known many Jews, and Beatrice's dark good looks and zaftig figure must have seemed to him exotic. Bebe was intelligent, educated, forthright, and so strong-willed that in 1876, in spite of, or perhaps because of, her parents' objections to her Gentile suitor, she converted to Henry's faith and married him.

In 1881, Henry and Beatrice were living in Manhattan with their two

* William Edward DeMill — Henry later added the "e" — was a merchant and local politician.

sons: three-year-old William Churchill and the infant Cecil Blount. When Henry's teaching job permitted, he wrote and produced amateur plays and worked as a play reader for the Madison Square Theatre. There he met and teamed up with a young stage manager, David Belasco, whose drive and commercial instincts complemented Henry's literary talent. Together they produced melodramas, mostly written by De Mille and directed by Belasco, which were popular enough to inspire this anonymous doggerel: "Nor should it be forgot that no fiasco/Existed for De Mille or for Belasco."*

Henry wanted more than commercial success; he wanted recognition as a serious playwright, and in 1891 he got it, for his adaptation of a naturalistic German drama about labor.† The play was well received, and Henry, at thirty-nine, was financially secure enough to buy seventy-six acres in Pompton Lakes, New Jersey. Here he built an imposing three-story Victorian house overlooking the lake. With a new baby daughter, Agnes Beatrice, his family flourished. He began work on a new play and preached as lay reader in the local Episcopal Church. Life may have seemed, after his early struggles, too good to be true. As is often the case, it was. In 1893, after he and his family celebrated their first Christmas in their new home, Henry De Mille contracted a fatal case of typhoid. Legend has it that on his deathbed he implored his wife to keep his sons away from careers in the theater. Beatrice, who loved the theater and had enthusiastically supported her husband's theatrical aspirations, directed this evasive reply to his corpse: "May your sons be as fine and noble and good and honest as you were. May they follow in your steps . . ."[1]

At forty, Beatrice was suddenly a widow with three children, a house, a $20,000 insurance settlement, and no savings. William was fourteen, Cecil eleven, little Agnes not yet two. Beatrice's feelings are not recorded, but her actions inspire awe: eight weeks after Henry's death, she opened the Henry C. De Mille School for Girls in her home. Almost simultaneously, she set herself up as the second woman playbroker in America, with an office on Broadway.

---

* There were ultimately five collaborations. The *Main Line,* in which Henry played the male lead, was produced at the Lyceum Theatre in 1885; it was followed by *The Wife, Lord Chumley, The Charity Ball,* and *Men and Women.*

† *The Lost Paradise* by Ludwig Fulda.

The speed with which Beatrice opened the school was dizzying, but the idea was logical enough. In the early days of her marriage she had taught elocution at a boys' school in Brooklyn, and in Pompton Lakes she had helped start a school for the children of underpaid steelworkers, a labor of love and of conscience. Now she needed to be paid for her labor; but she was better at negotiating money than at managing it, and the school's fortunes floundered. As they did, her career as a playwright's agent flourished.

In the business world of the 1890s, women were secretaries; at higher levels nobody took them seriously, least of all themselves, and certainly not in the Broadway theater. Her natural chutzpah reinforced by desperation, Beatrice barged into this bastion of sexism with every appearance of confidence. She had always negotiated her husband's contracts; now, shrewdly, she staked out virgin territory by building a client list of women playwrights, particularly those whose work promoted the controversial idea of women's equality. She even wrote, in collaboration with a young woman dramatist, an autobiographical play; it failed commercially, but it drew attention to her as an exponent of what would one day be called women's liberation, and like-minded women responded by becoming her clients.

Two years after Henry's death, little Agnes died of spinal meningitis. The unsinkable Beatrice carried on. She enrolled her younger son, Cecil, in a military school in Pennsylvania and arranged for William to study at a gymnasium in Freiburg, Germany. When William returned to New York, he attended Columbia University. Like both his parents, he was strongly drawn to the theater, but in deference to his father's deathbed request, he studied engineering instead. In his senior year, however, he signed up for a playwrighting class and began his life's work.

From Columbia, William went on to the American Academy of Dramatic Arts. He had his father's tall, lean physique, but he was stronger and more athletic; in college he had gone out for track, fencing, and boxing and had played tennis with a passion that would endure all his life. His curly brown hair was already thinning; his face, like his body, was long and thin, with a hawkish nose and mournful brown eyes. Girls admired him for his wit and enthusiasm, but from a proper distance, for his mother insisted that her sons remain pure until marriage, thus ensuring that any premarital sexual experience would be riddled with guilt.[2] His letters to Anna George during their engagement reveal a strain of deep romanticism and a profound ignorance of women — a dangerous but not uncommon combination in young men of his time and class. Still, compared to his bride-to-be, William was a veritable guru of sex. If William strove for virtue, Anna Angela George personified it.

Anna's childhood existence was poor and peripatetic. Her father, Henry George, had left school and his parents' Philadelphia home at the age of thirteen and supported himself as an errand boy, seaman, typesetter, printer, and gold miner, all the while reading omnivorously and developing his revolutionary economic ideas. In 1861 he eloped with the Anglo-Irish-Catholic Annie Corsina Fox, who had grown up in Australia. Henry was twenty-one, Annie just seventeen. Her family disapproved, and for good reason: Henry had no money.

Henry George's Episcopalian father had published religious books, but Henry invented his own religion, the Single Tax, and wrote his own Bible, *Progress and Poverty.* "He who makes should have," said George; "he who saves should enjoy." Taxes should be placed only on land, and on such natural resources as oil, natural gas, and minerals, all of which belong to the people; labor should not be taxed, but where there is a natural monopoly, the benefits should accrue to the people.

During the years George spent writing his great work, the couple's financial situation wobbled from precarious to dire while their family grew. Anna, the youngest of their four children, was born in San Francisco in 1877. Two years later, Henry's book was finally published.

Progress and Poverty would become a classic, but the family's life did not improve immediately. For a time George worked on a New York newspaper while his wife ran a boardinghouse in San Francisco. By 1881, however, the family was reunited in Greenwich Village, and Henry was internationally famous. In that decade, *Progress and Poverty* sold more copies worldwide than any other book except the Bible.

Henry George was a true American original, self-made and self-taught, honored at home and abroad for his economic philosophy and his outstanding oratorical gifts.[3] Among his admirers were Sun Yat-sen, John Dewey, Count Leo Tolstoy (in Tolstoy's novel *Resurrection,* the hero goes into exile in Siberia with a copy of *Progress and Poverty* under his arm) — and Henry De Mille. The two Henrys were friends, and their children attended the Horace Mann School.* At the age of eleven, Anna asked the twelve-year-old William to marry her. He declined.[4] Nine years later, he would change his mind.

Publicly, Henry George was an icon, an authentic Great Man; his wife and children revered him. In Anna George de Mille's biography of her father, both of her parents glow with saintliness. Henry is generous, humble, modest, devoted to children, his only fault a "trace of impatience" when he called his children to him. His wife never thinks of herself and never complains — even though, in the early years of her marriage, she was forced to pawn her jewelry and was so close to starvation after the birth of her second child that her husband begged money from a stranger on the street. In Anna's version of her childhood, her mother was a marvel of "tact and managerial genius" who could and did rise to any occasion, including providing meals for unexpected guests; the presence of two servants is noted only in passing. The family gathered in the "shabby, cozy sitting-room . . . for study, reading, games, and fancy needlework and mending."[5] As Annie, an expert seamstress, taught her daughters to sew, they all sang. Indeed, as Anna depicted it, someone always seemed to be singing somewhere in the house. Her mother sang the alto parts of operettas and grand operas; her father, when deep in thought, absentmindedly whistled a few bars of "The Battle Hymn of the Republic" or "Yankee Doodle."[6] To their youngest child, Henry and Annie George were perfect partners in an ideal marriage — a perception that would create impossible expectations in her own marriage.

In 1897, after ignoring doctors' warnings and wearing himself out in an unsuccessful campaign for mayor of New York, Henry George died suddenly of a heart attack, leaving his family in emotional chaos. Anna was twenty — only five feet tall, but with the energy of a titan. Her piercing blue eyes were "of an intensity to stop speech"; masses of golden red hair flowed to her waist, and her tiny hands and size one feet were a source of great pride.[7] William, whom she had adored since childhood, gave her his class ring, and they became officially engaged five years later,

* The De Milles lived at 119 Waverly Place in Greenwich Village; the Horace Mann School was nearby, on University Place.

in 1902. In his postproposal euphoria William wrote, with unknowing clairvoyance, "I have kissed you as no man has ever kissed you, or will again."[8]

He was teaching fencing at his mother's school in Pompton Lakes and writing one-act plays; Anna was living with her mother in New York. They saw each other only on weekends, but William wrote often, on notepaper headed "The Dreamery," his attic studio in his mother's house. He was by then twenty-four, but his letters are those of a painfully earnest adolescent. "If this isn't heaven it's as near as I care to get . . . You are my image of God . . . I am absolutely yours forever . . . I cannot live without you . . . As our engagement gets older my longing for you gets much more intense . . . I never believed that I could so madly crave any living mortal."[9] She is his ideal, "the truest, most helpful little woman that ever inspired a man to work and love . . . I worship you more than my honor . . . I respect you as I do no woman except my mother."[10] "You are the one woman in the world who can give me the perfect understanding which every man craves."[11]

The impatient fiancé occupied himself playing the piano, riding his horse, playing tennis, taking long walks "with my gun for company," and writing *Strongheart,* a play about an Indian chief in love with a white woman.[12] When Anna suffered from premarital tension, understandable if for no reason other than her total ignorance of sex, William attributed it to the fact that her mother treated her "as if you were about two years old. . . . It is your constant and intimate relations with your mother (sleeping in the same room etc.) that is keeping you in this nervous condition."[13] As the wedding day approached, his letters quivered with anticipation: "I want to clasp you in my arms and feel your beautiful tender body next to mine — and feel you thrill with the same intense passion of love that I feel . . . I adore you through eternity."[14] After all this excruciating suspense, they were married on March 30, 1903.

Anna moved into the Dreamery, but the new bride cannot have had an easy time in the house of her formidable mother-in-law.[15] By fall, she and William had their own apartment in Manhattan, with enough expectations for several lifetimes. He thought her an angel; she thought him a genius. They had both suffered the loss of their fathers — for William, this occurred when he was in the throes of puberty, which exacerbated the trauma — but they had otherwise been sheltered and spoiled and taught that their families belonged to the intellectual elite. William had become titular head of his family after his father's death, and the position had given him a disproportionately strong sense of responsibility. Anna, the baby in her family, would become a woman of awesome capabilities, but certain childlike qualities — some lovable, some maddening — would linger throughout her life.

Hardly had the couple been joined than they were parted, this time by out-of-town tryouts of *Strongheart.* On the road almost constantly from May to December of 1904, William wrote to his bride almost nightly. On Christmas Day he wrote from St. Paul, Minnesota, of the play's success and of his anticipation of their reunion in January: "I long for you much more than when we were engaged. You are the only woman in the world Sweetheart . . . I wish to devote my whole life to making you happy . . ." On December 30, "I can hardly wait . . . I want you so. . . . Soon my arms will clasp you . . ."[16] At last, after another successful opening, this time in Minneapolis, he arrived by train in New York. Exactly eight months and nine days later — on September 18, 1905 — Agnes George de Mille was born.

two

Golden Days

In deference to Anna's modesty, Agnes was delivered at home, by a woman doctor. The event took place in a long, dark "railroad flat" at 357 West 118th Street, in the middle of Harlem, at that time predominantly white and middle-class; the Cathedral of St. John the Divine was under construction nearby. The family lived comfortably with a resident cook and a nurse, for William had followed *Strongheart* with a series of commercial successes. He would never be in a class with James Barrie or George Bernard Shaw or other first-rate playwrights of his day — even Agnes, who adored her father, conceded that he was far from being the genius his wife and mother believed him to be — but he was a diligent craftsman and, brick by brick, he built a solid career.

When Agnes was three, a baby sister, Margaret George, was born. The following summer, William wrote from New York to his wife in the country: "My little family after all *is* my world, even more than fame and fortune."[1] Increasingly disenchanted with David Belasco, his father's former partner and now the producer of his own plays, he wrote, "It's rather irritating to feel with DB that you only have a piece of his attention and I've certainly done my last play for him . . . I'm through with waiting his convenience. . . . I long for you and Merriewold and the kiddies."[2]

Merriewold was a 2,000-acre section of land at the foot of the Catskills, near the junction of New Jersey, Pennsylvania, and New York State. In 1889, a group of Henry George's disciples had bought the land and built a house, in which the Georges spent their summers. After George's death, his children built a house nearby; their mother died there. William courted Anna at Merriewold; after their marriage, he and Anna spent two summers in a tent behind the George house, then occupied by Henry Jr. and his family. When Agnes was four, William bought his own cottage, and he eventually acquired thirty adjacent acres at $15 apiece. The compound consisted of about two dozen houses — a woodsy community of intellectuals, most of whom were Georgists and many of whom were related by blood or by marriage.

Merriewold was the enchanted center of Agnes's childhood, and it would remain her lifelong spiritual home. In Merriewold's woods, free from the strictures of city life, she felt most alive. "My hair got redder. I moved directly, like an animal. I was quiet. I listened . . . You heard with your skin; you breathed light and shade."[3] Like a student cramming for an exam, she memorized nuances of colors, flavors, sounds, smells, seasons, and the names of every plant. The most mundane activities delighted her: churning ice cream, making jam, swimming in the lake. When the gardener gutted animals and fish, she was an attentive audience. A garter snake in pursuit of a frog was "the grimmest procedure I ever watched" — but she continued to watch for more than an hour, until "the snake lay replete, one little leg dangling from its mouth, its eyes closed in content. The frog's agony was being quieted by digestive chemistry."[4] Discovering a fire in a house that was under construction, she watched, mesmerized, as the blaze advanced, never thinking to alert the adults.

The annual move to the country was a major undertaking, with the children clutching their favorite playthings and the servants lugging a summer's worth of supplies. Merriewold was only six hours from New York — by train, ferry, and buggy — but it was a half-century backward in time. Facilities were primitive — there was no electricity, gas, telephone, running water, or indoor toilet — but to Agnes, all the necessities were there. Music, for example: William, a frustrated performer, sang Schumann, Wagner, and Debussy, and Anna sang Mozart. There was live music at the Saturday night dances in the clubhouse, and the children performed in short plays and pageants.[5] Their audience was the compound's extended family (the children called all the adults uncle or aunt), which included writers, politicians, businessmen, high-ranking tennis players, and musicians. Tournaments were played with deadly seriousness on William's tennis court, the only one in Sullivan County; he had it rolled and painted with white lines every day. Houseguests included varied assortments of Georges and De Milles and William's theatrical colleagues. It was a privileged world, with carefully delineated rules and roles for men, women, children, and servants. The prevailing values were Victorian, for the Queen had not been dead so very long (to Anna, despite her theatrical connections, girls who wore lipstick were "not quite fine"). Doting wives and mothers, products of their time and training, sat in pastel dresses on shaded porches through the long, humid afternoons, embroidering. It was a lovely picture, albeit a false one, and the image of women waiting, perpetually pretty and fresh, for their men would become a leitmotiv in Agnes's work.

In the woods, there were deer, raccoons, possums, beavers, and even bear. Agnes monitored the "procession of flowers . . . mountain ash, jack-in-the-pulpits, trillium, huckleberries, wild ginger, strawberries, yellow and white . . . then came the violets," which she claims to have recognized from the age of two.[6] "There were moments," she wrote, "when I stopped being a member of a family, my parents' child . . . and became simply a part of the forest."[7] But it was her parents, or rather her image of her parents, that kept her universe in perfect order. Anna, "sitting in the leaf shadows, embroidering."[8] William, writing in a hut in the forest, catching trout in the nearby stream, and reading aloud, by lamplight, from *Uncle Remus* or Kipling's *Just So Stories,* while the whippoorwills sang. William was Agnes's storybook hero. When a neighbor's child needed a doctor one midnight, "Father dressed, walked the mile to Superintendent Moore's, borrowed a horse and rode without light the six miles to Monticello."[9]

> Mother and Father sometimes went canoeing at sundown to watch the deer come down to drink, buck and does. And occasionally, if I promised not to speak or move, they sat me between them. Father paddled Indian style, without taking the paddle from the water, merely turning the blade . . . we slid in the darkened waters.[10]
>
> That Mother and Father were in love I knew as I knew that the woods were green and budding. They walked hand in hand; I remember them picking lilies of the valley as the first birds called, and the look he bent upon her, and the blue dazzle of her return gaze.[11]

In the midst of all this familial devotion and communal activity, Agnes was lonely. She was too bright, too creative, too sensitive, and too strong a personality, even in her early years, to have been otherwise. She was a pretty child with a fair complexion, freckles, a thick cloud of curly red hair, a turned-up nose, and her mother's blue eyes. Margaret, three years younger, was a rival and, as a companion, beneath contempt. The boys on whom Agnes had crushes were not interested — she was too young and far too bossy. So she invented imaginary friends who lived in the trees, and games to play with them. She was not unhappy. But in her recurring nightmare, the forest was destroyed, leaving "nothing but city streets."[12]

Once ensconced at Merriewold, the women and children stayed put from May through September. When business took William to New York, or to some tryout town with a new play, he wrote to his wife often and at length. He sent cards to the children, who were always "my dear boys" or "the little fellers." "Kiss the two little fellers," he wrote in the summer of 1910, "and never let them go on the stage if you can help it. My arms are aching for you all."[13] On September 18, 1910, he wrote, "I have been thinking all day of five years ago, when Agnes was born . . . hope the little desk arrived in time and that she liked it."

Anna, conscientious to a fault, worried about her firstborn's willfulness (frustrated, Agnes would cry until she vomited) and her inability or unwillingness to show affection. William sent reassurance: "Don't worry . . . at times she is very demonstrative but she has her father's failing of following her own line of thought to the exclusion of all else. She chooses her own time for showing affection whether the time is appropriate or not. That is the side of her that her father will always understand better than her mother, for he understands that it does not imply any lack of affection, but independence of situation."[14]

Although William was away a good deal, and a habitual flirt, there is no reason to doubt his faithfulness in the early years of his marriage. Trying out a new play on the road in 1911, he wrote, "It's exactly 100 hours now since I saw you."[15] "I miss our talks dear, and the perfect understanding which has grown between us. Every time we are apart it comes home clearer to me."[16] Inevitably, though, his career disrupted his family life; Anna's feelings must have been mixed when she read his Christmas Eve wire in 1911, tallying the number of curtain calls his play had received in Chicago.

At six, Agnes was sent to the Horace Mann School her parents had attended, but at a new location, uptown at 125th Street and Broadway. A photograph taken that year of Agnes with her sister and her great-grandmother Samuel shows three aristocrats, two very young and one very old, in Morningside Park, wearing fashionable winter coats and hats trimmed with ribbons, feathers, and fur. Agnes looks pensive, inquisitive, and supremely confident. The only visible cloud in her sky was her sister, whose arrival had ended her exclusive claim on her parents' attention. But another of her relatives was about to set events in motion that would irrevocably change the course and the climate of her life.

Cecil De Mille — Uncle Ce to his nieces — was, like his parents and brother, incurably stagestruck. He had followed William into the field proscribed by their father, attending the American Academy of Dramatic Arts and then playing minor parts in shows in New York and on the road. At twenty-one, he had married an actress, Constance Adams, whom he'd met in a touring company. Constance was eight years his senior and mature in more than years. She was handsome rather than beautiful, and elegant, and warm. By all accounts, including those of disinterested observers, she was a paragon of wisdom, dignity, calm, integrity, patience, and every other virtue, all of which must have been strained mightily by Cecil — to whom she was, true to her name, constant for fifty-seven years.

After their marriage Cecil and Constance continued to tour, together and separately, leading a financially precarious existence. When their daughter Cecilia was born in 1908, they could barely afford a pram, and Cecil "often walked from Times Square to 110th St. to save the nickel carfare to buy milk."[17] Cecil's acting talents were limited but his ambitions were not; he wanted to write, direct, and produce. In contrast to William, who had his father's dreamy disposition, Cecil was an extrovert — his mother's son — and eventually he went to work for her.

Beatrice De Mille was now a significant presence in the theatrical world. She represented some top playwrights, including her older son, and also produced and financed plays. As general manager of Beatrice's company, Cecil took advantage of the opportunity to learn about every aspect of the theater, from casting to balancing the books. But Cecil lived in his older brother's shadow, as he had all his life; while he worked for their mother, William was an established playwright, whose only flops were the plays he wrote in collaboration with Cecil.

Temperamentally, the brothers complemented and competed with each other. William was responsible, introspective, practical. Cecil was the impetuous adventurer, in his brother's eyes a failed actor and playwright. William was right; Cecil's gifts lay elsewhere. But when Cecil proposed to set out in an entirely new direction, William scoffed.

Motion pictures had been popular since 1903, but only as seven-to-ten-minute two-reelers in nickelodeons or as intermissions in vaudeville theaters, where they were called "chasers" because they cleared out the house between shows. But in 1912, Adolph Zukor, a Hungarian immigrant, produced an hour-long film about Queen Elizabeth that achieved legitimacy via the reputation of its star, Sarah Bernhardt. The following year, three friends of Cecil's joined forces to produce feature-length motion pictures. They were Jesse Lasky, a vaudeville producer; Samuel Goldfish (later Goldwyn), a glove salesman; and Arthur Friend, a lawyer. Instead of making movies in Fort Lee, New Jersey, then the site of most motion picture production, they proposed establishing the Lasky Feature Play Company in Arizona, where the land was cheaper and the sunshine, cowboys, and Indians more plentiful than in New Jersey. Cecil would be their onsite administrator, with the title of Director General. Cecil invited his brother, who had loaned him money in the past, to stake him with $5,000.[18] But the enterprise was, by William's lights, irresponsible and extravagant. He put his refusal in writing and reproached Cecil for having had the audacity to make such a decision without consulting his older and, by implication, wiser brother. With colossal condescension, he reminded Cecil of his heritage: ". . . a cultured family, two of whose members have made honorable names in the field of drama, and I cannot understand how you are willing to identify yourself with a cheap form of amusement and which no one will ever allude to as an art. . . . When you get stranded out there in the West I will send you your railroad fare." He predicted that Cecil was throwing away his future and dooming himself to obscurity, then aimed at a nerve: "I suppose Mother is heartbroken. This must be a terrible blow to her for I know what hopes she had for you . . ." He grudgingly wished him luck and signed off "With love (which is akin to pity)."[19]

Cecil was not deterred. With a director, a cameraman, an actor, and the actor's dresser, and fortified by an optimism that his brother both ridiculed and envied, Cecil headed for Arizona. Finding the town of Flagstaff more built up than he had expected, he continued to the end of the line: Los Angeles. In the section of town known as Hollywood, then a virtual wilderness, he rented a barn.* He converted the horse stalls into dressing rooms, rounded up extras off the streets, and in six weeks produced the first feature-length film made in California. *The Squaw Man* would eventually gross a quarter of a million dollars.

Watching the first showing of *The Squaw Man* in New York, William, whom a friend had called "the Cassandra of the screen," experienced an epiphany.[20] "I saw unrolled before my eyes the first really new form of dramatic story-telling which had been invented for some 500 years . . . a potential theater of the whole people . . . within the means of the poorest family, accessible all over the country, and beyond into foreign lands."[21] What the new medium needed, Cecil told his brother, was a new form of dramatic writing — something William could help to devise. The timing was propitious. "I had been writing and producing in the theatre steadily for thirteen years," William wrote in his autobiography, "and had reached a point where nothing I wrote pleased me . . . having attained the ripe old age of thirty-six, I felt my youth departing and yearned for new adventures." In September, after his latest play (*After Five,* written with Cecil) had opened in New York with a whimper, William left for California. If things worked out well, he would send for Anna and the children. On the train heading west, "six or seven years dropped from my shoulders; I was young again."[22]

In 1914, it was easy to see why Los Angeles was called the city of the angels. With its temperate climate and its proximity to the pristine desert, mountains, and sea, it seemed to promise eternal youth and unlimited possibilities. In this utopian environment, and in an industry bursting with energy and potential, William began writing screenplays. His letters to Anna were euphoric: "This particular art is *really* in its infancy . . . This is the one company with which I can work unfettered and really have the opportunity to rise quickly to the very top." Within a week of his arrival, he instructed Anna to put their belongings in storage and bring the children west. "You will love the autoing around here. The roads are superb and you ride through desert, then suddenly you are in the midst of wonderful orange groves and olive groves. Miles and miles of them, with the

* Hollywood was so christened in 1896 by a transplanted Midwesterner, Daeida Hartell Wilcox, who, with her husband, bought 120 acres of land surrounding what would become the intersection of Hollywood and Vine, to establish a God-fearing, teetotaling, sinfree community.

desert lying between. And always as a background range after range of mountains. . . . You and the children must wear amber colored glasses at first until you get used to the semi-tropical glare of light."[23]

Until the end of her life, Anna saved the letters her husband wrote to her that autumn. To her, and later to Agnes, they proved that despite William's eventual faithlessness, there was a time when his wife was, in his phrase, "my best beloved."[24] They were passionate letters, full of longing and delicately phrased lust. The open-air life, he said, made him feel "very strong and energetic. I want so to kiss your dear arms, and to feel your breast throb against my own. I want to hold you tight and kiss your lips. I want to feel your smooth skin against my face. I want *you,* my sweetheart — all of you." The new life he envisioned for them was a romantic fantasy: they would live simply, with work (*his* work) "the chief amusement . . . This is man-sized work, dear . . . It requires absolute concentration and much labor, mental and physical, and I long for the rest in your arms. . . . Home is where you and my fellers are . . . Let us be prepared to start out here as pioneers, and work back to the East side by side . . ."[25] On October 17 he wrote, with all the impatient ardor of a bridegroom, "How I want to take your tired head on my breast and kiss you to sleep. GET THE STUFF IN STORAGE AND COME TO ME."[26]

t h r e e

The Kingdom of Shadows*

Agnes had been imprinted genetically by the Georges and the de Milles and environmentally by Merriewold. The years in Hollywood would provide an overlay that would shape her sensibility, inform her work, and create an irreconcilable conflict of values.

In 1914, Hollywood was an agricultural community of 7,500 souls, its ultimate destiny inconceivable. Its train station was opposite an ostrich farm, and the real cowboys who appeared in the early Westerns rode their horses on dirt roads that crossed the town's one paved main street. The de Milles' first home (at 1814 Hillcrest Road) was at the foot of a hill verging on wilderness — a far, dry cry from Merriewold, but hills nonetheless for the children to race around in. In the canyon grew wildflowers and sage, and brambles, and coyotes. Agnes and Margaret attended the Hollywood School for Girls, where classes were held out of doors, as at the Horace Mann School — but in a garden, instead of on a roof. Some of their classmates, such as Edith and Irene Mayer, had famous, or about-to-be-famous, surnames. The only boys in the school

* The phrase used in a newspaper review by Maxim Gorky after seeing the "*lumière* films" in the summer of 1896 (Macgowan, *Behind the Screen,* p. 98).

were Joel McCrea and Douglas Fairbanks Jr. — a chubby, good-natured little boy, who always got very excited when his parents showed up for any school function.

From its inception, the American movie industry inspired curiosity, envy, and contempt — first in its immediate community, eventually the world over. Hollywood's early residents, most of them transplanted Midwesterners seeking a climate to cure their ailments, enjoyed the excitement of the movies being created literally in their front yards. At the same time, some citizens found the "movie people" easy to snub. They banned them from their clubs and, ipso facto, from some neighborhoods. The movie people, preoccupied with their collective endeavor to the point of obsession, scarcely noticed. They were inventing an art form — sometimes at the rate of a movie a week!

William quickly developed a facility for writing for the eye rather than the ear; in 1915 he wrote nine screenplays, two of them based on his own stage plays.* He worked throughout the summer in a little

* *After Five* and *The Warrens of Virginia,* which introduced the fourteen-year-old Mary Pickford to the screen.

wooden house with screen doors to keep the flies out. He hung a sign on the door saying SCENARIO DEPARTMENT — the first time the phrase appeared in Hollywood. Then he began, in emulation of his younger brother, to direct.*

It was not unusual for the relatives of cast and crew to visit the set during filming, especially for the more spectacular scenes — Cecil burning Geraldine Farrar at the stake, throwing Conrad Nagel into a crocodile pit, or feeding Gloria Swanson to the lions. Anna took her daughters out of school for such special occasions, and during school vacations they were often taken to the studio. To any child, but particularly a child with Agnes's imagination, a movie set was wonderland, where work was indistinguishable from play. The actors often improvised their silent scenes, accompanied by live music (to supply rhythm and mood), and without the tedious repetition that the process acquired as it grew more refined. When Cecil shot the battle scenes for his first big spectacle, *Joan the Woman,* the family showed up at the Lasky Ranch in the San Fernando Valley with picnic baskets. William, assisting Cecil with the scene, wore a cavalry officer's uniform and commanded a company of actors. "I was a little afraid that Father would get hurt," Agnes wrote in her diary, "but he didn't. The French came charging across the field with Joan at their head carrying her standard. . . . They jumped the stockade and fought the English and they won. It was the most beautiful scene I've ever seen."[1]

In this environment, Agnes was stagestruck, moviestruck, and mad to dress up — skirts down, hair up, high heels (improvised by tying spools to her shoes). Inspired by what she witnessed at the studio, she commandeered the girls in the neighborhood after school and, like a pint-sized version of her uncle Cecil, supervised them in scavenging scraps with which they built "sets" in her family's garage. In the scenes they enacted, she was always the star. With her best friend, Mary Hunter, she played for hours at a game they made up called Castle, in which their opposing armies fought complicated, semimilitary maneuvers in Cromwellian England. Her moral standards were lofty — inspired by a book called *The Lass of the Silver Sword,* she and Mary each swore, "I will try to be good

* At that time, directing meant not only shooting a movie but cutting, assembling, and editing it, as well.

and true, honest and obedient . . . I will stand by you always and together we will fight the battle of life armed with the silver sword of love and the golden shield of truth . . ." The girls knighted each other and became "battlemaids of the silver sword. . . . We prayed a little. . . . We danced a little dance with our staffs."[2]

In drama class at school, Agnes loved the pantomime exercises, which she performed without the slightest self-consciousness (one of her favorite stories was of marching stark naked to the Merriewold tennis court as a child and enjoying the attention she received). Her idol was Geraldine Farrar, the opera star who played Cecil's "Joan," and she longed to emulate Farrar's acting. Acting was not what William had in mind for his flagship child, but making movies was then very much a family affair — Margaret played a part in one of Cecil's movies, Anna was an extra in *The Warrens of Virginia,* and Agnes was occasionally allowed a day's work in a crowd scene.* In the summer before her eleventh birthday, she told her diary, "At the studio . . . Father was taking [*sic*] *Anton the Terrible.* I hate it, and so does he. They were taking a scene where they were beating a man. There were great big lashes on his back and the blood was pouring down. It nearly made me sick. While I was looking, suddenly a strange feeling came over me, and everything got blurred. I could hardly see. My eyes acked [*sic*]. The people became dim figures moving all around. I sat down in a dark corner in the room where they keep the armor for 'Joan of Arc.' I declared the truth and slowly things began to be clear, til I was all right."[3]

Declaring the truth was a principle of Christian Science, in which Agnes was instructed by her mother's cousin, Alice George, who was William's receptionist. "Allie" was a middle-aged spinster whose marriage prospects either took advantage of her generosity, or died, or turned out to be homosexual. In Agnes's work and in her life, Allie would become a negative object lesson: the specter of lifelong virginity, synonymous with emotional starvation. Decades later, Agnes would write with

* Agnes's first professional appearance, for which she was paid $5 for one day's work, was in *The Ragamuffin,* written and directed by her father in 1915. The only picture in which she had a "real" part was *Witchcraft,* directed by Frank Reicher and starring Fanny Ward; in a courtroom scene, Agnes screamed, "I see the Devil like a tiny little canary whispering in her ear," and then had hysterics. The picture was never released.

uncharacteristic sentimentality of "poor Allie" walking the streets alone at night, peering with pathetic longing into lighted windows at the togetherness of what appeared to be happy families.[4]

Any unhappiness in Agnes's own family was masked by a blizzard of activity. In her diary, she kept the minutes of her life: French lessons, piano lessons, diving lessons, homework, painting, sewing, picking wildflowers, quarreling with Margaret. During a weekend trip to the Riverside Mission Inn, the organ "sounded like a girl's voice. It is the most wonderful organ I ever heard." After tennis at Jesse Lasky's and a visit to the studio, "Came home. Spent the rest of the afternoon on the throne of China. I was constipated."[5] One day she saw a dog run over; sickened, she did not turn away, for it was *drama,* as compelling as the frog-eating snake at Merriewold, or the actor's realistic streams of blood. "I never saw any animal or human being in such agony," she wrote with a touch of relish. "He was tense with pain, his eyes were glassy and staring strait [*sic*] ahead. His tongue was hanging out and his mouth was foaming. . . . Every time we thought he was dead he would move again. Finally he gave a little scream and then I think he started to die . . . I cried. I couldn't help it."[6]

Bear Valley, where William did some filming on location, was "the most wonderful view I've ever seen. The mountains on each side of you, the desert before you. The mountains beyond the desert are pinks and greys and browns. The desert itself is grey with great patches of grey shadow here and there . . ."[7] The description is extraordinary for a ten-year-old, but this ten-year-old was reading voraciously — classics, mostly, from Washington Irving and Frances Hodgson Burnett to Thackeray, the Oz books, and *As You Like It.* They were William's selections, for he was preparing Agnes to be the next literary de Mille. When she was nine, he was already critiquing her work: "I like the [poem] about mama being in the study. It was realistic and the style flowed without effort."[8]

In Hollywood, William cast himself as the Great Playwright, a role that had eluded him on Broadway, and played it to the hilt. To Agnes he was dashing, sexy, and elusive. He treated his children "rather like puppies, for whom he had the fondest regard but whom he did not choose to fondle much. He expressed himself in rude banter and awkward pats."[9] Sarcasm was his forte: at fourteen, when Agnes returned home after spending the entire summer at Merriewold, "He looked up from his cocktail and said, 'Oh, you back?'"[10] His approval was her Grail, and a constant goad. "I'd rather love you for what you do," he wrote in her autograph book, "than because you're mine." For his sake, she drove herself to excel at school and at every extracurricular activity he prescribed: reading, writing, tennis, photography (for her eleventh birthday, "Father gave me a new camera. I've resolved that that camera shall teach me a lesson and that as long as I have it I shall strive to do better and conquer my carelessness").[11] She studied piano as though preparing for a concert career; throughout her teens, she would practice four hours a day. But however intense her efforts, she rarely got his attention and never his direct approval. Excellence was expected; if she got a B, he asked, "Why isn't it an A?" She settled for crumbs: "I once overheard him reading some of my verses to Cecil, so I knew he was proud of me."[12]

Anna's attention, on the other hand, was direct and relentless. The reformer's daughter raised her own daughters like little Victorians. Until high school, they dined alone and went to bed at eight (after that, bedtime was nine!), and they were forbidden such vulgar diversions as the newspapers. They were never allowed to forget that they were the granddaughters of a Great Economist and the daughters of a distinguished Hollywood Director.

Anna was a tiny dynamo; she had considerable charm, the righteousness of a zealot, and the thrift of a miser. Time and money were meant to improve life in some observable way, and to waste either of those precious resources was a sin. "Do something!" was her motto and constant exhortation to her children. Agnes never thought to disobey, for "the way [Mother] did things was The Way . . . not even Mrs. Astor . . . knew better."[13] When the children painted wildflowers, the colors were exact; when they sewed dresses for their dolls, the plackets and French seams and buttonholes were perfect; and while they hemmed table napkins with tiny, perfectly spaced stitches, they took turns reading H. G. Wells's *A Short History of the World* aloud. They said their prayers in French, improving their language skills along with their virtue.

Anna was a crusader with too many causes, around which her formidable energy sizzled and lost its way. She was too much of a good thing, and her family would eventually have to escape, or perish under the weight of her good intentions. Mary Hunter was one of a group of twelve-year-olds whom Anna drove around Los Angeles to point out illustrations of the Single Tax theory. "What you did with Anna," she recalled, "you didn't think of as odd. She wanted an image of an almost English style of family life — private, domestic, full of family occasions — and she had a talent for it. And she pulled it off, despite the objections of her husband.

"Anna let you know there were standards of personal and social behavior that must be maintained — how a well-bred girl should look and behave, what you should read, what you should wear, what you should do for recreation. She had no interest in conventional fashion, only in what she believed to be right. In high school, Agnes suffered from having to wear things like hand-embroidered smocks when her peers were wearing sweaters and skirts. Anna would have a fit if a ribbon wasn't the right color or not in just the right place. To this day, I can hear Anna's voice in the background somewhere, never quite satisfied, saying, 'Agnes! You must fix your hair! Must you have this awful disorder? I can't bear to go into your room!'"[14]

The de Milles wore their culture and values in Hollywood like colonials dining formally in the African bush. They entertained a rich mélange of international figures: politicians, military leaders, and explorers, many of whom were followers of Henry George. Anna's brother, Henry George Jr., was a New York State Representative, but it was primarily Anna who carried her father's torch, received his admirers from all over the world, and addressed them at Single Tax conventions, through which her daughters yawned. There were world-class athletes, as well — particularly tennis players, with whom William played on his court — and some of the world's finest writers and musicians, including Rebecca West, Michael Arlen, Somerset Maugham, Rosa Ponselle, Efrem Zimbalist, Alma Gluck, and Geraldine Farrar. Actors below the status of Charlie Chaplin, Mary Pickford, and Douglas Fairbanks were not invited. After Sunday evening suppers there was always music, by family and guests. A new movie would be shown and critiqued. The conversation was pyrotechnical.

There was no common social ground with Hollywood's empire builders — the Goldwyns and Mayers and Laskys and Zukors, immigrant salesmen for whom English was a second or third language. The difference was apparent to Irene Mayer Selznick, Louis B. Mayer's daughter and Margaret's classmate and friend. "I was so flattered when they invited me to dinner," she recalled. "Their intellectual and cultural standards were new to me. They had more books than I had ever seen in one house in my life. I liked the simplicity of their house, their food. I looked up to Agnes, and she tolerated me. At table, the girls and I were treated like thinking people. It was a bracing climate." On the other hand, "The whole family was snooty, holier-than-thou. Anna was autocratic and stiff-necked, and Agnes was even more so. She knew she came from superior stock, and she showed it. At school she did more than anyone else — history, music, editor of the school paper, editor of the yearbook, best player on the tennis team, head of the upper school, vice president of the drama club. She was full of vim and energy, and a conviction that everybody was stupid — which they were. She looked down her nose at everyone, ignoring them or sneering and jeering in a very subtle way that probably went right past them. She had ambition, and a great appetite. She wanted to read, to know, to prevail. She had zeal and application. She was heroic! She put some of her teachers to shame."[15]

For all her success at school, Agnes was failing at the endeavor closest to her heart. She had danced from the age of three, when her mother played a mechanical organ — but most little girls dance naturally from babyhood (many little boys do, as well, although in our culture few are encouraged to continue). Dancing is a pleasant way for children to release emotion, to get attention, and to experiment with the relationship between their bodies and space. Agnes saw her first ballerina at the age of five — the Danish Adeline Genée — and was inspired to participate in "dance pageants" at Merriewold, with the other children.[16] Then, in her thirteenth year, she saw Pavlova, and was converted. The legendary ballerina seemed to her nothing less than "intoxicated rapture, a focus of energy, Dionysian in its physical intensity."[17] Pavlova was the doorway to obsession.

Blinded by the light of Pavlova's dancing, Agnes pleaded for ballet lessons. But to men of William's generation and class, dancers were barely distinguishable from prostitutes; the phrase "serious dancing" was an oxymoron, and lessons were out of the question. He would allow nothing more "serious" than the Saturday afternoon dance pageants and other homemade productions — a seemingly harmless form of self-expression, untainted by formal training — that took place in the garden throughout Agnes's youth. The war was far away in Europe, but Hollywood's children danced to raise money for French war orphans and staged school playlets to benefit the Red Cross. In 1917, the local newspaper reported, "After a charming one-act play . . . Miss Agnes de Mille gave an interpretive dance, 'The Birth of the Butterfly.' [Accompanied by Victrola music, she entered] "swathed in white, her slow movements shed this cocoon, and she stood revealed in a simple tunic with wings, which expanded as the butterfly grew in strength."[18]

This and similar performances owed a good deal to Ruth St. Denis and Isadora Duncan, whose "interpretive" dances were taught at the Hollywood School for Girls.* Agnes was forbidden to participate, but she observed and absorbed the barefooted freedom, the theatricalism, and, in the case of St. Denis, quasi-mysticism. The "modern" St. Denis was in no way comparable to the classical Pavlova — she relied on her instincts, not on formal training — but she was probably the best-known American dancer, and the school she had recently founded with Ted Shawn was considered the first serious dance school in the United States. "Miss Ruth" was a friend of Anna's, and an object of awe to Agnes. One day, "Miss St. Denis came and had tea with us. I DANCED FOR HER. I was trembling too, because I was dancing before one of the greatest dancers in America. She said I had talent, and that I must go to her school next year."[19]

In 1918, the de Milles moved to a big, rambling wood-frame house at 1970 Morgan Place, on a hillside. In its basement, Agnes and a supporting cast performed her adaptation of a children's book about the English parliamentary wars in the seventeenth century. The precocious playwright played Captain Jack Careless (the lead) and also directed her sister, her cousin Cecilia, and six other little girls, all of whom played

---

* Agnes actually saw Isadora perform on one occasion, but not until the great dancer was, at forty, "prematurely aged and bloated" (Agnes de Mille, *Martha*, p. 26).

male parts and wore military uniforms provided by the resourceful Anna (Agnes insisted on historical accuracy, down to the colors and insignia). The author of the book, Beulah Marie Dix, was a family friend; Ms. Dix was amused and astounded. Forty years later she would write, "It is such a wonderful thing ever to meet with someone who knows, from childhood, what they want to do and then does it, in the face of every obstacle," and recalled that the play was "quite amazing for a child of your years to shape."[20]

In *Dance to the Piper* Agnes wrote, "When pubescent girls have any inclination toward dancing at all, they are fairly driven by the frenzy."[21] Her own case was classic. Waking and sleeping, she dreamed of dancing. Finally, when she was fourteen, ballet lessons were prescribed for Margaret, to correct her flat feet. Lest William be accused of favoritism, both sisters were enrolled in the Theodore Kosloff School of Imperial Russian Ballet.*

Agnes judged herself the worst pupil in her class, but through no fault of her own, she had one foot figuratively tied behind her. She was five years older than the optimum age to begin ballet training — a major, but not fatal, handicap. The insurmountable handicap was her body, which was the antithesis of a classical ballerina's. She was built like her mother: short (eventually only five-foot-one), with full bosom, wide hips, and disproportionately short arms and legs. The other students attended class every day and practiced together at the studio. Agnes was allowed only two classes a week (one group lesson, taught by Kosloff, and a private lesson with one of his assistants), and her daily practice was restricted to forty minutes at a makeshift barre in her mother's bathroom, alone, without music or mirror or a proper floor. Kosloff later recalled that her father "complained to me that he was awakened night after night by a clump, clump in Agnes's bedroom. He told me she would also get up early in the morning to practice before school; and she would study her schoolwork through recess and lunch periods so that no home work would interfere with her piano and ballet practice. He said she would cry herself to sleep if her mother forbade her an extra half hour's exertion.

* Kosloff had been an original member of the Diaghilev Ballets Russes, and had danced with Nijinsky and Karsavina.

Mr. de Mille disapproved highly of Agnes's becoming a professional dancer. He begged me to discourage her."[22]

Agnes loved every minute of it — the pain and the discipline and even the difficulty (perhaps *especially* the difficulty) of attempting the impossible: to transform her body into that of a ballerina. In her mind, if not her body, "I had come into my birthright . . . I had found my life's work."[23]

Emerging from puberty, Agnes had the intellect of an adult, the body of a young woman, and the emotions of a child. Her childish winsomeness had evaporated and she had acquired, to her great dismay, her grandmother Beatrice's prominent nose. She still had her mother's wonderful coloring, but her skin was blotchy, and heavily freckled by the sun. Her blue eyes were also Anna's, but their shrewd gaze was Bebe's. And unlike Anna's soft red hair, Agnes's was frizzy and wild. Her teeth were crooked. Her clothes, selected by Anna, bordered on freakish; at fourteen, when a brassiere was called for, she still wore little girls' undershirts. She went to Junior Cotillions "clad in a pink or flowered crepe de Chine dress made by [Anna], a little sash tying my precocious torso in two like a sack, a frill at my neck and frills at my elbow, pink silk socks and sandals (all the other girls wore taffeta frocks and silver cloth slippers with pointed toes)."[24] In such outfits she sat out most dances alone, consoling herself with thoughts of how sorry the boys who ignored her would be when she was a world-famous dancer. If a boy did ask her to dance, he quickly discovered that Agnes was a solo act, more interested in performing than in being anyone's partner.

The dance pageants grew more elaborate. Agnes generally portrayed flowers or fairies; in "The Lily, A Story of Growth and Resurrection," she was "the first shoot of the lily, bursting out from the earth."[25] Mary Hunter, who played Sunlight, believed that "the audience was moved and impressed; even then, Agnes must have felt the power to reach an audience."[26]

f o u r

Fault Lines

The warning tremors that signified the collapse of William and Anna's marriage were felt by their children only in hindsight. Thirty-five years after her parents' divorce, Agnes wrote a short story describing the dynamics in her family during its period of disintegration. It begins, "Her mother kept a list of topics suitable for discussion beside her plate so that when conversation died they would not just sit there listening to one another eat. Father never helped. He listened without comment to the report on the last speaker at the Friday Morning Club, the Bridge decorations at Veda's, the quail they'd started up on the regular Tuesday afternoon walk, the cook's arthritis . . ." The nineteen-year-old daughter, "Agatha," worships her father and longs in vain for his attention. He sighs a lot and relieves his boredom and irritation with gin; after dinner, he will surreptitiously visit his mistress. The mother is a teetotaler and obsessively thrifty (to avoid the sin of wastefulness, she pours her undrunk water into the floral centerpiece). Agatha is sickened by the tension between her parents. Except for the omission of Margaret, the scene is authentic.

The plot is simple: A friend gives Agatha a beautiful white dress to

wear to a party. Her mother, who has always dressed her in fussy, unbecoming clothes, manipulates her into wearing another dress that accentuates her imperfections and deemphasizes her sexuality. When Agatha tries to protest, she finds herself comforting her mother, who feels betrayed and rejected. When the girl cannot hide her misery, her mother is solicitous; "She seemed in some way particularly fulfilled and pleased when her girl was in pain or grieving."[1]

Anna's devotion was inexorable, water dripping on rock. She monitored her family's behavior with vigilance, urging them always toward perfection. "Anna didn't try to control you," Mary Hunter Wolf observed, "but she had a genius for making you feel guilty. She smothered you with too much nurturing — hovering, with no discrimination between what was and was not important."[2]

Agnes was caught on the fishhook of her mother's martyrdom. So was William, but he was beginning to wriggle free. Margaret went her own way. She knew instinctively how to flirt from the age of nine and did so with great success. "Father used to chuckle and in the end give her what she wanted," said Agnes. "I was too haughty and proud, and I loved Father too much."[3] At home, Agnes was often moody and sullen; she chewed her nails to the quick and had problems with her complexion. Margaret sailed through puberty with flawless nails and complexion, and the aplomb of a swan. When she was fifteen she told her older sister, "You have your dancing, but I can handle a man."[4]

Irene Selznick remembered William as being "very crisp, with a hint of sternness. He teased, heckled, and challenged his daughters."[5] He took a perfunctory interest in Agnes's tennis and riding, but otherwise, as Mary Hunter Wolf recalled, "Bill was a very self-centered man, and he paid absolutely no attention to Agnes. Agnes had a tendency to think poorly of herself — her looks, and also in general — and she had a genuine need to be bolstered up. I think Anna was convinced that Agnes was talented, but except for what she did physically, she was more corrective than supportive."[6]

William was an absentee father who spent long hours at the studio and otherwise enjoyed himself riding, playing poker, and deep-sea fishing. Agnes's only excursion alone with him was to a tennis tournament in Santa Barbara. In the evenings, at their hotel, he played bridge. "I didn't play bridge, so I sat and read. He didn't speak to me on the way up, and he didn't speak to me on the way back! He thought that was very funny, that we made the whole trip without speaking."[7]

William's absence was at least in part an escape from his wife. Mary Hunter Wolf remembered him "sitting in their large screened-in living area, rather dreading what might happen next. Anna would bustle in, an onslaught of intense domesticity. Bill would draw back in his chair with an 'Oh, no!' expression. 'Who will we invite to the Sunday movie screening? Who will sit next to whom?' I don't remember Bill even saying anything! He didn't care, as long as the living conditions were comfortable and supportive to him. And that was something that Anna was trained to do! Anna did everything in her power to be the perfect wife, the perfect mother, the perfect hostess. For all her caring and warmth and concern, her fussing must have driven Bill senseless."[8]

Anna's parents had called her "the Child," and in some ways she remained one. It suited William to have a child bride, for he had played paterfamilias since his father died. But their marriage was encumbered with the sexual hypocrisies and inhibitions of their day. Before the wedding, William had asked her to try not to think of sex as a duty; "I know," he wrote, "you do not mean it."[9] But she did. She was proud of having known nothing of sex before her marriage and no more than was absolutely necessary after it.

Anna was possessive, and wanted constant reassurance of her husband's love. He wanted passion, and felt it was passing him by. In the summer of 1915, when she was at Merriewold with the children, he wrote, "You always keep the mystery of the unattainable" — but the attainable was endemic in his business, and tempting. His conscience struggled with his libido while he continued to hope that Anna might discover the joys of lust. "If I can make your love as great as mine for you, fate and death itself are powerless . . . You have worked your dear magic about my senses until I am on my knees before your wonderful tenderness . . . I long to kiss you in long embraces that reach to the very bottom of my soul." She is his "'grande passion' . . . such as comes to a man but once and for one woman only out of all the world. . . . You mean everything a woman can possibly mean to a man — and oh how *your* man is longing to tell you so face to face, breast to breast . . ."[10]

Anna felt neglected, but never seriously considered the possibility that her husband would commit adultery. With her usual zeal she tended her English garden, supervised her house, raised her children, proselytized for her father's cause, and involved herself in community projects. But although her marriage would survive until 1926, it received its death blow four years earlier, when a screenwriter with the improbable name of Lorna Moon gave birth to William's son.

The official story, concocted by William and Cecil (with Constance's approval), was that, in November 1922, Cecil's lawyer found a nine-month-old baby on his doorstep. Having already arranged two adoptions for Cecil and his wife, the lawyer asked if they wished to adopt the baby. They agreed, and named the baby Richard de Mille. The truth, even more bizarre than the fiction, was that the baby's mother had tuberculosis and hadn't the strength, or perhaps the desire, to keep the child. There is no record of the effect of this transaction on the child's mother or father. Richard grew up believing that he was an orphan. By arrangement between William and Cecil, he was not told that "Uncle Billy" was his father until after William's death. Anna was never told.*

William and Cecil had little in common but their history and their blood, and the differences in their tastes and temperaments are symbolized almost too neatly by the style of their surname. Both had used De Mille and de Mille interchangeably in their youth, but after *The Squaw Man* Cecil became permanently upper case while William remained resolutely lower. "Cecil is from Balzac, William is from Barrie," wrote Hearst reporter Adela Rogers St. John.[11] Cecil was visual, William was verbal. Cecil's productions were spectacles, William's were intimate dramas. Cecil was the most conspicuous of consumers; his theme song might have been "anything you can do, I can do more ostentatiously." His estate took up an entire hillside with not one but two houses, orchards, pool, tennis court, and gardens. He had a ranch, a yacht, and a collection of valuable jewels, art, and show horses. Will Rogers called him his own biggest epic.[12]

Both men relished the fact that they were laying the groundwork for an art form, but William disdained the industry's commercialism (yet claimed that it was money that kept him there when he would rather have been writing for the New York stage). Cecil was commercial with no compunctions; the only director whose name rivaled D. W. Griffith's as a box office draw, he wholeheartedly embraced the industry he helped to create. On the set, in his trademark jodhpurs and boots, he was as autocratic and powerful as the heroes of his movies. Cecil was an autocrat off the set as well, but an irresistibly charming one. William wanted to improve society, and much of his work dealt with moral issues: women's suffrage, racism, miscegenation. He was literary and athletic; he sucked on his pipe and made wisecracks. Cecil respected his older brother's intellect; "If there's a brain in the family," he said, "it's William."[13] Cecil, the enthusiastic optimist, acted. William, the pessimistic scholar, hedged.

---

* In an undated letter to Richard, Agnes said that she first heard the truth from her cousin Cecilia, years after Anna's death. "All I could say at the moment was 'Thank God, my mother is dead.' It would have broken her heart." Cecilia was the De Milles' eldest and only natural child; John and Katherine were also adopted.

ꝏ

Cecil's sexual magnetism and energy were legendary. His three long-term mistresses — an actress, a writer, and a secretary — knew about each other, worked together, and socialized with each other and with Constance, who told a reporter that the secret of happy married life was "freedom, lack of possessiveness, and frequent separations" and that she never asked where her husband spent his weekends.[14] Cecil maintained that a husband's philandering was "a matter of small importance, so far as his feeling for his wife is concerned," and bragged that in eighteen years of marriage he had never spent a single Saturday night at home.[15] It was an open secret that he spent his weekends at his ranch, called Paradise, where he played potentate-host to couples, all unmarried (to each other), in scenes that might have gone straight into his movies, but for the censors. (This was at a time when William's biggest hit, *The Woman,* was considered sensational because a character discovers that his wife lost her virginity years before he met her and, even more shocking, he *forgives* her.)

At home, Cecil was the warm, expansive patriarch, and the extended family gathered there fairly often. The matriarchal Beatrice was a large presence, stimulating and exciting. At sixty-two, the intrepid Bebe had begun signing up playwrights and their works for the movies and followed her sons to California, where she did her best to manage and manipulate their careers. Cecil cherished her; William was wary. Mary Hunter Wolf remembered her vividly: "a formidable, monumental old lady who drove around Hollywood in a silent 'electric' and wore a flowered turban, kind of a column of flowers that sat on top of her head — it touched the top of the 'electric,' which was very high. She steered it with a bar, and was quite a sight to see."[16]

Beatrice didn't much care for children. Agnes, who didn't much care for her, said, "Father thought she was after money all the time — bleeding the boys for money. She spent money on her personal adornment like nothing I've ever known. She was not so much large as portly, and she dressed like the Gypsy Princess in an operetta. Her taste was so abominable that it was a kind of taste in itself. She found someone in Hollywood that could make realistic poinsettias out of plastic, and realistic wild roses and realistic honeysuckle, and she had lamps of this, with twines and loops and traps. Now that wouldn't be enough — she put a *veil* over it. With *beads.* She was a quite handsome woman with *beautiful* silver-gray hair in masses and coils, with big combs, with big feathers . . . red silk petticoat, green silk petticoat, silk stockings and gloves with lace inserts. *Nothing* was left unadorned."

When her grandmother died, in 1923, Agnes was detached. "I went and sat with Bebe when she was dying of cancer, and she was in very great pain. I was a *kid,* but I thought then that it was somewhat ironic that I was there, with all the strength, and the right to live, and the power — and she, who'd *been* so powerful, and so unfriendly, was simply going in front of my eyes."[17]

Grandmother and granddaughter may have been too much alike to be comfortable with each other — two positively charged forces with tremendous drive, naturally repelling each other. Beatrice's sons were the models for Agnes's ideal man: the elusive, acerbic, intellectual William, and the flamboyant, domineering, adventurous Cecil. Both men betrayed people who loved them. But it was William, Agnes's idol, whose fall would create shock waves that would rock her life and resonate forever in her work.

In the spring of 1922, "Personality Portraits" of the members of Agnes's graduating class appeared in the school paper. Agnes's self-portrait (she was, after all, the editor) read, "Versatility. A kaliediscope [*sic*]. An artist's palate [*sic*] smeared with paint. Chop Suey. A piece of batic [*sic*] (goods)."[18] The brief entry reflected her character and foreshadowed her style — forceful, original, quirky, and candid. Chop suey is an improvised jumble of meat, vegetables, and gravy — a fragmented dish.

Agnes's deepest desires were in conflict: to dance and to please her father. Pleasing her father meant a college education. In Pavlova's time and place it had been possible to study music, literature, painting, history, and languages as well as ballet. But in the United States in 1922, dancing was not taught in universities. It required full-time study, and Agnes's prospects were dubious. No matter how prodigious her efforts, they could not overcome her late start or the basic structure of her body, and her resolve was fading. Dancing would be tantamount to life in a convent, "away from the verve of Father's company, the house and its parties, away from Mother's activities, the friends, the conversations."[19] Her decision to attend college was a foregone conclusion, but the reasoning on which it was based was false. A domestic earthquake was a certainty; the only question was when.

five

Earthquake

Yearning for independence, Agnes applied to Mills College, in Northern California. Anna, who had no intention of lengthening her leash, decreed that she would attend UCLA. It was within walking distance, and it turned out to be an excellent idea.

UCLA, then called the University of California, Southern Branch, was in transition from small college into major university. The faculty was deliberately being seeded with top young(ish) academics from the East, and the lecture halls sizzled with their ideas and idealism. Agnes, who had been a star in her high school class of nine girls, now found herself in competition with the cream of the state. An English major, she was shocked when she received C− on an English exam. She confronted the professor indignantly, saying, "I never had a mark like that in my life!" "Miss de Mille," said Dr. Lily B. Campbell, "I think we'd get on much better if you had a sense of humor."[1] Thus began a long love affair of the mind and spirit.

Lily Bess, as Agnes came to know her, was an expert on Elizabethan drama.* She was then thirty-nine — a thin, freckled redhead, witty and

* Robert Kirsch, writing of Dr. Campbell as one of the *Los Angeles Times* Women of the Year on December 19, 1962, called her a great teacher, scholar, and researcher. "When curiosity stops, you're dead," she told Kirsch.

enthusiastic, unmarried, with a wonderful smile. With Mary Hunter away at school in the East, Agnes made Lily Bess her confidante and the center of her odd social life, which consisted, in her freshman year, of tea parties with faculty members and a librarian. Her peers were understandably put off by her manner and her wardrobe, for well into her junior year she wore "a large gray tricorne with a cockade and a gray cloak and pretended I was a young man out of Dumas's Antoinette romances attending the Sorbonne."[2] Believing her own appearance inadequate, she became someone else.

Agnes had given up her formal dance lessons, but she continued her solitary practicing with neither teacher, class, nor moral support (William's comment was "All this education and I'm still just the father of a circus").[3] In her sophomore year, she began to create skits and dance pantomimes, which she performed with other students at campus rallies and assemblies. These numbers were heavily influenced by Ruth St. Denis, for although Agnes was never enrolled in the Denishawn school, her mother's friendship with "Miss Ruth" had made it possible for her to observe classes, browse in the school's library, and play with its costumes and props. (St. Denis would later recall, "My beloved friend Anna de

Mille used to bring her two brats, Agnes and Margaret, to Denishawn House. . . . Even then, Agnes seemed to know intuitively that she needed a different foundation from what our roses and veils had to offer").[4] But a far greater influence, which added a unique dimension to her dances, was the movies. She had observed, close up, the finest actors and actresses of the silent screen. She had watched them, studied them, memorized them, learned from them how to use pantomime and gesture to convey character and emotion and how to stretch that emotion to the limit, just short of where it would become ludicrous. In photo after photo, the adolescent Agnes — as Carmen, as an Indian dancer, as Pandora — projects the gamut of expressions she saw portrayed at the studio and at screenings in her father's and uncle's homes. That was her education in melodrama, comedy, and basic theatrical principles.

Agnes designed and made most of the costumes for her numbers herself, for her passion for fashion rivaled her love of dance. As a child, she had dressed up in the feathered hats, cloaks, and furs that her mother's guests left in the bedroom while they drank tea in the parlor.[5] At ten, she knew the names of all the French designers. She wrote and illustrated a book on the history of costume.[6] She made clothes for her dolls (with meticulous stitches, of course, under Anna's supervision) and cut paper dolls out of fashion magazines, painting wardrobes for them and filing them by category. In her uncle Cecil's library she had pored over his books about period costumes, noting details for future reference. Her dances were amateurish, but the costumes were authentic and of professional quality.

Announcing UCLA's 1925 "Press Club Vodevil," the university's Friday Morning Club *Bulletin* promised, "Those who have never seen [Agnes] dance will have something to remember when their youth is over."[7] For this program, she "expanded her customary zeal" in a group of dances, two of which presented characters that would recur in much of her later work: "an exuberant, exotic peasant girl, happy to be living" and "quaint bridelike girls [waltzing] in bouffant skirts and white satin bodices."[8]

The next semester, Agnes created a "dance-drama" to four of Petrarch's sonnets, each in a different mood, to twelfth-century music. The story told of Petrarch's hopeless love for a married woman, with the figure of Petrarch symbolizing "the material body of the man watching his emotional nature, which is pictured in the dance."[9] She costumed the dancers "exactly like Botticelli nymphs with draperies split to the crotch."[10] To her mother, who was out of town, she wrote, "I did the best toe work of my life . . . Miss Campbell said . . . (lying in bed at five o'clock with me snuggled up beside her) that she thought I could be a great tragic actress."[11]

If Dr. Campbell was sexually attracted to Agnes, she never acted on it, and her relationship with Agnes, though unusual, was not considered improper even by Anna; but Anna knew that the teacher's influence threatened her power, and Lily Bess knew that she knew. When Agnes's theatrical presentations led to an invitation from a sorority, Lily Bess urged her to move into the sorority house, away from her mother's domination. Anna forbade it, and tightened her surveillance. When she discovered that Agnes had a crush on Alfred Longueil, the young assistant professor of one of her English classes, she enrolled in the class!

In her senior year, Agnes met Douglass Montgomery, two years younger than herself but a kindred spirit. "Dug" was an actor — rich, handsome, glamorous, dashing, and lively. At the Pasadena Playhouse, where he was studying, he was considered to have brilliant prospects. Seeing Agnes perform, he offered her her first real encouragement. He told her that she had a rare ability to move an audience, not as a classical dancer but as a gifted and original performer, and that she could and should make a place for herself in the theater.[12] Naturally, she fell in love with him.

Anna had told her that nice girls wait for the man to take the initiative, so Agnes, who had never been kissed, waited to be kissed. But Dug's interest in her was platonic, and the kiss never came. He was, however, a loyal friend and supporter. Through his connections at the Playhouse, she was asked to stage a dance pantomime there.[13] The plot, adapted from stories by Hans Christian Andersen and Lord Dunsany, centered on a "wild thing" from the marshes who falls in love with a passing minister and for his sake enters the world. After suffering the minister's scorn and other horrors of mortality, she returns to the marshes. Agnes danced the lead on point, supported by students playing elves and fairies. Local reviewers praised her pantomime and noted, "Her white tragic face seems to show assimilation of the real heart of the matter."[14] By the end of the weeklong engagement, even William had to concede that nothing was going to keep her off the stage.

William had his own decisions to make, for he was facing a domestic crisis. Within four months of Richard's birth, William had become deeply involved with his new collaborator, Clara Beranger. Clara — married, but separated from her husband — had the sexual sophistication that Anna lacked, and she was understanding of William's past transgressions. She lived in New York with her daughter, so the collaboration was bicoastal; they worked in California in the summer and New York in the winter, with Anna joining her husband in the East when she could. She considered Clara a friend of the family and included her in supper parties on both coasts. Finally, in 1924, Anna thought the unthinkable and learned that it was true.

Over the next eighteen months, she and William tried to repair the irreparable. The tone of his letters from New York caromed from condescension to pleading to intimidation born of desperation. "If we cannot have the sex-relationship, there is so much we can have that I cannot have with anyone else. . . . Are you going to break up our home because I do not love you in the way I did? If you do, it is upon your own head. . . . Don't think for a minute that I fear the public scandal for myself . . . I fear it for you and the children . . . I am a free soul, dear, but I think you could learn to like me on that basis if you knew how much love and affection my heart still holds for you. I do not believe that I have done wrong. . . . If you insist on hugging your sorrow to your bosom; if you insist on being the wronged wife and deserted woman . . . if your grief interests you more than my companionship it is for you to choose . . . [but] I won't give up my children without a fuss."[15]

Anna was intransigent; he must give Clara up. William still hoped that, like his brother, he could have the best of both marriage and bachelorhood. "Believe me, dear," he argued, "you are making a great tragedy out of what need not be tragedy. You would be surprised at the number of our friends who are keeping up fairly happy homes without sexual intimacy. . . . We can either make a terrible smell in the world or we can realize that we are both very fond of each other — enough to 'carry on.' . . . If I can't love you as you want, why not let me love you as I can?"[16]

In the summer of 1925, Anna took her daughters on their first trip to Europe. The girls, unaware that their parents' marriage was crumbling, were much too excited to notice their mother's state of distress. In her journal, Agnes experimented with language and style. On the boat, "The foam on the waves is like torn lace. We passed great medallions of it floating intact on the ocean's surface. The froth is like thick dusty cobwebs rippling in a little wind." To Dug, she wrote love sonnets that owed much to Milton, Keats, and Shakespeare. The journal entries, sometimes illustrated with little sketches, contain detailed descriptions of people, scenery, architecture, gardens, sky, moonglow. The Eiffel Tower was "a taught [*sic*] bow, stretched ready for shooting. Giant musical instruments strung together with nervous vibrant wires . . . The spring and energy in a dancer's foot." Westminster Abbey's architecture had "all the elasticity, the steeled tension of a tiger's leap."[17]

In England, Scotland, and France, Henry George's descendants were feted by Single Taxers. Meanwhile, in California, William collaborated with Clara Beranger on a movie called *Lost a Wife.* When his family returned in the fall there was a reconciliation of sorts, but neither William nor Anna could accept the other's terms. There was no room for compromise. In June 1926, the day after Agnes received a cum laude degree in English, she learned that her parents' marriage was over.

Agnes was twenty years old, but her reaction to the divorce was a child's: the man whose love and approval meant more to her than anyone's had abandoned her. While she had yearned for his time and attention, he had given it to other women. He told her about the other women himself (but not about Richard). "I knew after your mother and I had been married for three or four years that we were not compatible," he said. "She has never done anything for me that a good housekeeper couldn't have done."[18] He may have believed it, but Agnes knew it was a lie, and she never forgave him for it.

The divorce was a cataclysmic end to Agnes's charmed childhood, an event that would taint all her future relationships with men. If the man she had trusted absolutely could betray her, could any man be trusted?

Real life, for which she was almost totally unprepared, had begun.

s i x

Alchemy

Anna fled to Europe, taking the bewildered girls with her. There was neither time nor perspective in which to assess the damage; that would come later. Agnes, who had looked forward to some independence after graduation, now found herself "dragged at the tail of Mother's grief."[1] The Europe that had charmed and thrilled the girls the previous summer now seemed dreary. In September, they sailed glumly back to New York.

Anna had a substantial divorce settlement and she intended, her frugality notwithstanding, to live and entertain in the style to which she was accustomed. The girls each received $400 a month from their father, who thought it would enable them to live independently; but Anna, ruling by fiat, pooled their resources and rented a duplex for the three of them on West 67th Street. Margaret attended Barnard. Agnes took dance classes and tried to sort out her feelings toward her father, no longer a god but a flawed and rather pathetic mortal.

William had given up his son, but he fought for his daughters. Agnes had a streak of her mother's martyrdom (William had once hurt her deeply by asking, "Who's persecuting you now, dear?"); seeing herself as an abandoned child, she began to revise history accordingly. Years later she would remember that Cecil's gifts were French hand-embroidered lingerie, while

her father always gave her books.[2] But for her thirteenth birthday, William had instructed Anna that Agnes should buy herself "something she really wants, not too useful,"[3] and for another holiday, she was to pick out a shawl of "up to $100."[4] She cherished a romantic memory of a simple life in which her father had walked to the studio carrying a lunch box. But William, with or without his lunch box, had earned up to $4,000 a week during those years, tax-free, and Anna had had two household servants, a full-time gardener, a Cadillac, and a sometime chauffeur.

In her revisionist version, Agnes did not write to her father for two years after the divorce — but a stack of his letters exists, and they were clearly in response to her own. At last, in these wretched circumstances, she had his attention. Discovering her power, she wrote punishing letters of condemnation. She accused him of neglect and self-dramatization ("Believe me, my dear," he replied, "it is not *I* who am dramatizing the situation").[5] He defended himself, but he would not beg for forgiveness or even concede wrongdoing. "You must live a little longer," he wrote, "to know that my 'hardness,' my 'coldness' and my 'cruelty' are a defensive mechanism. . . . Oh my dear girl, love is not always evidenced by caresses nor by conventional manifestations. . . . If I have not played with you enough, What of it? If I have been away from home a lot, what of it? I have never been so far away that my protection was not around you. You are very sure at twenty-one—you have judged your father and found him wanting. . . . How foolish it is to deny yourself all I have of myself for you because you cannot approve my actions in a very personal matter which you are not yet equipped to understand." He summarized his paternal deficiencies as simple fact: "I have been waiting for you two to become adults so that we could become friends. I've never been any good at playing with children, either my own or anyone else's."[6]

Agnes refused to see him when he was in New York, but he continued to write and to send money, even when it became increasingly difficult for him to do so. Eventually, there would be a rapprochement. But the shadow of her father would cloud her future relationships in a crucial way, for she would always be drawn to men in whom she saw his intellect and wit, and would suffer from their unwillingness to express their emotions and give of themselves.

She had inherited her father's best qualities: his intelligence, his sense of humor, and his writing ability. During the melancholy European trip of 1926 she had written romantic, fanciful fiction about a family with whom they had stayed in France and dedicated a plaintive poem to their son, Claude Fielding:

> My sex appeal lay comatose
> with virginal unpowdered nose
> I stalked through life, Nor roused the while
> One single heart. With sickened smile
> Men gaped at my teeth or languid hose.
> Oh gallant hour when first you rose
> Before me, firing, as one bestows
> Flame to a brand, with frenzied wile
> My sex! A peal
> of triumph tore the sky! . . .[7]

Her nose was indeed virginal and so was the rest of her, for her father's double standard had ensured that she had never even been kissed. A kiss, he told her, constituted an engagement. "I hope, my dear," he had said after seeing a middle-aged family friend's hand on her shoulder, "you're not one of those girls who allow men to handle them."[8] So strong was the taboo that she never consciously wondered about sex until she was in college, when she decorously asked her mother, "What is physical love?" Anna, who didn't know the names of the pertinent parts of the body, replied with euphemisms.

Agnes had been an innocently sensuous child; at Merriewold she had embraced the tree trunks, "holding my face against the bark until I was sure I could feel the sap move against my body."[9] Alone in the Merriewold woods under a full moon, she experienced a dizzy moment she thought must be "something like death, a sweet numbness wherein I sank through ecstasy to the fullness and quiet of all-pervasive rest, absorbed as in a tide, with the sensitivity of all things about my head beating and whirring like birds. Four times I had dreamed of sinking into this intoxicated oblivion and wakened just in time. I had lain shaking with happiness."[10]

In Anna's house, however, the twenties did not so much roar as converse, and sex was not a topic of conversation. Agnes had grown up primarily with women — mother, aunts, sister, female cousins, and classmates — and there were few opportunities to acquire firsthand knowledge of boys. At eleven, she was fondled by a male family friend and had been upset enough to tell her mother about it, but there was no discussion of the incident; the man simply vanished from her life. Anna's circle of Georgists included a lesbian contingent, but Agnes never heard the word until college; even then she had no idea what they did, except that it was "damned peculiar."[11]

Dancing is a channel into which many a young woman has redirected her sex drive. Agnes danced at every opportunity, even on the boat returning from Europe (preceded by a soprano and followed by a passenger who played selections on his dentaphone). But in New York, professional opportunities for dancers with Agnes's lack of training and experience did not exist.

The 1920s was a dazzling decade in America. Along with flappers and Prohibition came emancipation, Freud, free love, "talkies," and an explosion of experimentation in the arts. In 1928, *Vanity Fair*'s nominations for its Hall of Fame included Pablo Picasso, Thomas Mann, Jed Harris, Max Reinhardt, Walter Gropius, Serge Diaghilev, Sergei Eisenstein, and Ernest Hemingway. Stravinsky, Bartók, and Bloch had been "discovered." Charles MacArthur, Helen Hayes, Gertrude Lawrence, the Lunts, Gershwin, and Toscanini were becoming household names. "Modern" was a magic word. Possibilities seemed limitless — except in the dance world, where almost nobody realized that a revolution was beginning, with Martha Graham leading the way. There was plenty of activity, but all the big attractions came from overseas. There were no native ballet companies — and if there had been, Agnes's technique would not have been adequate for them. The few American dance companies in operation were small, unsubsidized, and built around their stars. Ruth St. Denis, Ted Shawn, and Isadora Duncan had followings, but their dancing was interpretive, not classical. Musical revues and movie theaters presented clumsily abridged ballets, or tap dancers, or precision chorus lines. The *New York Times* was the only newspaper with a dance critic on its staff, and the word "choreography" was virtually unknown.

Agnes took class and practiced. Providentially, Douglass Montgomery (for whom her unilateral love had, if anything, intensified after William's defection) had also moved to New York, to work in the theater. "Dug" was in love — not with Agnes, but with her unique combination of talents. He encouraged her to create character studies that told a story by combining pantomime, which she did superbly, and dance, which she used "as decoration and accouterment exactly like costumes, or lights, or music."[12] The dancing consisted of some classical ballet, some basic tap steps, and an inspired third ingredient: indigenous folk dances, in which Agnes had become interested when Lily Bess Campbell had her reconstruct medieval singing games for her class in English drama. Although folk dancing was considered too common to be taken seriously by artists or audiences, Agnes was intrigued by the history and the possibilities of dances that were created and performed by ordinary people who had kept them alive for more than a thousand years. Her unlikely marriage of folk movement with pantomime and ballet produced a hybrid style that was distinctly her own.

Dug was a mediocre actor but a reliable sounding board and a brilliant coach. He taught Agnes what every true artist knows is essential — *economy* — and made her justify every second, every gesture, every ribbon, until she was able to establish character, mood, and atmosphere in the first eight bars of movement, without such frills as scenery or orchestra. Together they carved, focused, and polished the material, camouflaging Agnes's lack of classical technique with her musicality, her keen sense of period, her exceptional acting ability, and her intuitive timing.

Timing can be perfected, but it cannot be taught. Agnes's timing was the equivalent of perfect pitch; she had refined it on movie sets and in front of movie screens, learning exactly "how to attack with a real impulse, how to round the gesture on the musical line, how to make the point on the last down-beat."[13] She had a natural affinity for the elemental rhythms of the earth and the body; she wasn't always certain how to move but she knew instinctively when and, just as important, when *not* to move, to clarify and heighten an effect.

Dug gave her confidence, but the characters came directly out of Agnes, who did not so much create as discover them, dredging her own background and experience; they reflected different facets of her personality and were the seeds of much of her later work. The first one, reprised in various incarnations throughout her career, was a sassy pioneer girl, traveling west with the Gold Rush in a covered wagon. Wearing a long calico dress, scruffy congress shoes, and a sunbonnet, she began with a slow walk and built to an ebullient hoedown for an imaginary group of people sitting around a campfire. The square dancing was punctuated with some elementary tap steps — time step, break, buck-and-wing — taught to her by an old vaudevillian; as the dance heated up, she exuberantly tossed her hat away. In the finale, she got the audience to clap in time with the music.* The girl personified the buoyant, adventurous American spirit, but she was not a symbol, she was flesh and blood. Agnes called the piece *'49.*

The second dance she created was closer to the bone — in fact, it revealed the bone. At the Metropolitan Museum of Art, she had seen Degas's statuette of a ballet child wearing a tutu. Degas had looked be-

* The music was Guion's "Walking to the Pasture," which she'd played on the piano as a child. It had reminded her of the first time she'd seen the prairies "and recognized the meaning and the love of those large lands" (*Dance to the Piper,* p. 107).

hind the artificiality and elegance of the ballet and portrayed the pain and sweat of the common, unglamorous, unattractive little dancer. The sight of the child's aching knees and back, the pride on her dirty face, and the fear of failure in her eyes gave Agnes a pang of recognition that inspired her Degas studies, which were as moving and effective as anything she ever did. *Stage Fright* was the first.

The concept of *Stage Fright* is hackneyed today, but in 1927 it was original. No one had showed barre exercises on the stage before or made fun of the classic formalities. The idea was brilliantly simple: a terrified dancer warmed up in the wings, just before the curtain was to go up at the Paris Opéra. The light from the imagined stage filtered from the wings onto the actual stage. As a pianist played something by Delibes, Agnes entered in pink tights and a short, stiff, yellow skirt with spangles. Her hair was pulled back behind her ears and hung long in back, and at her throat was a black velvet ribbon. She carried a watering can, with which she sprinkled the floor to avoid skidding before beginning her exercises. In a gradually brightening spotlight that magnified her shadow on the backdrop, she practiced her role, hanging onto a stepladder, trying to keep her tights from wrinkling, and at one point falling flat in the middle of a pirouette. Her mood ricocheted from anticipated triumph (practicing her bows) to panic (when she forgot some of her steps) until finally, almost ill with terror, she forced herself to be calm. When she heard her cue she pulled up her tights one last time, composed her face, crossed herself, and exited onto the stage.

Agnes called the piece "a comedy satire on the traditions of classic ballet, [using] the old hokey ballet steps, the formalized Italian pantomime, and the stiff poses and ballet grin."[14] But *Stage Fright* was more than the sum of its parts; it demonstrated her extraordinary ability to convey, without words, her thoughts and feelings to the audience. She saw the humor in the situation — couldn't *not* see it — but saw its life-or-death seriousness, as well. By making tragedy funny and comedy sad, she brought tears to the eyes of the laughing audience. It was a tour de force that would stop the show every time she performed it.

Literally step-by-step, she and Dug created a group of pieces for a New York debut. Meanwhile, she prepared painstakingly for auditions that bemused or confused agents and managers who had never heard of Degas. But on January 17, 1927, with at least a little help from a family friend (Edna St. Vincent Millay, a co-owner of the Intimate Opera Company), she made her first appearance on a New York stage, at the Mayfair Theatre. The production was Mozart's opera *La Finta Giardiniera,* and Agnes performed a dance-pantomime in the last act. The *Brooklyn Citizen*'s reviewer noted that the opera's "most striking scene was . . . at the grave of the dead Columbine, when the ghost of the lovely lady [played by Agnes] suddenly appears in a white hoop, and dances exactly as the coquettish ghost of a dancer would dance, before reuniting all the lovers."[15]

Two months later she performed *Stage Fright* at the Little Theatre's "Intimate Sunday Night" series. She was only one among twenty-one acts on the bill, but it was her first chance to present one of her own dances professionally. In April, at a Women's Glee Club concert at Cornell University in Ithaca, she introduced three new numbers, one of which debuted another signature character: a woman waiting for her lover. In *Jenny Loved a Soldier* she was "an Elizabethan hussy romping around the village green until her sweetie who happens to be a soldier gets through parading and can join her." She wore "tattered striped petticoats, a man's torn brocaded coat, a disheveled ruff, a cavalier hat and a pair of grand embroidered gloves."[16]

Onstage, by virtue of costumes, makeup, and movement, Agnes transformed and transcended herself. If the dance called for beauty, she was beautiful. She could be elegant, vulgar, flirtatious, innocent, regal, and even sexy. But offstage, where Anna still dictated what she wore, she had no confidence in her appearance, and her sex appeal remained comatose. She described herself as "the only unattractive one in the family."[17] Yet when Dug suggested that she have her nose and her teeth straightened, she dug in her heels and clung defiantly to her crooked features, determined to succeed in spite of them.

In May 1927, Dug went to Baltimore for a season of summer stock. Agnes somehow disentangled herself from Anna and tagged along as a very junior member of the company.* She earned $25 a week, out of which she paid her expenses. She dreamed of marrying the elusive Dug,

* In *Fata Morgana,* a comedy, she had one line: "Isn't George coming, too?" In *The Butter and Egg Man,* she had three lines — and got four laughs.

but he never bestowed the kiss he knew she would interpret as an engagement. For a time he had been flattered by her devotion, but now he felt burdened by it, and told her so, shattering her hopes and compounding her feelings of rejection by her father. When Anna learned of her daughter's distress, she wisely decided to spare her further indignity by whisking her away from the cause of it. She took her to Santa Fe, New Mexico, where Mary Hunter was living. But for Anna, there was no such thing as a vacation. Santa Fe, she announced, was a perfect location for Agnes's first dance concert — her opportunity to break in some new pieces and gain more experience before her New York debut.

Santa Fe was a painters' and writers' town, and its relaxed atmosphere was a welcome relief from the postdivorce tensions. Agnes met most of the artists' colony, and was taken to the Hopi Indian reservation to see the fire and snake dances. The first concert at which she was ever the main attraction took place at Santa Fe's Rialto Theatre, on a splintery stage made usable by Anna and Mary, who puttied and sandpapered it on their hands and knees. Agnes performed *'49, Stage Fright, Jenny Loved a Soldier, Hindu Dance of the Hands,* and two new pieces, soon discarded.* She was not happy with her performance. But Dug, who was in the audience, wrote on his card, "To an artist. The evening is yours — no matter what you do or don't do from now on. Lobby greatly impressed and chattering. Don't take your calls each time as though you thought you'd been rotten. Of course you do — but, believe me, I don't, my dear!"[18] The *Santa Fe New Mexican* agreed with Dug, and reported, "FURORE OVER MISS DEMILLE, REAL ARTIST OF THE DANCE. Her natural grace, her exquisite facial expression, her accomplished technique developed through years of training under a famous Russian master, will undoubtedly make her known soon as one of the great dancers of America."[19]

Anna noted that receipts for the concert totaled $128.46 — $46.83 less than expenses. Nevertheless, it seemed an auspicious beginning.

---

* *Who Is Sylvia?* (never heard of again) and *The Bride,* danced to a Paderewski minuet, which "pictured a party in the gardens of Versailles in the golden age of grace and beauty in France" (Program in scrapbook, AdM Papers, NYPL).

s e v e n

Entertainer

A New York recital was the essential showcase for a dancer in the 1920s. That meant renting a theater on a Sunday night — the night it was otherwise dark — and creating the dances, designing most of the costumes, and doing all or most of the dancing. The cost of the theater, management, publicity, pianist, and costumes could amount to as much as $1,000, a substantial sum in those days. Some dancers had patrons who subsidized them. Agnes had her mother.

Agnes always maintained that without her mother's financial assistance she would not have had a career — an argument impossible to prove. Anna did underwrite Agnes's dancing for fourteen years. Contrary to the impression she gave, her resources were limited but not strained. Anna, who was never in her life without household help, always felt compelled to count pennies — even though, in addition to her divorce settlement, she still had the money she had saved during years of economizing on clothes, household expenses, and travel (she had traveled first-class only when with William). If Agnes had not needed several thousand a year, the money would probably have gone to another good cause, for Anna lived to make sacrifices. But to Agnes, it meant that her mother

owned her financially as well as emotionally. Her collateral was her career. She kept careful accounts and promised repeatedly to pay her mother back, with no idea how or when that might be possible. In the interim, she paid by relinquishing control of her life.

In the child Agnes's autograph book, Anna wrote what could stand as her epitaph: "I who have always been known as the daughter of my father, and the wife of my husband, pray that some day I will be known as the mother of my daughter." When the second and central identity sank with her marriage, the third became a life raft. With the same fanatical dedication that had impelled her to convert schoolgirls to the Single Tax, Anna "managed" Agnes — plotting strategy, fighting for money and billing, printing flyers, hounding friends to buy tickets, handling public relations, planting publicity (cousin Allie was drafted to help), and embroidering Agnes's costumes. No detail escaped her attention and advice, even to how much of Agnes's body should be exposed when she performed. At the same time, this tough, capable, manipulative woman was seen by both her daughters as a shattered victim who cried easily, deprived herself for their sake, and required constant assurance of their love and appreciation. As William had predicted, she hugged her sorrow to her bosom and, by doing so, rendered Agnes incapable of challenging, let alone opposing, her wishes.

On January 22, 1928, Agnes shared a program with the dancer Jacques Cartier at the Republic Theater. Normally, a debut was the culmination of years of training and apprenticeship, during which mistakes could be made in relative obscurity. But Agnes *began* as a star — an aerialist with neither partner nor experience to catch her and with the impossible intention that every number should be a highlight. Of the seven numbers on her portion of the program, there were only two actual highlights, but they were brilliant: *Stage Fright* and a second Degas study called *Ballet Class,* in which she portrayed the same little dancer with the smudged and sweaty face, this time performing endless repetitive exercises to the beat of her offstage teacher's stick. Whenever she made a mistake, the stick beat faster; in a brief moment of rest, she dreamed of the dancer she hoped to become. As in her other pieces, she exploited her limitations so cleverly that the audience never imagined that the hapless pupil with more dedication than talent was herself. Natalia Rambova, one of her teachers at the Kosloff school, was in the audience. "That is exactly the way Agnes used to go on when she was studying with me," she told a reporter. "Up and down on her toes she would go hour after hour, getting away from the beat of the music, but sticking to it til she dropped. 'Agnes, will you stop that, you're driving me mad,' I would cry. 'Sit down to catch your breath!' And she would give me an agonized look and say, 'I can't. I'm going to be a dancer.'"[1]

Agnes has said, "I was born a dancer" — but a dancer is what, through sweat and perseverance, she would become.[2] She was born a performer. Her work needed polish and focus, but she had what was more important: *presence,* otherwise known as star quality. Presence is that mysterious combination of concentration, energy, originality, and an indefinable *x* factor that enables a performer to simply walk onto a stage and own it. Dug had seen her talent raw and recognized it. At her debut it was recognized by John Martin, the most widely read dance critic in the country. As dance reviewer for the *New York Times,* Martin had been the first to recognize modern, nonballetic dance as an art form. After a repeat of Agnes's concert — at which she added *'49,* which stopped the show — Martin wrote that "her rare and intuitive understanding of human beings is the heart and soul of her work" and compared her ability to see tragedy "through a lens of comedy" with Chaplin's.[3]

Encouraged, she continued to look for work, but all that turned up was two weeks at the Roxy Theatre (on the bill with the Roxy Grand Organ, the Roxy Symphony Orchestra, and Roxyettes, and a soprano who sang the "Bell Song" from *Lakmé*). Discouraged but undaunted, she worked on new dances, three of which dealt with the subject that increasingly fascinated, terrified, and preoccupied her: sex.

The prospect of sex and the marriage she assumed would accompany it remained remote, for her social life would have raised no eyebrows in a nunnery. "When Anna first moved to New York," Mary Hunter Wolf recalled, "she organized 'evenings' for Agnes and Margaret to meet young men, whom she corraled, and I do mean *corraled*. After the movies or theater they went back to the apartment for hot chocolate, which did not go over well with young people of that day."[4] One of the young men was Ferdinand Davis, nicknamed "Twitch" — a long, wiry newspaperman who first met "Aggie" in 1926. According to Davis, "Anna had a quality that made you a little uneasy. She was a soul blighted — so brave, so good, a pain in the neck. *Too* good. If you didn't believe in the Single Tax, you wallowed in the outer darkness and in a very nice way, Anna would lead you out." Agnes was "ardent, and very intense, an eager beaver, feeling a little put upon by the world. She told me that her father wished she were a boy, and was far more interested in her tennis game than in her dancing. She was full of virtue and plain dealings, and she seemed the last person on earth to be what she was planning on being. She looked less like a ballerina than you could believe.

"We kept each other laughing and certainly, on my part, loving. But at that time you didn't sleep with boyfriends, and neither of us had a dime. She was an impecunious dancer. I didn't want to live my life with somebody looking like a character out of Degas. I think we both were conscious that we had something going there, but that I was not the guy for her and she was not the girl for me. Aggie was so high-powered — you marry Agnes almost at your peril."[5]

As Agnes had waited in vain for Dug's kiss, she waited for Twitch to propose. And she sublimated, creating new dances about sexual frustration, seduction, and rape. But before she had an opportunity to perform them, she was offered a job on the road. It came about indirectly through Ruth Page, a Chicago-based dancer and choreographer whom Agnes had met through Ruth St. Denis. Agnes had written to Page after her success in Santa Fe, pleading for an engagement ("Oh, Ruth, if I could do just one dance! It would be a beginning for me. The first time I appeared under real management!").[6] As a result, Agnes appeared with Page on a children's program at Ravinia, Illinois. Through Page she met Adolph Bolm, a Russian who had danced with Pavlova in Diaghilev's Ballets Russes in Paris and who now had a small ballet company that toured the United States. A year after Agnes's Ravinia performance he invited her to perform three of her solo pieces with his company on a six-week tour in the fall.

The troupe performed one-nighters in third-rate venues such as women's clubs and rundown theaters east of the Rockies. The company carried elaborate equipment, sets, costumes, and a small orchestra. Bolm was a tired, aging, and ineffectual manager; he talked incessantly of his glorious past as Diaghilev's premier character dancer, creating an atmosphere Agnes likened to *The Cherry Orchard*. The tour was a succession of cheap hotels, upper berths, and uncomprehending audiences that rarely filled the halls. In Macon, Georgia, where they played to 3,555 empty seats in a 4,000-seat house, Agnes wrote to her mother that she wished the South had been allowed to secede ("The niggers have a certain amount of gusty humor and animal energy, but the whites none").[7] In Louisville, "People sit quietly [during *Ballet Class*] and seem to be interested but don't understand what they are seeing. I can't believe it is all my fault. I don't think the subject matter arouses their imagination. . . . I put so much strength into making myself believe I am in an important theatre performing before a real audience that there doesn't seem to be any left for anything else."[8] Anna replied that she must always dance her best no matter how small the audience, because "it may be that one important person was present."

Anna demanded constant reports, by phone and by post. Her own letters were insistent and reproachful, beginning "Dear Owie" (Agnes's name for herself as a baby) or "Dearie" and ending, "Devotion." "Get good food and simple food at clean places. Get certified milk in sealed bottles. Peel fruit. Do not eat skins of pear, apples, peaches without washing it first. . . . Be sure to keep your plumbing right. Take Cascara 3-grain pills, chocolate coated — or Phenalax." She sent detailed instructions, with illustrations, on how she was to pack her best hat. To Columbus, Georgia: "The minute you get to a town, leave word at the theatre as to what hotel you are at. Then you can be traced. . . . Watch your step with the company all the time. Be diplomatic. . . . Doesn't the clapping in *'49* come too far before the end?" Two days later (they had spoken on the phone the night before), to Pittsburgh: "As soon as you get to your hotel, tell the head clerk and the chief telephone operator that they *must* get all messages to you. Leave a tracer as to your whereabouts whenever you leave the hotel, and leave the name and phone number of the hotel with the stage doorman. . . . Be sure to insist upon the 'George' in your name in those places where your grandfather was so loved." To Des Moines: "I'm very disappointed not to have had a direct word from you since you left at 2:45 last Wednesday." In reply to a wire Agnes sent her from Washington, D.C.: "I wish you had sent me the whole 50 words. . . . Do not tell Bohm [*sic*] you have a publicity agent (Aunt Alice)." When Agnes received an invitation to a theater party given by Condé Nast, Anna wrote, "This invitation means that you are being taken into the group of clever ones — the swanky, successful group of literati. . . . This invitation is a statement that you are 'accepted.' So if the Bolm ballet does not feel like the last word in artistic achievement, hang on to your own dreams and know that lil ole New York has stamped its approval on you."[9]

Agnes had been born into the country of the arts, but until now she had traveled on her family's passport. While it is true, as she stated repeatedly, that neither William nor Cecil (with one disastrous exception) ever helped her get work, the de Mille name gave her entrée. Cecil's fame had continued to spread with the advent of "talkies," and in 1929, William co-hosted (with Douglas Fairbanks Sr.) the first Academy Awards ceremony. So when Agnes did work, it drew attention. Newspapers noted that her debut had been attended (thanks to Anna's efforts) by such luminaries as John Murray Anderson, Geraldine Farrar, Mary Garden, Alma Gluck, Fannie Hurst, Edna St. Vincent Millay, Lawrence

Tibbett, and Sigmund Spaeth. And it was not insignificant that Ruth St. Denis, Ted Shawn, and Ruth Page were family friends. Now, however, Agnes began to make her own connections in the dance world. The first important connection was with the conductor of Bolm's little orchestra, Louis Horst.

Horst was a large, homely, cigar-smoking German of forty-four, with prematurely white hair; Agnes thought him fatherly and slightly vulgar, and liked him immensely. He wrote and arranged dance music and had been accompanist, confessor, friend, and champion to nearly every concert dancer in the business. He taught choreographers how to use music to develop movements and structure dances, and they found him to be an invaluable sounding board. On the train, he entertained Agnes with stories about everyone who was or had been anyone in the dance world, including Isadora, Ruth Page, Mary Wigman, Ted Shawn, Ruth St. Denis, and three of St. Denis's former students: Doris Humphrey, Charles Weidman, and Martha Graham. Most of all, he talked about Graham.

Like Agnes, Martha Graham grew up in California (Santa Barbara) in a privileged Victorian family, had an adored father (a physician) who opposed her dancing, and began her training late. Unlike Agnes, she had eagerly parted with her virginity at an early age. At twenty-one she had entered the Denishawn school and then toured with the Denishawn company, whose musical director was Louis Horst; he became her guru and, although married, her lover. In 1924 she left Denishawn and moved to New York, where Horst eventually joined her.

Agnes had observed Martha at the Denishawn school in 1918 and noticed her the following year dancing behind Gloria Swanson in one of Cecil's movies. When Horst introduced them after the Bolm tour, Martha was thirty-five, and just beginning to be recognized for her radical ideas about dancing, choreography, costume design, music, scenery, and lighting. Her subject was the human condition; her approach was psychological, mythological, and mystical ("Your spine, dear, is the divine tree of life").[10] What would become known as the Graham technique was an entirely new way of moving — miles beyond where Duncan and St. Denis had gone but in the same general direction, away from traditional ballet.

The movements were generated viscerally (the opposite of external ballet technique), based on contraction and release — sensual, sexual, sometimes manifestly orgasmic. The effect was as electrifying and controversial as Cubism or the twelve-tone scale.

Agnes formed a lopsided friendship with the small, dark woman who liked to describe herself with Ibsen's phrase "doom-eager."[11] To the success-eager Agnes, Martha embodied the greatness she knew she lacked. Much as she admired Graham's technique, Agnes was a jumper, not a stretcher, and Graham's exercises were built on stretches. But Agnes was charmed by Martha's exuberance, her brilliance ("hers was one of the most provocative minds I had ever encountered"), and her experience in the sexual sphere.[12] Martha had lovers. Martha had acolytes, the dancers she trained. Martha had patrons. Martha was fearless, a nonesuch — a *monstre sacre* who could giggle. Agnes came to think of her as "a beloved older sister," seeking and usually following her advice.[13]

The presence of Graham and the other "moderns" — Doris Humphrey, Mary Wigman, Charles Weidman, José Limón, Hanya Holm, and Helen Tamiris — was energizing the dance scene. Their rivalry was not always friendly, but they had in common their contempt for ballet (whose practitioners despised them in return), and they were all fiercely interested in what the others were doing. On the evening of February 17, 1929, there were three dance recitals in New York, all featuring Americans: the New World Dancers at the Cameo Theatre; Marga Waldron at the Lucille La Verne Theatre; and at the Martin Beck Theatre, Agnes de Mille, assisted by Charles Weidman, borrowed from his partner, Doris Humphrey, for the occasion. Louis Horst, who had helped with the editing, arranging, copying, and rehearsing, was at the piano.

Agnes performed fourteen numbers, five of which were new and dealt with the themes that would drive much of her work: rejection, loss, and sexual frustration. In *May Day* she played a Tyrolean girl on a picnic with a boy who was more interested in food than in her. *Tryout,* with music by George Gershwin and Ray Henderson, showed a dancer auditioning for a vaudeville manager — a more sophisticated version of the Degas character, masking her despair with bravado. *Civil War* was a dramatic progression of *Jenny Loved a Soldier;* to a medley of patriotic songs, a girl whose Johnny hadn't come marching home performed a military drill complete with musket. "It was pretty sobby," Agnes said, "but John Martin liked it."[14]

Harvest was her first experiment in pure dance form and contained no ballet steps. To Percy Grainger's arrangement of Irish tunes, a drunken peasant girl in a plain blue dress danced at a harvest festival "with hell-fire in her eyes . . . in one spot endlessly beating out the rhythm, her arms hugging her body, in a Dionysian frenzy. . . . Her hands press against her throat. Her head hangs back. Her bare feet pound." When an unseen rapist approaches, "her lips are parted . . . her breath comes short. With a single gesture she falls on her knees, one hand ripping open the bodice of her dress" and falls backward onto the ground, her head rolling "in ecstasy."* The prose (in Agnes's notebooks) was overwrought, but the pantomime was subtle, the movement exciting and sometimes beautiful, even though the actual rape confused some members of the audience ("I just tore my dress open a little, and looked expectant, and then I rolled on the floor").[15]

Ouled Nail, inspired by Ruth St. Denis's *Cafe Dancer*, shocked Anna (as Agnes no doubt intended) and a good many other people, as well. According to Agnes's program note, Ouled Naïls were belly-dancing Algerian prostitutes who worked in cafés and public squares to earn the money to buy themselves husbands. They wore all their gold, to guard against robbers, and spiked bracelets "that could easily tear open a man's throat." For authenticity, Agnes observed "cooch" dancers at Greek cafés on Eighth Avenue and got Ted Shawn to teach her the basics of belly dancing. Her face darkened with makeup, her eyes black holes, she wore a long, dirty skirt and pounds of cheap jewelry that jangled as she danced, barefoot and sullen, to Kurdish tunes. While her hips gyrated, her hands and feet beat out contrapuntal rhythms; in pantomime she acknowledged the coins thrown by members of her imaginary audience, reproached the freeloaders, and even picked up a cheapskate's donation with her toes and threw it back at him. Finally, at the table of a favorite

* Agnes listed the movements as "Escaping circles — rays. Crack whip. Snake windup. Rayed sun. Mock rape. Swing cloak" (Notebook, AdM Papers, NYPL).

customer, she lifted her skirt for him to watch while she retrieved his donation from the table. Her back was to the audience, but her movement made the procedure perfectly clear. The betel-chewing character was vulgar, but the performance was not; it was titillating, funny, uninhibited, and convincing. "When she wiped her nose with the back of her hand," said an onlooker, "you imagined you smelled her and saw hair under her arms."[16] That Agnes could make this sleazy character as authentic as her vulnerable little Degas dancers demonstrated the remarkable breadth of her range.

Her reviews were generally good, but she was never entirely pleased. Her work defied categorization; she was neither a classical ballet dancer nor one of the "moderns" who eschewed all ballet movement. Nor was she, as one reviewer described her, "the Ruth Draper of the Dance."[17] (Draper, whose work she admired, was a monologuist.) Agnes was furious when she was called a pantomimist, which she believed meant she was not taken seriously. She did use pantomime, but as a garnish, not the main course; she could convey volumes of meaning with the flick of a finger or the lift of an eyebrow. She was praised for the "American" style of her work — its steps, gestures, and syncopated rhythms — but she was already experimenting with the characters and characteristics of other cultures. She was compared to Angna Enters, who also performed character studies — but Enters was, like Agnes, sui generis; her "monologues in movement" were solemn and dark, and while she used some dance steps, she was not a dancer.

No artist creates out of thin air; even Martha Graham, Agnes's idol, said she only stole from the best. Agnes did likewise. She borrowed from ballet, from folk dancing, and from Graham herself, for which she was censured by purists in each camp. But if the final product was a patchwork quilt, it was a fine one, and uniquely de Mille — each number a small slice of theater. *Tryout,* for example, began with a bare stage, gloomy and dusty. Agnes entered as though her name had been called, wearing a white silk blouse and black velvet shorts. She struck various poses to display views of her figure, showed her high kicks, jumps on pointe, and a showgirl routine with rolling eyes and counterfeit smile. The audience could imagine the producer's "Thank you," after which

Agnes picked up her belongings and walked off in defiant indifference. The strips of lights snapped off one by one, and she made her exit in complete darkness. John Martin called it "choreographic acting.[18]

At last, a job offer materialized. *The Black Crook* was a musical melodrama that had been staged countless times all over the continent since its original production in 1866. It was to be revived in Hoboken, New Jersey, and Agnes was asked to choreograph the dances — her first opportunity to choreograph for a group. She would also perform in the show, and she would need a partner. Serendipitously, John Martin sent her one.

eight

Warren

Before John Martin began his long and distinguished career at the *Times,* he ran the American Laboratory Theatre — the school that introduced Stanislavsky's theories, later known as The Method, to this country — in Manhattan. Martin was a Southern gentleman and a classics scholar, erudite and witty. He was also a homosexual with an understanding wife. When he took a liking to one of his students and the young man, Warren Leonard, insisted that their relationship remain platonic, Martin became his affectionate mentor.

In addition to acting, students learned tap and ballet technique, for which Leonard, an outstanding athlete in high school, had a natural aptitude. After three years at Martin's school he went on the vaudeville circuit as a specialty act, combining dance, acrobatics, and comedy. In February 1929, just off the road and looking for work, he dropped in on Martin, who had heard through the grapevine that Agnes de Mille was looking for a partner. He thought it could be a good move for Leonard, and beneficial to Agnes, as well. He wrote a letter of introduction, and Leonard presented it to Agnes in person.

Agnes sized him up: he was twenty-five, but a receding hairline added ten years to his age. Of average height and build, he looked neither

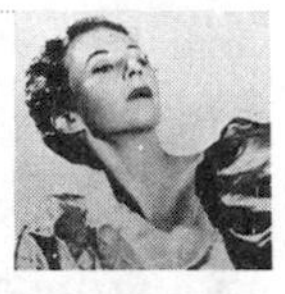

taller nor stronger than Charles Weidman, who had had difficulty lifting her (in *May Day,* he had accomplished it only by winding a large scarf around her waist, under her apron, and hooking his thumb into it to get leverage). Her first question to Leonard was "Can you lift me?" Leonard, who knew that a woman does most of the work in a lift, was surprised. He replied that in vaudeville he had worked with Avalon, The Girl You Can't Lift, who wasn't heavy but knew some trick of gravity that made it impossible to lift her. After members of the audience strained in vain to pick her up, she had climbed onto an eight-foot platform and dived into Leonard's arms. Agnes was impressed. Leonard seemed experienced and confident, and John Martin's recommendation meant a lot. She offered him $75 a performance. He took it.

Their collaboration was tense at first, for Agnes was used to working alone. Rehearsals were rigorous, and she was terrified that Leonard would drop her. "Afraid I'll drop you?" he asked. "Here, I'll drop you! It's not so bad!" He was tactless and blunt, but she appreciated his honesty and respected his professionalism. In *The Black Crook* he demonstrated a gauche charm that Agnes played off of with great effect.

Their first number in the show was "May Day," inserted with no regard for the plot, according to the convention of the day. It went so well that the director asked for another duet. With the help of a vaudevillian friend of Leonard's, they created "Can Can," danced to Offenbach's overture to *Orpheus in the Underworld*. In a number reminiscent of Agnes's dance pageants, she also performed as Stalacta, Queen of the Fairies, leading the corps of sixteen in two gently burlesqued ballets (one of which had mermaids dancing on their toes as though under water, breathing like fish, and using their arms for fins).

John Martin, who had no qualms about mixing business with pleasure, sent an opening night wire: SMILE TOWARD THE BALCONY BONFANTI AND ACCEPT MY UNETHICAL BUT HEARTFELT GOOD WISHES.* After the show he and his wife took Agnes and Warren out to eat, after which he went home and wrote a glowing review.

Audiences were receptive and sometimes rowdy, for the New Jersey theater sold beer, which was illegal in New York. After the show each night, adrenaline still rushing from the performance, Agnes and Warren rode the ferry back across the river to New York. For the first time, Agnes was in close physical contact with a man who touched her, held her, lifted her. She came to trust Warren's body, mysterious but familiar. She did not, however, trust the sexual feelings she expressed so freely on the stage. Louis Horst advised her to divest herself of her burdensome virginity, but, unlike Martha Graham, Agnes could not separate sex from marriage, and Warren was in no way a marriage prospect. He was a self-described street kid from Washington Heights, the son of a Christian Science practitioner and an entrepreneurial geologist who had tried unsuccessfully to get rich in oil; Agnes considered his family "mediocre."[1] So when she invited Warren to go home with her for chocolate cake after the show, chocolate cake was what she meant.

They ate in the kitchen and talked; her favorite topics were the divorce and Dug, and the suffering both had caused her. Anna chaperoned from upstairs, calling "Dearie, you have to get your rest!" if she heard silence. When Warren attempted a kiss, Agnes told him she didn't believe in sex before marriage. Naturally, her refusal to allow either of them to

---

* *The Black Crook* opened at the Lyric Theatre, Hoboken, New Jersey, on March 11, 1929. Ballerina Maria Bonfanti had starred in the original (1866) production.

act on their feelings only intensified them. One night during their "Can Can" number, when Leonard kicked backward at the spot where she was supposed to be holding a derby hat in the air, her nose was there instead. It broke with an audible crunch. When they left the stage she grabbed his shoulders and said, "You haven't hurt me, Warren. It was my fault."[2] At that moment, he fell in love.

If love was not blind, it was astigmatic. Agnes looked impeccable on stage, where every detail received her dedicated attention. Offstage, she considered her appearance a lost cause. She still wore the ill-fitting, unbecoming clothes her mother chose for her; her stockings were wrinkled, a hem hung down, a strap escaped its mooring, and her hair was an unruly red frizz that she rarely bothered to comb. A collection of nervous habits advertised her anxiety and frustration: she scratched her scalp, ran her fingers through her hair, and chewed her cuticles until they bled (a habit she tried to break by wearing white gloves day and night). Publicly, her demeanor, which she attributed to shyness, was no more appealing than her appearance; she was haughty and arrogant, bordering on pompous. Privately, however, Leonard found her to be warm, vulnerable, and when she spoke, bewitching.

Her commitment to *The Black Crook* ended in June, and she spent the summer in Europe with her mother, on the Single Tax circuit. On her twenty-fourth birthday she was back in New York; Leonard's gift was a copy of Walt Whitman's *Leaves of Grass,* inscribed "To Agnes — containing the most love any person can bestow on another." But all through the fall, as they worked on material for the next concert season, Agnes remained chaste, and Warren chastened.

Dug had nurtured her work in its infancy, giving her confidence and direction. Warren got her through her artistic adolescence and taught her to be a professional. The six years during which they worked together was a time of essential experimentation. Portraying a single character in an emotional situation had come relatively easily, but when she added a plot and tried to fit it to a piece of music, she was in trouble. She knew a good deal of theory, but her vocabulary of movement was rudimentary. In her work with Leonard, she provided the ideas and the tone; he provided the physical and psychological support that allowed her to dance to the limit of her ability. He contributed steps, what he had learned from practical experience, and everything John Martin had taught him about form, movement, and design. He was knowledgeable about music, interested in costume, and familiar with the technical aspects of lighting. He took a few classes with Martha Graham and showed Agnes what he had learned. Compared with the formal movements and fixed positions of classical ballet, the freedom of Graham's use of the entire body to convey and even create emotion was a revelation to them both. Agnes's body was no more suited to the Graham technique than it was to classical ballet, but Graham's revolutionary movement influenced her immensely, as it has influenced every dancer and choreographer since.

In November, "De Mille and Leonard — A Variety of Things in a Comedy Way" played a week at the Stamberger Theatre in Baltimore. "The audience hasn't the foggiest idea what I'm all about," Agnes wrote to her mother, but she added proudly, "I am no longer introduced as the daughter of the director but as Agnes de Mille, the dancer."[3] Anna replied, "Don't tell people you failed in Baltimore . . . be discreet."[4]

Agnes's first New York concert with Warren took place on February 12, 1930, at the Martin Beck Theatre. Agnes designed the costumes, shopping for materials herself at wholesale houses; Nette Duff Read, costumer for the Theatre Guild, executed them. They performed an ambitious program — eighteen numbers, solos and duets, with Louis Horst at the piano. Doris Humphrey thought *Harvest Reel* (formerly *Harvest*) "a little masterpiece; I thought you rose gloriously above the folk dance and were dancing the impetuous youth of the world. More power to you!"[5] The *New York Herald-Tribune*'s critic wrote, "Miss de Mille has grown and blossomed in her art since last seen here."[6]

The stock market had crashed and the depression descended, but the very rich could still pay $500 for after-dinner entertainment. Agnes and Warren performed at their private parties, at their estates, at the Plaza. Louis Horst sometimes accompanied them at the piano; Anna simply accompanied them, wearing an evening dress and standing in the back with the waiters. On one occasion, when the hostess was a former schoolmate of Anna's, Agnes felt inexplicable pangs of guilt that her mother had not been invited to the party.

In April, Anna made another trip to Europe, this time on behalf of her daughter's work as well as her father's. With a Dutch impresario, she planned a European concert tour for the fall. "You and Allie should refurbish your French in preparation for the tour," she wrote. Agnes should also study German, and she should begin working on publicity. "I'm glad you are keeping account of expenditures. You can probably stop leaks and have more money for your clothes etc. Please try to design dances with simple costumes for awhile. And when you buy personal dresses get them of figured material; it needs less cleaning. . . . So disappointed to have had only one letter from you in all this time."[7]

Anna had taken Margaret abroad with her, moving her cousin Allie George into the apartment in loco parentis; but in Anna's absence, Allie became so ill that she had to be moved elsewhere. Meanwhile, Agnes was having second, third, and fourth thoughts about Warren. For a year she had beckoned to him with one hand while fending him off with the other. He had been patient, but he was, as he pointed out to her, a healthy young man. He was not the knight she was waiting for, but he loved her, and she had come to believe that she loved him, too. Perhaps, with her encouragement, he might somehow transcend his background and acquire some polish.

Much later, after years of psychoanalysis, Agnes wrote an unpublished story called "Lorelei," about a young writer named Nancy who wears gloves day and night to hide the nails she bites to the quick. Nancy is superficially based on Constance de Mille's half-sister, but her sexual dilemma is Agnes's. "Highly sexed and easily roused," Nancy is tormented by sexual longings for a man who would gladly relieve them, but she is cemented to her virginity by the hope that a more suitable mate will come along. She fears that sex will dilute her creative energy; "If she became enslaved through her bodily needs, and she suspected that she had insatiable and terrible hungers . . . how could she write? She would be taken over." She is terrified of giving the extraordinarily patient man some claim over her, of losing her invulnerability. She toys with him, making love "but not altogether." Finally, the man makes an ultimatum: "I'm going to have you, or I'm going to have to go away."

In May, Warren Leonard made an ultimatum. To supplement the income he eked out with Agnes, he took a job in a Philadelphia production of *Lysistrata,* Aristophanes' play about women who give up sex for a principle. Before he left town, he informed Agnes that since she obviously didn't want him, he intended to find a woman in the show who did. Agnes was in no position to object. Then Allie's condition worsened and, rather suddenly, she died.

Agnes viewed Allie as a victim of poetic injustice — a pitiful, sex-starved spinster who died angry and cheated. The fear of becoming an Allie ultimately overcame Agnes's other fears, and she decided to take the only step that would irrevocably eliminate that possibility. One spring day, after a routine rehearsal with Warren in the apartment, Agnes produced the picnic basket they used in *May Day* and announced that they were going to New Jersey. Once there, via subway and ferry, they walked to the woods, spread a blanket on the ground, and endured what was, inevitably, a mutual ordeal.

"Lorelei" is a story suffused with regret. "Somewhere below thought," Agnes wrote, "was the sense that if she suffered enough it would be all right for her to have what she wanted. Her mother would have to forgive, because she was having no pleasure . . . She was left gasping for more, clawing for more, drowning for more. The deprivation wasn't exactly physical, it was emotional and spiritual. Rage consumed her. . . . It was not right she should be disappointed."[8]

n i n e

Aftershocks

"I have missed both of you girls more than you have suspected," William wrote to Agnes in 1929.[1] It was as close as he came to revealing his feelings. But he had given Merriewold to her (a believer in primogeniture, he provided for Margaret only much later, in his will). He stayed in touch, through chatty letters about weather and work. He searched for common ground: "The same difficulty you find in having no predecessors to teach you your line of work is what I am up against in my new work [talking pictures]. It is interesting that we should be pioneering in different fields at the same time."[2] He still hoped she would write, "maybe . . . because I don't know if I will write any more."[3] "Your novel of adolescence without sex sounds like an interesting angle. If I'm not mistaken, Tarkington made his greatest successes in a similar field."[4] Tentatively, he offered advice ("I am the only man you know who has your best interest solely at heart"); belatedly, he offered encouragement. For her debut he wired, WELCOME, MY DAUGHTER, INTO THE PROFESSION, and when *The Black Crook* opened, CONGRATULATIONS ON HAVING DONE IT BY YOURSELF. Agnes kept their correspondence going, even though her mother considered the mere mention of William's name an act of treason. He was her father, his money paid her bills . . . and she loved him. She sent him her reviews

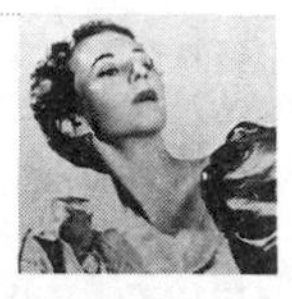

and proudly informed him that her dances made lowbrows laugh and highbrows cry. His praise was equivocal. "All the critics seem to feel that your big punch is in your human comedy," he wrote, "but I think you haven't suffered enough yet to *really* master comedy."[5]

William was determined to see his daughters and to have them acknowledge Clara as his wife, which she had become. In 1930, he offered to pay Agnes's railroad fare west. "I HAVE ARRANGED WITH METRO TO PERSONALLY DIRECT A PROPER TEST OF YOU TAKEN IN THE STUDIO HERE," he wired. "I FEEL SURE THIS WILL LEAD TO IMPORTANT WORK FOR YOU IN YOUR OWN FIELD IN PICTURES PLEASE LET ME KNOW HOW SOON YOU CAN COME LOVE FATHER."[6] Her future, he said, lay in the talkies; he would photograph "in sound one or two of your dances complete . . . I could give you a better break and show you to better advantage than someone who knew less of picture direction and was less interested in your success."[7] How could she resist?

Agnes arrived in Los Angeles in June, accompanied by Anna and Warren. Declining Cecil's invitation to stay in his home, she went to a hotel instead; she had come to establish a reputation in her own right. On the evening of June 24, the Windsor Square Theater was packed with an audience that would have made a statue bite its nails. "All the schoolmates, college friends, teachers and playmates of my lifetime and all Mother's and Father's friends came to see if their girl had the family spark," Agnes wrote.[8] The response from this illustrious audience was a dream of glory realized; the leading newspapers announced Agnes's triumph in six-column headlines, and the *Los Angeles Examiner*'s reviewer wrote, "She kicked into limbo with one nimble gesture all that balderdash about a prophet being without honor in his own country."[9] *The Stage* reported, "Agnes George de Mille instantly captured her house — not as a friend, or as anybody's daughter or granddaughter, but as a great artist in her own right . . . She's a story teller, an illustrator, a poet, caricaturist, portraitist, dramatist, pantomimist, comedian, satirist, humorist, designer *and* dancer. . . . Most terpsichorean performers dance with their feet; she danced with her head."[10]

Cecil threw a dazzling party for her, after which she and Anna moved into his house (leaving Warren on his own at the hotel). He offered to send her on the road with her own company. Wonderful, she said, but she would need a few years to create new dances and try them out in small concerts. Now or never, said Cecil — seize the moment. She could not. She asked him for work as a dancer; her face, he said, was not photogenic. Dance director, then? Costume researcher, perhaps? Music researcher? Assistant director? Impossible, he said, that would be nepotism — a common practice in Hollywood. Agnes was furious and hurt, but not devastated, for she was counting on the "important work" her father had promised.

She and William had exchanged a few words backstage after her concert, but their first real meeting since the divorce, an emotional reunion, took place in his office at Metro Goldwyn Mayer. He was vague about the screen test, but assured her that when she repeated her recital in July, he would see that every producer and agent he knew was there. First, however, she must move in with him and Clara. If she refused, he said, he would never speak to her again. Torn between primal loyalties, with Anna protesting "Haven't I suffered enough?" Agnes went to her father's.[11]

Clara was a kind, sensitive stepmother, but any positive feelings that Agnes felt for her brought on twinges of disloyalty to her mother, compounded by guilt over her relationship with Warren. Anna took Agnes's virginity for granted ("By the way," she asked, "*where* did [a friend] show you the modern French paintings and feed you nuts? Not at his apartment, I hope. Unless you took your own chaperone. I hope you were not unwise enough to go to a man's rooms. Such little indiscretions can become big"), but she knew that Warren's influence threatened her control.[12] He was acceptable as a dancing partner, but she made it clear that he lacked the intellect, background, and social graces to qualify as a suitor. To her annoyance, however, he refused to stay in the place to which she relegated him, and he actively subverted her authority. Because of him, Agnes was tentatively asserting her right to a modicum of privacy and independence. Agnes's wardrobe, Warren decided, was appropriate for a middle-aged frump; he took her shopping and picked out dresses that suited her. Because of Warren, Agnes would no longer let Anna see her work in progress until she was ready. Anna had forbidden Dug to take Agnes to a play about lesbians; Warren took her, without asking Anna's permission, to a drag ball. Most worrisome was his insistence that when Agnes returned to New York she must, for the sake of her sanity, get an apartment of her own.

Warren considered Anna "an old fuddy-duddy. She completely dominated Agnes's life. When we traveled across the country, she made sure we were separated by several Pullman cars. She thought Pullman cars were sinful — strangers sleeping in one room, with nothing between them but curtains. She brought out the worst in Agnes."[13] Certainly it was impossible for Agnes to relax in her mother's presence — or, as the summer progressed, anywhere at all. Whether she was with Warren, William, or Anna, she felt she was betraying at least one of the other two people she loved most in the world. Guilt sabotaged her infrequent sexual encounters with Warren and left them both unsatisfied and depressed. In public she shrank from any sign of his affection and never acknowledged that he was anything more than her dance partner. Her ambivalence made them both miserable; he was hurt and confused, but he loved her. They kept on dancing.

Their second Los Angeles recital was as well received as the first — but there were still no offers of work, and the promised screen test never materialized. The Dutch manager with whom Anna had negotiated now offered bookings in seven European capitals. The cost would be $6,000, which William agreed to pay. Days later, on the advice of a friend who warned of European managers who swindled and exploited Americans, he withdrew his offer — costing Agnes her nonrefundable $500 deposit and her last illusions about her father.

Anna and Warren returned to New York; Agnes stayed in Los Angeles, suffering from various minor physical ailments exacerbated by stress. An appendectomy further postponed her departure. Anna's letters dripped with martyrdom. "I think I have done the wrong thing in taking on the apartment for another year," she wrote. "With one of you [Margaret] planning marriage and the other living in a separate studio, I am left with a white elephant. . . . Life gets pretty thick at times and it is hard to see the way out. But a door will open."[14]

Margaret's fiancé was Bernard Fineman, a producer some years older than herself. Margaret had dropped out of college for a career on the stage and was working at the Pasadena Playhouse when she met Fineman, whom she immediately decided to marry. "Burn this letter," Anna wrote to Agnes; "I am much upset about Margaret and Bernie . . . I have nothing against Bernie but can't believe Margaret can find happiness in Bernie's set or in that life . . . Mr. and Mrs. Bernie Fineman may find hotel doors and other gates closed to them. It isn't just or pretty but it's true."[15] Agnes assured her mother that Bernie was "sweet and sensible . . . and not the least bit racial either."[16] Privately, she thought him "an upstart manipulator."[17]

As a child at Merriewold, Agnes had been spanked for repeating another child's remark about not wanting to play with some children because they were Jews. "Your father is half a Jew," Anna had told her, "and you are a quarter."[18] When Agnes took a Jewish boy to a sorority dance, she was asked, "Are you Jewish?" She replied, "I'm a quarter Jew, does that make a difference?" — but the question arose only because she belonged to a sorority that excluded Jews.[19] In Hollywood the de Milles' snobbery was democratic — they looked down on the Goldwyns, the Mayers, and a great many non-Jews, as well — but Anna's prejudices were ingrained and conventional enough that she could instruct Agnes apropos of getting a better rate on hotel rooms, to "Jew them down."[20] After Cecil's death, Agnes would accuse him of anti-Semitism because he always referred to "my English mother who is an Episcopalian" and because in his movies "he wouldn't cast Jews as the people in the Bible — he cast Charlton Heston as Moses!"[21] Yet she referred to the nose she believed had ruined her looks as her grandmother's Jewish nose.

In her books and her conversation, Agnes referred to Jews almost as though they held foreign citizenship. David Belasco, her father's onetime partner, was "the Jew in the clerical collar."[22] "Father was anti-Semitic," she said, "and I don't blame him, he had to work with those terrible Jews."[23] Early in her career, William was suspicious of "your Broadway-Jew manager" and advised her to consult him before signing a contract.[24] At the same time, with no apparent sense of inconsistency, he told his stepdaughter — whose mother, Clara Beranger de Mille, was Jewish — that he was "very proud of his Jewish heritage."[25]

Margaret had her wedding and Agnes her twenty-fifth birthday, after which she returned to New York. Using her allowance from William, she rented the ground floor of a brownstone on West 67th Street, near Central Park. It had a piano and a room big enough to rehearse in. She and Warren immediately set to work.

Over the next year and a half they gave only two concerts, representing incalculable effort and a continuing financial drain. They also appeared by invitation on a program with Martha Graham, Doris Humphrey, Charles Weidman, and Helen Tamiris — all modern dancers, as abstract as Stravinsky or the Impressionists. In a review that cannot have endeared her to her hosts, the *New York Herald-Tribune* reported that the humor and naturalness of *May Day* were such relief from many of the obscure and abstract works that preceded it that it stopped the show.[26]

Agnes tried everything, even a couple of skits with dialogue that were retired after one performance. The solo numbers Warren composed for himself were well received, but there was never any doubt about who was the star and who the supporting player. Agnes was quite capable of stealing a scene by flicking a finger or rolling an eye, but she was generous; she knew that a good straight man is hard to find, and Warren was a reliable one. *May Day* was always a hit, from the moment he strolled onstage in his Tyrolean costume, carrying a picnic basket and looking for a good place to eat. *Burgomaster's Branle,* inspired by Van Eyck's painting "A Flemish Merchant and His Wife," was more mime than dance; a stuffy Dutchman tried to teach antique Flemish steps to his wife, who refused to take either him or the steps seriously. In *Parvenues,* they were an overdressed nouveau riche couple trying to appear sophisticated at their first great ball, circa 1880. She wore a pink satin ball gown trimmed with dead birds; he wore a dress suit, black wig with long sideburns, handlebar mustache, and monocle. Everything went wrong, and finally, when her false curls fell off her head, he picked them up disdainfully, tossed them into the air, and they marched haughtily out of the ballroom.

John Martin, Agnes's most influential fan, wrote, "Her most persuasive creations are always those which deal with earthy people, even though sometimes they may masquerade in the garments of elegance. Under the sartorial fripperies of any courtier she can manage to find a lusty human being, and it apparently delights her to unmask him. Her more purely esthetic concerns she reserves for her ballet studies [which] are purely classic in tone and totally devoid of emotionalism and dramatic color, while her character sketches are equally free from both the movement patterns and the basic approach of the academic ballet." He pronounced her "one of the richest and most indigenous talents the dance has yet uncovered."[27]

Martin's praise did not cheer her, for she was more determined than ever to master pure dance movement. Comic acting, which she did superbly, was, if not too easy, not difficult enough. She was a brilliantly gifted clown who wanted to play the Swan Queen — never mind that she could do what no Swan Queen could ever do. Inspired by the paintings of Gozzoli and Piero della Francesca, she had begun to experiment with Renaissance, Elizabethan, and pre-Classical material. "To use movement more effectively," she said, "I began by working with rather unemotional classic pieces like Bach; composers such as Chopin were too loaded with emotional content for me to cope with at that time."[28] Her first successful attempt was *Gigue,* in which she danced in the eighteenth-century classic style to Bach's Fifth Fugue, following the formal structure of the music quite literally. The dance was built on the gigue (jig) step, the French version of an Irish shuffle, with light sliding steps in between. The first part was in fugue form; she announced the entrance of the first voice with her feet, the second voice with her arms, the third voice "by movement through the torso and the turning of the whole body; and when the fourth voice arrives, she jumps it, to indicate the vigor of four simultaneous contrapuntal voices, continuing the patterns of arms, feet and body uninterruptedly."[29] In the second part, the straight gigue form, she set the steps backward to match the inverted theme. "Bach's music is passionate," she said, "but underneath there is such a feeling of human adjustment to God and the Word . . . I was thinking of Christopher Wren's church, the Age of Reason, and the religious faith of the early founding fathers here — not the Puritans, but the men who made our Revolution and built those little white houses."[30]

These were years of false starts and demoralizing disappointments. Her confidence was crumbling; she was bewildered, for her childhood had prepared her only for success. But there were dancers who viewed her as a model. "Louie [Horst] was always telling us," said Dorothy Bird, one of Graham's dancers, "to be as professional and thorough as Agnes. She asked for criticism and she took it, and never defensively. Louie so admired that. She was so thorough about everything — costumes, lights, music, and she rehearsed herself black and blue. She fought like a wild thing, and she was totally an outsider."[31]

She was trying to learn to compose dances that were not pantomimes, not dramatic stories, but "planned sequences of sustained movement which would be original and compelling." But everything she attempted "seemed to develop either into trite balletic derivations or misconceptions of Graham. I tried to learn form and style through studies of English and American folk dances and through reconstruction [informed guesswork] of preclassic (1450–1700) European court patterns. It was slow work and it was bloodless. . . . I had nowhere to dance, and no company to work with."[32] When she did perform, the letdown afterward was a free fall into despair. No one could help her because she was exploring uncharted territory; there was no way *but* the hard way. Complaining every step of the way, she continued.

t e n

Sea Change

For two years Warren had been Agnes's dancing partner, production manager, confidant, and sounding board. He was a willing dogsbody whenever she needed him to set lights, shift scenery, mend a costume, or sweep a stage. They would work together for another three years on and off, during which time she continued to send him mixed signals about their future — but after 1931, he was no longer her lover. Her guilt precluded pleasure, and she knew now that he would never transform himself into a marriage prospect.

In the spring of 1932, she was actively looking for a more suitable mate. "Twitch" Davis was living in Paris, but there were two new candidates. Michael Kostanecki was an architectural student, from a Polish family so distinguished that not even Anna could disapprove. Michael actually wanted to marry her — but there was no chemistry, and furthermore he was Catholic, which to Agnes meant serial pregnancies.

There was also Sidney Mellon, who had been a Rhodes Scholar at Oxford. Sidney's family credentials were also impeccable; he was distantly related to the Mellon financiers and was an investment banker. He courted Agnes with charm, sophistication, wit, and determination, and

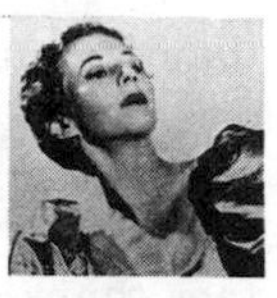

he got her. Dug had been a juvenile infatuation, Warren a romantic cul de sac; Sidney appeared to be the lover she'd been waiting for. For three months she was ecstatic, seeing him once or twice a week and believing that he was as seriously in love as she. Their relationship was disappointing sexually, but a doctor assured her that she was not frigid, merely terrified, and that she would enjoy sex when she relaxed. But before that could happen, Sidney suddenly announced that his feelings had changed; he wanted them to be friends, but not lovers. Perhaps her sexual fears exhausted his patience; perhaps he had sensed, as had Twitch, that marriage to Agnes could be perilous. The rejection scraped nerves still raw from her parents' divorce and left her bewildered. "He'd made such a determined effort to get me, over a long period of time," she said. "I wasn't pretty, I didn't have much money, and I thought, 'Why would he want me unless he loves me?' And he *seemed* to."[1] While she tried to understand what had happened, she and Warren were hired to choreograph a Broadway revue.

Flying Colors, so-called because half of the chorus girls were "colored," was an answered prayer of the kind Saint Teresa said makes the angels weep. The show was produced by Max Gordon, book and lyrics by Howard Dietz, music by Arthur Schwartz, all heavyweights in the musical theater.* On the strength of two hastily staged audition numbers performed by girls borrowed from Humphrey and Graham, Agnes and Warren were assigned to stage eleven dances and musical numbers in four weeks.

Except for *The Black Crook,* neither of them had ever choreographed for a group larger than two. The sixteen African-American girls were talented but inexperienced, and their Caucasian counterparts were not dancers but showgirls, foisted on the choreographers by Gordon, Dietz, and Schwartz. Due to a lack of communication and Agnes's lack of assertiveness, the costumes and sets were designed with no regard for the fact that dancers would be required to move in them. The best dance number, "Smokin' Reefers," was a sensational treatment of voodoo ritual; unfortunately, it had no connection with the song lyrics, which were about smoking marijuana.

Preparing for the opening in Philadelphia, they worked through the night, drowning in flop sweat. "I used to pray," Agnes wrote, "that something would hit the taxi that carried me to rehearsal."[2] Anna demanded a report. "I feel you must be ill," she wrote with deep sarcasm, "else I'm sure you could have sent me a line in one of my addressed envelopes . . . if you are too pressed to write ask Warren or one of your girls to [write] on the margin of a newspaper or bill of fare."[3] At the end of the second day in Philadelphia, the two choreographers were replaced by Albertina Rasch, who had directed dances for Florenz Ziegfeld's revues. (To add to their humiliation, Agnes and Warren had danced, not as guests but as hired help, at a private party Rasch had given in Hollywood.) When the show opened in New York a month later, "Smokin' Reefers" was the only remnant of their work. Monetarily, there was nothing to salvage, for their fee was to have been based on the length of the run.

The *Flying Colors* debacle was followed by dire financial news. At the nadir of the depression, Anna learned that her investments had been mismanaged and her income curtailed. William, one of thirteen million un-

* *Flying Colors* starred Clifton Webb, Charles Butterworth, Patsy Kelly, and Tamara Geva.

employed Americans, was recovering from a nervous breakdown. When he proposed cutting his daughters' allowances in half, they could not refuse. Nevertheless, when another opportunity for Agnes to perform in Europe arose, Anna decided that this time she would underwrite it and, unlike William, see it through. She cashed in some of her remaining stocks and bonds, Agnes borrowed $1,000 from Margaret's husband, and in October they sailed, with Warren, on the *Île de France.*

Agnes's personal depression was also at its nadir. She pined for Sidney Mellon as she had pined for her father, but this time there was no one with whom she could mourn. Her grief notwithstanding, the show and her career went on. On the Continent they encountered an obstacle course of crossed signals and complications, through which the resourceful, indefatigable Anna maneuvered them. In Paris, where reporters referred to Agnes as Cecil's daughter, Anna used letters of introduction from Geraldine Farrar and an influential local Georgist to fill the house. In Brussels, where Agnes was advertised as "Gladys de Nil of the Hollywood De Nils," Anna papered the house with an audience assembled by the American Consulate. In both cities they took a financial loss, and the trio headed for London with sagging morale. London would be still another auspicious beginning — but this one, unlike its predecessors, would lead Agnes toward maturity as an artist and as a woman.

Romney Brent, an actor and close family friend, was largely responsible for the success of Agnes's four London recitals. As the momentary darling of London's theatrical set, Brent salted Agnes's audiences with the friends of his friend Noël Coward and with other outstanding artists, most of whom Agnes won over completely. Critic Arnold L. Haskell called her "a dancer of contrasts, a whole ballet company in one" and ended his review, "Thank you, America, for de Mille."[4] W. H. Haddon Squire wrote in the *Christian Science Monitor* that "Miss de Mille's muse is light-hearted, and has that touch of nature that makes the whole world kin . . . Miss de Mille and Mr. Leonard are so happy in their work that he would be a surly critic indeed who did not share their enjoyment."[5] After this warm reception, made even warmer by the novelty of breaking even financially, Marie Rambert, who was in the process of establishing her own ballet company, invited Agnes to come back to London and study with her.

If Agnes had any doubts about accepting the offer, the next few months in New York dispelled them. To save money, she moved into her mother's apartment, where the tension between Anna and Warren was palpable. All around her, a renaissance of dance was taking place, sparked by the moderns: Martha Graham, Doris Humphrey, Charles Weidman, and Hanya Holm. No one, she felt, wanted or cared about her work. She feared that "whatever I did, no matter how expert I became, I would never be more than a glorified parlor entertainer, could not be for the very nature of the medium I had chosen. Martha moved; I grimaced . . . I had therefore obviously to learn to move."[6] A few months later, after President Roosevelt took office and closed the banks, the country began to climb out of its depression. On May 7, Agnes arrived back in England with her costumes, music, and press material, and began to climb out of her own.

The English dance world, being English, resisted change; ballet might be Russian, French, or Italian, but there had never been, ergo never would be, any great native ballet dancers. Only classical ballet was taken seriously; when Kurt Jooss took his "modern" company to London from Germany, they were received as a novelty. But Agnes's arrival coincided with the establishment of the first English ballet companies, both of which were founded by women who had belonged to Diaghilev's Ballets Russes. Not coincidentally, neither of these ambitious women was English.

The larger of the two companies, Sadler's Wells, was founded by the Irish Ninette de Valois, and would eventually evolve into the Royal Ballet. The Polish-born Marie Rambert operated her Ballet Rambert, then called Ballet or "B" Club, on a shoestring in Notting Hill Gate. "Mim" shared the building with the Mercury Theatre, which belonged to her husband, Ashley Dukes. Like Agnes and Anna de Mille, "Mim" had a tiny body that contained a large, contradictory personality. She was capable of great warmth, wisdom, and tenderness, but her miserliness and insults, her hysterical outbursts and off-the-cuff organizational style drove people mad. She was an intense, opinionated martinet, who could on occasion be outrageous — turning cartwheels in Piccadilly Circus, for example, when well past fifty. She had high standards, ambition far beyond her resources, and an unerring eye for new talent. For a pittance she employed, among others, dancers Hugh Laing, Alicia Markova, Peggy van Praagh, and Maude Lloyd, and two men who would achieve international recognition as the finest English choreographers: Frederick Ashton and Antony Tudor.

Six mornings a week, Agnes took a ninety-minute class in Rambert's cold, damp rehearsal room. The term "class" is deceptive; dancers at every level take class not to learn new steps, for the classical steps are basic, but to acquire strength and stamina and to refine their technique. For years, Agnes had artfully camouflaged the weaknesses in her technique. What little technique she did have was rusty, and her body had lost its youthful flexibility. In Rambert, she had a tyrannical teacher. Rambert had studied with Émile Jaques-Dalcroze and then with the Diaghilev's Enrico Cecchetti, whose rigorous method she taught. Agnes's body must have been astonished by the demands she made on it to bend, stretch, and move in ways that disregarded its proportions and proclivities. Slowly and painfully, it began to surrender. She could never overcome her shape, and her natural impulse to act was the antithesis of the pure, lyrical movement she sought. But her foot was as strong as her will, and she could jump. "My *entre-chats-sixes* [*sic*] are getting as neat as scissors," she told her mother proudly. "But, and this is vital, I have no line. . . . My God, if I could do one good pure arabesque!"[7]

Her presence in class mystified the other students. In the merciless fourteen-year-old eyes of Brigitte Kelly, "She was tough-looking, and so much older than the rest of us — except for Maude Lloyd, the oldest members of the class were in their early twenties. She had an unlikely figure for a dancer, very full-busted, and a tiny little waist. She was quite hippy, with short legs and tiny little feet. Everyone thought she was a rich amateur — there were always plenty of them about.

"My mother [Grace M. Kelly] was Mim's wardrobe mistress, and

Agnes enlisted her to help with her recitals. My mother came back from the first rehearsal and said, 'You won't believe it, in that Pompadour costume [the superb cream satin brocade dress she wore, with a white wig, for *Gique*], that woman has turned herself into a raging beauty!' This was the artist. . . . She had a kind of a go-getting aggressiveness that you didn't get in England. Her whole style was entirely her own, and very *unusual.*"[8]

Using Anna's parting gift of $400, Agnes had taken a room in the English Speaking Union in Mayfair. By de Mille standards, she had the barest necessities; a maid made her bed, tidied her room, and did her laundry, but "if I wanted a button sewn on or a stocking washed or a press clipping mailed or a ribbon bought, I had to do it."[9] Financially she was still her parents' dependent, but freedom from Anna's constant surveillance was exhilarating. She was twenty-seven years old.

In May, she gave three recitals on the tiny stage of the 120-seat Mercury Theatre. The absence of Warren and Anna was liberating but nerve-racking, for she had to break in a new pianist (Norman Franklin), find a partner (William Chappell), and attend to the secretarial and publicity details herself. Antony Tudor, who at that point in his career functioned as Rambert's secretary, accompanist, stage manager, and janitor as well as dancer and choreographer, operated Agnes's lights and curtain. With only a dresser to help her with nine changes of costume, hair arrangements, and makeup, she performed ten solos and one duet — a virtual decathlon of dance that incorporated drama, lyricism, and comedy — finishing in a state of exhaustion unknown to most mortals.

The public no more knew what to make of her than did Brigitte Kelly. Her pace made the English seem plodding by comparison; her attention to details astounded them, and her emotionalism made them flinch. "In London the ballet world was small, as it is everywhere," recalled Frederic Franklin, who was part of it. "We had heard that a dancer had come from America and her name was de Mille. Cecil De Mille came immediately into our minds. Anyone who came from America attracted our attention because of the way they dressed, and of course they spoke differently, and we always crowded around to hear them. She was a novelty to us — one of those Americans who wanted a career in England as a solo artist.

We didn't have that breed in England; no one would have *thought* of having a solo recital!"[10]

In *Balletomania,* the dance critic Arnold L. Haskell presented his view of the 1933 London concert scene and Agnes's place in it. "The dance concert," he wrote, "is usually a piece of monstrous impudence. . . . When we consider that Anna Pavlova, for all her art and personality, never appeared unsupported, and that her famous solos [e.g., *The Dying Swan*] lasted but two minutes each, what can we think of those who ask us to watch them for an entire evening in the triple role of artists, dancers, and choreographers?" Such performers, he went on, are inept exhibitionists and constitute "a whole class of 'inspiration' dancers, expressionist dancers and exotics, whom Nijinsky so happily labelled 'mushroom' dancers. Isadora Duncan is their goddess, but they have not understood her, for Isadora . . . was the great exception." Agnes, said Haskell, was something entirely different; her gestures and movements conveyed "a series of character sketches and impressions, ranging from the beautiful to the grotesque." Calling her "by far the finest *dancer-danseuse* I have seen," he explained that although she was the niece of Cecil B. De Mille, she was not a wealthy dilettante, but a hardworking professional who expressed herself so clearly in movement that program notes were unnecessary. He praised her range — "from the brutal realism of 'The Ouled Nail' and the satire of 'The Audition' ['Tryout'] to the white ecstasy of 'Hymn'" — and concluded, "De Mille is important, not just another wordless Ruth Draper."[11]

A few more recitals followed, but Agnes had not come to England to repeat herself. She had come to learn to choreograph, by dancing in the works of great choreographers and watching them work. Antony Tudor gave her that chance.

William Cook, a Cockney lad who had reinvented himself as Antony Tudor, was a year younger than Agnes, but considerably older in his experience of the world. Tudor had been a sixteen-year-old clerk at the Smithfield meat market when he saw a performance by Diaghilev's Ballets Russes and was imprinted for life. Rambert took him on as a student and employed his various talents as they became evident; in exchange, he had the use of her company, on which he taught himself to choreograph in a style all his own. His masterpieces were yet to come, but Agnes recognized from the start his extraordinary ability to do what she most longed to do: to convey emotion by means of movement, and nothing else.

Tudor had a working-class background — his father was a butcher, his formal education sketchy — but he and Agnes both knew that, artistically, he was an aristocrat. He was analytical by nature, an autodidact who based much of his work on literary and mythical subjects. His wit was sardonic but usually, in those early days, gentle. For a time, he was Agnes's most kindred spirit.

Tudor's muse, lover, and alter ego was the dancer Hugh Laing, a West Indian from Barbados. The twenty-two-year-old Laing had black hair, green eyes, skin invariably described as golden, a beautifully proportioned body, and the sculpted face of a matinee idol. By temperament he was as spontaneous and volatile as Tudor was reserved; he was famous for his tantrums and his taste. His artistic instincts seemed infallible, and his presence onstage made the audience hold its collective breath. The symbiotic partnership of Tudor and Laing, begun in 1932, would continue (with interruptions, notably Laing's marriage to the dancer Diana Adams) until Tudor's death in 1987.

Agnes took private lessons from Tudor, but their relationship was more than professional. With "the boys," as she called them, Agnes explored London's street markets, docks, antique shops, and outlying counties. Antony and Hugh provided her with a kind of delayed adolescence, the luxury of simply being silly; in order to keep other passengers out of their train compartment during an outing, for example, they put on a private show at every stop: Antony picked his nose, Hugh drooled or hung by his knees from the hat rack, and Agnes cried real tears.[12] With somewhat more decorum they attended the events of the dance season, including the new ballets and phenomenal dancers in the first London appearances of Colonel de Basil's Ballets Russes de Monte-Carlo.* Agnes thought of "the boys" as her cronies, her pals. But when they invited her

* The dancers included André Eglevsky, Igor Youskevitch, Irina Baronova, Alexandra Danilova, Anton Dolin, and Tamara Toumanova, "twelve years old and a true ballerina. I sat there and wept," Agnes wrote to Anna, on July 6, 1933.

to share their house near Rambert's studio, she was shocked. In her mother's eyes, and thus in her own, it would have been improper for a single young woman to share living quarters with two young men. The fact that the young men were homosexual would have made it scandalous.

Homophobia was rampant in the United States sixty years ago — before *The Kinsey Report,* Masters and Johnson, the Sexual Revolution, and Gay Liberation. In Britain, homosexual activity was a criminal offense until 1967. But in the arts, always a haven for misfits, there was tolerance. In her own attitude on the subject, Agnes assumed the missionary position, acquired from her father, who prided himself on his masculinity. William had accepted the lesbian Single Taxers who had come to his home to pay homage to Henry George's daughter; but in a 1929 letter to Agnes he wrote, "Homosexuality in any form has always been terribly repugnant to me — I hope you feel enough antipathy not to feel personally drawn to anyone who has this disease."[13]

The men she was drawn to were sensitive, witty, and bright; they loved the arts, but not necessarily women, and if they were not exclusively homosexual they were "just in the middle."[14] "My first real love was one of our family doctors," Agnes said. "He was about thirty-five, I was eighteen. He was debonair, funny, charming, and a pansy."[15] Douglass Montgomery, although he married twice, preferred men. As did John Martin, whom Agnes confessed she'd have married "in a minute" if he'd been single.[16] As did Antony Tudor, on whom she developed "a kind of crush."[17] Given the preponderance of homosexual men at every level of the dance world, it is not surprising that some of them became Agnes's valued friends and sometimes lovers — in fantasy, if not fact. Her relationships with them would have been complicated enough had not William inoculated her with his antipathy; thanks largely to his acceptance of the prevailing misinformation and prejudices of his day, Agnes believed that homosexuals were psychologically disturbed, their activities immoral. "The fact that many men who dance are neurotics cannot hurt the art as a form," she would write, "and we [the audience] may reach some understanding of the psychological problems of the unfortunate people involved. We can only do so by recognizing facts and I think what you call the typical American male will be influenced by the quality of the art and not by the morals of the practitioners."[18]

At this stage of her life, Agnes was not emotionally able to sustain a mature relationship with a man. Love was inseparable from pain, and sex from guilt. Sex was a perplexing proposition, a bumpy road she traveled with one foot on the accelerator, the other on the brake. When the object of her desire was homosexual, his foot was on the brake as well — which was frustrating, but relieved her anxieties about sex and commitment. She could feed her romantic fantasies *and* satisfy a need to replicate her unfulfilling relationship with her father. Tudor was simpatico in many ways; he appreciated her humor and her determination. He was poor, to a degree that far exceeded Agnes's idea of poverty — but he saw how hard she worked for little or no money and empathized with her. Her struggle, her strength, and her vulnerability made her a soul sister of sorts.

The triangle formed by two gay men and a straight woman has more than three angles, and a delicate balance of power. If the woman is attracted to one of the men, she may come to believe, at her peril, that she can change him. She may take his sexual reticence as a tantalizing challenge; she may become aggressive, imagining that any positive response from him is an expression of romantic interest. But if she exerts any sexual pressure, he may retreat even from her friendship. Or he might have hoped, in the repressive atmosphere of the thirties and forties, that a relationship with a woman would "cure" him.

For a woman as insecure about her sexuality as Agnes to put herself into competition not only with other women but also with men was masochistic and could only feed her fear that she was not "sexy," meaning desirable. But rejection only made her more determined.

During her first month in London, Agnes had met two men who would change her life and renewed an acquaintance with a third, who tried to change it but failed. The latter was Kenneth Fairfax — a fair-haired, clean-cut-looking upper-class Englishman, four years younger than Agnes. They had met at a Single Tax conference in Edinburgh in 1929 and since then had corresponded. Now he began to court her, which she enjoyed — but there were obstacles. One was his wife, who was out of the country and whom he promised to divorce. He worked for a publishing house, earning barely enough to live on. Agnes was impressed by his knowledge of economics, English literature, history, and philosophy — but he knew nothing about dancing or music, and her sense of humor baffled him. In his favor, he was a good companion and a presentable escort. Agnes was still grieving for Sidney, but her self-esteem required that there be a man in her life. So she equivocated, as she had with Warren, saying neither yes nor no, but maybe. As a last resort, hoping lightning might strike, she slept with him — but there was no spark. At the same time, she was sliding into still another impossible love affair.

e l e v e n

Ramon

Agnes sent her mother detailed, entertaining accounts of her days: whom she saw, what they wore and said and ate, what she earned and spent. The English Georgists, an eccentric collection of crusaders and cranks, were her devoted surrogate aunts and uncles, and she sometimes spoke at their meetings. Through them and her other family connections, she socialized with the political and intellectual and artistic elite: Bertrand Russell, Harold Laski, Krishna Menon, Oswald Mosley, Walter Lippmann, and assorted ladies and lords. As the granddaughter of Henry George, she was invited to lunch with Mr. and Mrs. George Bernard Shaw. She danced in a cabaret for the Prince of Wales and spent a weekend at the Raymond Masseys' country home. Writers Elizabeth Bowen and Rebecca West befriended her; West called her "a child of the house" and was a generous provider of gossip, wisdom, and entertainment. But it was through an American friend that she met Ramon Reed.

Reed's story has the elements of a Brontë novel, with overtones of *The Secret Garden:* great wealth, beauty, a dead mother, a cold father and stepmother, incurable illness, and hopeless love. At the age of sixteen, Reed had been stricken by a mysterious disease, possibly multiple sclerosis, which left him paralyzed and partially blind. Three years later, having

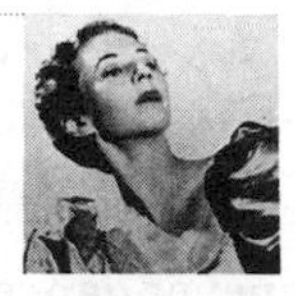

gradually regained his sight, he hired a male nurse (an inheritance had made him financially independent) and went to Oxford to read for a degree. But the physical effort was too much, and he was forced to leave the university.

When Agnes met Reed he was twenty-two, and looked like "a luminous, emaciated child."[1] In the Chelsea flat where he lived with his nurse, he spent most of his time in bed, too weak to sit up for more than a few hours at a time. He was able to read and write, even when horizontal, and to form original, and often amusing, opinions. Agnes responded at once to his intelligence and humor; his predicament, and the grace with which he coped with it, touched her heart. Taking charge much as her mother might have done, she brought to his flat the most stimulating people she knew in London: writers, actors, musicians, dancers, and the more presentable of the Single Taxers. She got him out of his invalid's cocoon, as well — to afternoon teas, to supper parties, to the cinema. When they attended the theater, in evening dress, the ambulance hired to convey them there attracted curious onlookers at both ends of the journey; they waved and blew kisses to the crowd.

There was nothing romantic about Ramon's tragedy, but both he and

Agnes tried hard to perceive it that way. He told her that he expected to recover; beyond that, they avoided the subject of his illness. Together with the nurse, Percy Thorpe, Agnes dealt with the frustrating logistics of transporting someone who cannot walk. The wheelchair was so heavy, the curbs were so high; "Are there no other paralyzed people in the world?" she asked.[2] A chauffeur drove them into the Kent countryside for an elegant picnic; when Ramon asked for some flowers, "I picked him a large bunch of buttercups and daisies. I wanted to run and tumble in the fields, but when I looked back and saw him watching me from the car and waving as I turned toward him, sitting watching until I returned, my heart broke and I couldn't romp before him."[3]

The first time he saw her in concert, "I danced *Harvest Reel* as I've never danced it before, as I've dreamed I could dance. The dancers stood up and shouted at the end. Ramon was all but out of his chair at the footlights. I gave him a moment of freedom, I know it. If I never do anything else, that's something."[4] The news that he was incapable of a sexual relationship dismayed but could not have completely surprised her and may even have been, at some level, a relief. And there were compensations. He was wonderful company. He adored her. His faith in her talent rivaled her mother's. And unlike her father, and Sidney, he could not run away. She kept her room at the English Speaking Union, but often slept in Ramon's parlor. Sometimes the hapless Kenneth Fairfax, still dangling, escorted her there and left her at the door.

In July, on the recommendation of Romney Brent, Agnes was hired to choreograph the dances for a new show, *Nymph Errant,* with music and lyrics by Cole Porter. Brent had written the libretto (based on the James Laver novel) and was also directing the show, which was produced by Charles B. Cochran. It starred Gertrude Lawrence as a young English girl who flits from man to man all over Europe, seeking real love. There were to be eight dances; one was a Greek Dionysian ritual set in the Acropolis, another a jazz number set in Harlem, another danced on a satin pillow in a Turkish harem. Irrespective of whether Warren had helped or hindered her on *Flying Colors* — in retrospect, she claimed the latter — this time, Agnes was on her own.

Cole Porter was the quintessential cosmopolitan sophisticate and, in Agnes's opinion, "the most powerful person in the theater." She admired his "fabulous" rhymes, and described him to her mother with precise detachment as "a small, finely boned and fastidious little man with a round doll head like a marionnette's (Charlie McCarthy), large staring eyes, and a fixed and pleased expression that I rather think has nothing to do with his emotions. . . . He walks mincingly and very gingerly with tiny steps, and he leans on a cane. . . . His voice is soft and husky and rather light. He purrs."[5]

Porter, Cochran, and Brent treated Agnes as an equal and saw that she had competent dancers and plenty of time to rehearse them. Porter even wrote music for one number to her specifications. Cochran asked her advice "about music, cuts, costumes, characterizations, things that are none of my responsibility, but on which he apparently feels my opinion is of some value." On the basis of her dances, Cochran promised to present her in recital. She believed she was "sitting pretty. . . . The people in the company are charming — include me in their lunches and beer bouts. I feel liked for the first time in such a group."[6]

The tryout city for the show prior to the London opening was Manchester. Ramon was installed in a rented house outside the city, and Agnes performed all the dances at his bedside — but he was not able to attend the opening, which took place on September 11, 1933, at the Manchester Opera House. It was a glittering event, for Cole Porter was always surrounded by the most amusing people. Agnes arrived in a taxi with Romney Brent, Douglas Fairbanks Jr., and Noël Coward, on whose lap she happily sat. Once again her work was received enthusiastically by a celebrity-studded audience, and for the first time her name appeared in a program all by itself, after "Dances and Ensembles by." If it all seemed slightly too good to be true, it was.

The press was unenthusiastic (Porter later told a friend, "We were so cocky about coming in with a success that we did not do the work that you normally do on a musical").[7] That work had to be done before the London opening. Agnes was asked to create a new dance, involving five girls playing with a beach ball, and to make changes in another. Her confidence crumbled, and she feared a repetition of the *Flying Colors* fiasco. As the pressure mounted, Ramon became ill and asked for her. With Cochran's permission, she went.

Percy Thorpe, whose devotion to Ramon approached fanaticism, was understandably jealous of Agnes. Now he informed her that Ramon's condition was far more serious than she realized — that he lived under the threat of kidney infection, blood poisoning, and gangrene, and that any excitement endangered his life. By raising false hopes where there were no grounds for real ones, he said, Agnes was shortening his already short life expectancy. She was daunted, but she believed that Ramon needed her. She sat with him through the night, until his fever broke and the crisis had passed. Next morning, back in Manchester, she learned that Cochran had brought in someone else to rework one of the numbers. This was not *Flying Colors;* her dances would remain in the show and her name in the program. But she sensed a change in the weather, and a well-meaning friend confirmed it. Cochran and company had lost interest in her, he said, "because I looked messy at rehearsals. I wonder if I shall ever learn. Every atom of my attention was going into my work . . . The fact that the audience cheered at the opening meant nothing, nor the fact that that night I looked ravishing."[8]

Throughout the period of anxiety over Ramon and the show, letters from Anna arrived with relentless frequency. Anna wrote when on trains and boats, in restaurants and department stores, in other people's homes and her own, wherever she happened to be, filling both sides of each page and then thriftily writing around the edges. One wonders how she found time for her other activities, of which she had a great many, for her word count must have rivaled Dickens's.

"I do hope you're wearing smart, chic things," Anna admonished, "and are carefully put together and made up, even at rehearsals. Spend money on grooming. Have a little manicure [*sic*] or shampooer go to you at the hotel, after hours if need be . . . have you learned to save your voice? Are you using a whistle or small megaphone? . . . I'm eaten up with curiosity."[9] Agnes dutifully assured her mother that she missed her and longed to see her — but when Anna actually booked passage for a visit, Agnes panicked, for the life she had created in London was too fragile to withstand the intrusion of Anna's meddling. She appealed to her sister to keep their mother in New York, but Anna, learning the truth, was deeply hurt. A tidal wave of guilt crossed the Atlantic and engulfed Agnes, who wrote begging forgiveness. Dancing around the truth — that Anna, who would gladly have hurled herself into a volcano for her daughter's sake, would only make everything more difficult by her presence — Agnes explained her difficulties with the show, her strenuous preparations for the Cochran-sponsored recital (two lessons a day, with her hips wrapped in rubber sheets to slim them down), and that anything left over went to Ramon. "I'm walking through tragedy," she wrote, "didn't tell you because I was afraid you'd fret, fear I was . . . rushing him toward heartbreak. Perhaps I am. I'm also bringing him life. . . . He asks nothing of me but my company, such affection as I could give him and the right to love me in return in an absolutely unpossessing way, no strings, no promises, no demands."[10] Of course she wanted Anna to come, but not now, when she had no time to play with her. She should come later, for the recital.

Placated, Anna sailed in November. While she was en route, Charles Cochran, for reasons that apparently had nothing to do with Agnes, tried to renege on his promise. In the end, he compromised: they would split the expenses and the profits (the latter, Agnes assured him, were academic). He then canceled all advertising for the concert, claiming that advance ticket sales did not justify any further expenditure. At this news, Agnes became hysterical. She recovered in time to write her own publicity blurbs, to which she signed Cochran's name.

The recitals, two of them, took place late in November. They succeeded critically, but the expenses, which Agnes believed were padded by Cochran's business manager, bankrupted her. Once again, what had seemed a step forward turned out to be the familiar treadmill. Once again, her career was becalmed. Anna returned to New York, but for once Agnes did not need her mother's sympathy; her own self-pity sufficed. "I had been compared to Charlie Chaplin," she wrote. "Who cared? I had hit dances in a London success — who cared?"[11] She envied Rambert, de Valois, Ashton, and Tudor for their sense of direction; "My path," she wrote, "meandered."[12] She clung to Ramon, who, for all his frailty, provided a refuge. "He gave me an acknowledgment of the importance of my work that I felt I must have or cease to exist as a personality. . . . And I had to have this recognition from a man."[13]

Sexually and professionally she was profoundly frustrated, and money was a constant concern. She had received nothing from her father since her arrival in London, and she now learned that he could no longer send her any allowance at all. Except for six guineas she was paid for researching old dances for a harpsichordist, Anna was her sole source of support. "Now I faced life like other dancers," she wrote.[14] But she would never be like other dancers, or share their frame of reference (when her father had suffered his financial losses, living more modestly meant cutting back to one house servant and combining the duties of his gardener and chauffeur into one job). Her surname, however, did lead people to think there was big money behind her, and she believed they increased their fees accordingly. "Living within the aura of wealth and yet so powerless," she wrote, like some Chekovian character, "I came to find extremely galling."[15]

In January she moved to cheaper lodgings — very near Ramon, just off the King's Road. She would later refer to this as a time when she "starved and froze in a garret."[16] It was true that her room had no central heating, that the gas meter had to be fed with shillings, and a bath cost sixpence — but what Agnes considered necessities were, to a great many people, luxuries. A maid lit her gas fire in the morning and brought her breakfast. Her former landlady did her laundry and refused payment. Her new landlady polished her shoes, ironed and mended her clothes, ran errands, and took messages for her.

All the same, if poverty can be a state of mind, Agnes was poor. She lived on £3 a week, a shining example of the Anna de Mille School of Thrift. Every penny she saved paid for her lessons with Rambert and her production expenses. At the same time, she was moving in the rarefied social circles that had been her element since childhood. If she had to travel by bus, she sometimes did so in evening dress (her sister's hand-me-downs), her destination a champagne party at Noël Coward's. If she could not afford expensive restaurants or the theater, she had invitations from Romney Brent, Douglas Fairbanks Jr., and other friends who could. This schizophrenic lifestyle led to some ironies only she could appreciate, as when Gertrude Lawrence drove her to the train station after a weekend at Charles Cochran's country house and stood beside her as she bought her ticket, forcing her, out of embarrassment, to travel first-class instead of third. A student of Rambert's recalled, "I didn't think Agnes had much money then. But I know that when we had baked beans on toast, she was taken to dinner at the Savoy."[17] "In her books she was crying poor," said a friend, "but not with us. She had terrifically interesting friends. I met her at the home of Commander and Mrs. Hawkins; one of their daughters, Diana [later to become Lady Yehudi Menuhin], was a student of Marie Rambert. Mrs. Hawkins had been a concert pianist; she used to have musicians who were going to play at the Albert Hall during the week come to her Sunday salons and play. I heard Schnabel play Beethoven. The kids, sitting in the corner without chairs and having tea brought to us, were Agnes, Diana, her sister Griselda and myself."[18]

Agnes had the use of Romney Brent's flat to work in during the day, and lunch was served to her there by Brent's valet. She was trying to devise gestures that were abstract but still conveyed an emotional impact. Tudor did it by dredging his subconscious. Agnes worked from externals, studying everything she could find in the British Library, from Darwin's *Expression of the Emotions in Man and Animals* to medical reports of the compulsive gestures of the insane. With Tudor and Laing she went to Cornwall to see the May Day ritual of the Maypole, celebrated with the ancient pagan rites. The Clifford Curzons introduced her to the Belgian Arnold Dolmetsch and his family, who played medieval and Renaissance music on dulcimers, harpsichords, and other original instruments — a great rarity at the time. The Dolmetsches were experts on pre-classical (sixteenth- and seventeenth-century) dancing, and Agnes plied them with questions. "I learned plenty. All the toe-pointing, bowing, and peeping under arms belongs to the cotton-batting-wig school of dancing, it seems. The real thing was restrained and quiet and flowing in a most lovely and expressive style. I learned everything I could, court bows, street bows, manner of holding hats and swords — everything. They had read all the contemporary works on the etiquette and dancing of five centuries in as many languages. It is wonderful always how much more effective the authentic gesture is than the vulgarized theatrical adaptation."[19]

In February 1934, Romney Brent, Agnes's guardian angel, commissioned her to create two ballets for a new revue he was directing called *Why Not Tonight?* One had to do with the wind and has not been heard of since. The other was based on a scenario by Ramon Reed, who had previously written stories and poems, but never anything for the stage. The story, borrowed from Boccaccio, was simple and funny: a young, inexperienced devil tempts three righteous virgins and tricks them into going to hell. The idea appealed to Agnes, and she began to stage it using Tudor, Laing, and some of Rambert's students. To one of them, Therese Langfield, "Agnes was rather like a schoolmistress in rehearsal. She seemed absolutely confident, partly because of the way that she walked and moved. She had this *wonderful* posture. When she came into the room, you sort of stopped and looked! Other ballet masters waddled in — 'Oh my back, Oh my hip, Oh what I did yesterday.' Agnes was always straight as a die. I was surprised whenever Mim treated Agnes the way she treated the rest of us, when she told her to stick her bottom in or whatever — I'd think, 'Oh, you can't speak that way to Agnes!'"[20]

Three Virgins and a Devil, as Ramon titled his work, was performed for the first time when *Why Not Tonight?* opened in Manchester on March 22. Agnes was not in the house, or even the country. Ten days before the opening she had turned the ballet over to Tudor, with detailed instructions, and left for Hollywood. Uncle Cecil had answered her most longstanding, fervent, and ill-advised prayer.

t w e l v e

Cecil and Cleopatra

The story of Agnes and *Cleopatra* is the story of David and Goliath, without the Hollywood ending.

Cecil had been impressed by his niece's Los Angeles recital and by reports of her work on *Nymph Errant.* With some nudging from Anna, he offered Agnes a job on his version of *Antony and Cleopatra.* Paramount would pay her round-trip railroad fare from New York, plus a salary of $250 a week for an estimated five or six weeks.

Her assignment was to dance one number and to supervise a sequence on Cleopatra's barge. In a three-page letter, Cecil explained that although she might be "considerably startled" by his non-Shavian, non-Shakespearean treatment of the story, his intention was to humanize the characters. He considered her "the most interesting dancer I know. Your dances are different and have drama in them, and something to make one stop, look and listen." Her brief was to create a dance that would accomplish Cleopatra's purpose of arousing the world-weary, sophisticated Antony. Cecil's idea was that the queen "has a net dragged over the side of the ship dripping with water and seaweed and dragged by slaves before the table and couch of Cleopatra and Antony, and then the net is opened and with the kelp wrapped around them, beautiful girls come to life, their

hair still dripping with the sea water, and lay before Antony the clams of the dinner's first course." This was to be "the most seductive, erotic, beautiful, rhythmic, sensuous series of scenes ever shown."

Cecil had suggestions for other dances, all with the same purpose and all recognizable anywhere in the civilized world as quintessential De Mille. One was a fire dance (using a man "who blows lighted gasoline from his mouth in a stream four or five feet high"). Another was a dance of Egyptian nymphs and fawns featuring "the hawkheaded man in gold with the Egyptian insignia of the sun between the horns of the bull on the head of the hawk, his ears feathered plumes, and his head feathered plumes." Agnes's solo he described thus: "When Antony tries to free himself from the spell being cast over him, I see a bull led before him, on the back of which lies a beautiful dancer, whose costume suggests, perhaps, the mate of the bull. Perhaps her headgear is horns, and her shoes are hoofs, like Edmund Dulac's 'Europa and the Bull.'"[1]

Cecil specifically told his niece "no numbers are seen from beginning to end. . . . The effects must be such that can be quickly seen and passed. In other words we will only see portions of each number."[2] Her work was to be peripheral. But to Agnes it was a chance to create something "mysterious, beautiful, new" that would impress not only Cecil but Martha Graham, as well (she had Graham's *Aztec Suite* in mind as a model).[3] To her mother she wrote, "If I can only persuade C.B. to let me have one print cut the way I want as an experiment, I know I could persuade him."[4] To Warren, who had met her at the boat in New York, she wrote, "[Cecil] thinks the dances are only flashes, but I'm sure that when he sees how effective they are he will include more than he now has."[5] Later she would admit, "I knew very well what he wanted, but have tried perversely to give something that interested me."[6] Never mind that it was Cecil's picture; her superior talent and taste would prevail. It was a miscalculation she would repeat, often to her cost, throughout her career.

Her Aunt Constance welcomed her into the fold and installed her in the west wing of the De Mille home on De Mille Drive. In those luxurious surroundings, she clung to her recently acquired perception of herself as her own advertisements presented her: "a distinguished European artist." According to her press kit, which she had assembled herself from her best reviews, she was a success. But by her uncle's standards, which she had long ago internalized, she was, at best, not a failure. She was not rich, and outside the self-absorbed dance world, only her surname was famous. Cecil called her "Baby." In his house, could she be anyone other than his niece?

Cecil had always been the most exciting man Agnes knew, and the only man whose approval meant as much to her as her father's. But the brothers were born rivals, and Agnes was loyal to her father, with whom she identified. She resented the fact that it was Cecil who had the power, the glory, and the international reputation, even though he himself admitted that William was his intellectual superior. "Cecil's commercial success ate at William," said William's granddaughter, "and I think he hated himself because he felt that it shouldn't have mattered, that you should be judged on your artistic worth, and not your box office pull. William did all right, but he didn't have a street named after him!"[7]

Agnes was enough like her uncle that the qualities about which she complained most bitterly — his stubbornness, his insistence on approving every minute detail and on having the final word — would later exasperate her own co-workers. For her, as for Cecil — largely, in fact, *because* of Cecil — failure was unthinkable. Furthermore, according to Warren

Leonard and other observers, her ambition was "bigger than Cecil's."[8] Ambition is, to be sure, a requisite of achievement — but the clash of these ambitions would shake Cleopatra's throne room — that is, on the Paramount set.

Cecil's attitude toward women was complicated. He admired women who were strong and independent, like his mother (one of his favorite lines in his movies, delivered by the hero to the heroine was "By God, you have courage"); but if he thought that a woman's power threatened his own, he felt compelled to dominate her.[9] According to Agnes, his idea of sex was "adolescent pipedreams, such as Swanson in her fantastic robes with her hair all swirled."[10] A regular feature of the famous weekends at his Paradise Ranch was the competition he encouraged between the women guests over the biggest and brightest prizes in a basket of jewels he provided. Cecil saw those women as amusing, flirtatious children and treated them accordingly.

At her first meeting with Cecil, Agnes informed him that he must decide who was to be in command, LeRoy Prinz or herself. Prinz was De Mille's pedestrian but reliable dance director, and his supremacy was not negotiable. In private, Cecil agreed to Agnes's suggestions — "the opening number with enormous feathers . . . the lotus dance (I've diminished the bull's importance), the Negresses' dance with the fire-eater and . . . a bacchanale with falling rose petals at the finish"[11] — but on the set, he deferred to Prinz. To "Dearest, dearest Warren," she wrote, "My position is not yet clearly authoritative, as I hope it soon will be. While [Cecil] professes to believe in my ability, he instinctively fears to trust a girl who grew up in his house, and falls back always on Leroy Prinz for the material which he knows from experience is surefire. Yet he wants to avoid what is banal."[12]

According to Agnes, Cecil told a staff member he wanted a dance that would represent "an orgasm, a copulation between an animal and a girl. Only he wanted it with 'class' and that's why he'd sent for me."[13] He asked her for something like her *Ouled Nail,* which he considered very sexy. She refused, arguing that the dance of a filthy, betel-chewing prostitute was inappropriate, and she offered instead a dance that incorporated movements from "Running Wild" and "Smokin' Reefers" (her production notes include references to Jaques-Dalcroze, snake hypnotism, "girls do phallic strike," Nubian Dance, squatting naked dancer, bumps, and "girls ride on each others backs, panting"). Every question and delay, whether concerning music, costumes, makeup, stills, or business arrangements, she took as a personal insult, an affront to her judgment. During the third week, she wrote to Warren: "Never in all my life have I been subjected to greater humiliation, rudeness, ignominy and indifference . . . [Cecil] has ignored my presence on the set, using the script girl as a model for the setting of business or positions while I stood by, offering suggestions to deaf ears. . . . He has continually announced his doubts as to the suitableness and effectiveness of my projected numbers . . . in front of any members of his staff who happened to be present when his fears assailed him."[14] But by then, she was out of the picture.

What had begun as farce ended in melodrama. Because Agnes was devising something far more elaborate than was called for, her work was not ready when Cecil wanted to see it. When he insisted that she at least describe what she was working on, she acted it out for him herself: semi-naked dancers would sway orgiastically, then stop suddenly "and sink backwards to the floor in the slow Graham fall I used in the Greek dance — the arms and bodies would lower to reveal the bull [with Agnes on its back] standing above them. He would advance over a floor carpeted with swooning bodies. The idea is sufficiently sensational to appeal to CB, and visually it would be interesting, if not entirely in good taste."[15]

Tasteless or not, Cecil was unimpressed. Agnes told him she was convinced it was excellent; otherwise, she said, she wouldn't have suggested it. He replied that he was the director; maybe, he said, she would have her chance some day. Meanwhile, he relieved her of all her responsibilities except her own solo, in which he warned her not to show the camera her profile (because of her nose) and not to open her mouth (because of her crooked teeth).

She performed her solo for him the following evening, in full body makeup and costume. "My costume," she reported to Warren, "is held on with adhesive. In pulling the old tape off to put fresh ones on for the audition, they tore the skin so that gouts of blood came out all over my shoulders and back. The trained nurses took this last taping off me the following day. All's well now. I add this detail because I simply can't resist it."[16]

The "audition" took place on the huge set that was Cleopatra's throne room. In Agnes's account, "The entire staff was present. They sat on the steps of the throne. The floor was polished black, and reflected my white dress. I had three spotlights on me. . . . I did the dances [to a Rachmaninoff–Rimsky-Korsakov medley]. Twice my brassiere broke; the costume department had not taken into consideration the muscles in my back. CB took it all quietly, but the mood was gone." When she finished, "CB frowned and shook his head. 'Won't do. Wouldn't rouse anybody." The censor, on the set to protect the American public from anything that might be salacious, concurred. "When the censor said there was no risk of indecency, Uncle Ce became grim. He warmed to the subject. 'Means nothing. Has no allure. It does nothing to me.'" What he wanted, he said, was "'lots of girls. Beautiful, naked girls, making love to a bull. I want that bull to stand for Antony. I want it to mean something unmistakable to the audience. I want something like the dance in The Ten Commandments. Like the dance in The Sign of the Cross. Prinz, take charge of this number!'"[17]

The next day, Agnes told Cecil she was leaving the picture. He did not try to dissuade her. She moved from his house to Lily Bess Campbell's, to nurse her wounds and her anger. Her uncle's rejection of her work was hurtful — but she could, after all, tell herself that he was incapable of appreciating it. What was worse, what burned like acid where she was most vulnerable, was his pronouncement, in front of his staff, that her attempt to be sexy "wouldn't rouse anybody."

t h i r t e e n

"Something of a Portent"

Within weeks, Agnes resumed her life in London. She spent the month of August in the Welsh countryside with Ramon – an enchanted time in spite of Thorpe, whose hostility had escalated; he now implied repeatedly that Agnes was a fortune hunter whose motive in befriending Ramon could only be greed.

By September, she had created four new dances and regrouped. In the United States, she knew, American ballet was finally receiving some respect. Louis Horst had founded a magazine, *Dance Observer;* as its editor, publisher, and major contributor, his mission was to see that modern dance, particularly Martha Graham's, was accepted as a legitimate and important art form. Graham's company was now established in New York. Ted Shawn had formed his own all-male touring company. Helen Tamiris was involved in an ambitious dance project funded by the Work Projects Administration. Agnes yearned to be a part of all that activity. Her plan was to break in the new dances in London and then perform them in New York, after which she would go west and "wage a regular campaign on Hollywood."[1] She had lost the battle with Cecil, but she intended to win the war.

She spent her days taking class and rehearsing; after dinner she

sewed while Ramon read aloud to her. He had not been so happy, he told her, since his childhood. Agnes was not *un*happy, but she was acutely aware that time, a dancer's priceless asset, was inexorably passing while she waited in a sort of emotional limbo for the prince who would awaken her with his kiss. Meanwhile, she danced.

Agnes would later write at length about dancers and sex, often in terms of sublimation and control. Her views were informed, incisive, subjective, and revealing. Ballet dancing, she wrote, is "probably the most erotic form of dancing known to us, [and can be] a complete although unconscious substitute for physical love."[2] Women turn to dancing to achieve "power and Dionysian release on their own terms. . . . It is a physical release as no other performing art can be, because it is practiced on the whole body. . . . [It has] often been chosen as a vocation because a woman's life, sexually speaking, has become in our civilization unsatisfactory, uncertain and expensive to the individual. . . . It guarantees satisfaction and control to people who are afraid they will not otherwise know them. A dancer can do more than pray or hope [for a man to satisfy her needs]; she takes matters into her own hands."[3]

She was less sanguine than ever about her chances of marriage and motherhood. Objective observers thought that the combination of her personality, intelligence, and humor made her at least as attractive as her glamorous sister; but Agnes had internalized Hollywood's (Cecil's) definition of beauty, compared to which she saw herself as an unappealing, if not ugly, duckling. Offstage, out of defiance and distraction, she ignored her appearance to the point of neglect. Onstage she felt beautiful. In dancing, she wrote, "the face matters least and the body is beautiful if it functions beautifully. . . . The woman appears at her absolute best, infinitely desirable. She is beloved. She is cherished. But never at any moment is she threatened. Nothing this great impersonal lover [the audience] can do or feel will compromise her physically."[4] Her handsome partner "must take her if she is the best, not the prettiest, mind you, but the best and the most skillful. And there for all to see, in public, she will perform with him the ritual of romantic courtship." Her rewards are "attention, admiration, emotional release, and they remain always under the performer's command. She never surrenders her will . . . and for any female who doubts her powers this is a temptation of frightening persuasiveness."[5]

Like most educated women in the thirties, Agnes accepted Freud's theories about frigidity and believed that if her sex life was unsatisfactory, it must be her fault. Many dancers, she wrote, "possibly a majority, are partially frigid . . . certain deep rejections and fears prevent easy sexual release. In any case, the dancers have evolved a substitute expression and do not mind the state so bitterly. This, of course, is no good answer to the fear of life. But it is an instinctive and practical one."[6]

In Wales, she devised a new dance that dealt, like *Harvest Reel* and *Three Virgins and a Devil,* with sexual tension. As she described it, *Witch's Dance* represented "a striving toward release through repetitious and progressive rhythmic patterns."[7] On a dark stage, with only her white face visible, she pushed her hands through the folds of the black cloak she wore, palms outward at shoulder level. She then dropped the cloak, revealing herself in a white slip, "dyed dark purple in shaded stripes with a flit gun and accentuated with swinging stripes of black crepe. The dress is off one shoulder and on that arm I wear a loose jagged sleeve which looks as though it had slipped down. Hair wild. Skirt unhemmed and ragged. Whole appearance slightly hexed."[8] In this costume she moved "like an animal, crouching, somersaulting, a final straightening to ecstasy and a contortion on the ground in spasms of convulsive insanity."[9] The music was Stravinsky's *Le Sacre du Printemps.*

Witch's Dance was one of four new creations; in another, *Dance of Death,* she emulated Ramon, going not in defeat but in defiance to her doom. In all there were sixteen dances in her fall 1934 recitals — most of them solos, in a broad range of styles and moods. The countless details of such an undertaking required the help of a staff, and Agnes had none. She did, however, have her mother's power of persuasion. "Even with all that drive and energy, you always wanted to help Anna," Mary Hunter Wolf observed; "she always seemed as if she were coming apart. There's something of that in Agnes."[10] She managed to find people to handle her printing, publicity, business affairs, and even morale. She had always designed her own costumes quite beautifully, but she lacked, as she put it, *"fantaisie."*[11] Now she commissioned the dancer-choreographer Andrée Howard to help, and she described the results with relish. For her *Mozart Minuet* she wore a "brown brocade over a short hoop, the length of the court ballet dresses, split and looped up to reveal puffs of cream satin and cloth of gold and edged with gold fringe. The sleeves are of flesh-colored invisible net criss-crossed with gold fringe which hangs in cascades down my arms to the wrist. I wear cream satin shoes with square gold heels and diamond buckles. My wig is of yak hair stiffened and painted with gold on the highlights."[12] In *Galliarde,* based on the lively Elizabethan court dances she'd learned from the Dolmetsches, she wore "moss green taffeta latticed with black horse-hair braid, at every junction of the braid is nailed a flame-colored Tudor rose. There is an enormous farthingale and a high silver gauze collar edged with lace. The neck is cut very low with a transparent yoke of net and pearl lattice finished off at the throat with a small double ruff and necklace of pearl. The bodice is studded with emerald buttons and tassles of pearls. My wig is drawn in a high pompadour off the forehead and a roll on top of the head . . . the hair is flaming pink."[13] In this dress she played an Elizabethan woman who took revenge on a dignitary who had spurned her by throwing coins and jewels on the ground for him to pick up (as a final touch, she stamped her shoe on his fingers as he grabbed the jewels).

In November she gave a series of four recitals, each one a tour de force; a stunned reviewer wrote, "Miss de Mille indeed is something of a portent."[14] Although her share of the box office was only £11, the final recital, she reported to her mother, was "the best I've ever given. . . . I feel alive for the first time in about six years."[15] She did not trust her mother with the additional reason for her rebirth: a German Jewish refugee named Edgar Wind.

Agnes had met Wind (pronounced Vindt) at a party the previous year. A professor of philosophy and an art historian, he had been instrumental in relocating the prestigious Warburg Institute from Nazi Germany to London. She had not thought of the professor again, however, until red roses arrived backstage after her recital, with an ardent message. His intellectual credentials were impressive; he knew four living languages and two dead ones, and he played the piano beautifully. "I was intoxicated," Agnes said, "by a mind of that caliber. For the first time in my life, a man of position, of stature, of achievement, was courting me."[16]

Edgar was a large man, fifteen years Agnes's senior — not handsome, but impeccably groomed. He thought her work brilliant and even went to class with her, to observe. He was understanding about her relationship with Ramon, even promising to look in on him while she was in America and send her reports. Agnes had seen Edgar only four times when she sailed for New York, in December. When he kissed her goodbye — her first real kiss in a year and a half — it was easy to confuse chemistry with love.

On the other side of the Atlantic, Warren kissed her hello — but on the cheek, at her insistence. It was a strained reunion, for they brought to it conflicting expectations. Agnes had assumed that Warren would be available to her, as in the past, as a dance partner and a friend. Warren, however, assumed that she was still in love with him. He had acknowledged all along that her talent was superior to his own; "When she stepped onto a stage," he said, "she had the aggressive, indomitable courage to think she was the best at what she did. And she made the audience think so, too."[17] But he had been her straight man, her foil — her other hand, clapping — and he still believed they might become the Lunt and Fontanne of the dance world. She had, after all, written to him often and affectionately; as recently as the past spring, while working on *Cleopatra,* she had written, "Oh my darling, I wish sometime I might be associated in your mind with something besides pain. . . . My feeling for you is deep and poignant."[18] She had never told him about Sidney Mellon, and she did not tell him now about Ramon or Edgar, but her coolness was unmistakable; she spoke of "my" plans, not "ours."

Warren felt a knife in his heart; years later, when she began to publish autobiographical books, he would feel it turn. Authors exercise editorial license to keep the story moving; but Agnes not only wrote of Warren as having been nothing more to her than a dance partner, she erased him from several specific events in which he had participated, such as her first European tour (she and Anna had traveled, she wrote in *Speak to Me, Dance with Me,* "quite alone").[19] "We were so close, we might as well have been married," Warren said. "She told me *everything.* But in *Dance to the Piper* she wrote about me so cavalierly, with no emotion. I knew all along that I wasn't the most important thing in her life. Her *career* was. But I wasn't just along for the ride — I was *part* of the ride!"[20]

In *Dance to the Piper,* Agnes wrote that when she returned to New York, Warren informed her that "he had decided I was too dominating an influence in his art life [and] he intended to try his fortunes alone — a very manly decision but ill-timed, I felt, since our Guild concert was scheduled four weeks later."[21] The concert was actually six weeks away, and Warren's decision was based on something that had been a source of contention between them for years: billing.

Before their very first concert together, Warren had objected to the words "assisted by" in front of his name on the program. "Magicians have assistants," he said, "dancers have partners." He had his own solo numbers, he set lights and served as her sounding board, and he felt he deserved better. From his point of view, things changed only for the worse. On some flyers her name was twice the size of his; for their Paris concert, it was five times as big. He told her that either her name was too large or his was too small. He asked for equal billing. She refused. "He was unknown!" she said; "I was a known concert dancer!"[22] On *Flying Colors,* he had had equal billing. Now he refused to work without it. He miscalculated. In London, Agnes had discovered that he was expendable.

Agnes replaced him with two men (one of whom, Robert Lewis,

would direct the original *Brigadoon*), both of whom were satisfactory. But although the *New York Herald-Tribune*'s dance critic considered the concert "the most momentous occurrence so far in the current dance season," Agnes considered it a qualified disaster. Tastes had changed; while she had sweated to improve her ballet technique, "modern" had become the rage, and ballet dancing temporarily passé. The public's appetite for evenings by a solo performer (such as Angna Enters, Cornelia Otis Skinner, and Ruth Draper, none of whom were dancers) had peaked. Agnes wanted praise for her dancing, which had improved. But some reviewers preferred her early "character" pieces, such as *'49,* and suggested that she restrict herself to dances "incorporating the American spirit, the American character and American history."[23]

In the 1930s, dance was still reviewed largely by music critics who knew little about dance. John Martin was an exception; his knowledge of all the arts was solid, and his power enormous. His praise in the *New York Times* could make a career, for his opinions were quoted all over the country. Martin had championed Agnes's career enthusiastically from its start, and even more so after she teamed up with his protégé, Warren Leonard. She had thought of him as a friend — a conflict of interest in which Martin colluded — and until this first concert without Warren, his reviews of her work had been unequivocally positive. Now he wrote that she had lost her warmth and ebullience, and asked, "Has she gone aristocratic on us?"[24] He also deplored the absence of Leonard. It may have been, as Leonard believed, that Martin admired Agnes's work less as he came to admire modern dance more. Or he may simply have expected too much and been disappointed. Whatever his motive, Agnes took it personally, assuming that Martin's fondness for Warren, and her break with him, was a factor. But Martin also had the wisdom and foresight to write, "It would be extremely interesting to see her work in a larger theatrical medium than the concert stage can provide. As a potential creator of that nebulous native ballet for which we are all waiting and watching she has marked, even unique, qualifications."[25] Something of a portent, indeed.

f o u r t e e n

Such Sweet Sorrow

Agnes's wounds from *Cleopatra* would never heal completely, but enough scar tissue had formed in a year to allow a return to Hollywood. Two recitals were booked, and Warren was to be her partner. "My love for Agnes had been killed by lack of nourishment," he said, "but she wanted me to be in a concert with her in California. She said, 'You will have everybody in Hollywood see you.'"[1] She installed him in an extra room in her father's office, and herself at Margaret and Bernie's, in Beverly Hills.

They rehearsed at the studio of Carmelita Maracci, a fiery, twenty-three-year-old, chain-smoking, five-foot-two-inch dancer who claimed to have been born in Uruguay. As her soul seemed to be Latin, no one doubted her. Not until the end of her life did her husband discover that her birthplace was Goldfield, Nevada. Her intimates called her Tootie; Agnes called her Carmi, and attended her classes when she could. Like Agnes, Carmelita was a powerful, ambitious woman who created and performed her own dances in an unorthodox hybrid style — in her case, a combination of ballet and Spanish dancing. Technically and creatively, she had everything: strength, delicacy, passion, imagination, and intelligence. No one was like her. Agnes prophesied that she would be an international success within five years, an opinion that was shared by John

Martin and by subsequent students of Carmelita's (a group that included Jerome Robbins, Robert Joffrey, Leslie Caron, Gerald Arpino, Erik Bruhn, Allegra Kent, Cynthia Gregory, and Carmen de Lavallade, who likened the sound of Carmelita's castanets to Arthur Rubinstein playing the piano). The relationship between Agnes and Carmelita, both more and less than a friendship, would last over fifty years.

When Agnes first wrote about Carmelita, in 1952, it was not a particularly flattering portrait (Carmelita never forgave her for saying she had "the head of a precocious monkey" — or, for that matter, for misspelling her name), but it was worshipful nonetheless.[2] She described Carmelita's feet as the most beautiful in the ballet world (dancers are obsessed with feet) and called her "close to genius . . . a staunch friend and a great teacher."[3] To the best of her knowledge, everything she wrote was accurate. After Carmelita's death in 1988, Agnes revised and expanded her original portrait. She still extolled Carmelita's brilliance, still thought her best dances "the most passionate and powerfully devised solos I have ever seen."[4] By then, however, she could tell the rest of the story — that Carmelita was "a fugue of neuroses" whose emotional knots strangled her career.

But in 1934, Carmelita was great fun to be with, and she introduced Agnes to a Los Angeles she had not known existed. Living off her mother's and sister's largesse, Agnes considered herself a pauper. With Carmelita and Lee Freeson, whom Carmelita later married, she discovered the city of the truly poor. Chinatown. Little Tokyo. Black churches, with gospel music. Spanish services in the Mission Church, where Annie George had been taught by nuns in the 1850s. Night court, where prostitutes were brought in for arraignment. Dollar Days on Hollywood Boulevard, where Agnes, to whom shopping meant an upscale department store, proudly bought shoes for two dollars and gloves for fifty-nine cents. There were wonderful parties, where Carmelita cooked as creatively as she danced; among the guests were such embryonic legends as Edward Weston, Ansel Adams, and Robinson Jeffers. People danced, in couples or alone. Lee Freeson remembered Carmelita and Agnes dancing together, wild and abandoned. "Agnes had a great, childlike enthusiasm for the experiences she had with us," he said. "Carmelita loved that about her."[5]

When Agnes acquired some power in the dance world, she would use it determinedly on Carmelita's behalf — singing her praises, arranging introductions with influential people, writing rhapsodic referrals for fellowships and teaching positions, sending a check whenever Carmelita's situation was desperate and sometimes when it wasn't. But Carmelita was bedeviled, and her gratitude was poisoned by jealousy. Her affection for Agnes was real, but so were the fears and the rage that drove her. In 1976, she wrote a spiteful description of Agnes as she had first known her, "a passionately unhappy person. . . . She had beautiful feet that she pushed around as if she disliked them. . . . She jumped or tripped to conclusions, with a disregard for the truth. Research took time. Facts were boring. Since she always arrived ½ hour late, and left early, she never knew why or what or how a movement began. She had, I am sure, the idea that it always exploded in mayhem and frenzy. Her legs and feet were never properly stretched or warmed to any of the intricacies of the dance. I'm afraid her assumptions to friendly intercourse were just as sketchy, but Agnes never asked to enroll in a less advanced class, nor did she want friendships to start from the beginning. She was used to making fast sketches of people. . . . Assumptions, always assumptions!"[6]

It was true that Agnes at times had no patience for details and formed opinions with lightning speed. Carmelita, at the other extreme, pursued an impossible perfection. Her failure to achieve it fed a bitterness that corroded her life.

Amnesia is endemic in Hollywood, and five years had passed since Agnes had danced there — but the name de Mille, whether upper case or lower, guaranteed attention. Once again she played to sold-out audiences sprinkled with motion picture luminaries. Once again the reviews were excellent. Once again, she waited in vain for offers of movie work (their failure to materialize was due at least in part to bad timing, for it was the era of the Busby Berkeley musical extravaganza, the antithesis of Agnes's subtle, intimate work). And once again, when all seemed lost, her mother stepped in.

Anna had been a founder of the Hollywood Bowl; Agnes had attended its first seasons while she was in college, listening under the stars to music she would never forget. Thanks to her mother's efforts, Agnes was commissioned to stage three numbers at the Bowl — ten weeks' work, for which she would be paid $2,000. She would be lucky to cover her expenses, but it was a challenge she could not refuse. Warren agreed to assist her (the billing read "Choreography by Agnes de Mille, Production directed by Warren Leonard"), and a friend, the director Mitch Liesen, edited and advised. Barbara Parry, one of her dancers and also a student of Carmelita's, remembered Agnes as "a terrific worker — a sweating, eight-hour-a day, tough, hard-working dancer. In Carmelita's class, she worked til I thought she would drop. The dancers in the Bowl ballet were young — I was only fourteen — and Agnes was just the dearest person with us. Later she acquired the reputation of being tough, but that was her gentle period."[7] Finances were strained to the point that on days when Agnes needed an accompanist she called the rehearsal pianist in the morning, using a code — ringing once and hanging up — to save the cost of a phone call.

Agnes kept a heated correspondence going with Edgar Wind, but he hadn't the resources to visit her in California. Ramon, on the other hand, did have the resources, the devotion, and, miraculously, the determination for what would be his greatest adventure. With Thorpe and his customized car, Ramon traveled by freighter to Los Angeles via the Panama

Canal. He arrived during Agnes's rehearsals for the Bowl, when she had time for virtually nothing else. For Ramon, she made time.

She settled him in a little house, to which she brought, as she had in Chelsea, the most interesting people she knew. She took him to see everything she loved in Los Angeles: the beach, the wildflowers in the foothills, the Hollywood Bowl concerts, the Spanish missions, Chinatown. She took him to parties — elegant ones, at the homes of Hollywood's cultural elite (at Edward G. Robinson's, Stravinsky played chamber music), and cozy, amusing ones at the home of her friends David and Michael Hertz. All this took place around her rehearsal schedule, which intensified as the date of performance neared.

Agnes was accustomed to the constraints of Rambert's tiny theater; now she struggled to accommodate to a stage that was 104 feet wide and an amphitheater that seated 17,000 people. She came closest to success in a Czechoslovakian folk dance, using a brilliant variety of flags and costumes that were designed and made by folk experts at UCLA. But the length of the dances, and the electrician's failure to bring up the lights on cue for one number, made the evening less than a success. The *Los Angeles Times* told the sad story: "Had the lighting been better, the peasants would have been revealed clad in beautiful soft autumnal colors and their dancing the jigs and reels of Ireland would have delighted the audience. As it was, it took too much imagination."[8] The *Hollywood Citizen-News* was harsher, calling "Dance of Excitement" reminiscent of many a night club routine, but much, much longer."[9]

Agnes tried to be philosophical; nobody outside Los Angeles, she told herself, would see the reviews. Within days she and Ramon were touring California with the resentful Thorpe, who sulked, complained, and issued dire warnings all along the way. They drove north to the redwoods, then east to Fresno, where Agnes boarded a train for Colorado. Ramon followed with Thorpe in his car, joining her in Steamboat Springs, where she had a two-week teaching job.

The Perry-Mansfield Summer School of Dance and the Drama was actually a ranch, in a glorious setting at the top of the Rockies. The students, all girls, took classes in ballet, ballroom dancing, drama, and art. Agnes was somewhat nervous, for she had never taught before, but she was a great success. She and Ramon, with the ubiquitous Thorpe in tow, went on a two-day camping trip, sleeping on the ground, surrounded by what Agnes thought "the most beautiful scenery I've ever experienced in this country."[10] Ramon had fallen in love with the desert; now he was enchanted by the majestic mountains.

Every sight, sound, taste, and event was charged with intensity for Ramon. At the beginning of his holiday, doctors in Los Angeles had examined him and diagnosed multiple sclerosis and a severe spinal curvature. Like the English doctors, they had pronounced him incurable. They did not tell him what they must have suspected — that he could not live much longer — but he must have suspected it, too. However much time he had, he would make the most of it. En route back to Los Angeles, with Agnes and Thorpe, his adventures continued: a violent rainstorm that stranded them in the mountains; a coincidental meeting with Martha Graham and Louis Horst at the train station in Santa Fe; a side trip to Zuni to see the Indians perform their authentic rain dance. But in early September, as the days grew shorter, Ramon headed back to London, via New York, with Thorpe driving.

Agnes remained in Los Angeles. The director George Cukor had asked her to choreograph the dances in his movie version of *Romeo and Juliet,* to be produced by Irving Thalberg, but the starting date was months away. While she waited, she continued her lessons with Carmelita and contemplated her financial situation. The Hollywood Bowl venture had left her $127.85 in the hole; her Perry-Mansfield money had barely covered her living expenses, and at the age of thirty-one, she was once again her mother's dependent. *Romeo and Juliet,* however, promised what was by Agnes's standards a fortune. In those days, a choreographer on a major film, especially one with important dance scenes, had the luxury of two or three months of preparation and rehearsal, followed by an extended shooting schedule. Agnes would earn $8,000 for four months' work.

She pined for Edgar. He wrote weekly, professing his love and promising fidelity until she returned, but she was doubtful. By the time her *Romeo and Juliet* work was finished, sixteen months would have elapsed since he kissed her goodbye, and her father and Sidney Mellon had conditioned her to expect betrayal. She appealed to her mother to finance a quick trip to England — in steerage, if necessary. "I think I'm falling in love with Edgar Wind," she wrote, "and I'd like to find out."[11] Anna replied, "You must be free to do what your heart dictates," but she was concerned about how Agnes's change of heart would affect Ramon, whose health was so precarious that any upset could cause an episode of fevers, nerve spasms, and worse. "That whole situation has been ghastly," Anna wrote, adding, "You know my heart's desire is your happiness."[12]

"Please don't think my experience with Ramon has been or is 'ghastly,'" Agnes replied. "My experience with Dug was and with Sidney . . . because they were mean and egotistic and cowardly. But association with someone noble and brave and discriminating, no matter how tragic, can never be anything but stimulating. . . . He was the first completely strong [she wrote "virile," then crossed it out] man, emotionally speaking, that I've ever associated with."[13]

In the end, Agnes decided that nothing could be settled in such a short trip and that, whatever the outcome, her work on the movie would suffer from the stress. Hoping for the best while expecting the worst, she began taking lessons in German. She went to a skin specialist, who put her on a strict diet to improve her complexion. Borrowing Carmelita Maracci's studio, she taught a class in Movement for Actors to five young actresses, only three of whom (Kitty Carlisle, June Lockhart, and Katherine deMille, Cecil's daughter) could pay; Agnes earned less than the pianist. After class, she lectured the students on her grandfather's theory of the Single Tax, to which she had subscribed since reaching the age of reason. With Warren (whom Anna had recruited into the Single Tax fold), she organized a seminar for the reading and discussion of *Progress and Poverty.* But from late November, when she went on the MGM payroll, there was time for little but *Romeo and Juliet.*

It was a million-dollar production, a giant step beyond anything Agnes had done before. With the support system of her dreams — dressing room, office, the use of a secretary, researchers, musicians, whatever else she needed, and no interference — she felt like a newly discovered treasure. For the first time in her life she was earning real money, most of which she hoarded, some of which she spent on clothes. Never before had she felt so certain that the breakthrough in her career was at hand.

Warren was her assistant, and he danced the male lead in the production number at the Capulets' ball, where the lovers meet. Leslie Howard was Romeo; Juliet was played by Norma Shearer (Mrs. Irving Thalberg). For Juliet's entrance into the ballroom where Romeo and five hundred extras awaited, Agnes created a pavane — a stately Renaissance court dance in which the feet rarely left the floor — danced to madrigals played on lutes, virginals, serpents, and other authentic instruments.

Cukor visited rehearsals daily and never uttered a negative word. Agnes completed the dances in three weeks; with the filming still months away, the company remained on the payroll. To keep them occupied, she and Bella Lewitzky and Mary Meyer, two Lester Horton dancers who were in the movie, gave classes in ballet and in modern dance. Agnes arranged performances of her dances for studio executives, guests, and anyone who expressed an interest. The atmosphere was so civilized that afternoon tea was served every day.

Bernie Fineman had taken a job in London and moved his family there, so Agnes moved into the spare room of their friends, John and Eda Gershgorn, in Beverly Hills. Her closest friends were Michael and David Hertz; he was a playwright, they had very little money, and Agnes thought them "the happiest couple I knew, and the most fun."[14] Ramon had thought so too, and he corresponded with Michael. His letters were light, cheery, and newsy, but between the lines, it was clear that he missed Agnes terribly. In January, he wrote that while watching the sleet outside his window, he was thinking of the flowers that would bloom in the desert in spring. "I authorize for you both a really gay and scintillating 1936," he wrote, "and I authorize our swift reunion. . . . Drive out to the desert for me, please. . . . Very Much Love, Rover."[15]

It was Agnes's understanding that Irving Thalberg had been kept informed of her plans, but he did not see her dances until filming was about to begin, and he was not prepared for "something that would do no disparagement to the head of the Holy Roman Empire."[16] Cecil might have approved, but Thalberg was appalled. He complimented Agnes on her work, but ordained that the "story pace must be maintained even at the cost of choreography, a point of view I naturally did not share."[17] When the dances were filmed, they became what Thalberg had originally envisioned: background. Agnes was crushed; "This time," she wrote her mother, "glory slipped right through my fingers."[18] As consolation, she had money in the bank and the satisfaction of reviews that called her dances "some of the most beautiful phases of the picture" and "so very lovely, they make such beautiful pictures in their groupings and bodily movement that they . . . stay in your memory with a check to look again more carefully the next time you see the picture.[19]

"Dear Michael," Ramon wrote in March, "I wish to Christ we were all sitting round lowering a bottle of gin instead of me writing a letter that's got to go six thousand miles to reach you . . . We could have the hell of a fine party — Michael, you'd be one ecstatic smile; David, you'd be witty; Ag would stand in fifth position; and I, uninhibited, could wave a finger." He commented with humor and insight on events in the larger world — politics, mostly, and the rise of Fascism — and then confessed, "Today I have been a little melancholy: reflecting on the fact that today a year ago I sailed out of London docks on my way to California. . . . My love to sunny California, to the Hollywood hills at night, to the deserts if by chance you cross them, to the soon imminent scent of orange groves."[20]

To Ramon, whose life was measured in ticks and tocks, Agnes's absence must have seemed to last an eternity. But when she returned, in May, Edgar was her first priority. Only after Edgar had met her at the dock, taken her to a quiet room, played a little Mozart on the piano, and become her lover in fact as well as fantasy did she visit Ramon — and then it was to tell him that while she still loved him dearly, she was *in* love with Edgar Wind.

Agnes viewed Ramon as a father figure by virtue of his maturity, and as a son by virtue of his helplessness and youth. She viewed Edgar, who was older, as father, lover, and teacher, and idealized him as she had William. He was, she believed, "the answer to everything in my life."[21] That included marriage and a child, without which she believed she could never be a complete woman. She was enthralled by Edgar's intellect, his prestigious position in the art world, and his appreciation of her work. And although their relationship had been almost entirely epistolary and was not sexually satisfying,[22] her need made her euphoric with optimism, setting her up for a series of betrayals that would play themselves out over the next two years.

For all his maturity, Ramon was human, and he was deeply hurt. He had believed that he and Agnes were a couple and Edgar their friend, and nothing had prepared him for a different configuration of the triangle. Eventually, as his physical condition worsened, he refused to see her. Then Edgar, suddenly and with no apparent reason, also refused to see her, establishing a pattern: he lied, he compounded the lies with excuses, she made excuses for him and forgave him. Seven times he would abruptly break off with her; six times she would blame herself and take him back, or somehow *get* him back. When he admitted, under duress, that there was another woman, Agnes blamed her long absence. When he swore he was finished with the other woman, Agnes believed him. When he promised romantic holidays together, her anticipation and tension were almost unbearable — as was her despair when he reneged at the last minute. He accused her of being "spiritually greedy, that I trusted nothing, that I tried to run the universe myself, that I couldn't rest. Of course, he'd personally just made it impossible for me to draw a quiet breath, but aside from that the accusations were true."[23] Not surprisingly, by June, she felt she was on the verge of a breakdown.

She tried to concentrate on her work, devising new dances for the next London season. First, though, she must make another transatlantic crossing. Leslie Howard was to play *Hamlet* on Broadway in the fall, and he wanted her to choreograph the play within the play.

Ramon agreed to see her before she sailed. He had been dangerously ill, but he believed he was recuperating — or perhaps he was whistling in the graveyard when he wrote to Michael Hertz that he planned to start a novel. But when Agnes saw him for what would be the last time, he had had a relapse and his condition was critical. She offered to forgo the *Hamlet* job and stay with him, but he would not allow it. He sent her on her way with a sort of benediction, wishing her happiness and predicting success.

Ramon had loved her unconditionally, as no one else had done. When she had drifted in a dark sea of doubt, Ramon's devotion and faith in her talent had kept her afloat. While *Hamlet* was in rehearsal, she received word of his death.

f i f t e e n

Cobweb Love

It was the vision of *Hamlet's* director, John Houseman, that the play within the play be performed by a medieval troupe of actors. Agnes's choreography, set to Virgil Thomson's music, was so elaborate that shortly before the opening Houseman and Howard decided, as had Thalberg during *Romeo and Juliet,* that it was too much of a good thing and threw it out. Grieving for Ramon and fearful of losing Edgar, Agnes paused only long enough to collect her $800 fee and to perform her new dances for Martha Graham (who approved) before returning to London.

She rented a spacious room in a house in Pimlico, not far from Victoria Station. With Ramon gone and Edgar unreliable, she turned for moral support to Rebecca West, Elizabeth Bowen, Joan Reed (Ramon's cousin), and Lisa Hewitt (Rambert's factotum and Agnes's wise, calm, and supportive business manager). Nora Stevenson, her rehearsal pianist and a motherly soul, always had tea and empathy at the ready. Tudor and Laing regularly invited her to Sunday lunch at their house; the place was cold, damp, and reeked of smells contributed by the dogs neither Antony nor Hugh bothered to housebreak, but the hospitality was warm and the company stimulating.

Through a colleague of Edgar's, Agnes met Lillie Oberwarth, a Jew-

ish refugee from Nazi Germany who ran a boardinghouse for other refugees. "Mrs. Obie" had the nurturing instincts of Gaia and the survival instincts of Mother Courage. "How it is dished out, so you must swallow it down" was the advice she gave herself, but she had more sympathy for the misfortunes of others. For Agnes, her parlor became "a nest of comfort."[1]

Agnes was physically and mentally exhausted. Ramon's death had been a shock, and Edgar's unpredictable behavior, which careened from solicitous to callous, made her unbearably tense. She was terrified that he would, like Sidney Mellon, suddenly call the whole thing off. Whatever was wrong, she believed it must be her fault. She lost weight, energy, and hope; sleep eluded her, and at times she wept uncontrollably. So although psychoanalysis was anathema to her mother, who considered it an admission of weakness and a betrayal of family privacy, she consulted an analyst.

The analyst reassured her; she was suffering from emotional fatigue, not losing her mind. The tension caused by her fear of failure and rejection had been compounded by the tensions between her parents, between Anna and Warren, between herself and Thorpe. The analyst "was sure," she wrote to Michael Hertz, "that I had come to the end of one life and was about to start another . . . he thought I needed a doctor's help so I could go on into the new experiences fresh and not inhibited with old habits, that I must stay away as much as possible from my family, particularly my mother."[2] The analyst moved away from London after only a few sessions, but his assessment had at least temporarily averted a breakdown.

In February and March 1937, her exhaustion notwithstanding, Agnes gave six recitals of her own dances (eight of which were new), made her ballet debut in a new work of Tudor's called *Dark Elegies,* and choreographed dances for a film. She was still serving her apprenticeship as a choreographer, learning from her mistakes and building a foundation for future work. Unfortunately, she had to make those mistakes in full view of a paying public, and her high standards led her to equate mistakes with failure.

In recital, her partner was Hugh Laing — a difficult man, but the most satisfactory partner she ever had. Together they performed the numbers that had been most successful with Warren and also her "Pavane" from *Romeo and Juliet.* Most of the new dances, described by one reviewer as "short stories in movement,"[3] were American, with self-explanatory titles: *The Harvesting, Strip Tease, Hornpipe. Boston Brahmin,* like *Parvenues,* was a burlesque of nineteenth-century New England society. The themes of some of the others — war, death, impotence, and destruction — reflected Agnes's emotional state. *Dust,* for example, concerned the plight of a starving, hysterical woman in the Dust Bowl ("Everything in my life," she wrote melodramatically to her mother, "turns to dust").[4]

Her choreographic notebooks from this period document how she drew from ballet, modern dance, and mime, and how she revised and recycled movements that would become staples in her vocabulary. In *Strip Tease,*

> knees quake, hands shake, face shows shame, she tears off clothes, bumps, shakes shoulders in "frenzy," struts. . . . Cowboy jump twist. . . . Toe strut. Markova. Mae West. . . . Rhapsodic adagio strut, rhapsodic adagio pawing ground . . . liquid hips . . . Open and shut skirt walking upstage back to audience . . . twist hips . . . undulating plié.

Notes for *Hymn of Youth* read,

> on knees rotate hips, rock on knees, arm beat from Armistice [Day], rock on knees doffing hat, leg swing, arm swing, swing both arms with crouch, military foot rhythm, frozen goose step, gallop with elbows, horse-back re-levé, knee up . . . lick ground, rotate hips, hat doff, mark time knees, walk pompons with hips, pas de bourrée drill-pirouettes, Spanish jerk stamp, pas de b., smothered hysterical walk, run in place."

For *Hornpipe* she wrote,

> Sea swell, side to side, bigger and slower. Side to side, extra steps to catch balance, suggest pitching ship. Slow one side uphill, race down together traveling sideways and backward. Breasting billows. Hauling rope—foot beats. Pulling. Pushing. Running at first, stopping to call en route, ribaldries. Slapping thigh. Enormous rocks. Skids. Swabbing decks. Knee work. Running up ropes. Sailing into distance.

Such were the nuts and bolts with which she created works that became, through her artistry, more than the sum of their parts.

For the film *I, Claudius,* directed by Josef von Sternberg, Agnes built on movements from *Nymph Errant, Harvest Reel,* and *Dance of Death* to create a Roman orgy in dance. But on the day the number was to be filmed, the production company went bankrupt and shut down for good, owing Agnes two weeks' salary. At another time she would have been devastated, but the film mattered far less to her than the upcoming premiere of Tudor's *Dark Elegies.* She thought it a masterpiece and hoped it would establish her as a dancer in a company of dancers, untainted by mime.

Tudor was not the first choreographer to set an important ballet among ordinary people (as opposed to princes and swans), but he was the first to add a psychological dimension. His *Jardin aux Lilas,* in which a Victorian woman is forced by social propriety to forsake her lover and marry another man, had been the hit of Rambert's previous season. In *Dark Elegies,* a community of peasants mourns the death of their children to the music of Mahler's *Kindertotenlieder.* Using technique that was basically ballet but incorporated steps, gestures, and body motions suggestive of modern dance, the soloists express grief, despair, and, finally, acceptance of the tragedy.

Tudor had chosen Agnes on the basis of her stage presence and acting ability, and he coached her privately on the movements — some of which, such as circular swoonings backward to the floor, she found exceedingly difficult. It was the first time she had ever worked under someone else's direction, and Tudor, who in later years was often described as cruel, showed her nothing but patience. She was onstage throughout the ballet; her five-minute solo, set to the fourth song, consisted of "a gentle, lyric, fragile, heart-breaking series of movements performed mostly on one leg with no expression on my face."[5] She did so with such conviction that one reviewer wrote, "Her sense of personal disaster is an exact complement to the music."[6]

Agnes's relationship with Marie Rambert was ambivalent and probably competitive. "Aggie wasn't *quite* a member of the family, because she wasn't in the company," Maude Lloyd recalled, "but she came to class with us every day. She and Mim had the same drive, and power. They were strong, strong characters. They could be very kind. They could be very unkind."[7] After her March recital at the Ballet Club, Agnes decided that she had nothing more to gain from Rambert. Tudor and Laing had reached the same conclusion, and the three of them decided, on the premise that Antony's and Agnes's work could provide a complementary contrast, to form a company of their own, to be called Dance Theatre. Agnes borrowed some money from Romney Brent, Hugh Laing raised some more, and they prepared for a week's concerts in Oxford, in June.

The situation with Edgar had gone from chaos to worse and was a steady drain on Agnes's energy. She described him to Michael Hertz as "two people, the finest and most stimulating person I have ever known and on occasion the most sadistic and brutal."[8] But Edgar could not have "mangled" and "shattered" Agnes without her collusion.[9] By virtue of his intelligence, erudition, and remoteness, he was the shadow — the very dark shadow — of her father. However badly he behaved, she made excuses for him: overwork, neurasthenia caused by the lingering trauma of the Hitler experience, and the evil machinations of the "other woman," over whom he claimed to have no control.

Her friends despised him. To Carlheinz Ostertag, one of Mrs. Obie's refugee boarders, he was "supercilious, superior, standoffish, brooding. He was a *very* established art historian, one of the top people in his field. He had an extraordinary mind, and he was rude to anyone who was not his caliber. Agnes was just wonderful — witty, funny, full of beans, exuberant. Edgar Wind was an ice cold fish, full of sarcasm — a total egomaniac."[10] Therese Langfield, who observed him at rehearsals and social occasions, said, "None of the girls liked him. He had the usual sort of charm that was turned on and off. He was sort of a charming phony."[11]

He gave Agnes just enough attention to sustain her hope of marriage — a fantasy with roots that reached back into her childhood, when her whole family had colluded in a fiction of who they were and how they felt about themselves. The divorce had been a cold shower of reality, and Agnes had never worked through her feelings about it. She felt she had somehow failed to make her father love her enough, failed to love her mother enough, failed in her profession. Now she was failing with Edgar.

Through Mrs. Obie, Agnes met the Freudian psychoanalyst Hilde Maas, another German Jewish refugee, and became her patient. Her obsession with Edgar persisted, but she began to realize that it was a symptom as well as a cause of her problems. Quite soon, hope returned. "I'm finding out," she wrote to Warren that summer, "why I always just miss getting what I want. You're going to see a new Aggie."[12]

With Dr. Maas, Agnes began the painful exploration of her psyche. Gradually, she came to understand what would become a cliché in the age of self-help groups: that whatever the sins of her parents, she was responsible for her life. To change it, she must change her own perceptions, attitudes, and behavior. When she had lacked the assertiveness that might have averted the *Flying Colors* fiasco, she blamed her father. William had declined culpability. "As for your 'weakness of character' which you claim to have derived from me," he wrote, "I can only say that since you were very small I have tried to make it possible for you to be yourself. You are your own problem, and must work out your own life and character."[13] It was good advice, and analysis helped her to accept it, but never completely. In *Dance to the Piper,* she still blamed her father for "having allowed us to be shackled from early childhood with the cobweb love of Mother's insistence," without conceding the extent to which William had been shackled, as well.[14] No one Anna loved could say no to her without being made to feel guilty of not loving her enough; but no amount of love could have *been* enough. Nor had Agnes been able, as a child, to say no to her father, for pleasing him had been her raison d'être. As a result, in the early stages of her career, the woman Jule Styne would one day call "a killer" was incapable of contradicting anyone in authority when presented with unsatisfactory costumes, sets, dancers, or policies.[15]

Even in the golden days of her childhood, Agnes had had a tendency to see herself as a victim ("Who's persecuting you now, dear?"); in adulthood, denied the success and recognition she believed were her birthright, she had grown angry and confused, and had acquired a permanent sense of grievance at the unfairness of life.

Working with Dr. Maas, she decided that since her parents' divorce she had unconsciously sabotaged herself so that her father, out of pity, would love her more. It hadn't worked; the only person who pitied her was herself. No matter how hard she worked, "there was self-defeating behavior in everything I ever did. I used to be late. I wasn't too well-dressed. And in my dances there was a sour note, always. That was my hallmark—a bitter, sour note. People didn't really like it, it left a bad taste in their mouth. Through analysis, I lost my taste for failure."[16]

It was more difficult, in fact impossible, to lose the guilt bestowed by her mother. When she had bought her mother presents with her *Romeo and Juliet* money, Anna, whose self-imposed martrydom required Agnes's feeling of obligation, returned the gifts to the department store and had them credited to her daughter's account. Years later, when Agnes was firmly established on Broadway and tried to repay her debt, Anna never cashed the checks, but endorsed them over to the Henry George Institute instead.

Nothing was too minute or mundane to escape Anna's attention ("I wish you'd wear wooly shirties and underpanties as Margaret does," she told Agnes in her twenty-ninth year).[17] With an ocean between them, Agnes could at least escape her mother's physical presence; but in the spring of 1937, when Margaret was also living in London (and in the process of divorcing Bernie Fineman), Anna proposed a visit. The sisters were frantic. Which was the lesser evil, Anna's presence or the guilt of keeping her away? There ensued a blizzard of letters and cables from Agnes, within whom daughterly duty struggled with self-preservation. Harsh truths were followed by profuse apologies and protestations of devotion. Cautiously, Agnes confessed that a doctor had advised her to see as little as possible of her family. She and Margaret, she explained, were going through "the most crucial period of our lives. This year will determine whether or not we are going to develop into healthy happy (more or less) women or continue the half-crazy, restless, undirected existence we have led for the last ten years. . . . Can you come over in a suit of armor, take what comes of fun, and not give a damn about the rest? As though you were a trained nurse with two bad-tempered and very ill patients who are not capable of courtesy or good manners? . . . What will really do us damage is . . . anguished sympathy, Questioning, Watching, The responsibility of someone we love bewildered, hurt and lonely." What she asked was, she knew, against her mother's nature — that she withhold "the attentions . . . which the love you have for us drives you and has driven you to show, even against your better judgment. I'm not condemning, I'm explaining . . . I must not be sympathized with or indulged in my moods of self-pity (I work myself up in your presence to absolute orgies of martyrdom). And you must not eat your heart out with loneliness if Mag and I simply ask to be let alone. But we do want to see you — tranquilly and gayly. With no tension. If I lose control of myself during the next two months I lose my love."[18]

Anna, to her credit, rose to the occasion. She wrote an understanding letter and stayed in New York.

s i x t e e n

American Suite

In September 1937, Agnes crossed the Atlantic for the twelfth time in as many years. She would cross it twice more before she would settle in a home of her own, and then it would be for life.

This trip was prompted by an offer from Vincente Minnelli to choreograph the dances for his first directorial assignment, a show appropriately called *Hooray for What!* The offer was timely, for Dance Theatre had folded after its week in Oxford. Agnes and Tudor had presented their best work — four of his ballets, ten of her solo concert pieces, and a new *Elizabethan Suite* that she danced with Laing, all with new costumes. The programs must have been memorable, but due to weak publicity and bad timing — it was exam week, and students had no time for entertainment — few people were on hand to see them. The company limped back to London, disappointed and broke.

Hooray for What! meant six weeks in New York, at $350 per week — a prospect that sent Agnes into emotional turmoil. Louis Horst had nicknamed her "Agony de Mille," and she did have a flair for angst, especially when the longings of her heart contradicted the demands of her ambition. Edgar had just returned from two months in Italy, during most of which

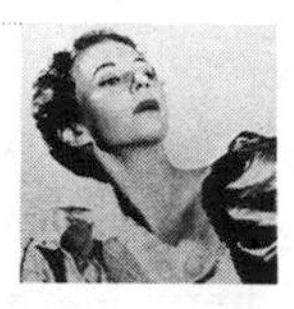

time she hadn't even known where he was and had been too distraught to sleep, eat, or concentrate. Their reunion was "joyous," but she was not inclined to risk another separation.[1] Edgar encouraged her to go, for the sake of her career. Dr. Maas also urged her to go. As it turned out, she might have saved herself the trip, for the show was another exercise in frustration and humiliation.

Hooray for What! was a social satire that is overlooked in most histories of Broadway musicals and scarcely mentioned in the autobiographies of Minnelli and E. Y. Harburg, its lyricist. Its problems were many, but lack of talent was not one of them; in addition to Minnelli and Harburg, it had music by Harold Arlen and a book written by Howard Lindsay and Russell Crouse for its star, Ed Wynn. It also had Kay Thompson, Hannah Williams (better known as Jack Dempsey's wife), Jack Whiting, Sue Hastings' Marionettes, and Al Gordon's Dogs.

Hiring Agnes was Minnelli's idea; he had twisted the arm of Lee Shubert, the producer, to get her. Shubert's business manager, Harry Kaufman, was Agnes's bête noire (she would later refer to him in print, with some satisfaction, as B. M.).* Kaufman objected to the trained dancers Agnes wanted to hire; he banned her from auditions, at which he and his friends chose the chorus girls they preferred. It was, said dancer Dorothy Bird, "Sugardaddy land."[2] In most cases, Kaufman got his way. Agnes got her own back by requiring the chorus girls to perform real work and by refusing to give management's pets special things to do. "I might have played ball just a little," she said, "but I scorned to and worked my own ruin."[3] It was becoming a familiar refrain.

The show had an antiwar theme, and Minnelli aimed to create an ironic effect by using a variety of war paraphernalia, including guns with bayonets. To the horror of management, who wanted skin, he almost completely concealed the girls' torsos with simulated barbed wire and their faces with gas masks. "We were seen simply as a harem," said Dorothy Bird. "No one cared a thing about social comment or satire."

The big dance number was the nine-minute "Hero Ballet" (suggested by the Jooss Ballet's famous *The Green Table*). The soloist, Paul Haakon, was a superb Danish dancer, remembered as the Baryshnikov of his day. Haakon had studied with the great Michael Fokine, and he did not believe that a woman choreographer, especially one unfamiliar with his particular strengths and weaknesses, could make the most of his capabilities. But Agnes's perfectionism (which other perfectionists understood, but which drove everyone else crazy) won him over, and he danced the dramatic part of a crazed soldier who kills his own men with great effect.

Agnes knew she was in trouble when the Broadway dance director Robert Alton was brought in to "fix" the dances. At the dress rehearsal, which lasted three days and two nights with scarcely a break, she learned that Minnelli, who had designed the sets, had changed the shape of the stage and eliminated three of the four exits by which dancers could leave it. With diminishing emotional and physical reserves, she adapted her dances to the changes. As background accompaniment, screaming fights raged among Harburg, Minnelli, Kaufman, Crouse, Lindsay, and the stars, all of whom were — accurately — predicting disaster. The show

* "It is the custom to speak kindly of the dead, but having entertained nothing except loathing for him when he was alive, I see no reason now to veil my opinion" (*Portrait Gallery,* p. 99).

opened in Boston on Halloween, and it was clear to all concerned that it was a mess. The B. M. fired Agnes the next day.

Once again she returned to London, feeling more than ever that she was the only failure in the de Mille family. But in that family, quitting was never an option. Every time a defeat knocked her flat she struggled to her feet with renewed determination, like the battered underdog hero of a prizefight movie. Convinced that the natural audience for her work was not in England but in the United States, she planned "the most brilliant return to America I could possibly have."[4] She would take Tudor, Laing, and a nucleus of girls (to be supplemented by some American dancers) to New York, and possibly California, to perform her work and Tudor's. That would lead, she believed, to a major concert tour and some lucrative commercial work. Edgar, she hoped, would join her at some point. Financing was a "snag" she would somehow work out.[5]

For years Anna had urged Agnes to use Rambert's dancers as "pawns" with which to choreograph group work, and she had done so on occasion, choosing girls she thought could adapt to her style.[6] She had used them on the short-lived *I, Claudius,* for which they were paid; mostly, though, they rehearsed for nothing. She reassembled a handful of them now, and resumed work on a long piece she'd begun the previous summer, called *American Suite.* Of its four parts, three were enlarged versions of dances she had previously performed alone: *The Harvesting, Dust,* and *'49.* The other part was called *The Rodeo.*

The girls were young and naive, but not unaware that they were being used as pawns. They didn't mind; they thought Agnes a fascinating phenomenon. "We hadn't seen many American people in the flesh," Therese Langfield Horner recalled. "We only knew them from films. Agnes was the cinema come to life! To me, she was something like Myrna Loy and William Powell. She was dynamic and so witty — she had the answer like *that* when something happened, there'd be a silence and then we'd all *collapse* with laughter. But when she worked on her ballets, all the authority was there."[7]

"Temperaments flew around like bats on a wall," said Elisabeth Schooling, "but Agnes always seemed perfectly calm. Easy and nice and encouraging, always extremely helpful."[8] One of the girls, Charlotte Bidmead, eventually told Agnes that she could no longer afford to work for nothing. "She said, 'What's the least you can live on?' I said, 'Thirty bob a week.' Agnes accepted that, and she paid me.

"I was her protégée, her pet. I think we were under a sort of spell. *I* was; she mesmerized me. She was so very sparkling and vivacious and funny, she had so much energy. I'd never met a personality so strong. I'd have done absolutely anything for her, I just adored her. I suppose it was a schoolgirl crush.

"She was in no way masculine, but I couldn't imagine her being one whit affectionate, or in love with anyone. She had such drive, you couldn't imagine her being sufficiently pliable to fit in with anyone else's life. Almost as though she was locked up in her ambition. She wasn't cold or remote, but I couldn't see her giving up her personality enough to share her life with someone else."[9]

Bidmead was perceptive beyond her years, for Agnes was struggling with exactly that dilemma. At this point she could not envision a life without Edgar, but he would not even commit himself to spending Christmas with her, let alone a lifetime. For all her bravado, she had spent the last of her Hollywood money on costumes, music, and rehearsal costs, and she was again living, frugally, off her mother. Dr. Maas continued to see her, although she could not pay. There was no money with which to underwrite her plans for a company—and if it did materialize, it would mean another long separation from Edgar. At the same time, the political situation in Europe was volatile, the atmosphere tense, and Hitler's invasion of Austria imminent. Agnes was ready to go home—but she could not leave Edgar, with whom she now believed she had "a good honest chance to be happy."[10] Emotionally, she had run off the edge of a cliff and continued to run in midair, like the cartoon character that plummets to earth only when it looks down. In January she looked down and collapsed.

Fortunately, Mrs. Obie was on hand to put her to bed in one of her rooms, look after her, and keep the world away. She was wracked with aches, chills, fever, weakness, and general emotional disarray; a doctor diagnosed flu and exhaustion and ordered rest for six weeks. Her fatigue was profound; "After every conversation I sleep for hours, and the slightest confusions infuriate me."[11] The New York trip was postponed until the fall.

Her letters to Anna during this period are recitations of calamities interspersed with bursts of manic optimism. "Edgar is good and sweet and cherishes me," she assured her mother and herself, and attributed his problems to "exile," alluding to his refugee status.[12] In a letter in which she declared, perhaps echoing Dr. Maas, "Our greatest fault, yours and mine, is that we don't plan sensibly. We always attempt too much," she went on to predict, "within two years I'm going to have my own school and company."[13] As her energy returned, she worked on her technique and on her new group dances.

The idea for a dance always came to Agnes as an emotion, around which she would devise a scenario. To induce and intensify the emotion in herself, she listened to music — something other than what she intended to use, lest it become too familiar. Bach, Mozart, and Smetana were her favorites. With her feet up, drinking pots of strong tea, she envisioned each character in detail, down to the colors and textures of the costumes. Then she began to move.

Some choreographers block the larger movement first and work out the details later. Agnes began with the particular. Believing that "in every good gesture pattern there is a world, a cosmography," she stood in front of a mirror and acted out the natural, everyday gestures with which people reveal themselves — a shrug of the shoulder, a tilt of the head, a glance.[14] When the right gesture eluded her she sometimes could summon it, following Martha Graham's suggestion, by articulating what she wanted to convey.

For this process, which could take weeks, Agnes had a broad range of references on which to draw. Her firsthand experience encompassed city and country, East and West, theater and film. She had studied the arts, especially painting and sculpture. She was knowledgeable about world history, particularly with respect to customs, costumes, manners, and morals. Her special gift was her ability to find the precise gesture that conveyed a universal emotion and express it through a specific character in a specific time, rhythm, and place.

Eventually Agnes began to compose, expanding the gestures into the steps that were the DNA of the dance. "Acting gestures that reveal character are quite easy and instinctive for me," she explained, "but the dance gestures, the stylized gestures that reveal the emotions are hard come by."[15] Using the actual music, if it was available, she worked out the dance pattern. The piano studies she had begun at the age of six, for her father's sake, had led to a deep appreciation of musical form and literature and an understanding of the subtleties of a score. Agnes constructed a dance like a piece of music: state the theme, restate it, develop it; state a second theme, recapitulate the first, and build toward a climax. She understood that if an action began and ended on a downbeat, it provided a sense of completion. It also gave weight to each motion, even the seemingly insignificant ones such as lifting the head or opening the eyes — a technique, she wrote, that "will tend to retard pantomimic action to a pace slower than what a nonmusical actor would employ. But . . . the retarding ensures clarity; holding back the significant forceful end to the final beat guarantees a decisive point, particularly in comedy."[16]

Next, armed with extensive notes and diagrams, Agnes brought in the dancers. She demonstrated, they imitated. She developed the gestures, breaking them down into their components, reassembling them, reversing them, broadening them. If two hours' hard work produced two or three good gestures — five seconds, perhaps, of movement — she was satisfied.

Agnes loved the vitality of folk dances, and they were the basis of her dance composition. Once the key gestures were set, she added movements from folk dances of the appropriate idiom, rearranging them in new sequences and incorporating her own ideas. She appreciated the rules and courtesies of folk dancing, the definition of male-female roles, and the fact that ordinary people had performed them for generations, making them "literally the footprints of untold numbers of human lives."[17] Folk dances were living history, and Agnes revered history.

She brought in more dancers, and the revision process continued. She edited and refined the gestures and folk steps, adding movements inspired by classical ballet, modern dance, tap — whatever styles and techniques seemed felicitous. The final design seemed simple, spontaneous, and authentic. In fact, almost nothing was authentic — except the spirit and meaning of the dance. Variations on this recipe would comprise the core of her work for the next fifty years.

Of her new group of dances, Agnes was happy only with *The Rodeo.** It derived from a square dance she had attended in 1935, at a ranch near the Perry-Mansfield Summer School in Colorado. She had observed square dancing before, but never participated. On that occasion, when "Turkey in the Straw" was played on an old upright piano and a fiddle, she had been inspired to dance a hoedown — alone — and found it exhilarating. She thought the old-fashioned courtesies romantic, the ranch hands the epitome of masculinity, and the designs of the dances intriguing. She had idealized cowboys since her childhood, when the extras who worked in her uncle's movies would ride into Cecil's yard, swoop her and her cousins up, and gallop around the block with the children clinging to the horns of their saddles. She remembered the smell of sweat and leather, and the "great male laughs which we found pleasantly terrifying."[18] It was exciting and sexy.

Agnes first described *The Rodeo* as free arrangements of running and riding rhythms

> set for eight figures who appear together only at the climax of the Arkansas Traveller. The rest of the time they run on and off in loose patterns travelling always across the stage. Giving the sense of tremendous space and long informal trails. The movement is vigorous, gay and for all its violence dignified — with the exception of the solo figure who is always in trouble, off balance, off beat, frequently progressing backwards or sideways, once on the ground. As long as the indicated rhythms and number of measures are preserved, I don't care what is done to melody, accompaniment or key sequence. But the composition should remain simple and native, because although the steps are in no way authentic the feeling of the dance as a whole is graphic and folk. It is explicitly a southwestern rodeo and must smack of nothing else.
>
> The dancers are at once horses and horsemen — a sort of American centaur. The emotion behind the composition is dynamic, forthright and humorous. Vigor and speed are essential.[19]

---

* *Rodeo* was first performed publicly on April 25, 1938, in Norwich.

This embryonic version of *Rodeo* contained all the basic movements Agnes would use in its final incarnation — the riding; the roping; the rhythms and movements of horses galloping, trotting, prancing, pawing, and swaying; the skidding slides across the floor. The English girls who first executed those movements were intelligent and willing, but had no sense of American humor or tempo or posture, let alone the sheer energy of the American West. To these gentle natives of a small damp island, Agnes tried to convey the feeling of riding for days across vast spaces under a blazing sun. "We were all ballet-trained," said Therese Langfield Horner, "and at that time there was little that was not ballet. Graham had not been here. Agnes used our ballet training, but there were some extraordinary movements we'd never done before. She said 'You've got to feel as though part of you is the horse, and the rest of you is controlling it.'"[20]

The riding movements incorporated influences as disparate as classical ballet, Isadora Duncan, Martha Graham, and tennis. To show that the rider was actually propelled by the horse, Agnes combined movements of the diaphragm and pelvis — the spasmodic, involuntary movements associated with coughing, laughing, and orgasm (similar to Graham's famous contractions) — with large, free movements of the back and arms. Peggy van Praagh, one of Agnes's soloists in *The Rodeo* at its London premiere, described "a series of attitude turns renversé with the arms sweeping to the ground [that] represented a cowboy's trick while riding his horse. The cowboy's natural movement was cleverly assimilated into classical movement."[21] All the girls wore culottes, tailored shirts, and neckerchiefs. Agnes was, as in life, the solo figure who was always in trouble. The music was a medley of cowboy tunes; when Agnes couldn't afford a rehearsal pianist, she hummed. Her old friend Twitch Davis recalled one of the first performances: "Aggie came bounding across the stage from the left, fell off the horse and shook her fist at it. That was *Rodeo*. I thought it was wonderful."[22]

In the summer of 1938, Agnes's optimism was dangerously high. Her group's first London recital, which included *The Rodeo,* had been a great

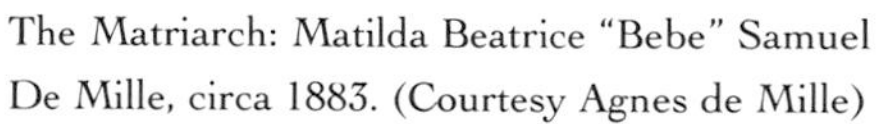

The Matriarch: Matilda Beatrice "Bebe" Samuel De Mille, circa 1883. (Courtesy Agnes de Mille)

Anna George de Mille. (Courtesy Agnes de Mille)

Cecil de Mille, before he began using the capital *D*. (Courtesy Agnes de Mille)

William de Mille, 1890. (Agnes de Mille Collection, New York Public Library)

Agnes and Margaret at Merriewold. (Courtesy Agnes de Mille)

Golden Days. (Courtesy Agnes de Mille)

Dance pageant, 1915. (Courtesy Agnes de Mille)

At the studio with Douglas Fairbanks, Sr., Agnes wears a Revolutionary War hat made by her mother. (Agnes de Mille Collection, New York Public Library)

Anna and William, in a symbolically subordinate position to a bust of her father, Henry George. (William de Mille Collection, University of Southern California)

Agnes with Pop, 1923. (Agnes de Mille Collection, New York Public Library)

Margaret, Anna, and Agnes in 1929, after the divorce that smashed their illusions. (Courtesy Agnes de Mille)

Ballet Class. (Soichi Sunami)

Ouled Nail. (Courtesy Evelyn Taylor)

Agnes and Warren Leonard in *May Day.* (Soichi Sunami/New York Public Library)

Elizabethan Suite. (Courtesy Agnes de Mille)

Agnes with Cecil and his daughter, Katharine (in costume for a Mae West movie), on the *Cleopatra* set. (Agnes de Mille Collection, New York Public Library)

Agnes with Ramon Reed in Wales, 1934. (Courtesy Agnes de Mille)

Joe Anthony. (Courtesy Joseph Anthony)

Rehearsing the original *Rodeo* studies in England, 1938. (Agnes de Mille Collection, New York Public Library)

"Rodeo"

III Front group stationary
back group whips +
galops.

IV - back - galops in circles
pivot - pivot turns

pivot slow   slow developé turns -
V - stretch neck + balance

VI - all galop in confusion -
rope accents jumped high -

Freddy Franklin's solo -
beat hat around neck of
bucking horse
wave hand
touch feet mid-air
2.   3 4
4 counts

tacit
Tacit 4 counts
bend way, way back!
4 pirouettes (can he?)

Agnes's early notes for *Rodeo*. (Agnes de Mille Collection, New York Public Library)

ıes as the Priggish One with Annabelle Lyon and Lucia
ıse in *Three Virgins and a Devil.* (Agnes de Mille Collection,
v York Public Library)

Rodeo's Cowgirl with Frederic Franklin. (Agnes de Mille Collection, New York Public Library)

nbi Linn and James Mitchell in the *Oklahoma!*
am ballet. (Courtesy Bambi Linn)

Wedding day — June 1943. The bride was much happier than she appears. (Agnes de Mille Collection, New York Public Library)

She said David was in [illegible] and
due home in February or March. This was
written before the German push. My heart
aches for her now. Please God David has
been spry in stepping backward!
Judy is at work hard on the floor
book shelves. A dandy girl! She has
got a generous amount of white paint in
her hair which I shall have to cope with
presently. She is now lying flat on her
stomach painting the bottom shelves.
I must chase her up and go back now my
love. I hope you have a fine
birthday and a fine 25th and a fine
boxing-day,
All my heart's love —
your own Mouse

mouse wassailing
a touch triste

Agnes signed a wartime Christmas letter to Walter "Mouse wassailing, a touch triste." (Agnes de Mille Collection, Smith College Archives)

Agnes with some of her leading female dancers: Annabelle Lyon, Allyn Ann McLerie, Betty Low, Joan McCracken, Katherine Sergava, Bambi Linn, Pearl Lang, Gemze de Lappe, Lidija Franklin, Dania Krupska, and Amy St. Just, 1945. (Agnes de Mille Collection, New York Public Library)

success.* Edgar had sent orchids, tiger lilies, and carnations. He had moved his Bechstein piano into her room in Pimlico and himself into an upstairs room in the house — feeding her fantasies but still evading commitment and seeing her only at his convenience. Agnes interpreted proximity as a deepening of their relationship and told Anna, "I think we may well be clear of trouble."[23]

That summer she danced at the Westminster Theatre in the premiere of another Tudor ballet. *Judgment of Paris* was Tudor's satirical version of the Roman myth in which the shepherd Paris judges a beauty contest among three goddesses. Tudor set the scene in a sleazy café; the goddesses are tough, over-the-hill prostitutes who dance for a patron (Paris) as he drinks himself into a stupor. Each dancer used a comedic prop: Therese Langfield Horner (Juno) had a fan, Charlotte Bidmead (Minerva) a bedraggled feather boa, and Agnes (Venus), wearing a long blond wig and a bored expression, listlessly manipulated and wriggled through two hoops. The patron, who was played by Tudor, eventually passes out, and the women pick his pockets. Laing played the waiter. The music, excerpted from Kurt Weill's *The Threepenny Opera,* perfectly suited the lewd, cynical, yet very funny entertainment. It was the third ballet in which Tudor created a part for Agnes. The second, which had debuted during their week at Oxford, was *Gallant Assembly,* in which Agnes portrayed an aristocrat who was, under the skin, as depraved as the prostitute in *Judgment of Paris.* In Tudor's ballets, as in *Ouled Nail,* Anna George's proper daughter relished the chance to be vulgar and lewd.

For four years, Agnes and Tudor had been close friends and colleagues. By the autumn of 1938, they were neither. With no explanation, the impenetrable Tudor, whose motives were never successfully analyzed by anyone, perhaps even himself, withdrew his friendship. Agnes attributed it to jealousy: "After the first performance of *Dark Elegies,* he didn't get a good press, and I did. The critic was wrong — I wasn't that good, and his ballet is a masterpiece. But it was after that that he turned against me."[24] Whatever his reason, it cannot have been purely coincidental that the days Therese Langfield Horner remembered — "the lazy, sunny,

* May 26, 1938, at the Fortune Theatre.

summer days when Antony and Hugh and Agnes were all friends, eating ice cream beside the Thames, either Agnes or the boys keeping us laughing" — dwindled down as Tudor grew increasingly frustrated with the progress of his career.[25] The English resist change until it is forced on them, and change was what Tudor was about. There was no place in England for him to work, and recognition came only from a discerning few.

For all her competitiveness, Agnes was always a great and unselfish admirer of talent, and she heralded the accomplishments of Graham, Maracci, and Tudor with a generosity rare in the arts. Even during the hectic *Hooray for What!* experience, she had found time to tell a young dancer, Ruthanna Boris, "about this great choreographer in England, and trying to teach me his ballets. She just loved his ballets so much, and she wanted me to know about Tudor because she thought he was great."[26] She was determined to introduce him to America, where she believed he would find the respect and success he deserved.

She was right, but her timing was premature. When the American contracts she tried to negotiate fell through, they fought, not for the first time but with the most ferocity, and accused each other of all sorts of perfidy, including stealing steps and movements. Tudor announced that he had found a sponsor and was to have his own theater and company, in which there would be no place for Agnes — because their styles were incompatible on the same program and because she was too old. Agnes later apologized for what she had said in the heat of the moment. Tudor replied that he had spoken coldly, intending to do the greatest possible harm.

In years to come, there would be considerable speculation about Tudor's influence on Agnes's work and very little about influence flowing in the opposite direction. All choreographers draw on styles of movement they admire, and Agnes readily admitted doing so. Dancers who worked with both choreographers in England considered their relationship symbiotic, for they were together during a formative period and they used the same dancers. Peggy van Praagh, a soloist in *Dark Elegies,* called Agnes "a very strong force with Antony," particularly in the creation of Agnes's role in *Elegies,* in which folk movement played an important part.[27] According to Agnes, the style and the use of hands in her *Romeo and Juliet* pavane form the basic idiom of the ball scene in Tudor's 1943 *Romeo and Juliet.* And when Tudor began to use modern dance movement in his own work (in *The Planets,* in 1934), the only modern dancers he had seen were German expressionists; his introduction to Martha Graham's work, certainly an influence, was through Agnes's detailed descriptions.

The similarities in their work were superficial but the differences were deep, for their styles reflected their characters — one translucent, the other opaque. They were both fascinated by psychology, but Tudor was drawn to its darker aspects; Agnes's characters were "normal," or trying to become so. They both strove for authentic emotion, but they approached it from opposite directions. Agnes gave her dancers a movement, then injected the feeling. Tudor began with the feeling and devised a precise movement that conveyed it. His dances are paintings — subtle, multidimensional, and ambiguous. Agnes created posters in primary colors; dramatic and comic effect mattered more to her than replicating a movement precisely. Her characters are diverse but not complicated (even Lizzie Borden, the most tormented is basically a "good" person). Tudor, a product of a rigid class system, created characters whose destinies were generally preordained, by fate or by something within their psyches. In his work, life is a competition for sex, love, and power; nothing is simple, least of all sex. Agnes came from a culture that revered individuality and power; her characters determine their own fate. Their ultimate happiness is traditional heterosexual love — her romantic, child's-eye perception of her parents' marriage. Her men are men and her women are women, with no no-man's-land in between.

The men in her real life were harder to read. Even Edgar, she decided in hindsight, had "a strong streak of homosexuality."[28] In August 1938, undeterred by his history of broken promises, she was feverishly anticipating a promised fortnight with him in France. At the eleventh hour, he canceled. Angry and hurt, she contacted her friend Michael Kostanecki, who was in Paris, and had her holiday with him. She was too humiliated to tell her mother the truth, so while she traveled with Kostanecki, she sent detailed reports to Anna about what she and Edgar were eating, seeing, and spending on their idyllic holiday. For another seven months, "in order to fend off family enquiries and sympathy and dismay," Agnes maintained the fiction that she and Edgar were engaged.[29]

In September, events in the larger world eclipsed personal considerations. Britain's Prime Minister Chamberlain, whose name would become synonymous with cowardly appeasement, signed his infamous nonaggression pact with Hitler, who had already invaded Austria and Czechoslovakia. Within weeks, the English began to evacuate women and children out of London, preparing for the war they believed was imminent. Then the Home Office refused to extend Agnes's work permit. Hoping that a miracle would somehow reunite her with Edgar in America, she prepared to leave England for good.

She still hoped to transplant the core of her company to the States. But Hugh Laing refused to leave Tudor, and Tudor would do nothing without a contract. Therese Horner could not travel because of a small child, Peggy van Praagh had teaching commitments, and a dancer who had agreed to pay her own fare reconsidered and withdrew. That left only Charlotte Bidmead, Agnes's protégée, to help her reconstruct her work in New York.

According to Bidmead, "She said, 'I'll send for you,' and I, like a little rabbit, said, 'Oh, yes!' It was all vague, and I was such a dimwit, I didn't ask Agnes where I would live, or anything. Once she'd gone and I was away from her influence, I began to think — did I want to go on doing Agnes's work, having worked all my life to become a classical ballet dancer? I asked Antony, but he ducked the responsibility and told me to ask Margaret Craske. She was a marvellous teacher, we went to her for classes. She said, 'I think you have a chance of being successful if you can get some weight off your thighs.' Well, there's never just one reason, is there? Anyway, I wrote to Agnes, probably a very naive letter. She was understandably upset. But she had offered me nothing but promises. She couldn't possibly understand that for me, doing her work was like a branch line — extra experience for me in the dance world, but the whole thing I'd worked for was ballet. We were all so in love with dancing, to get experience was our only goal. But Agnes was eaten up with ambition. She hung her ideals on a distant star and believed in it so strongly that anyone who spoilt that was letting her down. She thought that Antony had poached me, influenced me — but he hadn't."[30]

In Agnes's version, Bidmead deserted her; "promised bits by Antony for his new project [she] was accordingly reluctant to accompany me to

New York, although I had trained her and paid her for a year with this precise goal in mind."[31] Fifty years after the fact, she would still be indignant about Tudor's treachery and how "Lottie" had deserted her.

At thirty-three, Agnes was beginning to grow up. Although she was still financially dependent on her mother, their geographical separation had given her some autonomy. Her relationship with Ramon had given her a sense of responsibility for another person. She still clung to her fantasy of a life with Edgar; that protracted exercise in denial had yet to play itself out. But the sessions with Dr. Maas had identified some of the psychic obstacles that impeded her progress and had strengthened her confidence in the future. Professionally, she had acquired the experience she would need for an opportunity that might never materialize. The test would come in America, where nothing was certain — except that Anna waited, with arms outstretched.

s e v e n t e e n

Regrouping

Agnes had asked her mother to find her a cheap apartment. Her plan was to live on $25 a week from Anna and to finance her working expenses by teaching. But the apartment Anna rented for her, which was within shouting distance of her own, was not cheap enough for Agnes to begin climbing out of debt. The unacceptable alternative, which Anna frequently suggested, was that they live together. They compromised: Agnes went to her mother's for dinner most evenings, but Anna was not allowed to enter her daughter's apartment without ringing the bell.

The apartment, a second-floor walkup at 42 East Ninth Street in Greenwich Village, had a large front room with an open fireplace, hardwood floor, and floor-to-ceiling French windows all across the front, facing north. In the back was a closet-sized bedroom, a cubicle kitchen, and a bath. The furniture consisted of a bed, a chest of drawers, a piano, and eight mirrors, creating an ascetic, vaguely New England effect.

Agnes took a two-hour class in ballet technique every morning at a studio shared by Paul Haakon and two young choreographers, Michael Kidd and Eugene Loring, who took turns teaching class. Agnes taught two classes a week at the Young Men's and Young Women's Hebrew Association. The "92nd Street Y," as it was known, was famous for pre-

senting the cream of the culture to some of the most sophisticated audiences in the country. Professionals who could use the $20 per class taught and lectured on all the arts. Agnes taught "Exercises for bodily control, strength and range of gestures," including jumps, falls, and "Walking and Running with emphasis on style and deportment"; exercises in "emotional expression"; and "the producing of tragic, comic and ironic effects, and the representation of personal and folk character in both dancing and acting." Also "Exercises for Style in Dancing. Pre-Classic Ballet Forms. Folk Dances."

In November, she found herself in the position Robert Alton had been in when he replaced her in *Hooray for What!* — doctoring another choreographer's dances for a show. In this case, the choreographer was Eugene Loring, the show a jazz version of *A Midsummer Night's Dream* called *Swingin' the Dream.* Unfortunately, there is no filmed record of this short-lived "vast jitterbug carnival," which featured Dorothy Dandridge, Benny Goodman and his sextet, Jackie "Moms" Mabley as Quince, Butterfly McQueen as Puck, Dorothy McGuire as Helena, Louis Armstrong as Bottom, effects by Walt Disney, and lines from almost all of Shakespeare's plays.[1]

Experimentation was exploding in all the arts in the late 1930s. The audience for modern dance was growing, due in large part to the work of Martha Graham, Doris Humphrey, Helen Tamiris, Hanya Holm, and, of the next generation, José Limón. A great many American modern dancers gave concerts in Broadway theaters on Sunday evenings. Kurt Jooss's company, composed of German exiles and dancers from ten other countries, made similar appearances. But as far as the general public was concerned, ballet was Russian.

The Soviet Union's loss of imperial dancers and choreographers after the Revolution had been America's gain, for the schools run by distinguished Russian émigrés — Theodore Kosloff, Adolph Bolm, Michel Fokine, and Mikhail Mordkin — had trained and nurtured a generation of dancers who were ready when their opportunity arrived. When impresario Sol Hurok brought Colonel de Basil's Ballets Russes de Monte-Carlo to tour the United States in 1933, a wave of balletomania ensued. Expatriate Russian companies, consisting of English, French, and American dancers, thrived. Because Americans agreed with Hurok that only European dancers and choreographers were first rate, some dancers "Russianized" their names; Lillian Alice Marks became Alicia Markova, Sydney Healey-Kay became Anton Dolin, and so forth. Hurok presented other international talents, as well: Mary Wigman, Vincente Escudero, Uday Shankar, and Trudi Schoop.

Bennington College had legitimized dance in academia by offering summer school lectures and workshops taught by Louis Horst, John Martin, and other leaders in the modern dance world. Bennington also provided space, costumes, scenery, and technicians for Graham, Humphrey, Weidman, Limón, Hanya Holm, and their companies. Agnes was never a member of this exclusive group. Even though the moderns were beginning to realize that they needed to learn some technique, and ballet dancers that they needed some freedom, Agnes was considered a crossover dancer, an outsider. It posed a persistent problem: "It is difficult to keep one's own style intact and robust," she had confided to a friend, "when all around recognizable greatness reveals itself (particularly in dancing) in forms quite alien to my means of expression. I have to shut my eyes and keep moving arbitrarily, by instinct. Most people think I am going wide of the important line of developement [*sic*] in my field, and when I vary my course slightly, the others claim I am being untrue to my own line of progress."[2]

Whatever her professional problems, Agnes had a rich social life. Everybody knew just about everybody in the small, incestuous art world, and the Upper Bohemian salons that enlivened the social scene were the nerve centers of gossip, the most popular indoor sport. One such salon took place every Sunday during the "r" months at a four-story brownstone on East 61st Street.

Kirk Askew, the small, bright-eyed host, ran a prominent art gallery; his elegant, "Junoesque" wife, Constance, came from Connecticut society.[3] Their guests, generally numbering fifty or sixty, were actors, playwrights, designers, directors, writers, poets, art dealers, painters, and photographers. Musicians included Roger Sessions, George Antheil, Elliot Carter, Aaron Copland, and Virgil Thomson. From the dance world came, among others, George Balanchine, Lincoln Kirstein, critic Edwin Denby, and choreographer Frederick Ashton, when he was in New York. The conversation, mostly shoptalk and politics, was witty and nonstop. Tea was served from five o'clock, followed by Prohibition gin and cocktails, and splinter groups often went on to an all-night party in Harlem. Couples might be interracial or hetero- or homosexual, and the *mariage blanc* (Paul and Jane Bowles, Lincoln Kirstein and Fidelma Cadmus, Carl Van Vechten and Fania Marinoff, Marc Blitzstein and Eva Goldbeck) was accepted, but flirtations were discreet. Homosexuals had tremendous power in the theater of the day, but there was no camping at the Askews, and it was considered bad form even to allude to the subject openly. To Agnes it was "just a great big salon, with *every real* artist, and all the hangers on, and the pansies of both sexes *swarming*."[4] She attended alone, wearing a flame red dress or a green-and-gold Indian sari. Another regular, the designer Oliver Smith, recalled, "It was in the depression, and all the poor people of that world could go to the Askews and get something to eat and something to drink, and exchange ideas. They didn't take Agnes very seriously. Aaron [Copland] did, but some of the others didn't."[5]

Agnes still intended to form her own company. Through colleagues and referrals and her observation of dancers in the various classes she attended, she recruited eleven young women — one of whom, Sybil Shearer, would become her muse.

As a young student, Shearer had seen Agnes perform in New York and been moved to write her a fan letter. She was invited to lunch at Anna's apartment, where her first impression was that "when Agnes smiled, she didn't look a day over twelve. Her clothes were quite Dali and she wore little straw bonnets with flowers in front. So did her mother. Agnes looked like a replica of her mother — the same bonnets and tricornes, the same size and shape."[6] Shearer had since become a soloist with the Humphrey-Weidman group, but she was, like Agnes, a maverick, destined to travel alone. For a time, however, she felt an artistic kinship with Agnes and wanted to dance with her. She was slightly taller than Agnes, slender, with brown hair and strong features. She wore no makeup, and except for her penchant for wearing riding boots as everyday footwear, she was unremarkable to look at. But Sybil had an unearthly, mystical quality. She had a special affinity for nature; "her friends would find her at dawn with her ear in the grass, listening to the sounds of the earth."[7] Her dancing was simple, passionate, evocative, and brilliantly inventive, and she was a gifted pantomimist. Where Agnes was witty, Sybil was fey. For any idea Agnes came up with, Sybil could invent a movement, often a hysterically funny one. "I'd say, 'Sybil, that is divine; now, what did you *do?*' I wrote it all down and used it. Working together, we laughed until tears streamed down our cheeks."[8] Watching them, audiences had the same reaction.

"Agnes had this *terrible* stage fright," said Shearer. "She was so *vulnerable,* but she always felt she had to *audition.* Once she borrowed Martha Graham's studio to show her new dances to all the important people in New York. Afterwards everybody filed out, not knowing what to say. Agnes wasn't *ready* to show those dances on the stage, but she wanted criticism from 'important people.' She always had an exaggerated respect for their opinions. Once Ernst Lubitsch [the director] was in town, and Agnes felt she should audition for him. It was in a dance studio that was a five-flight walkup, with the bathroom and dressing room at the back. When Agnes saw Lubitsch in that setting she said, "This is terrible, I can't go on! Why did I do this?' He was very polite, thanked her and left. She wanted him to see her work, but why would he ever want to use her? Auditions seemed to be part of the ritual of being in the theatre for her, something she had to go through."[9]

Through her old friend Mary Hunter, Agnes found a new partner. Mary had moved from Sante Fe to Chicago to New York, establishing herself as an actor and director along the way. In the late 1930s she brought together a group of young, unknown actors from all over the country — Horton Foote and Jerome Robbins were among them — and formed the American Actors Company. Using improvisational techniques, they developed material about where they grew up and the characters they'd known there. Agnes occasionally visited the workshop sessions, and it seemed to her that Joseph Anthony, a tall, handsome leading man in the company, would make a suitable partner.

Joe Anthony was seven years younger than Agnes, and an unlikely combination of unsophisticated Wisconsin country boy and flamboyant performer. His dance training was nil, but he was intuitive and inventive; like Warren Leonard, he had studied fencing, acrobatics, and gymnastics to supplement his acting talent. He was hardworking, reliable, and courteous — a welcome relief from Hugh Laing's hysteria. Joe also set lights, hung scenery, mended costumes, and was generally as helpful to Agnes backstage as he was on it. "Her previous partners had been better dancers," Anthony said, "but I was a better actor, and I could see a dance as a play. She was smart enough to make me *look* like a dancer. I could only turn in one direction. I was very good on great leaps from left to right, but I couldn't reverse it! Agnes knew all that, and used it.

"She was interested in much more than just the steps; they were a means of revealing the person's character and the quality of their life. What interested her was dramatic conflict, especially as revealed in male-female relationships, and the social attitudes that determine why people dance this way instead of that way. When we did the *Pavane,* she said, 'Joseph, it's not just stylized court dance, it's about the relationship of *characters.*' She explained that I was a young man, an ordinary citizen reaching out for the first time to a person higher than himself, my idea of a princess. It was courtly — a gentle, subtle social encounter between a man and a woman. She'd say, 'Don't just flirt with me. Flirting *then* wasn't like flirting today. It was their only opportunity to express affection. It had to be masked, not exposed.' Agnes made it a piece of history—not just puppets up there but real human characters. When she did a country dance you *knew* those were illiterate people, enjoying sexual interplay and not just making faces. And if she invented something, you couldn't tell that it wasn't authentic."[10]

"Agnes was obsessed with money," said Sybil Shearer, who believed that dancers should take alms. "She was always saying that *dancers should be paid!*"[11] But she could pay her dancers only $10 for each performance and nothing for rehearsals. "Little did we know," said Eleanor Fairchild, "that we were going to rehearse for months and only do about three concerts! She had wonderful dancers—Sybil, Marguerite De Anguera, Ruthanna Boris. I was nowhere near on a par with those girls, and I was totally awed by Agnes. I'd never known a woman who did anything on her own before, who wasn't subservient to a man, and I'd never seen anybody dance with that vigor and vitality, knowing exactly what she wanted to do. When she danced, she was *one*. But she never seemed to laugh or be very happy. She used to tell the girls, 'If you see a man, bring him back, I could use one.'"[12]

Ruthanna Boris walked to rehearsals, "from 66th Street to Agnes's studio on Ninth Street, because I didn't have carfare. After rehearsal, Agnes would ask me to stay and take tea with her. Then she would tell me all her troubles—about her lack of money, how her mother had to sell another bond, and how hard it was for a woman to get along in this world. I didn't tell her I didn't have money for carfare. I didn't mind! Then I'd walk home, and on the way I rehearsed in my head what we'd done. We were a different breed then. We didn't know what it was to be tired. I would have gone to Alaska to dance for nothing!"[13]

It would never have occurred to Agnes that one of her dancers could not afford carfare (in England, she had been shocked to learn that a friend could not afford cream). Nor would it have occurred to her that the single-minded pursuit of what one wanted most in the world was a luxury to all but a fortunate few. To Agnes, her career was as much a necessity as a roof over her head. She regarded herself as poor because she took buses instead of taxis, because she was financially dependent on her mother, and because she had to borrow and scrounge to support her career.

To that end, she counted every penny spent and earned with the diligence of a tax collector. She had committed herself to a January concert at the 92nd Street YMHA without knowing where she would get the money to rent the theater, run advertisements, print and mail flyers, pay the stagehands — and the dancers — and take care of incidental expenses, such as renting a piano. There was also the matter of a $125 management fee for the woman who had made the arrangements. The total expenses came to $830.

It was generally assumed that Agnes somehow had access to her uncle's fortune, when in fact he had never given her a cent. She had always been too proud to ask — until now. "I'm trying to borrow money from the old bastard," she told a friend, "so I can get my concert on here in New York."[14] She asked for $1,500; as a joke, Margaret offered to put up her wedding diamonds as security. "Send them over, we'll have them appraised," said Cecil. In a letter to her uncle, Agnes thanked him for his kind offer of a loan and his interest in her career. "Happily," she concluded, "I now find that I will not be forced to impose on you, as I can get more advantageous terms here, from a pawnbroker," and signed herself "Your grateful and affectionate niece, Agnes."[15] But she never mailed the letter.

She borrowed the money from friends, and rehearsals proceeded. "Agnes worked into the mirror," Ruthanna Boris recalled, "with the company behind her. While she was working out the *Rodeo* material on us, Sybil would be off in a corner behind her, working on something by herself. Agnes would see in the mirror something Sybil was doing; she would stop dead and say, 'Sybil, I want that movement! I'll take that movement, that's mine!' Sybil was transfixed, I don't think she even knew what Agnes was talking about. But I felt like saying, 'Agnes, that's stealing!'"[16]

No one has ever precisely located the line between research and plagiarism — but as Shearer saw it, "Agnes was a *researcher*. She *researched* everyone's work, and she *used* it. To work with her was an education. I enjoyed her — she was fun to work with, but she needed me more than I needed her. She once said, 'I don't think I know where I leave off and where Sybil begins."

"Most dancers don't see drama, they're just legsters. Agnes was a headster. All her solo dances had movement themes that came from actual dances — ballroom dances, the Ballets Russes, Western-style dancing and court dances. But her subject was *people,* so that acting and dancing were combined into one whole. She had lots of ideas, but she was not good at original movement. She wasn't satisfied with her solo work because she thought of herself as an inadequate dancer. But in a good solo concert, a whole company is packed into one person. To me, her real greatness was her solo dances. Most of her solos were little theatrical masterpieces."[17]

Three years had elapsed since Agnes had appeared on a New York stage, and she felt she must prove herself all over again, as a choreographer of group dances as well as solos. In the months following the YMHA concert she performed with her group at the Guild Theater and participated in two benefits to raise money for the Spanish Loyalists. The reviews were generally good; the critic Edwin Denby confessed that he preferred her work to that of modern dance groups because her dancers looked human and seemed to enjoy dancing. But she still billed herself as Agnes George de Mille, and her illustrious relatives, living and dead, were her severest critics. Internalized, they peered over her shoulder and showed no mercy.

In September, the last vestige of a balance of power in Europe vanished. Hitler marched into Poland, and Britain and France declared war on Germany. The United States would remain uninvolved for another two years — but Agnes, like every other American, could feel the pace of history suddenly accelerate, taking her life, like a leaf in the wind, in directions no one could foresee.

e i g h t e e n

"A Really Fine Night-Club Show"

The war's most noticeable effect on the insular ballet world was that Russian touring companies, stranded in the United States, produced a new wave of Russian émigrés. The first wave, which had been displaced by the Revolution, included Mikhail Mordkin, who had partnered Anna Pavlova in her first appearances in this country. Mordkin had eventually started a school in New York, as well as a ballet company, into which his best students matriculated.

The manager of the Mordkin Ballet, a young man named Richard Pleasant, had a grand vision: an American ballet company with an international repertory that would encompass the best of every type and style of dance. In 1939, Pleasant joined forces with Lucia Chase, a Mordkin dancer who had inherited an enormous fortune.* When Chase shifted her support from Mordkin to Pleasant, Ballet Theatre was born.

The company's catholicity and its emphasis on ballet as theater seemed made to order for Agnes, and indeed she was one of the diverse

* Her family had owned Chase Brass and Copper of Connecticut, and their firm made the Ingersoll watch.

group of choreographers (Anton Dolin, Bronislava Nijinska, Michel Fokine, Yurek Shabelevsky, Adolph Bolm, José Fernandez, and Eugene Loring) who were invited to contribute to its sensational first season. The dancers were Russian, French, and, primarily, American, with American names: Patricia Bowman, Miriam Golden, William Dollar, Annabelle Lyon, and Donald Saddler (one American member of the corps de ballet, Nora Koreff, changed her name after the first season to become Nora Kaye). The soloists, sets, costumes, and lighting were also first-rate, for Lucia Chase refused to stint on anything. The staging would be contemporary and the music either new or reorchestrated — by the composer, if possible — for the company's chamber orchestra. "Not since the Renaissance court ballets," Agnes wrote, "had such a display of costumes, music and performances been put into simultaneous work. Diaghilev may have established higher standards artistically, but our scope and verve were unmatched."[1]

In its initial season, Ballet Theatre presented twenty-one ballets — six of them world premieres, five others American premieres. Fokine restaged his classic *Les Sylphides* and *Carnaval;* Dolin restaged *Giselle* and

Swan Lake. Antony Tudor, who was imported to join the company only because Agnes had urged Lucia Chase, who had never heard of him, to do so, was the hit of the season with *Jardin aux Lilas, Dark Elegies,* and *Judgment of Paris.* In *Paris,* Tudor and Hugh Laing and Agnes recreated their original roles, and Chase danced Minerva. But Tudor gave Agnes's role in *Dark Elegies* to Chase.

Long after Lucia's death, Agnes still maintained, "I acted better than anyone, but Lucia was considered the great pantomimist in that company, so why should they have me? But as a choreographer, they'd take me."[2] She was referring to the fact that when Pleasant commissioned a ballet from her, he stipulated that she not dance in it herself. Whether or not Lucia was a consideration, Pleasant astutely realized that what Agnes designed for herself could not be successfully recreated by another performer; it would have been like someone trying to replicate Chaplin's Little Tramp. "He contended that I would never develop a true choreographic technique until I stopped using my own acting style as model. . . . He offered me for cast the choice of the company but he refused to allow me to think in terms of my own limited technique and special acting talents. 'I am going to save you,' he said flatly. 'I will not permit you to cripple your talents.'"[3]

A performer without an audience is a sail without a breeze — but for all her romanticism, Agnes had a tough, practical streak. At thirty-six, she knew that as a dancer, she had gone as far as she could go. "There is no definite age limit to performing once you have reached the top," she wrote in *To a Young Dancer,* "but you must get there while you're young."[4] If she was to have a future in dance, it would have to be choreography.

Balking at the thought of creating a comedy role for someone other than herself, but afraid to compete directly with the company's other choreographers, Agnes decided to do something completely different. *Obeah,* or *Black Ritual,* was an exotic piece about Haitians. To complicate matters, the best job to which a black dancer could aspire at that time was in the line at the Cotton Club in Harlem; black dancers had never been taken seriously in a major production, so there was no pool of trained dancers from which to choose. Agnes hired sixteen women, most of whom were untrained, undisciplined, unprofessional, and underfed. Two of them had studied with Graham, one with Lester Horton; three were nightclub dancers, one was a trained nurse, another a gym teacher.

It would be the first full-length ballet she had ever done — two scenes, running twenty-five minutes, with a jazz score by Darius Milhaud. At one point she considered going back on her word and improbably dancing the lead, which called for a black woman, herself. "How I hungered and thirsted," she said, "to have the large stage and the orchestra, the dressers and crew I'd never had."[5] Her ego screamed, "Look at me!" She told it to shut up.

For the sake of the dancers with day jobs, rehearsals took place at night, by which time they were tired and tense. Agnes fed them hot soup, bread, and pep talks; they were pioneers, she told them, breaking new ground for Negro dancers. In the end they were adequate, but the ballet was "pseudo-voodoo."[6] At its opening,* the music was inexplicably played at half tempo, causing Agnes to run outside the auditorium and beat her head on a pillar. The audience was enthusiastic; the critics were not. John Martin called the ballet "an interesting novelty."[7]

Black Ritual was not a failure, but it was not the success Agnes longed for, and no new commission was forthcoming. Spring arrived, and the news was disheartening. The Germans, having already occupied Holland, Belgium, Norway, and Denmark, entered Paris. As the world shuddered, dancing seemed at once trivial and more essential than ever. In the fall, Richard Pleasant suggested that Agnes restage *Black Ritual* — with white dancers! By then, however, she was in Omaha, on tour with her own company.

An agent had booked a two-week, bargain-basement tour of schools, colleges, and drama clubs — nine dates in the Midwest and four in Chicago. Once again Agnes borrowed from friends to pay expenses. Her company consisted of Sybil Shearer, Joe Anthony, Katherine Litz (a leading Humphrey dancer), Louis Horst, and herself, all of whom helped with the music copying, sewing, and a multiplicity of errands. Agnes took

* On January 22, 1940, at the Center Theatre in Radio City.

care of all the paperwork. Joe set the lights, Horst cued the curtain, the women pressed and packed the costumes. They traveled by train and in private cars, with Sybil and Louis arguing in the backseat. It was a grueling schedule: packing, unpacking, pressing, briefing a new dresser in each town, making up, and, in Agnes's case, performing in eight of the eleven numbers. They opened in Kearney, Nebraska; during the *May Day* duet, Joe inadvertently slammed his hand down on Agnes's steel knitting needle, which entered his palm and exited through the back of his hand. With the same stoicism Agnes had displayed when Warren broke her nose onstage in *The Black Creek,* Joe braced the hand between his knees, pulled the needle out — miraculously, there was no blood — and went on with the show.

Agnes was gratified by the positive response of audiences who were seeing her work for the first time, but she never lacked for things to complain about. "We called her the wailing wall," Sybil Shearer recalled. "*So* melodramatic. She always had some huge problem — money, rehearsal time, inadequate dancers. She took everything personally — she almost *asked* people to mistreat her, because she was such a good complainer! She appreciated herself, which was not conducive to other people appreciating her. She could be hoity-toity and deliberately not hear you. She was highly emotional, and that was on view. People said deprecating things about her. It was as though suffering made life meaningful for her."[8]

The tour ended triumphantly at the Goodman Theater, in Chicago. Reviewers praised Agnes's humor, taste, and technique, and Joe's "exceptional gift for characterization."[9] By this time, Joe and Agnes were lovers.

Anna disapproved of Joe; he was the son of immigrant German farmers, and his education was limited. She referred to him as "the boy with the weak face." When she thought he was in Agnes's apartment she walked up and down the sidewalk, patrolling like a jealous lover, shooting radioactive guilt-inducing arrows through the walls and causing Joe to announce, "For a woman your age to be so afraid of your mother is obscene!"[10]

From Joe's perspective, Anna "had an aura of disdain. She thought herself *chosen* because of Henry George. She would generally sit without a word, surrounded by a coterie of intellectual people talking about matters of great moment; she would smile and hand you a canapé. When she did speak, everyone was supposed to shut up and listen."[11] At table, Anna would tell Joe he was using the wrong fork. "She didn't approve of my clothes, either. *Noise* was gross. *Vulgarity* was disgusting. She was a *practiced* lady; I never saw her cross her legs. I used to want to grab one of her legs and *throw* it over the other one!"

As Anthony recalled it, "My relationship with Agnes was the biggest challenge of my life. Neither of us wanted to be serious, but I loved her deeply, and quite violently, for a while. She has always been a mysterious creature, so strong and so vulnerable, and the conflict of those qualities are as tough on her as they are on any relationship."[12]

Agnes still loved Edgar Wind, whom she considered superior to Joe in almost every way—but Joe, unlike Edgar, was a satisfying lover, and she had waited a long time for that. Joe, however, was wary. "I was daft for her, but wise enough not to get hooked. I knew she could never ever respect me as a partner. As a man, yes, but never as her match in wit, education, background. She needed another outlet. She was very powerful. Sexually she was on the edge of violence, and very much in need."[13] Sex and propinquity kept the affair going until the summer of 1941, when Joe went to Hollywood to act in a movie. Agnes followed him, uninvited, setting herself up for the rejection that awaited her ("He told me I had been a mistake"), and returned to New York alone.[14]

For Ballet Theatre's second season, Richard Pleasant asked Agnes to create a comic character part for Lucia Chase. He wanted it in a hurry, and badly enough to retract his condition that Agnes not dance in her own work. *Three Virgins and a Devil,* the piece Tudor had completed for her in 1934, served both purposes neatly. Agnes replaced the original music with a sixteenth-century galliard in 6/4 time, orchestrated by Respighi, and revised the movement and the ending, which had never been resolved in London. For three weeks she worked frantically with Sybil Shearer, who translated her ideas into movement ("I really should put

Sybil's name on the program," Agnes said, "but I don't know how").[15] The role of the devil was almost entirely Shearer's creation; she "suggested an Hieronymous Bosch animal whirling and scrabbling over the floor."[16] Agnes played the Priggish One, who is dragging her reluctant friends — the Lustful One (Annabelle Lyon) and the Greedy One (Lucia Chase) — to church when the Devil (Eugene Loring) intercepts them. He plays a tune on his cello, which he also uses as a pogo stick, as they clasp their hands and piously attempt to pray. To their horror, their pelvises involuntarily begin to bump and grind to the rhythm. One by one, the Devil tricks them into entering his cave, the gateway to hell, each victory accompanied by a puff of infernal smoke. The Priggish One is the last holdout; when the Devil weeps, hoping to gain her sympathy, she dries his eyes with the end of his tail. A church bell sounds offstage and she waves her arm in a gesture that says, "God, you'll have to wait!" Finally she grabs the Devil's tail and triumphantly drags him toward the church, intending to save him. He escapes; she chases him, he steps aside, and she spins into his cave, carried by her own momentum.

The ballet is highbrow burlesque, a broad satire of piety, self-righteousness, and chastity; the virgins' shocked surprise can be hilarious. "It looks easy," said Sallie Wilson, who later danced Agnes's part, "but it was relentless. You had to bend in a way that stopped your breathing."[17] The Devil's movements were classical, with beats, pirouettes, and tours en l'air; the virgins' movements were modern and free. The costumes and the setting, based on a Flemish painting, were medieval. *Three Virgins and a Devil* premiered on February 11, 1941, and was a great success with both audience and critics. But Ballet Theatre would not commission another work from Agnes for three years. By then, they would need her more than she needed them.

Agnes had only two other showcases for her work that year. In May, Mary Hunter's American Actors Company gave three off-Broadway performances of *American Legend,* a celebration of Americana. The show opened with Agnes's "running set" — a classic square dance, accompanied only by the sound of clapping hands and dancing feet. The audience had never seen anything like it, and the effect was electric. Songs, dances, tall tales, and a one-act play by Horton Foote followed, and the evening concluded with Agnes's *Hell on Wheels,* a play within a play with songs, dances, and pantomime. "Hell on Wheels" was the name given to the car behind the caboose on the work trains used in the construction of the transcontinental railroad in the mid-nineteenth century. With a huge replica of the American flag behind them, the workers sang an authentic folk song, "Great Pacific Railway, from California Hail," and pantomimed laying the tracks that joined east to west. The dancer Mary Meyer, Agnes's close friend since *Romeo and Juliet,* gave a speech as "Miss Liberty," wearing Grecian robes and a laurel wreath. Then the workers were entertained by a troupe of broken-down entertainers, prostitutes, and gamblers who toured the work camps. The onstage "audience" shouted its approval of the dance-hall girls and its disapproval of a woman who tried to recite a poem. Finally, Agnes, "with the nervous agility and mocking hauteur which distinguished many of her comedy portrayals," danced a hoedown, daring anyone to dance her down and making it clear that whoever did so would be her sweetheart.[18] The character was the pioneer girl Agnes had created for her very first dance, *'49* — hearty, honest, and energetic, touching and inspiring, with a heart of gold and a will of steel. She was the quintessential de Mille character, the idealized spirit of the American West, and audiences always cheered her on with delight. In this incarnation, she was seen by the management of the Rainbow Room, a ne plus ultra New York nightclub, and booked for a six-week engagement.

The era of dance concerts was ending, and nightclubs had become one of the few places where concert dancers could be seen. For the Rainbow Room, Agnes, who had negotiated a rapprochement with Tudor and Laing, recruited the beautiful-but-difficult Hugh as her partner. The room was the epitome of sophistication, but there was no glamour there for Agnes. Her friend, the dancer-pantomimist-clown Lottie Goslar, helped her carry her costumes from a car to the dressing room. "We put them in bedsheets," Goslar recalled, "and tied the opposite corners for a grip to carry it with. We each carried a bedsheet with each hand, and when we got to the Rainbow Room, we had to walk through the room and up a spiral staircase to get to the dressing room. Paying customers were sitting there, sipping champagne. They must have wondered 'Who are these two washerwomen?'"[19] For her labors, her partner, and herself, Agnes received $400 a week.

In his review, Walter Terry pointed out that unlike theater audiences, whose specific purpose is to be entertained, a nightclub audience almost defies the entertainer to hold its attention. "You really can't be bothered with food or chatter," he wrote, "when Miss de Mille and Hugh Laing launch into their lusty cancan with kicking legs, come-hither glances and associate highjinks. In another number, Miss de Mille turns to a good old American folk dance, 'Hoe Down,' and on opening night she had a sophisticated audience clapping out the rhythms and egging the dancers on to greater efforts. . . . Mr. Laing and Ray Harrison . . . fought for the honor [of dancing her down]. . . . A really fine night-club show."[20]

n i n e t e e n

Walter

Agnes had struggled through twelve years of wild-goose chases and dead ends. Her professional successes were fleeting, the time between them bleak. She still loved Edgar, but her fantasy of a life with him was fading. Her emotional state was, she wrote with an uncharacteristic lack of exaggeration, "despair."[1]

Her mind was as meticulously organized as a space station, but her appearance was still a disaster. Sybil Shearer remembered her "with a run in her stockings, her hair flying, her neck black from the soot of the city because she'd only thought to wash her face. She was just unconscious of how she looked."[2] Consciousness was dawning, however; for the first time in her life, she was making an effort to clean up her offstage act, even going so far as to get her teeth straightened. Dr. Maas had urged her to continue her analysis in New York — but not, under any circumstances, at her mother's expense, for that would give Anna another means of control. With no other source of money, Agnes delayed. But during her affair with Joe Anthony, Edgar Wind had surfaced in New York. For a brief time, she was sexually involved with both men — in her view, a dangerous step toward promiscuity. Concerned, she appealed to her maligned but understanding stepmother, who agreed to subsidize her

analysis with another Freudian, Dr. Florence Powdermaker. Ultimately — but not until she had met the man she would marry — she was able to break off with Edgar for good.

Anna's household now included Margaret (remarried, to a soldier who was overseas) and her ten-year-old daughter, Judy. Margaret had made fashion her profession, and she had progressed from a job as Elizabeth Arden's personal assistant to an editorial position at *Mademoiselle*. Judy remembered the family as one in which "everybody did their own thing. My grandmother had a dual mission: to tell the world about Henry George, which included handing out Single Tax tracts to strangers on buses, and to promulgate Agnes's career. My mother worked in retailing, and she had beaus. Agnes worked 'til she dropped when she was on a job. She was always beset by the powers that be, dragging herself in at the end of her rope, physically exhausted. Suki [Anna's nickname] would say, 'Would you like a little sherry, dear?' My grandmother didn't really approve of drinking, and a thimbleful of sherry was her idea of a big walloping drink. On Christmas Day, Suki always used to have a big open house; she'd whomp up a big bowl of eggnog and she would flavor it ever so delicately with a little bit of sherry or what have you. My mother would come in, stir it up and take a little sip. She'd go to the liquor cabinet and bring out a bottle of booze, give it a good healthy pour, and leave the room. Later on Agnes would come in and do the same thing — stir it up, taste it, and add another big dollop of liquor. My grandmother never could understand why the guests left so happy. She'd say, 'It's *almost* as though they're *tipsy!* And I only put a *little* bit of sherry in!'

"Suki was a warm, demonstrative person, with an antic sense of humor. But if she thought something impinged on moral principles she might say, 'Margaret, don't you think that dress is cut too low? Let me pin a little lace in.' As an Edwardian lady, she had a whole drawerful of little lace triangles to pin into dresses if they were cut too low. She was deeply shocked and offended by sex. Once I was talking about sex, I think in the sense of procreation. She said, 'We don't talk about that!' I said, 'But you must have *done* it, because you have two children!' She went beet red and refused to talk about it any more.

"Agnes and my mother loved each other dearly, but there was a lot of rivalry between them. My mother felt that she had to be the beauty because Agnes was the brains. They were equally brainy, but the roles were partially thrust on them, and they fostered them. I remember coming back from spending the night at Agnes's and telling my mother she was wearing the most beautiful pink dress — and my mother said, 'Yeah, and I'll bet she was wearing orange lipstick with it!' My mother was very glamorous, very soignée; Agnes sort of made a fetish out of being a frump. Although onstage, when she was all put together, she was a *devastating* woman — much more attractive than my mother, I always felt. My mother had style, and projected an aura of beauty and glamour — but she was not any more conventionally pretty, feature by feature, than Agnes was!"[3]

While Anna and Margaret conducted an ongoing argument about how Judy should be raised, Agnes argued with herself about whether or not to continue pursuing the success that eluded her. In the fall of 1941, the Jooss Ballet presented her *Drums Sound in Hackensack,* a satire about Indians in New Amsterdam, iniquitous fur traders, and a Dutch girl lost in the jungles of New Jersey. The movements owed a good deal to Sybil Shearer, but the timing and characterizations were all Agnes. For the first time, reviewers characterized her blend of romance, melodrama, and humor as "the de Mille touch."[4]

Agnes's little company — consisting of Joe Anthony (no longer a lover, but a friend); Sybil; two other dancers, Katherine Litz and Lilli Mann; and pianist Trude Rittman — made one more tour of the Midwest before fizzling out for good in New England. Sybil wanted to create and perform her own dances. Joe had been drafted. With neither partner, company, nor work, Agnes toyed with the idea of getting a job as a salesgirl at Macy's. Anna had had a heart attack, which made Agnes feel more than ever a burden. Still, she took class every day at the Ballet Arts Studio in Carnegie Hall, where some of the finest dancers of the day practiced and taught: Alexandra Danilova, Frederic Franklin, Edward Caton, Vera Nemtchinova, Rosella Hightower, Leon Danielian, and the members of the Jooss Ballet. As was always the case, her name, her age (thirty-seven), and her dogged attempts to keep up in spite of her unballetic body made her something of a curiosity to the other dancers. The class provided some structure to her days, and stimulation and release for her body and mind. The daily practice was a prayer, a rosary that her muscles recited.

She taught a class of her own, Acting for Dancers. "She gave us sensory exercises," a student recalled. "She had us walk into a lake and stand on one foot and, with the other foot, feel the way the water moved. She had us walk around the room the way cowboys walk, after riding a horse a lot. She had a thing where we had to do a contraction and then an 'up' breath, a very Agnes thing; she said, 'In an emergency you don't breathe, you take a breath in and you hold it, so that your ears will work!'"[5]

Another student — Bambi Linn, who would dance to stardom in Agnes's next show — pointed out that "until Agnes, dancers were fairies and dolls. Agnes asked us to be *people.* When you've been stuck in fifth position for years and someone says, 'How do you *feel* in this situation? How would you act? What would your body do?' suddenly you're relating everything you do as a human, not as ballet schtick! She would say, 'It's snowing, feel the snow.' Some people would be invigorated, other people got wet, other people got cold. We were just walking, there were no dance steps involved. I don't think there was even music. Then she'd say, 'Now it's stopping, and the sun's coming out.' And we'd all blossom forth. Then she'd have us run across the room toward an Evil Force — we didn't want to go, but something was pushing us. It was all to get us out of these stupid steps we'd been stuck in for years. For me, it was like being born."[6]

At the end of 1941, Germany, having conquered much of Europe, invaded the Soviet Union. When the Japanese bombed Pearl Harbor on December 7, the United States declared war on Germany, Italy, and Japan. On the national level, everything changed. But life on a personal level, at least for civilians, was largely business as usual. Agnes's life was not directly affected, and she maintained an active social life. She saw a good deal of Martha Graham, who lived across the street. Early in 1942, Graham invited her to a concert at Town Hall, and even provided her with a date: Graham's strikingly handsome manager, Walter Prude.

Few people knew anything about Walter Foy Prude's background other than that he had been born and raised in Texas. He had left Texas at nineteen, closing the door firmly behind him. He never discussed more than the bare facts of his youth — not even later with his wife, his son, or his closest friends.

From the age of two, Walter was a motherless child — a status that made him a misfit from the start and that, if it did not shape his personality, certainly colored his sensibility. Agnes was also a misfit, but her family was an anchor, a bedrock of devotion and strength and pride. Walter's only emotional connection as a child appears to have been with his mother's youngest sister, who was only six years older than himself; he spent his summers with her family in a small West Texas town. Annie Vee, as she was called, remembered Walter as a sweet, stubborn, perfectionist child, decent and reserved — adjectives that would apply to him throughout his life. During the school year, he lived with his paternal grandmother, a righteous Fundamentalist, in Dallas. His father, a clothing salesman, eventually remarried, but there is no evidence of love between Walter and any of the Prudes.

In his teens, he fell passionately in love with Brahms and became an accomplished, self-taught pianist. His other passion was tennis, at which he also excelled. Academically he was precocious, graduating from high school at fourteen. At Rice Institute, in Houston, he prepared for medical school; but in his fourth year as an undergraduate, he dropped out and followed a friend, Craig Barton, to New York, where his real education began.

"I want to really live," Walter wrote in his journal, "and I want to accomplish; but I have not the slightest notion of how to begin either." He polished his manners and refined his tastes. He read Proust, wrote romantic, Byronic poetry, and considered the piano "my real mistress."[7] He diluted his accent until it almost disappeared, but he would always look like the star of a Western movie — over six feet tall, with a long, lanky body, fair hair and complexion, and deep-set gray eyes. Agnes thought him "a nice combination of Gary Cooper and George VI of England."[8] Like Cole Porter, another small-town American boy, he transformed himself into a paradigm of sophistication, his wit as dry as his martinis. He seemed, people said, almost English. No one would ever have guessed Walter Prude to be the son of a Texas haberdasher.

He scrutinized people, including himself, with a merciless eye and noted the details in his journals with excruciating self-consciousness. He was hired as secretary to the concert pianist Olga Samaroff, and entered the inner sanctum of the music world, where he felt very much at ease with the people he met. His artistic standards, already high, rose. In 1931 he met Paul Nordoff, a composer, who fell in love with him. He wrote lyrics to Nordoff's music, lived with him for a time, and traveled across Europe with him. Eventually, he left Nordoff and took a job with a Chicago-based concert agency. In 1941, Martha Graham was one of his clients.

He had never heard of Agnes until Graham introduced them. At their first meeting, he was intrigued. She was enchanted. They met again the next day — and the next, and the next. They both loved language and good music; they played a game of listening to a string quartet and identifying the period and composer. They made each other laugh. "Our relationship ripened precipitously," Agnes said, "there was no time for finesse" — meaning that within three weeks of their meeting he was drafted and ordered to Biloxi, Mississippi.[9]

Agnes was "madly in love," but the war made everyone's future dubious. Walter kept his feelings guarded; like her father, he was "never wholly within reach."[10] He told her he loved her and that he had never been in love before; but the closest he came to a commitment was to leave his poems with her, and his journal. She wrote to him, often and at length; paradoxically, the physical distance between them generated letters that brought them closer. Still, they scarcely knew each other. He had met her mother once (Anna was not impressed); they had slept together twice; he knew little and cared less about dancing, except Graham's. But their lives, although neither of them could have known it, were already inextricably linked. Nor could Agnes have known that her fourteen years in a professional wilderness were over and her grandest dreams of glory were about to come true.

twenty

"Full Out, with Enthusiasm!"

Agnes was in the vanguard of a new generation of choreographers who were moving from the classical style to a more representational one, building on the gestures and rhythms of real life. As a corollary to that development, Americana had begun to be taken seriously as a subject for ballet. In the mid-1930s, choreographers Catherine Littlefield, in Philadelphia, and Ruth Page and Bentley Stone, in Chicago, began using American themes in their work. At approximately the same time, Lincoln Kirstein, a wealthy young patron of the arts, founded a ballet company and a school, in Manhattan. To run them, he imported the thirty-year-old George Balanchine, a onetime protégé of Diaghilev's at the Imperial Ballet in St. Petersburg.

Kirstein's American Ballet suspended operations after its opening season (it would be reincarnated fourteen years later as the New York City Ballet), but his school flourished. In 1936, he formed a touring group called Ballet Caravan, which presented new works by Balanchine and by Lew Christensen, both of whom added jazz rhythms to the classical technique. In Balanchine's *Alma Mater,* Christensen's *Filling Station,* Page and Stone's *Frankie and Johnny,* and Littlefield's *Barn Dance,* dancers played college football, pumped gas, murdered unfaithful lovers, and

square-danced. Graham based her *Letter to the World* (1940) on the work of an American poet (Emily Dickinson), and Doris Humphrey used American folk sources in *Square Dances* (1935).

Ballet Caravan premiered the first widely successful all-American ballet, Eugene Loring's *Billy the Kid,* in 1938. The scenario, written by Lincoln Kirstein, told the story of the mythic outlaw's gambling, gunfights, sweetheart, capture, escape, and execution. But in 1942, the only ballet company in this country that most Americans had heard of was still the Ballet Russe de Monte-Carlo,* the unofficial successor to Serge Diaghilev's Imperial Russian Ballet.

Every year from 1933, when Sol Hurok introduced the company to the United States, the Russians had played a season in New York and toured the provinces. With Colonel Wassily de Basil as its director and Leonide Massine its principal choreographer, the Monte-Carlo Ballets Russes, as it was called in New York, had an enviable roster of stars that included Alexandra Danilova, Alicia Markova, Igor Youskevitch, André Eglevsky, and Frederic Franklin. The repertoire consisted of

* Originally the Ballets Russes de Monte Carlo.

old Diaghilev productions and new ballets, some quite experimental, by Massine. In its initial New York season, the company had presented its first "American" ballet: Massine's *Union Pacific,* with a libretto by Archibald MacLeish about the completion of the transcontinental railroad. But although Nicholas Nabokov's score incorporated railroad and cowboy songs of the 1860s, and the dancers chewed gum, slapped their thighs, and tap-danced, Massine's style was unmistakably Russian. The same problem afflicted *Ghost Town,* the company's next venture into Americana; its subject (the gold rush), composer (Richard Rodgers), and choreographer (Marc Platt) were American, but Platt's training and technique were Russian, and *Ghost Town* had the *look* of a Russian ballet.

Intrigue is endemic in the insular ballet world, and Russian intrigue could hold its own with Machiavelli's. The Ballets Russes, in all their variously named incarnations, were rife with artistic and political rivalries. In 1938 the Russian-American Sergei Denham organized what was known as the Ballet Russe de Monte-Carlo, with Leonide Massine as its artistic director. Denham needed new choreographers, preferably American. Into the breach danced Agnes, with a scenario that had been rejected by Ballet Theatre: *Rodeo,* or *The Courting at Burnt Ranch.* She sold it to Denham for $500, on the condition that she would dance the lead on opening night.

In *Rodeo,* Agnes grafted a story of adolescent love onto the movements of her London "Rodeo" studies. The setting is a Colorado ranch at the turn of the century. The ranch hands stare into the distance, squinting in the sun; the gum-chewing Cowgirl, wearing pants and a pigtail, imitates their posture and attitude. When the rodeo begins, the men show off their riding and roping skills for some town girls, whose starched gingham, sunbonnets, and parasols arouse the Cowgirl's envy and contempt. She has a crush on the Head Wrangler, but she can express her feelings only by thumping him in the ribs. Seeking the men's acceptance and approval, she tries to ride and rope as they do — but they refuse to take her seriously, and the girls make fun of her. When her horse throws her, she climbs right back on, thumbing her nose at the town girls; but when the Wrangler banishes her from the corral, she is crushed. The Wrangler goes off with the rancher's pretty daughter, and the Cowgirl dances a poignant solo, then collapses on the ground in despair as the scene ends.

In the dark, the audience hears the sound of hands clapping and feet running — the unaccompanied "running set" from *American Legend.* The lights go up on four couples and a caller performing a brisk square dance that intensifies in speed and excitement as it builds to a climax.

In the next scene, couples in party clothes are waltzing inside the ranch house but the Cowgirl, still in riding pants, is outside, without a partner. The Champion Roper befriends her in a big-brotherly way; he spits on his hands to smooth her hair, dusts off her pants, and begins teaching her to dance. But when the Wrangler again pairs off with the rancher's daughter, the Cowgirl falls to the floor sobbing.

In the final scene, boys and girls line up to choose partners; once again, the Cowgirl is odd girl out. Humiliated, she runs offstage. A hoedown, taken verbatim from *Hell on Wheels* (itself an evolution of *'49*), ensues, with each dancer trying to be faster or funnier or more inventive than the others. The Cowgirl reappears, wearing a bright red dress and a ribbon in her hair. The caller yells, "If you don't dance her down, you can't marry her," and the Cowgirl outdances everyone. Then, according to Agnes's original scenario, the Wrangler "suddenly grabs her, forces her to dance his way and wears her out by sheer brute strength. He releases her. . . . She stumbles into his arms" and, presumably, they live happily ever after. (In the final version, the Roper challenges the Wrangler and kisses the girl, who immediately realizes that it's the Roper whom she loves.)

The story was a fairy tale, with humor. The men were cardboard cutouts — strong, but gentle with the women. The town girls had slightly more dimension; Agnes even tried to explain to the dancers how their characters' movements would have been affected by the corsets they wore. But in the Cowgirl, the independent but vulnerable pioneer girl of *'49* reached her apogee. The Cowgirl is Agnes — the outsider with her heart on her riding breeches, allowing herself only a moment of self-pity before picking herself up after a fall. Agnes's description of her is a pithy self-portrait: "always trying something a little beyond her, and whether she succeeds or fails she is as cocky as hell."[1] All the men who withhold their approval are, of course, William de Mille. Like Agnes, the Cowgirl simultaneously yearns for a man who ignores her and fears she will lose her identity if she "surrenders." The Cowgirl — awkward, romantic, wistful, hiding her shyness with bravado — is a wonderfully theatrical character, and a universal one.

Contemporary feminists would disown a girl who considers herself an outcast without a man and adopts the superficial accouterments of a woman to get one, but the situation is true to the social custom of its time. That Agnes clung throughout her life to that mentality, as espoused by her mother, only added to the character's authenticity. "Without a man," she wrote, the Cowgirl "can have no love, no children, no land, no home, no occupation, no reason for being. She will be wasted."[2] The Cowgirl conforms, but she retains her individuality. The dress she puts on is simpler than those of the other girls, without the frills. In the uniform of a woman, she is taken seriously; but she ultimately wins by using her talent, not her looks.

For the first time in her career, Agnes demanded control of her work. Egged on by Martha Graham, who counseled arrogance, she negotiated a clause in the contract that allowed Denham to make suggestions and recommendations but not to "obstruct, hinder or interfere with de Mille."[3] She then requested that Aaron Copland compose the music.

Agnes knew Copland casually; he had accompanied a performance she gave on the *Île de France* in 1932, and he was a member of the Askew salon. Like Agnes, he had been born and raised in New York, but in Brooklyn, not uptown; his father, a Russian-Jewish immigrant, had parlayed a pushcart into a department store. Copland had composed music for concerts, radio, and films, including *Of Mice and Men* and *Our Town,* and he was a major figure in American music.

At forty-two, the balding Copland thought himself ugly. He had prominent teeth, and on his oversized nose rested glasses with thick lenses. Copland was as steady and diplomatic as Agnes was melodramatic and tactless; he reserved his passion for his music.

His classical foundation, his deceptively simple style, and his occasional incorporation of American folk songs (he had interpolated cowboy songs into his score for *Billy the Kid*) made him the perfect choice for *Rodeo.* And he was intrigued by the prospect of a cowboy ballet that was light and bouncy — unlike *Billy,* which was earnest and tragic.

Agnes sent him the scenario, showed him the quality of the steps, and gave him a "time-plot" that broke sequences down into minutes, such as:

> Hoe-Down, 4 min. Intro — 16–24 measures — girl appears. Pause and silence for about 4 counts while she faces boy. Dance begins on walk — hit a fiddle tune hard. Verse and chorus with brass yells and whoops. Vamps in-between, long tacet toward close for tap cadenza, 9 measures of frenzy.

Copland worked out some sketches and played them for Agnes, who made comments. The first time she heard the entire score (played by four hands — Copland's and those of a twenty-three-year-old Leonard Bernstein) she whooped and danced with excitement. The music was rich — exuberant, emotional, and distinctively American. "You couldn't hear those long sequences without the sense of enormous distance and space and strength and loneliness," Agnes said. "Everybody thinks of America as such a bustling, big, busy place, but it was lonely for so long" — a description she might have applied to herself.[4]

To design the sets, Copland recommended his friend Oliver Smith, another Askew salon regular. Smith was a tall, redheaded twenty-three-year-old who had trained in architecture and art; the previous season, he had designed Massine's *Saratoga* for the Ballet Russe. "I went to Agnes's studio on a very hot summer morning," Smith recalled. "I could hear a lot of foot-stamping going on upstairs, and some piano playing. I knocked on the door and this rather intense, perspiring woman with lots of red hair said, 'Come in and sit down and listen!' She was improvising while Mr. Copland played. She explained to me what she felt about the ballet, that the characters should be dwarfed by space and height and isolation."

Smith's backdrop for the first scene was a hot, orange-red sky. As background for the running set, he designed a curtain painted with wild horses galloping across a bright blue sky. The idea was Smith's, but it grew out of his conversations with Agnes. "It was a real collaboration," he said. "I'd sit in a comfortable chair and she'd sit in a little rocker and sort of rock slowly back and forth, and jump up occasionally. We drank a great deal of coffee. Agnes speaks from emotion first, rather than intellectually. Her great sense of vitality and life expressed itself in her face."[5]

Happy with Copland's music and Smith's designs, Agnes joined the

Ballet Russe company in Los Angeles, in July. "We were on tour," the dancer Robert Pagent said, "and the first inkling most of us had that Agnes was going to do a ballet for us was on a hot, hot, hot summer day at the Hollywood Bowl. We were rehearsing Massine's *Rouge et Noir*. All of a sudden we saw this little lady walking around in that vast amphitheater. She had a little blue-and-white printed cotton dress, lots of red curly hair cascading down, and an enormous navy blue straw hat. She carried a briefcase. She made her way to the stage and introduced herself."[6]

Pagent was one of the Americans and Canadians who comprised about one-fourth of the company. The stars of this Americana piece were to be a Yugoslavian (Casimir Kokich, the Wrangler), a Bulgarian (Lubov Roudenko, the Cowgirl after the premiere), and an Englishman (Frederic Franklin, the Champion Roper). "The English-speaking people understood what she wanted," Franklin recalled, "but some of the Russians could not speak English, and I could see them falling by the wayside. The strange, bucking motions and horse motions went against the grain for them. Down the nose they'd look, as though she was an invader. A lot of them lolled against the barre and wouldn't move. 'When do we do the big stuff, to get the applause?' So out they went, eight out of eighteen of them. Sheer willpower kept us going. 'Let's take it from the top,' Agnes would say. 'Full out, with enthusiasm!'"[7]

Franklin was one of Agnes's four right hands during rehearsals; the others were pianist Rachel Chapman, Robert Pagent, and another dancer, James Starbuck. She needed all the support she could get, for rehearsal time was limited and the dancers were exhausted. They carried in their heads a repertory of thirty or forty ballets; they traveled like a circus, covering more than 20,000 miles in a season, performing until eleven-thirty nearly every night, sleeping more often in Pullman cars than in hotels. Understandably, they were not eager to learn a new ballet at ten-thirty the next morning, especially from a woman. The Russians were not accustomed to taking orders from a woman; their only female choreographer, Bronislava Nijinska, had at least been Russian. Among themselves, they sneered at Agnes's ignorance of the niceties of ballet etiquette. When she called them 'People!' instead of boys and girls, or ladies, they interpreted it as rudeness, when in fact she was emulating her uncle Cecil, who used the command to get his actors' attention on the set. "The Russians' attitude," said Starbuck, "was, This was their Art, she was an outsider! They had worked with Massine, Fokine, Balanchine. To Russian ballet, Agnes de Mille was nobody!"[8]

To Agnes, who had never before worked with more than one male dancer at a time, the Russians were "great muscled brutes leaning against the barre and staring with watchful, smoldering eyes."[9] They considered ballet legitimate only if it was based on classical tradition (*Swan Lake, Les Sylphides, Giselle*), or a Russian folk story (*Petrouchka, Schéhérazade, Gaîté Parisienne*), or a symphony (Massine's *Rouge et Noir*). Dancing meant steps and positions that had been rigidly prescribed and handed down through generations. Agnes respected tradition, but not convention; in her ballets, the acting was as important as the dancing. But to the Russians, the idea of characterization was as foreign as the syncopation of a timestep. While Agnes sweated to get them to stand naturally (rather than posing in fourth position) and to walk bowlegged (like cowboys, without pointing their toes), they wondered what that had to do with dancing. When she worked for hours on one comic moment, the regisseur, a diehard from the Diaghilev company, accused her of reducing the Ballet Russe to the status of a nightclub.

"If we can find how a man stands and walks," she said, "we will know the basis for his movement in any situation — dancing, riding, fighting." The cowboy is "slow of speech, sunburned, humorous . . . out of his element when he walks, but when he rides, a Centaur." To convey "his emotions, his exhilaration, his sense of power, his domination, his pride in strength," she took what she needed from every technique, including tap, and forced the men to move like athletes — not, as they had been trained to do, like "windblown petals."[10]

The prancing, bucking, and galloping horse movements did not imitate horses, but evoked them — "the way their legs shoot out when they gallop, the way their necks stretch, their trotting, the way they stand and shiver, the way they look at you before they do something outrageous, the way they buck." The men also had to give the impression of being thrown and jerked forward by an unseen horse. "It was very, very, *very* strenuous dancing," said Robert Pagent, "and of a type that none of us had done. We would come out of the rehearsals with every muscle in our bodies aching. The Russians used to complain like crazy."[11] They got headaches from the jerks and pulls and tremendous back movements, which are not balletic — percussive gestures, borrowed from Martha Graham, and sports movements — an overhead tennis smash, pitching a baseball.

"At rehearsals," one dancer recalled, "Agnes sat on a chair, in second position. She could do every single part herself, to perfection. She was absolutely in charge. She talked about the plains, and the earth, and the great American West, and cowboys, and courting."[12] But the company's skepticism was demoralizing, and much of her assurance was bravado. She burst into Carmelita Maracci's house one afternoon and collapsed on the couch — "sobbing," said Lee Freeson, "as though her heart had been torn to pieces. The company had insulted and humiliated her, the dancers acted as though they were doing her a favor."[13] Next day, like the Cowgirl, she dusted herself off and went back to work.

The company continued its tour across the country, rehearsing in hotel ballrooms, high school gymnasiums, whatever space was available. To subsist on her three-dollar-a-day per diem — the usual expense allowance at the time — Agnes lived on sandwiches and coffee, traded in her first-class tickets for coach, and avoided porters. The servicemen who filled the trains were constant reminders that the war was going badly in Europe, North Africa, and the Pacific. Walter, now a corporal stationed in Tennessee, expected an overseas posting soon.

During the Second World War, Americans viewed their country, its history, and its role in the world with an uncomplicated innocence unknown to members of later generations. Agnes was hardly an innocent, but she was a romantic, and Copland's music evoked for her "generation on generation of men leaving and falling and the women remembering. And what was left of any of them but a folk tune and a way of joining hands in a ring?"[14] She knew that her work, compared to larger events, was trivial. At the same time, she knew that her career was on the line.

In September the company returned to New York and six-hour-a-day rehearsals. Some of the Russians started to understand and to like *Rodeo,* and it began to acquire "the smell of success."[15] At the end of a list of minor musical changes submitted to Copland, Agnes added, almost as an afterthought, "Oh, Aaron, maybe I've done something good."[16]

The company went on vacation, leaving Agnes to practice her own part for opening night. The role of the Cowgirl, with its bravura exits and entrances, its off-balance turns and suspensions, requires a solid technique and, just as important, the comic timing and acting ability at which Agnes, who used her face as much as her feet, excelled. Of all the women who have danced the role since its premiere, many have surpassed its creator in technique — but none have flung themselves into it with such abandon, or projected pathos and joy with the same conviction. "It *mattered* to me," Agnes said, "that girl fighting for her happiness. I used to stand there with real tears pouring down my face."[17] Morton Gould said, "Agnes gave the Cowgirl an edge. She never became too coy or arch; you felt sympathy, liked her, and smiled with her, were sad with her. She moved as though she would fly."[18]

Agnes had found her Head Wrangler *and* Champion Roper in Walter. She had visited him in Tennessee in August, on her way back to New York, but it had been a tense and unsatisfactory forty-eight hours. "I have to settle my mind to coping with his resistances to marriage or just walk out," she had written to Mary Meyer from San Francisco. "I do truly love him . . . I must not think so much of my own needs and fears."[19] And from Seattle: "I don't think [Walter] can know how deeply lonely I am — or how the insecurity of the future frightens me. This isn't brave, I know."[20] While the company was on break, she visited him again. This time, they were more relaxed. She played a record of Copland's music for him and danced every part. It was, she believed, the most moving choreography she had ever done, and she credited their love for each other with "grounding" her enough to make it possible. *Rodeo,* she wrote to Walter on the eve of its opening, was "Texas and the way I feel about you."[21] Indeed, one reviewer would observe that the characters had "the authentic blend of drawling ease and trigger quickness that makes Texans, for instance, unlike any other people in the world."[22]

The event for which Agnes felt her whole life had been preparation took place at the Metropolitan Opera House on October 16, 1942. Mistakes were made, but all the laughs she had promised the dancers would come, came, and there was applause in all the expected, and some unexpected, places. The audience was swept up by the theatricality of the choreography, music, and set, and by the characterizations, especially the Cowgirl. "Agnes's part was terrifically difficult," Frederic Franklin recalled, "and the music was too fast, and her collar was too tight. When we got to the hoedown, she was failing, and I could see it — in the face, and the breathing. The kind of stamina that it takes — she thought she had it, but when you're sitting in the dressing room and three-quarters of your energy is gone in nerves, you've got one-quarter left to dance on. I hung on to her, helped her, pushed her and really lifted her, because she was going! When the curtain came down she was almost on the floor, hanging on to me."[23] As she took curtain call after curtain call — seventeen or twenty-two, depending on who was counting — Agnes thought, "Once more I had been incapable of the perfect effort."[24]

What she had achieved was more exciting than perfection: she had opened a window through which fresh air flooded. She had studied her craft, submitted to its discipline, and learned how, within its constraints, to be free. May Gadd, an acknowledged authority on American country dances, contrasted Agnes's work with "the death-dealing touch" of choreographers whose idea on folk dancing was "old-fashioned 'quaintness' and a hearty or grotesque (the men) or dainty (the girls) peasantry, all wearing the same fixed smile" while performing elaborate steps with very little pattern.[25] *Rodeo,* although light and amusing, had reality. As an inspired cook combines commonplace ingredients into an original recipe, Agnes added new textures and flavors to traditional American folk material. The painstakingly crafted, evocative gestures — the cowboys squinting in the sun, the Cowgirl stopping herself from hitching up her skirt as she had her pants — appeared improvised, and their meaning was clear. The jaunty, bowlegged male dancers lurching across the stage on their imaginary horses were so sexy, Agnes's sister noted, that you could smell them in the tenth row.

By Agnes's own merciless standards, *Rodeo* had one serious flaw: the horses and riding movements were stylized, while the rest of the ballet was realistic. The inconsistency did not trouble the critics; to them, *Rodeo* was "heartwarming . . . full of flavor, effortless, and extraordinarily well composed"; "the success story of the season"; "a grand show"; "a smash-eroo"; "blessedly free from pretentiousness and chi-chi"; and "a brilliant theater piece."[26] Alfred Frankenstein called it "the kind of ballet that Mark Twain might have written if his mind had run to ballets.[27]

Because both *Billy the Kid* and *Rodeo* had Western settings, cowboys, horses, riding movements, and scores by Aaron Copland, comparisons were inevitable. Agnes's *Rodeo* studies had been performed in London months before *Billy* had premiered (in Chicago, in 1938). But because *Billy* had reached New York nearly three years before *Rodeo,* it was suggested that Agnes had based her style on Eugene Loring's. Loring himself called *Billy the Kid* "the prototype for the later 'western' ballets of de Mille, Robbins, and others."[28] And Alexandra Danilova, whom Agnes revered, stated in her memoirs, with stunning inaccuracy, "Loring showed [Agnes] the nail, and she hit it on the head."[29]

Contemporaries grow up subject to the same influences, and they influence each other, as well. But it was Agnes who devised the big, violent riding movements from sports movement, and Agnes who used virtuoso tap dancing in a ballet for the first time. And while both *Rodeo* and *Billy* have themes that were revolutionary in ballet, those themes are entirely different. *Billy the Kid* is an epic melodrama, highly stylized and symbolic. The hero is an outlaw, not a cowboy, who is destroyed for the sake of establishing law and order in the Wild American West. *Rodeo* is an intimate, gentle, unaffected, and funny romance about real people and timeless emotions — a shining model of an Agnes de Mille ballet.

In November, Agnes danced the Cowgirl in Los Angeles, appearing as guest artist with the Ballet Russe de Monte Carlo. "What higher satisfaction could there be," she asked rhetorically, "than to go back after all the troubles with the most famous ballet company extant, in my own work, a score by our leading composer, brilliant decor, and for my partner a great virtuoso?"[30] In front of a packed house that included Carmelita Maracci, Theodore Kosloff, Lily Bess Campbell, George Balanchine, and, most important of all, her father, she took a dozen curtain calls. "I faced about at the end, dripping and breathing and spent, my arms filled with carnations and roses, toward the wings and there, in the exact spot

I had stood as a girl waiting to see Anna Pavlova . . . stood Pop, smiling and radiant."[31] It was a sweet triumph, but William's approval came decades too late. Psychoanalysis helped; Walter's love helped; but nothing would ever completely assuage Agnes's yearning for her father's unconditional love.

But in the professional arena, all the slot machines into which she had invested her resources for fourteen years suddenly paid off. Offers of work came from both coasts, and she had already accepted her next assignment: the choreography of a new musical called *Away We Go,* to be produced by the Theatre Guild. Its final title would be *Oklahoma!*

t w e n t y - o n e

Oklahoma!

Before movies and long before television, Broadway was the source of popular culture, and musicals were its most popular product. When a show was a hit, the whole country sang its songs. So the announcement that the Theatre Guild would produce a musical version of Lynn Riggs's *Green Grow the Lilacs* was exciting news. The show was to have music by Richard Rodgers, lyrics by Lorenz Hart, and a book by Oscar Hammerstein II. But the announcement was premature. Hart, severely debilitated by alcoholism, was approaching the end of his long collaboration with Rodgers, and of his life, with the inevitability of a Greek tragedy. Hammerstein would ultimately write the lyrics and, in doing so, history — for it is as impossible to imagine *Oklahoma!* without Oscar Hammerstein's lyrics as it is to imagine it without Agnes de Mille's dances.

Agnes had asked Lawrence Langner, head of the Theatre Guild, if she might choreograph *Away We Go.* Langner sent Theresa Helburn, his second-in-command, to the opening of *Rodeo.* Rodgers and Hammerstein went with her. Within days, Agnes was hired to create the dances that would add the word "choreography" to the vocabularies of millions of Americans who had never seen a ballet, never heard of Fokine or Balan-

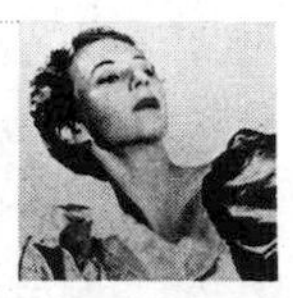

chine or Tudor or Graham. Asked to name a choreographer, they would know only one: Agnes de Mille.

The American musical theater had only recently begun to take itself seriously. Historically, the book of a musical had been merely a contrivance on which to hang the show's songs, jokes, girls, star turns, production numbers, novelty numbers, and grand finales. It was more important that a song match the set than the plot. A dance, either by a high-kicking chorus line or a specialty performer, usually followed a song, but not necessarily for any logical reason.

Show Boat, in 1927, was the first musical play, as opposed to a revue, musical comedy, or operetta. Its songs, by Jerome Kern and Oscar Hammerstein II, evolved from an authentically American story (based on Edna Ferber's novel) in which dimensional characters dealt with serious problems, such as miscegenation. *Show Boat* was a breakthrough, but it did not start a trend; for although the composers of the thirties were giants (Harold Arlen, Irving Berlin, George Gershwin, Jerome Kern, Frank Loesser, Cole Porter, Richard Rodgers, and Sigmund Romberg) and the lyricists brilliantly literate (Ira Gershwin, Lorenz Hart, and, again, Cole Porter), their subjects remained, for the most part, frivolous.

Doris Humphrey, Charles Weidman, José Limón, and other modern concert dancers and choreographers had begun working on Broadway in the early thirties, but the next stylistic milestone was provided by George Balanchine for Rodgers and Hart's *On Your Toes* in 1936. Balanchine's *Slaughter on Tenth Avenue* was a sophisticated jazz ballet performed by trained dancers, and it propelled the story line. *On Your Toes* gave audiences a taste of ballet, but did not actually change the course of dancing in the musical theater. *Oklahoma!* would do that.

Oklahoma! was de Mille territory. Set just after the turn of the century, before Oklahoma joined the Union, it had cowboys, horses, pioneers, romance, melodrama, and even a hoedown. The flimsy story concerns the love of Curly, a cowboy, for Laurey, a pure young woman. To make Curly jealous, Laurey goes to a box social with the sinister ranch hand, Jud; but Curly bids everything he owns for Laurey's picnic basket, and Laurey marries him. Jud picks a fight with Curly and is accidentally killed, and the happy bride and groom ride off in — what else? — a surrey with a fringe on top.

The collaboration of Rodgers and Hammerstein was a new one, and problematic. Rodgers, a smallish, compact man with the appearance and persuasiveness of a high-powered business tycoon, had produced some of this century's most beautiful melodies. He was only three years older than Agnes, but while she had labored in the wilderness, he had enjoyed a long string of successes. With Lorenz Hart, he had written nearly five hundred songs, many of them standards, for twenty-nine theatrical productions and eight movies. Their partnership had lasted twenty-four years, and Rodgers's ability to work well with another lyricist was unknown.

Oscar Hammerstein II had been writing direct, simple, often sentimental lyrics with many composers, for stage and screen, for twenty-one years. His honesty, thoughtfulness, and lack of neuroses made him an anomaly in show business. He was taller and broader than Rodgers, with the face of a failed prizefighter. Like Agnes, he had been born in Harlem, into a family that had been in the theater for three generations (his father,

Willie Hammerstein, had managed a vaudeville theater owned by his grandfather, Oscar Hammerstein I, an impresario). He had written lyrics and libretti for some of the biggest hits of the twenties, including *Rose Marie, The Desert Song,* and *Show Boat.* But in 1942, he had not had a hit for ten years.

Hammerstein wrote *Oklahoma!*'s dialogue and lyrics, and "spotted" the songs so they kept the plot moving. To indicate Laurey's ambivalence about marrying Curly, he ended the first act with a dream ballet in which the characters became circus performers. Agnes pointed out that the idea lacked suspense — and sex. Dr. Powdermaker's patient wrote a scenario that had both, and provided a dramatic contrast to the otherwise light, folksy show. "Laurey Makes Up Her Mind" reveals, in a dream, the young woman's repressed sexuality and her conflicting longings, not unknown to Agnes, for carnal sex and romantic love.

In her scenario, Agnes defined what would come to be known as a typical Agnes de Mille ballet: "lyric, non-realistic and highly stylized, but salted with detailed action that is colloquial, human, recognizable. If . . . the dancers are used as minor characters in the other scenes their main characteristics must be maintained in the ballet." This ballet would be revolutionary because it was essential to the audience's understanding of the characters. It would express emotions that words could not convey, in terms that a nondance audience could understand.

The eighteen-minute dream ballet, set to a medley of the songs in Act One — "The Surrey With the Fringe on Top" became, for example, a wedding march — begins after Laurey sings "Out of My Dreams" ("and into your arms, I long to fly") and falls asleep. Using overlapping pantomime, she and Curly change places with their dancing counterparts. At their wedding, Curly lifts Laurey's wedding veil to kiss her and "the whole scene freezes with horror — Suddenly she doubles up and tries to run. It is not Curley [*sic*] but Judd [*sic*] whom she has married — No one moves — She runs between them in nightmare terror. Judd does not move either. He waits for her to realize that the unavoidable has happened — She faces him panting."

The girls in Jud's collection of French postcards now come to life, costumed as stereotypical Western dance-hall girls, and put on "a kind of

Whore's Parade . . . dirty, lusty, dreary and funny." They dance with the somnambulistic cowboys, and the leading whore pushes the frightened but fascinated Laurey into the parade,

> ripping her dress off her shoulders in a businesslike way. When the girls have had enough they depart like a company of glutted spiders, turning before they go over the crest of the hill for a last appalling salute to their partners. (Turn at top, rotate knees, hands on hips, shoulders square). Men leave in a group — spent, empty, dogged (not exactly pleased with themselves). Laurie [*sic*] immediately!!! into screaming run, lifts and run lifts, low pirouettes (deep plié) — very low turn, like a flame over the grass. Jud drags her by the hair of her head. She bites fists in agony. He pulls her hands from her eyes, from her breast. Little begging hands. Pulse, numb fingers, neck awry.
>
> Laurie kneels on the stage, dress torn, exposed, ashamed, exhausted. [The sky darkens, a woman] with skirts and sunbonnet blowing runs terrified across the background as though to escape a tornado. Judd rushes on Laurie — swings her over his head and runs.
>
> (If it is possible to suggest a rape accomplished in midair in the heart of a hurricane, I want that there.)
>
> The action is brutal, violent, melodramatic and reminiscent of all the old woodcuts of the villain doing the heroine in . . . That the movement will be also beautiful is my chief concern.
>
> In the moment of extremis, Laurie throws back her hands and finds Curley standing beside her. . . . He pulls out his gun and shoots Judd. . . . Judd continues to advance. They struggle and Judd strangles Curley to death.
>
> Laurie crouches by Curley. Judd comes toward her . . .
>
> Quick Dimout
>
> The real Laurie is discovered not feeling her freshest.[1]

Dream ballets were not new on Broadway. The most successful had been Balanchine's for *On Your Toes, Babes in Arms,* and *I Married an Angel;* Robert

Alton's for *Pal Joey,* in 1940; and Albertina Rasch's *three* dream ballets for Kurt Weill's *Lady in the Dark,* in 1941. But *Oklahoma!*'s dream ballet was the first that both advanced the plot and revealed a character's psyche and heart. It was also, as John Martin would point out in the *New York Times,* the first time Agnes had created an "altogether objective work; in everything that has preceded it she has built a central role so specifically for herself and her highly personal idiom as a dancer that no other dancer undertaking it could hope to be much more than a little imitation de Mille."[2]

As the dream lovers, Agnes cast Marc Platt, formerly of the Ballet Russe de Monte Carlo, and Katherine Sergava, of Ballet Theatre. Broadway dancers had historically been hired for their looks, not their training. Agnes chose dancers — not just the leads, but all of them — for their technique and their ability to project personality — that is, character. Instead of a line of interchangeable chorus girls, she wanted individuals. "I believe that the dreamy [looking] girls don't deliver the performances," she told a reporter; "they've usually had things too easy."[3] *Rodeo*'s town girls, with their pretty faces and empty heads, had been Agnes's comment on conventional standards of "dreamy" good looks.

When the auditions began, according to stage manager Elaine Anderson Steinbeck, "Dick and Oscar and Rouben Mamoulian [the director] were terrified they weren't going to get pretty girls. It was, 'Who cares about how they move their legs, we care how they look!' They fought for good-lookin' girls with good-lookin' legs and pretty faces, and Agnes fought for the good dancers."[4] Richard Rodgers, said his wife, "felt that Agnes went out of her way to pick girls who were especially unattractive or had ugly legs. There were a lot of jokes about Agnes's unattractive dancers."[5]

At auditions, Agnes told dancers to walk across the stage with some emotional purpose, to see whether they could do what dancers had not heretofore been asked to do: act. Mamoulian objected strongly to one girl who looked about twelve and had enormous thighs, and braces. The girl, who was actually sixteen, had been the youngest member of Agnes's Acting for Dancers class. She had a natural spring in her body; her leaps were longer and wider than anyone else's, without the visible "preparation" that telegraphs most dancers' jumps. Without warning she soared, skimming the stage with an ease that made other dancers gasp. "If she goes," Agnes said, "I go!"[6] Rodgers, whatever his private opinion, backed her up, and Bambi Linn was hired. She and another girl originally chosen for the chorus, Joan McCracken, would become Broadway stars. The tall, classical Diana Adams, also in the chorus, would become one of Ballet Theatre's and, later, Balanchine's, greatest ballerinas.

Bambi had a fresh, childlike quality that Agnes used throughout the show. She costumed her as a little girl, to make her stand out, and gave her little character bits such as handing a bouquet to the dream-bride and nervously bursting into tears. In the course of rehearsals Bambi graduated from the chorus to a character listed in the program as "Aggie," a name she chose herself. "Agnes was like another mother to me," she said, "and Joanie [McCracken] was like a big sister. Joanie was older than the rest of us, about twenty-four. She taught me a lot of things. Tampax had just come out. We had to wear blobby old Kotex, pared down, and I saw that Joanie had a Tampax. I said, 'How do you use that?' and she said, 'It's not good for you to use it, you haven't had sex yet, it might hurt you.'"[7]

For McCracken, Agnes created the character of Sylvie, "The Girl Who Falls Down." McCracken had straight brown hair, enormous eyes, and a glorious smile. Like Agnes, she was only five-foot-one and not beautiful, but onstage she was exuberant and funny, and commanded attention. Sylvie was a hoyden, sister to the Cowgirl — awkward, always out of step, looking or kicking in the wrong direction, pluckily picking herself up after every fall. She was featured in "Many a New Day," a dance that was Agnes's idea; Rodgers and Hammerstein had intended the song as just a song, sung by Laurey and her friends. To Agnes, it was a chance to expand on one of her favorite subjects: young, innocent girls on the brink of womanhood, getting dressed for a picnic, silly and self-absorbed and charming.

∞

In the hierarchy of power, Agnes was at the bottom, Rouben Mamoulian in the middle, and Richard Rodgers, who made all final decisions, at the top. Mamoulian was an articulate, cultured Russian émigré with impressive stage and film credits, but he had done only one Broadway musical — *Porgy and Bess* — and seven years had elapsed since then. Both he and Agnes were accustomed to being in charge, and each accused the other of being autocratic. When rehearsals began, in the Theatre Guild building on West 52nd Street, Mamoulian preempted the stage, leaving Agnes and her two assistants to conduct rehearsals in the downstairs men's and women's lounges and in an airless room on the splintery top floor. Agnes claimed that he watched her rehearsals and stole movement ideas, such as having people sit or crawl as an alternative to the comparatively static patterns of previous musicals. She was particularly frustrated by his habit of pulling dancers out of her rehearsals, having them stand around for hours while he staged the songs, and sending them back exhausted. But she had finally learned to fight for what she wanted, and she quarreled often and violently with the director. Finally her agent, Richard LaMarr, took the two of them out for drinks and a peace conference. After two hours of discussion, Mamoulian agreed not to take the dancers unless he absolutely needed them. "You see," he said, "I'm not a very difficult man. And you must admit, what other director do you know who can stage crowd scenes the way I do?" Agnes said, "My uncle!" Mamoulian was not amused, and he continued to interrupt her rehearsals.[8]

One of the wonders of *Oklahoma!* was that in spite of the egos that collide like bumper cars in the course of a collaborative creative effort, everyone kept faith with the overriding priority that each element must serve the story. Dialogue had to lead naturally into songs, songs into dances, reality into fantasy and back again, with the audience never feeling a bump. The concept suited Agnes perfectly; in her recital pieces, she had always combined acting with dancing. Within three weeks, she set forty minutes of dances (nearly half of which would be cut before the opening). "I was like a pitcher that had been overfilled," she wrote, "the dances simply spilled out of me."[9] Her vocabulary of movements was limited, but because each step was grounded in character, it had its own unique color and shading. Her approach was a kind of Method Dancing; she knew that it took more than a sunbonnet to convincingly portray a pioneer woman, and she talked to each dancer about the character's experience and thoughts. In certain situations, merely standing still — anathema to a dancer — was more dramatic than any movement might have been. Even a simple movement such as running was theatrical because it was executed in character, augmented by facial expression, hand movement, and gesture. The way a character tilted her head, angled her arms, or smoothed her hair could be more telling than pages of dialogue. Characters had their individual gestures, some so subtle that the audience noticed them only subliminally. Others were obvious — Bambi's "bells" (kicking her heels together in the air), for example.

When a section of the ballet took shape, Agnes showed it to the orchestrator, Robert Russell Bennett, with whom her communication approached telepathy. She explained or acted out accents or certain definite movements on beats, and Bennett arranged Rodger's melodies accordingly, providing harmonies and counterpoint that perfectly matched Agnes's intentions. He was especially fond of cellos and French horns. "When the dancers first heard Bennett's magical orchestral sounds," said conductor Jay Blackton, "it gave them a terrific lift."[10]

Throughout the company, excitement began to build. "When I first saw the script," said Elaine Steinbeck, "I said to [technical director] John Haggott, '"There's a bright golden haze on the meadow. There's a bright golden haze on the meadow. The corn is as high as an elephant's eye and it looks like it's climbin' clear up to the sky. Oh what a beautiful morning. Oh what a beautiful morning. Oh what a beautiful day." *What in the hell is this?*' And when we found out there was no music under that — this play starts a cappella, with Curly singing offstage, and the orchestra comes in under him — we knew this was going to be a pretty peculiar show! Then all of us who worked on the show began to catch on to what they were doing. You could see it beginning to work! There was a very good feeling. But the management was nervous, because there was a lot riding on it."[11]

The management had reason to be nervous, for the Theatre Guild was in desperate financial straits, and it was not reassuring that the major roles were played by unknown actors — Joan Roberts, Alfred Drake, Celeste Holm, and Lee Dixon. The out-of-town crises began in New Haven, where *Away We Go* ran four and a half hours. In Boston, everyone worked around the clock in a frenzy of activity and anxiety. It was there that the show was christened *Oklahoma!*, the title of the final song — and when the entire company assembled at the front of the stage and sang it, leaning forward into the audience, the audience spontaneously joined in on the final "*Yow!*" — an encouraging sign. Even though Walter Winchell reported, "No legs, no jokes, no chance," everyone was optimistic — except Agnes. "The direction and dialogue are bad,' she wrote to her mother, "and no trimming can make them good."[12]

Oklahoma! opened at the St. James Theatre in New York on March 31, 1943. Agnes stood at the back of the theater, wearing a plain black evening dress and her mother's Victorian opals, and clutching Robert Pagent's arm so tightly that it was black and blue the next day. From the moment that Alfred Drake strode onstage in front of a backdrop of sky that seemed to stretch for miles over the plains of Oklahoma, the audience sensed that it was witnessing something extraordinary. After the dream ballet there was tremendous applause, and during the intermission the lobby buzzed with the electricity that charges a theater when history is being made. During the second act, which opens with the rousing "Farmer and the Cowman" hoedown, there was no doubt about the outcome. At the end of the play, the applause was overwhelming, and it echoed in the next day's reviews. "Wonderful is the nearest adjective," Lewis Nichols wrote in the *New York Times;* "There is more comedy in one of Miss de Mille's gay little passages than in many of the other Broadway tom-tom beats together."[13] But it would be weeks before anyone would begin to grasp the dimensions of the show's success.

Oklahoma! was the first musical in which the libretto, score, character development, plot development, decor, stage direction, and choreography all came together; the show worked seamlessly as a whole, without sacrificing the integrity of its parts. As Judy Garland would observe, "The corn *is* as high as an elephant's eye" — but the emotion was real, and the show was perfect for its time.[14] People needed the prospect of a beautiful morning. Like *Rodeo, Oklahoma!* had a core of American optimism, ebullience, and humor that evoked nostalgia for what seemed a simple, comprehensible past. The pioneers, carving out a new state, mirrored the determination with which Americans were fighting the war. The show would outlast the war — but until the war was over, servicemen stood three-deep at the back of the theater each night, often with tears in their eyes.

Until *Oklahoma!* most theatergoers had equated ballet with swan queens and princes, tutus and tights. Agnes's dancers wore jeans and gingham dresses; their leg movements were balletic, but they did not assume the classical ballet positions. They were characters in the play, not interchangeable members of an anonymous chorus, and their gestures were idiomatic American. Their dancing was sharp and focused, often funny, and sometimes quite beautiful.

The ensemble numbers that swept the entire stage with joyous, free movements, the huge slides, the men lifting saucy girls with swirling skirts, would become a de Mille trademark. So would the soft, turning arabesques and the lyrical lifts: tender, as when Laurey is poised outstretched on Curly's shoulders as though they were flying together through the air; or spectacular, as when the running Laurey stops abruptly, tiptoes to Curly, places her head against his chest, spirals down into a bunched-up position on the floor, and then ascends as though by magic, still bunched, to his hip. Agnes's work was so influential that forty-six of the seventy-two Broadway musicals to open during the next three and a half years would include ballets. Twenty-one would have dream sequences, many of them bad imitations of *Oklahoma!*'s. After *Oklahoma!*, it was taken for granted that show dancing would include ballet and modern dance, in whatever proportions the show required.

In the midst of the cheering, Agnes fixated on the discouraging words of Robert Lawrence in the *New York Herald-Tribune:*

> Taking a leaf from the pages of her composer colleagues on Broadway, who borrow to advantage from Ravel and Stravinsky, she has gone not only to

> her *Rodeo* for source material but to Eugene Loring's *Billy the Kid* for the three honky-tonk girls . . . and the pirouettes which precede the silent shootings in Loring's ballet; also to Antony Tudor's *Pillar of Fire* for certain new and effective lifts. This procedure could not be followed in producing a new work for Ballet Theater; but in the melting pot of Broadway, where the best contemporary idiom is melted down and redistributed with universal consent, she has violated no ethical canons.[15]

Agnes, who freely acknowledged various influences on her work, was livid. Responding to what she perceived as an accusation of plagiarism, she wrote, in a righteously indignant letter that the *Herald-Tribune* declined to publish, "I try to invent freshly, but one builds upon what one has done. An entire fresh idiom is not attainable with every new work." Her rebuttal is an illuminating account of her methodology. She conceded that she had quoted "quite deliberately" from *Rodeo* in the riding passage; no steps were identical, but the rhythm and style are "so similar as to make quibbling groundless." In addition, she had borrowed "three arm gestures from the Indian dance in *Drums Sound in Hackensack;* one arm position from *Black Ritual;* a hip rhythm from the dance-hall girls in *Hell on Wheels;* a fall and lift from a short recital piece (*Night Scene,* 1941), and running movements from another (*Hares on the Mountains,* 1939); and several buck-and-wing square dance gestures used throughout my concert career in native folk dance studies and later developed in *Rodeo.* They were varied and developed further in *Oklahoma!*" The use of honky-tonk girls in a southwestern environment was "characteristic of the subject — even trite," and the only similarity between her girls and Loring's "trollopes" [*sic*] was that "both sets swing their hips." The lifts that Lawrence likened to Tudor's "were invented in the basement of the Guild Theatre with the exception of one very spectacular roll on the floor and jump from a prone position onto the man's hip. I composed something like it in 1940 with Sybil Shearer's help. It was performed by her and Hugh Laing at the time he was rehearsing *Pillar of Fire.*" As for the silent turns preceding the shooting, "if they are contained intact in the choreography of *Billy the Kid* then I can only say that unconsciously I remembered when I consciously believed I invented. This happens to every creative person.

. . . But steal? That can only happen when the thief brings no personal creative comment to the matter in hand. I respectively [*sic*] submit that this is not the case with my work."[16]

There were some additional debts: to Sybil Shearer, for her spiral falls; to Tudor, for his tired, cynical, comical whores in *Judgment of Paris;* to Martha Graham,* for the women's staccato cupped-hand movements away from their open mouths, signifying their voices going out (the gesture became part of Agnes's vocabulary); to Marc Platt and another dancer, George Church, a onetime wrestler, for working out the violent, dangerous fight scene (at one point Curly stands on Jud's shoulders, is thrown, and must land in a certain way to avoid injury); and again to Church, for devising his own tap routine (Agnes, who used tap fairly often in her work, claimed to know only four basic tap steps herself). No artist, however, creates in a vacuum, and whatever Agnes's sources, the creative vision was hers. She worked to her strengths — character and theatricality — and when she put the components together, the result bore her unmistakable signature. By vernacularizing the classical and elevating the vernacular, Agnes had altered the collective consciousness of Broadway choreographers forevermore.

* Per *Martha* (p. 88), Graham first used the device in *Poems of 1917* in 1928.

twenty-two

The de Millennium

Five days after the opening of *Oklahoma!* Agnes was on her way to Omaha, where the peripatetic Walter was stationed. Walter was still struggling with his resistance to marriage, but Agnes considered that a technicality; between rehearsals of *Oklahoma!*, she had planned her trousseau. During the frantic Boston tryout, she had found time to write, "I'm going to fall asleep dreaming of the clothes I shall buy to ravish you with. I want your battalion to gape with envy and Prude's Ag to become synonymous with all that's provocative."[1]

In Omaha they became formally engaged and planned a June wedding. "It's an astonishing thing," Agnes wrote to Mary Meyer, "what making up your mind will do. I loved Walter from the moment I knew him but on sort of a blind hunch. And now I find he's all the gracious and dear things I ever wanted in a man — sweet, tender, steady — not at all capricious or difficult or strange. Much, much steadier than I."[2] But Agnes still had some ambivalence about marriage. Like Laurey, she had a dream. She consulted her analyst. "Your dream is the key to the problem," Dr. Powdermaker replied. "You can't settle down and enjoy Walter until you forgive your mother — more important, forgive yourself for lov-

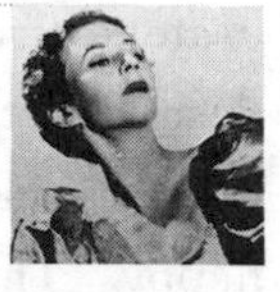

ing your father more than you did her. You make her (in your dream) do horrible things to your lingerie — so that you will have an excuse to be angry with her without feeling guilty. Your real anger is due to feeling possessed by her and you feel that it's wrong to resent her for that. Also I guess you enjoy the turmoil and the battle and aren't quite ready to give it up for the peace of Walter. The relation with Father was probably never really as exciting to you as the fighting relations with mother which is probably one of the main reasons why you kept it up. . . . Have a beautiful wedding and a really glorious honeymoon."[3]

Agnes had reason to feel guilty about Anna, for although she allowed her to help sew her trousseau, she excluded her from the wedding. For logistical reasons — Walter would have only a two-week furlough before he had to report to a new posting, in New Mexico — California seemed the logical place to be married. William would give his daughter away. Anna had missed Margaret's wedding also; both girls did their best, with good reason, to keep their mother away from their men. "Dear Child," Anna wrote on the eve of the wedding, "Think of me — and Margaret — and Allie. We had all hoped to be at your wedding . . . I had always hoped to be able to fuss over the 'wedding feast,' to make the wedding cake — but those are material things that do not matter really, after all."[4] The sighs between the lines are almost audible.

The ceremony took place in an Episcopal chapel in Beverly Hills with just nine people in attendance, including Clara de Mille, Mary Meyer, David and Michael Hertz, and Agnes's Aunt Constance. Uncle Cecil was not invited. Instead of a traditional wedding dress, which Agnes thought inappropriate in wartime, the bride wore a simple brown gabardine suit that matched the groom's khaki uniform (her hat, an elaborate latticelike creation, provided a festive touch). Afterward, Walter described the event to Paul Nordoff, who had declined an invitation to be best man: "For better or worse, it's done. She's mine, and I'm very happy." The ceremony and the honeymoon had been "pure magic." The organist had suggested

> a little Norwegian wedding march instead of the Lohengrin . . . gay and sweet and full of the deepest joy. As we listened to it on the small, sweet-toned organ in the beautiful little chapel we could only nod at each other dumbly and fight back the tears that kept coming to our eyes. It was all so right! . . .
>
> At last we could hear music coming softly from the chapel, along the winding cloister and through the blossoms straight into our hearts. It was the D-minor Toccata. . . . As we stepped out everyone was standing and I could feel a wave of pure emotion move to meet me as palpably as the suddenly louder music . . . [when] the little wedding march began its gay lilting tune, everyone turned and a sort of sigh went up softly over the chapel. . . . I'd never seen [Agnes] look so lovely. There was a sort of glow, a radiance, about her and as she came up the aisle it was as if she were singing the music, or as if she were the very simple song itself. I found it best to look away . . . until she came up beside me and smiled up into my face.
>
> The music dropped to the softest murmur. "Dearly beloved," began the Rector. Agnes's hand was in mine, our shoulders just touching. . . . We were being married. Tremendous, magical moment. I could feel with every fiber of me the actual sensation of love surrounding us. I thought, "This is the

> way it should be; the way it must always be!" [As the Rector joined their hands together] a phrase the organ was quietly singing pierced me straight to the heart. It was the *Jesu Chorale* . . . It was like unbearable pain. It was too great to be borne. I closed my mind. Closed my ears and fastened my eyes desperately on the Rector again, praying that I should be able to make the responses.
>
> A moment later Agnes was in my arms and we were giving each other the first long kiss of greeting and of acknowledgement of one of the great experiences in our lives together. There can never be a more perfect and lovely one.[5]

The honeymooners spent a week, arguably the most blissful of Agnes's life, in Los Angeles, in homes loaned by Agnes's friends. They had three more weeks together, in Hobbs, New Mexico. Walter left their hotel every morning to report for work on the base, leaving Agnes to revel in having attained the magical identity of wife. It was "the first time that the word 'our' had meant anything in my life. . . . I had a stake in life beside my own wits and, more important, beside my own wants."[6]

Walter wisely corresponded with his new mother-in-law, letting her know that Agnes had "managed to make the wretched little [hotel] room almost homelike, with improvised tables, wildflowers in a waterglass, and the inevitable books propped up in an imposing array between two bottles of paste. She's even getting some work done, both daily bars [*sic*] and considerable composition for 'Venus.'"[7] *One Touch of Venus* was to be Agnes's next show.

She felt she must do another show immediately, to consolidate her position. *Oklahoma!* had paid off handsomely in prestige, but she had earned only $1,500 for her six weeks' work, plus a bonus of $50 per week throughout the New York run of the show. For *Venus,* the Theatre Guild offered $20,000 for ten weeks' work. Walter was nervous; if he wasn't killed in the war, which he thought was likely, he would return to civilian life with very little money and no job. It could not have escaped his notice that the newspaper accounts of his wedding identified the bride as a celebrity in her own right as well as the daughter, granddaughter, and niece of her illustrious relatives, while the groom was merely "Lieutenant

Walter Prude of the Army Air Force." But whatever his private trepidations, he encouraged Agnes to pursue her career. On August first she was back in New York, where *Oklahoma!* was being proclaimed the greatest theatrical success of the century.

She returned to find herself the Queen of Broadway, in demand by everyone. The press reported that it was Agnes de Mille Year on Broadway; she was bombarded by requests for interviews and photographed with her dancers for *Vogue*. Women of all ages emulated the "Oklahoma look" that was so adorable on Bambi Linn and Joan McCracken: flat "ballerina" shoes, pinched waists, full gingham skirts, ponytail or topknot, straw hats with feathers and flowers. Helena Rubinstein asked her to name a perfume representative of her dances (the idea was dropped when she suggested "Exhaustion"). But Agnes could not rest. "On every subsequent show," she believed, "I knew I would have to hazard my whole career, the rule in show business being that you are as good as your last job."[8] She remained tense and nervous; she still bit her nails and carried a knitting bag with her wherever she went, lest her hands have a moment's idleness. She watched *Rodeo* performed by replacement dancers and found it not good enough. There was "no way of ensuring lasting beauty. Verily, I wrote in water and judging my work with a dreadful dispassionate vision, perhaps it was as well."[9] But when she said as much to Martha Graham, her idol shrugged; the idea that no artist is ever satisfied was hardly news to Graham. "There is only a queer divine dissatisfaction," Martha said, "a blessed unrest that keeps us marching and makes us more alive than the others."[10] With that crumb of comfort, Agnes went into rehearsal for *One Touch of Venus*.

With *Venus*, Agnes intended to prove that she could choreograph a show without cowboys. The story, based on a novella by F. Anstey, concerned the statue of a goddess that comes to life when an unsuspecting mortal playfully puts a ring on its finger. The goddess and the mortal, a humble barber, fall in love; but when Venus sees, in a dream, what her life would be like in his bourgeois suburban world, she becomes a statue again. The music was by Kurt Weill, the German émigré composer best known for

The Threepenny Opera (in collaboration with Bertolt Brecht) and *Lady in the Dark*. The lyrics and libretto, were written, respectively, by the popular humorists Ogden Nash and S. J. Perelman. The show's young director, Elia Kazan, had recently had a hit with Thornton Wilder's *The Skin of Our Teeth*. Neither Kazan nor Nash nor Perelman had ever worked on a musical.

The star, Mary Martin, had been a sensation five years earlier, singing "My Heart Belongs to Daddy" in Cole Porter's *Leave It to Me.* Since then, she had been seen only in some terrible movies, but she would prove herself to be the perfect choice to play the statue of a Greek goddess.

On her way home from New Mexico, Agnes had stopped in upstate New York to see Sybil Shearer, whom she had consulted about all her choreographic projects for the past five years. For two days, she worked with Shearer on comedy ideas for the new show. It was their last professional session together. "Agnes was *always* talking about money," Shearer said, "about how nobody was getting paid enough. She used my stuff in *Venus*, and later she sent me a check for fifteen dollars, and a note — 'I hope you don't think I went up there to pick your brain for nothing.' That was the end. I didn't care if she used my stuff, and I didn't care about money! But fifteen dollars was an insult!"[11] Shearer, who had ambitions of her own, subsequently moved to Chicago, where she pursued a solo career.

Agnes would never find another Sybil, but she would henceforth have a cadre of dancers on whom she worked out movement. During rehearsals for *Venus*, she persuaded Dorothy Bird, one of Graham's dancers, to give her a crash course in Graham technique — skipping, flying through the air, and falling. "Agnes prodded me with questions," Bird said. "I felt guilty, but I knew Agnes would change it. Which she did."[12] She also observed some of Graham's rehearsals, attended every performance Graham gave, and hired two of Graham's dancers, Pearl Lang and Nelle Fisher. Her other featured dancers were Peter Birch, Robert Pagent, Diana Adams, and the extraordinary Sono Osato.

Osato had joined the Ballets Russes de Monte-Carlo at fourteen, and had recently resigned from Ballet Theatre to be with her soldier husband, a decision that Agnes admired. She was now twenty-four — tall, with long straight dark hair and a slender, perfect body. Her face was an exotic amalgamation of the loveliest attributes of her Irish, Canadian, and Japanese ancestors. "Look up her pictures in any old Ballet Russe program and drop dead with joy," Agnes told Weill. "She looks like a Japanese Joan McCracken but has the body of a sylph."[13] Agnes discovered that Osato, like McCracken, had a rare ability to be sexy and funny at the same time, and she featured her in the show's major dance numbers. "Forty Minutes for Lunch" was a lighthearted treatment of a "city traffic" theme that had been portrayed with deadly seriousness by modern dance groups. In the midst of Rockefeller Center at noon, Venus would flirt with a sailor, cavort in a shop window, and transform frantic New Yorkers (indicated by nervous finger snapping and rhythmic walking, in directions reversed by traffic whistles) into a state of happy infatuation with life and with each other.

The big dance number, "Venus in Ozone Heights," was the show's finale. It could have been called "Venus Makes Up Her Mind," for Venus, like Laurey, had to choose — in this case not a man, but a world. On a summer evening in Brooklyn, she sits on the stoop, contemplating a lively pantomime version of suburbia as neighbors gossip, children play, housewives clean. Husbands return from work and mechanically kiss their wives, mow their lawns, eat their dinners, and read their papers. Venus, wearing lacy lingerie, cannot distract the barber from the sports pages. As she turns away, the children onstage become nymphs, fauns, dryads, and satyrs. Joined by Dionysus, the goddess Diana, and her hunters, they bewitch the husbands, wives, and adolescents of the neighborhood, all of whom dance in a wild pagan rite. There is thunder, lightning, and, suddenly, silence.

> Venus stands up with an ancient and terrible cry — it should be a long musical wail in descending quarter tones (I once heard a Basque battle-cry from the 15th century and my blood hasn't warmed up since), sliding into the melody at the bottom.
>
> The houses fade and slide away. The stars blaze out all over the sky. [Venus] and the dancers stand in a wilderness. . . . a drum starts to throb softly . . . the dance builds to absolute madness . . . very free, built on leaping and running. Venus should be heard crying — and shouts (what was the

Greek cry invoking Dionysius?) — the rhythms should occasionally break off short leaving the dancers rushing and pounding in silence, or silence punctuated by shouts (Did you ever see a southwestern American Indian ritual?)

The crowd finally streams out . . . Venus appears naked, translucent, Olympean, awful — and walks in wreathings of mist against the stars. The enormous and terrible figures of the Zodiac appear in the heavens.

People's hearts should be bursting when this is over.[14]

Agnes considered the bacchanal to be far superior, in its composition and development of themes, to *Oklahoma!,* which told a relatively straightforward story. The management found it confusing. Throughout the sweltering days of August, without benefit of air-conditioning, Agnes cut, added, and rearranged, until the dancers were exhausted. She had acquired the habit of wearing the hand-embroidered petticoats her mother had worn as a bride. By the end of the day, the starch in the petticoats had wilted, but Agnes had not. To Osato, "her invention and energy seemed limitless."[15]

According to Robert Pagent, the most inspired addition to the ballet was its climax. "Venus comes from backstage in a body suit, but to all intents and purposes, she's nude. She has a scarlet cape flowing from her shoulders — and as she steps out, with this cape rolling out behind her, an aviator comes out and he's holding a young girl in his arms. She has her head on his shoulder. He waltzes with her, against the rumba rhythm of 'Speak Low,' across the stage towards Venus. And when he gets in front of Venus, she holds out her hand and she has gold sequins that come shimmering down. Then he goes waltzing off."[16] After that touching moment (made even more so by the war), Pagent carried Mary Martin off to Olympus on his shoulders, leaving the forlorn barber alone on the stage as the curtain fell.

Most artists are very protective, with good reason, of their work in progress. None was more protective than Agnes, who sometimes stationed a guard at the door of her rehearsal room. Her admiration for Kurt Weill was so great, however, that for him she made an exception. She was particularly impressed by how willingly he cut six minutes of music he thought was the best he'd written since leaving Germany, because it was too long and slowed down the show. For Agnes, cutting work that she knew was good was like amputating a limb, or at least a digit. Her attitude, as expressed to Weill, was, "Let's give it as much time as we possibly can in the show because, by God, it's good."[17] Before rehearsals began, she had sent Weill the scenario for a proposed third ballet. "Please, please," she implored, "don't make me put this lovely dance in a corner of the stage while they make a scenery change."[18] The dance, a touching pas de deux about adolescent love, was cut after the first run-through because it had nothing to do with the plot.

Unlike most Broadway composers, Weill orchestrated his own music — a boon for Agnes, whose dances required stronger, more interesting orchestrations than the relatively pedestrian ones of the past. "At that time," observed Maurice Abravanel, the show's musical director, "there was a big abyss between Broadway music and serious music. With the success of *The Threepenny Opera,* Weill had become about the most successful theater composer in the world. But he didn't mind at all sitting down with Agnes and tailoring his music according to her needs, giving her eight bars of this kind of music, sixteen bars of that. It was the way that, in the old days, Petipa worked with Tchaikowsky."[19]

Until Broadway dances became organic to the show, they simply followed a song and were accompanied by orchestral repetitions of the melody. After *Oklahoma!,* composers hired dance arrangers to adapt the score for the purposes of movement, shaping and developing the tunes in ways that reinforced the texture and dramatic content of the show. Dance arrangers compose additional material when it is called for, such as for a ballet, keeping in mind both the choreographer's intentions and the integrity of the score. If the choreographer needs a waltz, and there is none in the show, the dance arranger finds a tune in the score that will work as a waltz and remain recognizable. Trude Rittman, Agnes's rehearsal pianist, would become the first and best-known dance arranger in the American theater. On *Venus* and eight subsequent shows, Trude would do for Agnes musically what Sybil Shearer had done with movement. In the rehearsal hall, Agnes relied on Trude to come up with music that would make her want to dance.

Agnes had hired Trude Rittman as accompanist for her little troupe in 1940. Rittman was a German Jew, a onetime wunderkind who had fled the Nazis in her early twenties, leaving a promising composing and performing career behind her. She was slightly taller than Agnes, an unremarkable-looking woman with brown hair, thick glasses, terrible headaches, infinite patience, and uncompromising musical standards. The dancers marveled at her ability to simultaneously play, count for them, and make musical and choreographic suggestions. Rittman had a ghost writer's talent for capturing Agnes's style and a jazz pianist's gift for improvisation. "I could sort of *smell* what she was after," she said, "it was like a seventh sense."[20]

Agnes's collaboration with Elia Kazan was not so felicitous. "In those days," said Maurice Abravanel, "either the director or the star would be the very big shot. But in this case, *Agnes* was a big, big star, and she was very jealous of Kazan. And Kazan's attitude was 'I'll show that woman — she is not the boss!' He admired Agnes's work, but he complained that she treated him like a stage manager whose job was merely to set the lights and keep the set out of the way of her dancers."

In spite of their personal feelings, said Abravanel, "Agnes and Kazan together created some wonderful little things in the staging. When Venus visited the barber in his barbershop, the sinks all filled with roses, and flowers appeared around all the pictures, and fountains appeared. It was magic time. They cooked that up between them." But her policy of closed rehearsals infuriated the other members of what was supposed to be a team. "Kazan felt she was too independent. We all wanted to see what she had done, but she was in her own cubicle. She was invited to our meetings, but she didn't take part."[21] The danger, as always, was that total absorption in her dances could skew her perspective about the show. Producer Cheryl Crawford recalled "incredible" scenes. "[W]hen [Agnes] felt something was right, she could be stubborn and obstinate. If we tried to cut one minute from one of her ballets all hell broke loose. Usually she was right about the ballet sequences, but they were sometimes a little too long and cutting was a painful process for both of us — a minute here, a minute there, then a compromise."[22]

In 1943, if a show didn't make it out of town, it had little chance of success in New York. At the dress rehearsal in Boston, *One Touch of Venus* was in trouble. The scenic designer, Howard Bay, had framed the proscenium with battleship-gray velveteen drapes to be moved mechanically to varying lengths, creating an effect that Perelman likened to the inside of a coffin (to Mainbocher, who designed Mary Martin's costumes, they were "testicles hanging down and ruining Venus's costumes").[23] Agnes complained that the suburban houses for the "Ozone Heights" number ruined her ballet. Mary Martin's costumes, Grecian draperies and gowns, were so lovely that the audience applauded them, but Kermit Love's costumes for the bacchanal did not work at all (one of his inspirations, quickly overruled, was to sew dark plush onto the satyr's body suits, to simulate hairy genitals).

Because of the bacchanal's complexity and the larger demands of the show, Agnes had to produce at least five versions of the number. Every morning, Trude Rittman had a new arrangement to the exact counts that had been rehearsed the previous day; in the escalating pandemonium, hers was sometimes the only voice of sanity to be heard. Agnes's last instruction to the dancers before the opening was "'Do the ballet as rehearsed in New York until Sono's second entrance, then the Saturday-matinee version until the change into E major, then the sixty-four bars we rehearsed this afternoon but not the ending — that's not ready. When Sono jumps do what we did last night. We'll do the last thirty-two bars tomorrow night the way we rehearsed them today.'"[24]

When the show opened at the Boston Opera House on September 17, the scenery and costumes had been improved, but the underlying problem was glaringly obvious: the audience was not laughing. Kazan told Perelman that "his stuff may have read well in *The New Yorker,*"[25] but it didn't play on stage, and Perelman replied that Kazan had no sense of humor. The dialogue was gradually reduced to little more than introductions to the musical numbers, which was just fine with the audiences. Then it was decided that the show needed a more upbeat ending, and Agnes came up with one as corny — and as effective — as *Oklahoma!*'s. After Venus disappeared into the clouds, leaving the barber alone, a clap of thunder sounded and the stage went dark for a moment. When the lights went back up, Venus was a statue again, on her pedestal in the museum. The barber asked, "Why did you leave? You said I'd never be alone again!" Whereupon a girl who looked amazingly like Venus entered and exchanged a few words with the barber. He offered his arm and they went off, gazing into each other's eyes. Curtain.

Every man in the audience fell in love with Sono Osato. So did Kazan, and he asked Agnes to create a dance just for her, to Weill's beautiful ballad "My Foolish Heart." In her autobiography, Osato described the way Agnes, in a deserted hotel ballroom, "tossing her coat, pencils and notepad to the floor, began to dance. She took what looked like one step of a slow-motion running stride, punctuated by two quick upward flicks of the hands toward the breasts, then a step with a cute, naughty leer backwards over the shoulder, with two snaps of the fingers, then repeated it . . . She stopped as suddenly as she had started, gathered up her things and, without a pause, bustled off to rehearse [another] version of the bacchanal, calling back over her shoulder, 'and after *that,* I'll think of something else.'" In a subsequent session she told Osato, "'An American sailor [Robert Pagent] will saunter in. He'll lean on the proscenium and ogle you. He'll stop you dead in your tracks. You'll go balmy over him, he'll go balmy over you and offer his arm. You'll stare at the audience thumping your foot, thinking it over. Then bolt straight up, slap your skirts, hitch your bosom, tweak your roses, and perk your head in his direction. He'll stride over to you. You give him the eye, he gives you the eye. Take his arm, bend over, do some snappy little foot patter towards the wings, and then, just before you go, lurch back with one quick take at the audience and strut off!'"[26] Agnes told Weill that in that spot she needed a sea chanty; she suggested "What Shall We Do with a Drunken Sailor?" and Weill interpolated the song into his score.

Despite the anxiety attacks that preceded the show's opening at the Imperial Theatre in New York, *One Touch of Venus* was the musical success of the season, praised for its beauty and its brains. Sono Osato's solo stopped the show.

Venus was not, as some reviewers pointed out, another *Oklahoma!*— but nothing could have been. More important, from Agnes's point of view, were sentiments like those of Howard Barnes, who wrote in the *Herald-Tribune* that the "wonder girl of Broadway" had outdone herself; "she has given the cue for fantasy, without which *Venus* would have been merely mannered."[27] Or Edwin Denby's: "She again succeeds in touching the heart of the average audience through the dance numbers in a way no other musical comedy dance director can . . . There is no doubt that the public loves any show Miss de Mille touches."[28] The only sour note was struck by the critic Burton Rascoe, who hit a nerve with his observation that the "Ozone Heights" number, while lovely, "leads one to suspect, from the other dance numbers in this show and from *Rodeo* and *Oklahoma!,* that Miss de Mille is at her best in satire and in funny pieces but not so imaginative in depicting voluptuousness or ecstasy."[29] But John Martin, the critic whose opinion still carried the most weight with Agnes, was full of praise. The current era of musicals, Martin wrote, was the "de Millennium."[30]

t w e n t y - t h r e e

Power

"Theatre people like you when they see you," Agnes had decided in her youth, "and if they don't see you they only like you when you're powerful. The thing is to get powerful."[1] *Oklahoma!* gave her power. At the end of 1943, she was the most-sought-after choreographer on Broadway. She was also, as her letterhead proudly proclaimed, Mrs. Walter F. Prude. All she wanted, she told Walter, was to be with him and to do good work — a conflict of interests they would both underestimate until their civilian life together began. During the war, survival eclipsed all other considerations. Days after the *One Touch of Venus* opening, Agnes joined her husband at his temporary posting in Lemoore, California; but after a fortnight together in an off-base boardinghouse that offered little privacy, he was transferred to an embarkation area and then overseas, to England.

In the drama that was Agnes's life, there were no intermissions; she careened from climax to climax "full out, with enthusiasm," playing every role in which life cast her with the fervor of an evangelist whose religion was herself. It was not a question of acting; she was sincere to a fault, even at times when a little guile might have been prudent. The intensity of her emotions fueled her creativity but exhausted everyone around her.

So it was not surprising that she would play the wife of a soldier with all stops out.

She had been working for some time on a ballet called *The Frail Quarry*. Since *Rodeo,* both the Ballet Russe de Monte Carlo and Ballet Theatre had been asking for her work. But Ballet Theatre's rejection of *Rodeo* still rankled, and she had felt slighted when Lucia Chase offered a contract to Tudor but not to her. She was no happier with the Ballet Russe de Monte Carlo. The company had performed *Rodeo* seventy-nine times in its first two seasons; the quality of the performances had gradually deteriorated under the stresses of touring, and Agnes informed Sergei Denham that she would not do another ballet for him until he gave her enough rehearsal time to get *Rodeo* back into a condition "that I will not consider a disgrace to my reputation."[2] *The Frail Quarry,* therefore, went to Ballet Theatre.

Having demonstrated in *Venus* that she could work without cowboys, Agnes now wanted to show that she was not limited to Americana. *The Frail Quarry* is a ribald and romantic burlesque of French court life in the eighteenth century. A wife whose scholarly husband is immersed in his books becomes the shy but curious "quarry" of a prince, with whom she enjoys a fling in the woods on a summer afternoon. When her husband realizes her adultery, she is stricken with guilt and begs forgiveness, jolting them both into a new realization of the joy of married love.

Three recurrent themes in Agnes's work are romantic love, forbidden sex, and the natural world; *The Frail Quarry* includes them all. Pre-Revolutionary France is a long way from Ozone Heights, but in both *Frail Quarry* and *One Touch of Venus*, a bored, neglected wife is lured from domesticity into sexual delights — in the first instance by nature, in the second by the gods. Agnes used authentic antique dances as a springboard, knowing that exact replication would be boring; each movement was expanded, exaggerated, satirized. She drew on her knowledge of the period's manners and customs; the women's heads wobbled, she explained to a reporter, because of the elaborate headdresses they wore, and the movement also expressed their vanity and frivolity. No nuance escaped her attention: the degree at which the head was inclined (it depended on the person's rank), the formal position of the courtier's hands, the depth of a commoner's curtsey before a prince, the way that a man removed his hat "in such a way that the lady could not see inside it — probably because it was so dirty."[3] The juxtaposition of elegance and comedy that had worked so well in her recital pieces made the ballet, while not a great piece of choreography, a thoroughly enjoyable piece of theater.

To please Walter, she commissioned his friend Paul Nordoff, who had composed music for some of Martha Graham's ballets, to arrange and develop music from various operas by Gluck — a decision she later would regret, although Nordoff's music worked perfectly well. Nordoff, who owed Agnes money and undoubtedly resented her marriage to Walter, was not available at times when she considered his presence essential. Afterward, there was an angry exchange of letters; the friendship was fractured, but salvaged (Nordoff later married and had children, then earned Agnes's lasting displeasure by leaving his family to live with a man).

Agnes's scenarios were little playlets, rich with details; they boiled down in rehearsal, she said, like spinach. *The Frail Quarry*'s setting and costumes had the grandeur and romance of a Watteau painting. In the shade with the Husband, a cardinal in scarlet silk, and the wife in pearl colored satin. The Husband and Cardinal are playing chess at a small table. The wife is bored . . . This tableau is held for a few seconds. A girl runs on and stands poised in a patch of sunlight like a winged insect. She holds a tambourine which she shakes delicately a few times . . . The wife grows excited . . . The girl breaks into a brisk, provocative little hornpipe, then drifts off in pas de bourrée [a series of small, even steps on pointe], beckoning the wife to follow. Voices call; a couple of girls whisk out of the bushes, race through the shadows and are gone like rabbits. Enter two girls with tambourines. . . . The wife is beside herself with desire to join the fun. Enter three girls . . . the ultimate in tantalizing, provocative walks [also funny — a de Mille specialty] . . . To the beat and roll of drums the prince and his men come on. . . . A hunting horn sounds.[4]

Like the nuns in *Three Virgins and a Devil*, the wife, while affecting propriety, is surprised to find her fingers snapping and her shoulders jerking. "A girl's legs bang up in the bushes as she disappears from view. The husband makes an important chess move."

Agnes toured with the company during the rehearsal period, when the usual rigors of touring were compounded by the exigencies of wartime. From New York to Chicago, St. Louis, Kansas City, Denver, Seattle, and San Francisco, the trains were packed with soldiers, to Agnes a constant reminder of the comparative frivolity of her work. She had cast herself in the lead, with the understanding that Janet Reed, on whom she worked out the part, would play it when she was otherwise engaged. For Lucia Chase, who insisted on a role for herself, she created the character of a young woman unilaterally in love with the Prince, played by Hugh Laing. Agnes had cast him with misgivings, for although he was perfect for the part, he and Tudor had pointedly ignored her since the opening of *Oklahoma!* During rehearsals, Laing treated her with the same rudeness with which he often treated Tudor — but Agnes, unlike Tudor, was not in love with him, and after he called her a goddamned fool in front of her cast, she vowed never to work with him again.

To further poison the atmosphere in rehearsals, Laing and Anton Dolin, the other leading man, hated each other. Agnes had thought that the contrast between Laing's understated style and Dolin's flamboyance would be funny; but as rehearsals progressed, their styles seemed irreconcilable. Beyond that, "the basic trouble," Agnes later realized, "was a deep inner confusion that I couldn't think through . . . I didn't know which man that woman was in love with. The story isn't thought out. If I'd known my intentions clearly neither Hugh nor Dolin could have unnerved me because I'm stronger than either of them. But I didn't."[5]

For reasons never made entirely clear, management renamed the ballet *Tally-Ho* (over Agnes's objections), and premiered it in Los Angeles on February 25, 1944. It went on without Agnes; not having had time to prepare, she decided to "save my thunder for the Met" and had Janet Reed dance the role.[6] The audience loved it, and gave the dancers seventeen curtain calls. But up to and even after the opening in New York, Agnes continued to revise, with the dancers struggling to keep up with the changes. Eventually, *Tally-Ho* was a qualified success; it was "confused and obviously unfinished," John Martin wrote, "but the parts of it that are good are tremendously and outstandingly good." More than any other critic, Martin had the background, and the knowledge of Agnes's work, to appreciate how well her choreography "translated excellently into theatre terms and contemporary ballet dimensions."[7] "*Tally-Ho* is so brilliant in its best sections," he wrote, "that it will be unfortunate if the summer does not afford her an opportunity to fix it up in its less good ones."[8] But Agnes had already signed the contract for her next show, and her summer was fully booked. Four decades later, she would still be devising improvements to *Tally-Ho.*

By raising the standard of dancing on Broadway, *Oklahoma!* had also raised the position of choreographers, who had previously been relegated to the bottom of the totem pole. None had risen higher than Agnes, but she was too busy shoring up her position to enjoy the view. And her triumph, while delicious, had a bitter aftertaste. It had taken too long. She said as much to her friend Kitty Carlisle Hart when they happened to meet on Madison Avenue one windy afternoon. "She said, 'People are so charming to me now, and I'm the same person. I have the same talent.'

I still have a vision of her with that red hair and a black cloak, kind of billowing out behind her in some cosmic wind. She was always larger than life. It wasn't just the cloak was blowing out behind her on an ordinary March New York day. It was a *cosmic* wind. And she was always *fulminating* about something — a critic, or a producer!"[9]

In the summer of 1944, she was fulminating about E. Y. Harburg, who had written the lyrics to Harold Arlen's music for *Bloomer Girl.* Agnes, whose previous experience with Harburg and Arlen was on *Hooray for What!* (from which the despised B. M. had fired her), was doing the choreography for *Bloomer Girl.* When the director of the show was fired midway into rehearsals, Harburg, whom Agnes considered "one of the most fascistic, sadistic, bullying hypocrites I've ever met in my life," insisted on taking over.[10] As a director, he proved to be a fine lyricist, and the show was ultimately staged by Agnes and the producer, John C. Wilson. But to Agnes's great annoyance, Harburg got the credit.

Bloomer Girl continued the trend set by *Oklahoma!* of wholesomeness, nostalgia, and patriotism. The story,* set at the beginning of the Civil War, is a fictional treatment of Dolly Bloomer, a historic crusader for moral and political reforms, who urged young women to abandon sexist hoopskirts in favor of the more revealing garments that bore her name. Dolly's disciple and niece, Evelina, defies her father by embracing both bloomers and a slaveowner, who arranges the escape of one of his own slaves via the underground railroad. The show was a light romance, with the underlying theme of emancipation for slaves and for women.

Agnes felt a double kinship with women who waited for their men. Long before she had awaited Walter's return, she had waited, throughout her childhood, for her father. In 1929 she had created a "Civil War" solo for herself and had later danced a duet version of it with Joe Anthony. After *Oklahoma!* she had written a scenario for a more ambitious treatment of the theme; she viewed *Bloomer Girl* as "a chance at last to put on the stage what was in my heart . . . about women's emotions in war."[11] But unlike the ballets in *Oklahoma!* and *One Touch of Venus,* which had evolved organically out of character and plot, the twelve-minute ballet

* Book by Sig Herzig and Fred Saidy, based on a play by Dan and Lilith James.

Agnes devised for the end of *Bloomer Girl*'s second act was not central to the story. A grim depiction of loss, it showed the departure of the soldiers, the grieving women left behind, and the joyful reunion — darkened by the onstage body of a dead soldier, around which was performed a sort of funereal square dance. Agnes was "delighted to find such tragic strengths within me."[12] But when she proudly showed the dance to Harburg and Arlen and the producers, they were horrified. Expecting *Oklahoma!*, they were presented with *Mother Courage.*

The "bosses," as Agnes referred to management, asked her for something light and bouncy, like the other numbers in the show, which had no dance steps as such; simply through pantomime, patterns of movement (mostly walking, alone and in groups), and a few descriptive lyrics, the characters revealed themselves and their relationships, and conveyed the feeling of a small town on a Sunday. Couldn't she make the war ballet wistful, instead of grim, the producer asked — incorporating the ringing of victory bells, perhaps? But Agnes thought her ballet the best she had ever done, and throughout the rehearsal period she campaigned relentlessly to preserve it.

Arlen had composed a rich score for the show, and Harburg's lyrics, particularly "The Eagle and Me" ("We gotta be free"), were as appropriate for World War II as for the one between the states. *Bloomer Girl* starred Celeste Holm (*Oklahoma!*'s Ado Annie) and featured Joan McCracken, who sang as well as danced. The war had drastically curtailed the supply of male dancers, but one young man who showed up for the open audition immediately caught Agnes's interest. At twenty-five, James Mitchell had the look and the quality of a young Hugh Laing — dark and mysterious, with a beautifully chiseled face. Unlike Laing, Mitchell was well mannered, totally professional, and constitutionally incapable of throwing a tantrum. He had started dancing late, at nineteen, with the modern dancer Lester Horton. He had very little ballet technique (he would later acquire it), but he had a powerful stage presence and physical strength that belied his slight build. To overcome the back problem that kept him out of the Army, he had developed such strong arms that he could easily lift a partner with his arms outstretched — a movement that made the girl look weightless, and which

Agnes loved to use. At the audition, she offered him a job on the spot. Within three days, he was her assistant and lead dancer.

For Mitchell, a Californian who had only recently arrived in New York, "It was a very exciting time. Suddenly I was working with a very successful choreographer on a big Broadway show, and being paid for it! I'd never been to a musical before in my life, and Agnes took me to the St. James Theatre to see *Oklahoma!* from the back of the house. The second show I saw — a portion of it, from backstage — was *One Touch of Venus*. I think she was educating me, showing me what the work looked like on the stage."

Agnes's work, with its emphasis on acting, was "right up my alley," Mitchell said. "I was young, I was good-looking; the body seemed to be able to wrap itself around a particular movement. I had studied acting in college, so I understood what contact with the audience meant. I could create an atmosphere. There were a lot of dancers who could dance circles around me as far as technique went, but I seemed to be able to hold the stage when I walked on. And that's what Agnes looked for. So she was able to use me very well. And I was able to use Agnes. So it was a nice meld."

Mitchell had the intelligence and sensitivity to anticipate what Agnes wanted. His looks, ability, and affinity for her work made him the quintessential male de Mille dancer, and Agnes would use him whenever she could over the next twenty-five years. "The Civil War ballet was a particularly tough nut to crack," he said. "One evening she called me, late — nine or ten o'clock — and asked me to come to the studio. She wanted to work out the beginning of that piece. Her idea was a figure 'in one' [in front of the curtain], with a soldier's jacket that she had me whirl around my head, as though in triumph, but calling people together, to a drum roll. And people ran back and forth, in one, before the curtain went up. It was an electrifying moment. Because all of a sudden there was no song, there were no words, just pure movement. And that captured the audience."[13]

By September, when the show was to open in Philadelphia, Agnes had showed the bosses four different versions of the Civil War ballet. John C. Wilson offered a compromise: on the first night, the dancers could perform a nine-minute version of the ballet, one without the dead soldier on the stage. After that, he would replace it with a singing chorus. But one performance was all Agnes needed to prove her point. The ballet worked brilliantly as, among other things, a dramatic counterbalance to the lighter elements in the show; the audience was moved to tears and cheers, and one woman quietly handed Agnes her son's Navy wings.

The ballet showed the women attempting to lead normal lives, suddenly giving way to their anguish and despair, then recovering control and resuming their routines. When the men returned, there was silence until one dancer suddenly stamped and threw her head back, signaling the rush into the men's arms. Betty Low, who played the widow of the dead soldier, recalled, "There was a moment on stage every single night that I will treasure all my life. The whole company was quiet; everybody had got their man back but me, and I found out from people's faces that he wasn't coming back. I had to kneel down and put my hand on the earth, as though on top of his grave; there was a feeling of continuity and the future and reassurance. For me it was a spellbinding moment. On the night Roosevelt died [in April 1945], at that moment there was a hush in the audience at the Shubert Theater. They recognized a kind of symbolism — America wasn't going down the drain, we were going to go on."[14]

John Chapman called the Civil War ballet "pretentious, dullish and funny when it wasn't meant to be."[15] Horton Foote, writing in the *Dance Observer,* thought it dull and boring, its ending "sentimental to an extreme."[16] *The Nation's* reviewer compared its style with that of Tudor's *Dark Elegies* "with even a Tudor Woman in Black and Red [Betty Low] and Girl in Rose [Lidija Franklin] and Her Soldier [James Mitchell] who looks like Hugh Laing."[17] But Linton Martin wrote in the *Philadelphia Inquirer* that the ballet was "as emotionally moving and eloquent in its way as the impressively tooted and touted Tudor ballet, *Pillar of Fire,*"[18] and most of his colleagues considered it to be Agnes's finest work. "Thanks to Miss de Mille's ballets," said Howard Barnes, "one can even find considerable significance in [the show]."[19] Richard P. Cooke praised the "phenomenon [of] a ballet which had something to say and which said it so the average first-nighter could understand it."[20] Walter Terry applauded the depiction of "the courageous attempt to lead a normal life as the women move serenely along, suddenly breaking down into movements of anguish and despair and then resolutely wrenching back their self-control as they continue to wait," and concluded that the ballet was "an absorbing contrast to the surrounding levity."[21]

If Agnes needed any further vindication, she got it from "Yipper" Harburg, who admitted that he'd been wrong. "To think," he said to her, "that a lousy little bit of movement can make people weep, and me among them!"[22]

t w e n t y - f o u r

Rodgers and Hammerstein and de Mille

During the first two years of their marriage, Agnes and Walter spent a total of ten weeks together; the rest of the time, they conducted an intense, literate, and loving correspondence. Agnes had a gift for epistolary romance; Warren Leonard had compared her letters favorably with Elizabeth Barrett Browning's, and she took great pride in Walter's opinion that "Martha [Graham]'s not a patch on you at writing letters. Her letters, I realize now, are brilliant but selfconscious—and literary. They haven't got the incredible projection of humanness, warmth, and guts that is so altogether and uniquely you . . . My *sapient* little mouse!"[1]

Unlike Agnes who broadcast her feelings to the world, Walter kept his emotions firmly buttoned up. But with his wife, he let down his guard. "I know that my own thoughts and tender love will be around you like a mantle when you have time to receive them and need for them," he assured her.[2] About sex, they were both oblique. He supposed that the waiting was harder on her than on himself because "a man is actually the more carnal beast and can fritter away a part of his hunger or dream it out successfully. That's why I'm so glad you have the outlet of your work."[3] Agnes wrote, "I cannot go in heavily for promiscuous drinking

or fornication . . . so if I wreak my animal spirits and flowing heart on some good resistant choreographic problems don't you say a word."[4]

Romance, not sex, was their forte. For the opening of *Tally-Ho,* Walter had managed to have a bouquet of violets delivered to the theater, and a small apple tree, in bloom, to the apartment. He assured her of his faithfulness ("I haven't had time to pursue me a wench even if I wanted to . . . I'm all too certain anyway that a bright little face would come between me and my frail quarry") and confessed, "at all unexpected moments in the day and night, I grieve for you. I remember how your head nestles on my shoulder when I pull you down beside me and how you murmur then like a sleepy night-bird. I remember how your hand looks for mine when we're walking down a street and how your footsteps patter along at my side, preoccupied and oblivious of pitfalls. But most of all I remember the quick, unfailing response of your bright mind and spirit to my random moods. Did ever a man have such a dear, lovely, wonderful wife!"[5]

Newly domesticated, Agnes redecorated her apartment and sent him detailed descriptions and sketches. "O sexy and gay," he replied to one such report, "is my mouse's sweet chez."[6] On their first wedding anniversary, she wrote, "I never quite believe that you are you and pledged to me, that I know you well. Every time I see [your face] on the pillow beside me, every time I see it over a coffee cup I am surprised that you are there. . . . Most of my adult life has been spent quite alone, sleeping alone, walking alone, eating alone. To think of coming home with someone, knowing someone is at work in the next room, being certain that the next day and the next I will have a companion to gossip with, listen to — It doesn't seem possible to me that I can really have these things."[7]

When she learned that he had waited months to tell her that he had participated in the demolition of land mines, to avoid worrying her while she was in rehearsal, she wrote, "As someone who is a virtuoso self-pittier [*sic*] and clamorer, I am stopped short by the simple kindness of your care for me."[8] And on the eve of the new year: "I used to be afraid of what absence could do to us. I'm afraid of nothing any more. . . . You are my strength and my replenishment and my wisdom . . . Oh darling, whatever good or use I am as an instrument you made possible by clearing my heart. I hope you will never not be proud of me."[9]

When *Bloomer Girl* opened, Walter asked, "How will it feel to have three hits on the street at once? Will you rest on your laurels a while or will this stimulate you to look for new worlds, I wonder."[10] For Agnes, laurels were as restful as poison ivy, and she was already negotiating with the Theatre Guild to choreograph Rodgers and Hammerstein's second show, *Carousel.* At the same time, she was exploring ways of circumventing the Army's rule that prohibited the wife of a soldier on active duty overseas from leaving the country. She organized a dance show for Army camps, hospital wards, and embarkation centers in the New York area, using dancers from her shows and performing some of her old recital solos. She hoped to persuade the USO to send her to Europe, but they declined. She appealed to military officials, to the British Ambassador, and even to Mamie Eisenhower, who was a friend of her sister's, all with such persistence that Clare Luce suggested that she appear before Congress, predicting, "They'll send you overseas just to be rid of you."[11]

The war news had improved steadily since D-Day — June 6, 1944. Now the Allied troops were advancing on Germany, and the war in Europe was expected to end in a matter of months. But early in 1945, Agnes was asked to choreograph a movie in London, for $40,000. She accepted immediately, hoping that Walter would not be transferred elsewhere before she could get to England. The uncertainty was "nerve shattering. . . . Should I refuse all work here on the chance that I can get over within the next 2 months? Or should I carry on and grab the opportunity as it comes? . . . I'm going to cancel *Carousel* if [the producer] will take me over now."[12] But the movie was postponed until June. In March, *Carousel* went into rehearsal.

ꝏ

For the musical adaptation of Ferenc Molnar's *Liliom,* originally produced as a play in 1921, the Guild reunited its winning *Oklahoma!* combination: Rodgers, Hammerstein, Mamoulian, Agnes, and costume designer Miles White. Jo Mielziner, probably the most talented designer of his day, replaced Lem Ayers as scenic and lighting designer. Like most theatrical ventures, *Carousel* began with great good will and intentions, but Agnes was disenchanted with the Guild. "They are taking the stand that they discovered me, and that I should be grateful and work for very little. This is not my attitude since I worked for nothing on *Oklahoma!* and they never saw fit to recognize my services."[13] She had indeed earned very little for *Oklahoma!:* her $50 a week bonus would be augmented in 1947 to one-half of one percent of the gross (after taxes) of the London and national companies only. She had no share in the residual rights. In 1943, no one could have predicted that the value of those rights would reach historic proportions,* but it was clear even then that the show would make some people very rich and that Agnes would not be one of them. Agnes endorsed her grandfather George's economic theories, but all the de Milles respected the material symbols of success. *Oklahoma!* was a gold mine from which Agnes was excluded, and a malignant worm of resentment had begun to grow.

Everyone involved in *Oklahoma!* agreed that as a theatrical production it was a paradigm of teamwork. "It was only after it was a tremendous success," said Elaine Steinbeck, "that they started arguing about

---

* During the next fifty years there would be more than 30,000 productions of *Oklahoma!,* generating an income of $2.5 million for anyone who invested $1,000 in the original production.

who deserved credit for what." In their autobiographies, both Richard Rodgers and the Guild's Lawrence Langner credited Rouben Mamoulian with the marriage between the musical and dramatic elements in *Oklahoma!* Typically, the choreographer stages the songs in a musical — that is, gives the singers, most of whom have not been trained to move anything below their jaws, movements that emphasize the lyrics and mood. Agnes had staged the songs for *Venus* and *Bloomer Girl,* but Mamoulian had done so for *Oklahoma!* (except for "Many a New Day," which was Agnes's), and it was his responsibility for *Carousel.*

Agnes had considered Mamoulian her nemesis on *Oklahoma!,* and she was not eager to work with him again. The director shared her reluctance, for she had made no secret, around town, of her opinion of his talent ("small") and taste ("vulgar").[14] Rodgers arranged an emotionally charged reconciliation, and saw to it that her rehearsals were forty blocks away from the theater, where Mamoulian could not interrupt them. Throughout rehearsals, Agnes and the director maintained an exaggerated politeness. (Mamoulian "is behaving like a lamb and his direction is just about as intelligent," she reported to Walter).[15]

Carousel is about life and death: boy meets girl, boy gets girl, boy dies. Rodgers and Hammerstein, two urban Jews who never wrote about Jews and only once about a city, set Molnar's European melodrama in a Maine fishing village, in 1873. The antihero, Billy Bigelow, is a young carnival barker who loves and marries Julie Jordan, a factory worker. He loses his job and, to earn money for their expected child, he commits a robbery, in the course of which he dies. Years later, God allows him to return to earth to see his daughter, Louise, graduate from school. He gives her a star he has stolen; she refuses it, but he manages to give her hope and love before returning to Purgatory. Like *Oklahoma!, Carousel* starred two unknowns — in this case, Jan Clayton and John Raitt.

Rodgers and Hammerstein supervised every detail of *Carousel,* from the props to the vocal inflections. On *Oklahoma!,* Agnes had found both men sensitive and responsive. Like herself, they were perfectionists, extreme in their demands on themselves and on others, but good at cutting the tension with humor. Agnes had a deep affection for Hammerstein, and she had called Rodgers "an angel."[16] But it seemed to her that after

Oklahoma! Rodgers became harder, arbitrary, and autocratic. "His success gradually corroded him," she said.[17]

Throughout Agnes's recital career, her control over music, lighting, costumes, scenery, props, advertising, and performance had been absolute. In the theater she had power, but not control — a frustration compounded by her difficulty in disengaging her ego from her work. And although that ego could expand to fill any space available, it was as vulnerable as a soft-shell crab. Her defensiveness bordered on paranoia; combined with her innate arrogance and undiluted candor, it earned her the reputation of a virago.

Agnes fought fiercely for what she believed in, and quite often she was right. But in a business run by men, there was real antagonism toward a woman who spoke her mind. Furthermore, her variation on the Golden Rule was to criticize other people's work as mercilessly as she did her own. She could treat people she considered her inferiors with stunning rudeness — cutting them dead or vaporizing them with a wit tipped with curare. At auditions, her remarks ranged from "She's doing the lift as though she's climbing into an upper berth" to "He wears his jockstrap well," and she often commented in a stage whisper on the sex lives of the dancers. Some unfortunates were addressed directly: "You! the one that looks like a female impersonator!" or told at a rehearsal or, even worse, after a performance, "You're terrible! You really should give up! Why are you here?" Her targets never forgave or forgot.

With an artist of Richard Rodgers's stature she was respectful, but their collaboration was increasingly tense. Rodgers was a realist who liked to quote a line attributed to Irving Berlin: "I'll never work with that Ethel Merman again as long as I live — until I need her!"[18] To build on *Oklahoma!*'s success, he needed Agnes. According to his wife, Dorothy, "He thought Agnes was a not-very-attractive woman with an enormous amount of energy and talent, and a little too sharp to have as a friend. She was intimidating and demanding, and she had no tact."[19] Rodgers's daughter, Mary, was more succinct: "My father thought she was a pain in the ass."[20] When Rodgers and Lorenz Hart had worked with choreographer Robert Alton, no one thought of their shows as anything other than Rodgers and Hart's. Rodgers had no intention of allowing *Carousel* to be identified in anyone's mind as Rodgers and Hammerstein and de Mille.

The score of *Carousel,* which includes "If I Loved You" and the seven-minute "Soliloquy" in which Billy pledges himself to his unborn child, was Rodgers's favorite of all his shows. The music was orchestrated by Don Walker, but it was Trude Rittman who, as dance arranger, wove Rodgers's themes together to suit the action of the ballet, supplying transition, development, and referral as needed. Music helped to stimulate and clarify Agnes's ideas, but she had no interest in musical theory, such as harmony and keys. Her tonality was good, and her rhythm was excellent; she had a good ear for syncopation and an effective way of using it to break formal patterns with natural, spontaneous movement such as a dancer suddenly changing an action or direction.

Agnes trusted Trude's judgment and taste absolutely. They spent hours at the piano together, sometimes with one or two dancers, improvising. Trude understood, as few composers did, what music a dancer could and could not use. Agnes told her the mood she wanted, and the length, and she produced it.

Rittman, who worked with every top choreographer and composer in the theater, observed "a very deep difference between Agnes's musical consciousness and Balanchine's and Jerry Robbins's. Agnes's relation to music is a very lyric one and you can work very freely with her — whereas Jerry, for instance, almost forms the music of his movement. Jerry is more than anything musical, and Balanchine was a musician! They take the music as pure music, abstractly, with nothing attached to it, as music in fact *is.* That doesn't mean you don't have recollections, or pictures — when you hear a Schubert lied, you do think of certain things. But they have no plots, except once in a while. In Agnes's work, music plays a more *dramatic* role. She begins with a *story* that develops into a dance. She conjures up emotions and pictures that music awakens in her mind. Agnes is musical; she played the piano quite well. But her foremost talent is theatrical. The danger was that every so often she would go overboard — too much, too long, too self-centered."[21]

All but two of the eleven musicals running on Broadway in the spring of 1945 had emulated *Oklahoma!* by employing trained dancers instead of a line of kicking chorus girls or elegant, bored-looking showgirls. In *Ca-*

rousel, Rodgers broke with another tradition by dispensing with the overture. Instead, an opening prologue, set to Rodgers's wonderfully evocative "Carousel Waltz," introduced the characters and established the mood for the play.

The show had two big production numbers: the rousing "It Was a Real Nice Clambake" and the bouncy "June Is Bustin' Out All Over," featuring Pearl Lang, a Martha Graham dancer. The "June" dance was light and airy; little touches, as subtle as the sound of the girls hitting their wrists together, conveyed the sense that the girls were intoxicated with the thick, rich aura of spring. Agnes told the dancers to think about feeling "*ripe* — ready for love, life, fruition, as though you are smelling wet earth, wet grass, the sun on wet leaves, after rain. The palms of your hands are very sensitive . . . Your fingers tremble, hands and feet seem to be shaking off the droplets of rain. Everything presses upward, toward the sun. There is an impulse like a sharp breath, and then you just dissolve into numinous air."[22]

"Blow High, Blow Low" was eight minutes of walking, skipping, sidesteps, runs, lifts, and a comedic flirtation when a very small girl (Annabelle Lyon) dares a very tall boy (Peter Birch) to dance with her. The dance, which includes the lightning-swift steps of an eighteenth-century jig and ends with the boy lifting the girl high in the air and carrying her, arms outspread, offstage, is an expansion of *Clipper Sailing,* which Agnes had performed with Joe Anthony (and which had in turn evolved from *Hornpipe,* a solo she had done in 1936).[23] The number ended with the actors, singers, and dancers forming the shape of a ship and swaying, to the sound of sails flapping, so that the whole stage seemed to roll with the waves. The sailors went off to sea, leaving women and children behind — a theme that had moved Agnes ever since her father had, as she perceived it, abandoned her.

The ballet that ended the show was one of Agnes's finest theatrical achievements. It was Hammerstein's idea to show, in ballet and pantomime, the first fifteen years of Louise's life. The girl, who lived on the wrong side of the tracks and was the daughter of a thief, was another lonely outsider with whom Agnes could identify. The role required acting as well as dancing. Agnes created it for Bambi Linn, who excelled at both.

In its first version, the ballet lasted an hour and fifteen minutes. It included every character in the show, some of whom spoke lines of dialogue, and had numerous subplots ("It's wonderful," said Jan Clayton, "I give birth to Bambi right on the stage!").[24] It began with Billy looking down from heaven on his wife, in labor in the center of the dark stage, a pinspot on her face. The women gathered round her for a "birthing" dance, and then Bambi entered, performing a series of grand jetés around the circumference of the stage, leaping and soaring as though repealing the law of gravity. Barefoot, with her hair in a ponytail and wearing a simple, clinging jersey dress that matched the sky, she personified the freedom, innocence, and promise of childhood. In ensuing sequences she is snubbed and tormented by her schoolmates, and enticed by the rough energy of the carnival people who represent her father's world. A young man attempts a seduction, and Louise, like Laurey, is repelled but fascinated by her newly discovered sexuality. But the boy decides she is more child than woman, and leaves. Julie appears, comforts her, and sends her off to a children's party, where no one will dance with her. The carnival people return and dance "in a great ring on the outside of the children's circle. Louise is lost between and skips back and forth endlessly. The two circles, children inside, circus folk outside, are now moving in slow motion like a nightmare. Louise skips and skips normal tempo on and on. . . . Her low crying follows her father to heaven."[25] At the end, the characters form a big carousel with their bodies, with everyone circling around.

By the time the show reached Boston (via New Haven), the ballet was pared down to forty minutes, and the dialogue reduced to Louise shouting "I hate you!" at a taunting child. As was customary during Boston tryouts, everyone connected with the creation of the show watched every performance of the three-week run, afterward participating in midnight conferences that were pervaded, Agnes said, by "a wonderful spirit of sacrifice . . . I gladly cut what I consider inspired pieces of choreography if it is agreed that the show will benefit."[26] Her letter to Walter told a different story: "The bosses cut my big ballet in two," she wrote, "and forced me to expose a truncated version for two weeks. I forced my [version] on the stage last night in the teeth of their disapproval . . . My version brought the house down and we got the first genuine audience response of the run. Oscar found me in the lobby and threw his arms around me. I cried. He thanked me for holding out and making dramatic sense. Later Dick embraced me. And Mamoo, who had argued and argued . . . said, 'Didn't I tell you?' . . . When will people trust me to handle my own department like an expert?"[27]

The pressure preceding the New York opening was tremendous, for everyone knew that critics would compare the show with *Oklahoma!* At the eleventh hour, the Prologue still wasn't working. "Mamoulian had insisted that he was the mover of crowds," Bambi Linn recalled, "that he could handle it. Finally he had to say, All right, Agnes, you can do it. So Agnes did! She set up the whole thing [a combination of pantomime and musical movement, as in *Bloomer Girl*'s "Sunday in Cicero Falls"], and made it all work. She saved that Broadway opening."[28]

Carousel opened at the Majestic Theatre in New York on April 19, 1945. It was an immediate hit. The ballet enriched the show with its action, fantasy, characterization, and emotional range, and Bambi Linn was everyone's sweetheart. "Bambi doesn't come on until twenty minutes before eleven," said *Dance Magazine,* "and for the next forty minutes practically holds the audience in her hands . . . Her dance in its directness and sincerity is an artistic achievement."[29] Howard Barnes, writing in the *Herald-Tribune,* took a longer view: "It has waited for Miss de Mille to come through with peculiarly American dance patterns for a musical show to become as much a dance as a song show."[30] In other words: Rodgers and Hammerstein and de Mille.

t w e n t y - f i v e

Home

On May 7, 1945, the Germans surrendered to the Allied Forces, and peace broke out in Europe. Agnes ricocheted from anticipation to despair, fearing that Walter would be sent to the Pacific, where the war still raged, before she could get to England in June. Officially, she was to choreograph a movie, but she had taken the job only in the hope of seeing Walter and had not even read the script.

There was little satisfaction in her return to the country she had left seven years earlier with her career and her heart in shreds. The war had ravaged London. Agnes was shocked by the obvious devastations, and also by subtleties that grieved her aristocratic sensibility — the women's hands, for example, "destroyed with doing all their floor-scrubbing and washing for five years. On top of everything else, no one had a char for the duration."[1]

She settled into a flat in Pimlico for a six-month stay. There were happy reunions with old acquaintances, the titled (Lord and Lady Sandwich, Lady Colefax, Lady Wedgwood) and the plebeian (dancers, mostly, and her beloved Mrs. Obie). But when Agnes read the script of the movie, called *London Town,* she was appalled. The costumes were "old-fashioned and cheap. The music poor. The ideas behind the numbers con-

fused, muddled. . . . I am given no control of their structure. . . . I know [Wesley Ruggles, the producer] is frightened of the loss of prestige if I make it known publicly that I cannot work with him. . . . I do not wish to give him a good ballet idea, which Lem Ayers [*sic*] and/or Minelli [*sic*] could help me turn into dance history. Ruggles would emasculate and ruin it. I wish to have as little of my work recognizable in this picture as possible."[2]

The producer, Agnes informed her mother, was "nervous and domineering and dictatorial. In fact, he is just like Cecil."[3] Since *Cleopatra,* she had learned how to fight. But Ruggles was inflexible. Their battles were standoffs, and she would eventually pay him $4,000 to remove her name from the credits.

She recruited some of her prewar dancers, among them Brigitte Kelly. "Ruggles didn't want dancers," said Kelly. "He wanted Agnes to use beautiful models. Agnes dug her toes in and refused. There was a row, and she went ahead and got her little group together. It was universally thought that Agnes picked the lame ducks almost perversely, girls who were not particularly good-looking, with muscular legs. She may have merely sympathized with the underdogs, or she may have felt that a very pretty girl had an image of herself that would be too hard to break down. Probably it was a little of both."

Rehearsals took place in an unheated church hall in Camden Town. "Agnes would arrive in a kind of *Oklahoma!* outfit," Kelly said. "Straw hat, skirt with yards of material, braid, bows, flowers — a different outfit every time she came to rehearsal. We had all been deprived of material for so long, we were aghast!

"Agnes had been used to money, studios with central heating. One felt she was spoilt. She was obviously used to having a lot of attention, which she wasn't getting. One of her dancers was always having to run across the road to get her a cup of coffee. She never stopped complaining about the hall. She was the sort of person who, if the studio floor on which we were dancing barefoot was wrong for us in some way — whereas another choreographer would say, 'I'm sorry, that's the way it is' — Agnes would say, 'My dancers can't dance on this floor!' But we all loved doing her work because you didn't just dance, you were expressing something. She demanded that her dancers be characters, not just ballet fodder."[4]

Reunion with Walter remained uncertain until one afternoon in July when he appeared, unannounced, at her door. He had three weeks' leave, after which he expected to be shipped to the Pacific. But the day he left London — August 6, 1945 — the first bomb was dropped on Hiroshima, and within weeks the war was over. Walter was a civilian, looking for work in New York. Agnes was stuck in London, working on a movie she hated. And she was pregnant.

It was not an accident; she was approaching forty, and motherhood had been on her mind for some time. She had recently written to Walter, "I feel as fecund and as strong as the earth."[5] Walter, who was not eager to become a father, may have thought, or hoped, that she was referring to her work. On their last night together, Agnes, believing that he was "going into the hell of the Japanese invasion and there was no time for debates . . . acted on a deep instinct."[6] But when she surprised him with the news, his response was more apprehension than enthusiasm. He had no job, no money except his accumulated Army allotment (Agnes had banked it and lived on her own earnings), and a deep concern about "the enormous gap between our positions."[7]

Agnes was aware of the gap and its dangers. Since *Oklahoma!,* she had had first refusal of every important Broadway show; dancers now referred to the theater district as de Mille Gulch. She had turned down offers to direct the Salzburg Festival, to direct the Paris Opéra Ballet, and to earn $4,000 a week in Hollywood. But with her husband, she played down her achievements. "It is plain fact," she wrote, "that I and my very recent little success crowd you a little — and I and my life-long highly cultivated ego do make you at times uneasy. But oh, dear heart, I'm learning. I'm learning what really counts to me, what really matters. You do, your happiness."[8]

The war had postponed a dilemma she could no longer avoid. "I had drunk the Milk of Paradise and known power," she later wrote. "I could not think to give this up. I could forfeit my life, and my comfort, riches and convenience, for love — but not the magic release of work! This was my identity."[9] She loved Walter, but her work was her passion. Yet her attitude toward it was conflicted. During the war, the societal stigma imposed on women who worked outside the home was suspended, but it was reinstated when the men returned home after the war, expecting to reclaim their traditional roles. Agnes believed in equal rights for women, but she never considered herself a feminist; like the male establishment, she defined "feminism" by its radical fringe, and rejected it as anti-men, anti-family, anti-looking-pretty. She was more pragmatist than feminist — yet at a time when women were still considered freaks for even *wanting* to work outside the home, she exemplified feminist principles and demanded equal rights. Long before the formation of an organized women's movement, Agnes's young female dancers viewed her, with curiosity and awe, as a one-woman movement. "Agnes liberated me," said Bambi Linn. "She gave me the opportunity to be me — to stand on the stage and be a girl, a woman, a female who had importance. In Agnes's shows, it's almost always the woman who's the top dancer, never the man. Agnes presented women who made a difference — who went out into the prairies, who made it happen! Without the women, we'd be nothing! Agnes kept pushing and pushing and pushing, and people hated it — men, particularly. No one ever recognizes her as the one who first made you realize that women are not just mothers and wives, they are the driving force!"[10]

Yet Agnes believed that whatever a woman accomplished, she was incomplete without husband and child. Her need for male approval and affirmation was extreme. Although she considered herself unattractive, she made sporadic attempts to improve her appearance, to wear stylish outfits and hats that, someone observed, made her look as though she was on her way to speak at Barnard College (she had a penchant for feathers). She could be girlishly coquettish and could refer to Walter, tongue only partially in cheek, as "my lord and master."[11] The women in her family had believed in women's rights — Anna had carried a banner in suffragist marches — but only up to a point, beyond which they served the ambitions of the husbands in whose reflected glory they basked. The women she most admired — Isadora Duncan, Martha Graham, Lily Bess Campbell, Rebecca West — had succeeded professionally in their own right, but Lily Bess would die a spinster, Duncan's relationships with men were disastrous, and West's were painful. Graham chose art over life, and never looked back. Agnes insisted on both.

"I wanted it all," she wrote, long before the phrase became a cliché. "I wanted wifehood, motherhood and creativity in art . . . In the tremendous pride and exuberance of my present great happiness, I felt capable of encompassing all." But during her pregnancy, she had doubts. Could she overcome her lifelong self-absorption enough to consider the needs of a husband and child? Would Walter embrace fatherhood once he saw the baby? Would he understand and put up with the demands of her work, as she would have been expected to do if the situation were reversed? During his final leave in New York she had taken him to see *Oklahoma!,* his first exposure to her work. He said he loved the show, but did not comment on the dances. When she pressed him for an opinion, he disqualified himself on the grounds of being too close for objectivity. She pressed harder: had the dancing moved him? Not the way music did. The way Martha Graham's work did? Hardly. It did not take a Freudian to see that in her marriage Agnes had replicated her relationship with her father. If it was at times painful, it was, at least, a familiar pain.

Walter was proud of her, but he loved her in spite of her success, not because of it. Bill Hayden, another de Mille in-law, advised, "You are going to have to do some tall ordinancing not to fall into the miserable limbo of forgotten husbands of famous people, namely wives. . . . Just don't get too badly shot up trying to avoid it."[12] Walter managed the ordinancing adroitly. He would never become Mr. de Mille.

Agnes disentangled herself from *London Town* in November and sailed home. Walter had already found a job: assistant to Sol Hurok, the already legendary impresario. "We are for the first time knowing real domestic quiet," Agnes told a friend. "The first week I kept waking during the night and wondering how anyone could be so happy."[13] But the adjustments she and Walter faced were drastic. They had spent most of the past three years apart, and what little time they had spent together had been intensely emotional, nothing resembling normal life. He was starting over; she was the Queen of Broadway. Their combined experience with children was nil; and as parenthood approached, so did middle age. To further complicate the situation, the baby was born with a life-threatening illness.

Jonathan de Mille Prude was delivered by Caesarian section on April 20, 1946. He was of normal size and weight, but he had a rare intestinal malformation, Hirschprung's Disease, which made normal bowel movements impossible. The only treatment was to administer high colonic enemas to the screaming baby when the pressure of accumulated fecal matter built up. Periodically, violent vomiting and diarrhea dehydrated him to the point of requiring hospitalization and intravenous feeding. A crisis occurred about every five weeks; when it passed, the household lived in dread of the next one. When the baby was ill, Agnes said, "Walter would come home after a long day working at his office, wanting to have a nice drink with me in peace and quiet or see his son and have some fun; he'd hear a wail from the nursery and mix himself a martini, his mouth like a thread."

She also said, "What I got from childbirth was the sense of belonging to a race, being part of a big organic natural thing. Everything I'd done had been so full of effort! And here I was, without thinking about it, having produced a baby with eyelashes, joints, viscera . . . it just happened! Without answering a question! Or *counting!*"[14] During the first weeks of Jonathan's life, when only medical personnel were allowed to hold him, Agnes was shocked by the ferocity of her maternal instincts. Walter, she confided to a friend, was "very disturbed that he has so little paternal feeling, but I'm not worried about this. I've seen him with puppies and Jonathan has every bit that much charm."[15] Her efforts to accomplish the impossible task of satisfying husband, child, and ambition were heroic; "All parts of me," she would write, "are set against each other."[16] Rehearsals for a new show were to start in December, and she worried about how Walter would react to his first exposure to her obsessive working mode. To store up marital credits, she went to the country with him for three weeks, leaving Anna in charge of Jonathan and his nurse.

Her studio apartment had no room for a nursery, but there was a serendipitous solution. Anna was living alone (Margaret, now twice divorced, was living elsewhere with Judy), and health problems had curtailed her activities. It seemed practical, with Agnes needing more space and Anna less, for them to swap residences.

The building in which Agnes would live for the rest of her life was a brownstone at 25 East Ninth Street; it had once belonged to Washington Irving and, later, to Mark Twain. The eighth-floor apartment had high ceilings, large windows, two large bedrooms, a formal dining room, and a spacious living room that overlooked New York University. The atmosphere was informal; a brick fireplace, a grand piano, some antique dance prints Agnes had picked up in London and books, books, books everywhere set the tone. Agnes was partial to Victorian and French provincial antiques; she mixed styles and periods, insisting only that whatever she bought was the best. She had collected some good pieces of furniture, china, crystal and porcelain figurines, and a 1604 Swiss cabinet, her gift to Walter. There was also a small maid's room.

Before Agnes could go back to work, she had to find a reliable housekeeper. She imported Lily Cantello, who had been her maid in London. Lily's husband, Charles, came along as chauffeur and general handyman. With Lily and Charles in place, Agnes began preparing for a guest appearance with Ballet Theatre. She also resumed teaching her Acting for Dancers classes, in which every dancer in New York, hoping to be discovered and become the next Bambi Linn or James Mitchell, wanted to enroll.* Since *Oklahoma!*, every ambitious dancer and singer studied act-

* In an interesting reversal, the American Theatre Wing later sponsored a class called Dancing for Actors.

ing (as actors and singers tried to learn to dance) and Agnes's classes served as a sort of pre-audition sieve. When the dancer (now choreographer) Glen Tetley arrived for his first class, "I was about five minutes late, and I ran into a teachers' dressing room and threw off my street clothes and pulled on my tights — and this absolutely hysterical woman with her hair flying rushed into the room and without even looking at me just turned her back, threw all her clothes off and started pulling on tights and an awful old leotard. To my horror, I realized it was Agnes de Mille! Still without looking at me, she said, 'Would you please pull up this zipper, I'm so late for this class!'

"The class was Agnes doing de Milleisms from her ballets — teaching you to be the shy cowboy, how to be moon-faced, how to be Shucks and that sort of thing — or the strong, stern Western figure of masculinity. Or, on the other side, the sort of wooing of middle-American sweethearts. It was a lot of fun, a very interesting premise for a class. For her movement vocabulary, she used elements of American folk dance and tap dance."[17]

"Her classes were large," another student recalled, "maybe thirty people in a *huge* room, for an hour and a half. Most of us were trained ballet dancers, and what she taught was very new to us. She would have you do things like walk down the street in a big hurry, it was up to you to decide how you were dressed — you could create a character that way, with high heels or whatever. Or she would have you walk into a room where it was very dark, and there might be broken boards in the floor. She told us that the expressions that conveyed opposite emotions matched one another in physical appearance, like laughter and tears, and you would have to find a way to make it mean one or the other."[18]

On October 27, Agnes performed her original role in *Three Virgins and a Devil* with Ballet Theatre. Walter Terry wrote, "Her gestures of ardent piety, her stances of self-righteous determination and her wild alarm when she discovered her hips doing bumps and grinds (quite against her will) to the devil's satanic music were projected with the wonderful de Mille gusto. It was good to have her back again."[19]

t w e n t y - s i x

Brigadoon

Oklahoma! had opened the field of musical comedy dancing to serious choreographers. The best work was done by Jerome Robbins (*On the Town,* 1944), Helen Tamiris (*Up in Central Park* and *Annie Get Your Gun,* 1945 and 1946), and Michael Kidd, who won one of the first Antoinette Perry awards for his choreography for *Finian's Rainbow* in 1947. An identical award — there was a tie — went to Agnes, for another Gaelic musical fantasy: *Brigadoon.*

Lyricist Alan Lerner and composer Frederick Loewe had previously collaborated on three musicals, two of which were barely noticed; the third, *The Day Before Spring,* had run for five months in 1945. Lerner had grown up wealthy, privileged, and American; not yet thirty, he was a generation younger than Rodgers and Hammerstein. Loewe, an Austrian in his mid-forties, had been a musical prodigy as a child; his influences were the classics, Broadway, and the Viennese operettas of Lehar and Strauss, and his melodies were considered to be in a class with those of the great Jerome Kern. Like Agnes, Loewe had a gift for stamping the idiom of another culture with his own inimitable style, so that *Brigadoon*'s music and dances, while indubitably Scottish, were also recognizably Loewe and de Mille.

Lerner and Loewe were both small in stature. "Fritz" Loewe, who wore lifts in his shoes, boasted of having been a professional boxer, a gold miner, and a whorehouse piano player. He was excitable and rumpled, his most prominent feature a disproportionately large head. Alan Lerner was blond, blue-eyed, and debonair, but his gnawed fingernails, painful to see, betrayed the existence of private demons. He wrote lyrics with the same attention to details of character, story, and mood that dramatists give to their plays (a practice he would perfect nine years later in *My Fair Lady*), and he could agonize for a week over a single line. When the circumstances were right, the two men produced wonderful songs together — such as, for *Brigadoon,* "Come to Me, Bend to Me," "The Heather on the Hill," and "Almost Like Being in Love." But Lerner's sugary script made *Oklahoma!*'s seem cynical in comparison.

Two men from Manhattan, on a hunting vacation in Scotland, stumble into an enchanted 1747 village that comes to life for just one day in every hundred years. If any one of its inhabitants should leave on this magical day, the village will disappear forever. When the Americans arrive, the villagers are preparing for a wedding — but the bride, Jean, has chosen one suitor over another, and the rejectee announces that he is leaving Brigadoon. To prevent that catastrophe, the men of the town chase him and he is accidentally killed. Meanwhile, one of the New Yorkers has fallen in love with a local girl and must decide whether to stay in Brigadoon forever or leave, and never see her again. He chooses Brigadoon.

Oliver Smith, who designed the show, told Robert Lewis, its director, that he had stopped reading the script at the point where one of the strangers asks the twinkly old schoolmaster, "So you're all perfectly happy living here in this little town?" The old man replies, "Of course, lad. After all, sunshine can peep through a small hole." Smith said, "If I had read any further, I'd never have been able to design the show." Lewis met with Agnes to discuss, over martinis, "the problem of how to neutralize the operettalike goo in the story. The question we asked ourselves," said Lewis, "was, 'How do we set about killing Jeanette MacDonald?'"[1]

Like Elia Kazan before *One Touch of Venus,* Lewis was a seasoned director of plays but had never directed a musical. Unlike Kazan, Lewis understood movement, and he got along famously with Agnes. Working together, they devised antidotes to Lerner's whimsey: the spectacular sword dance that ended the first act, the violent chase that opened the second, and a powerful funeral dance.

Agnes had first experimented with Scottish dancing in 1930, when she outfitted Warren Leonard in a kilt as Bonnie Prince Charlie and took him to a Scottish dancer in Brooklyn for lessons. To ensure the authenticity of *Brigadoon*'s dances, she hired May Gadd, a folk dance specialist who had helped her with the running set in *Hell on Wheels* and also on *Oklahoma!,* and James Jamieson, a champion Highland dancer from whom the dancers learned the reel, the fling, and other traditional seventeenth- and eighteenth-century dances. Agnes then expanded and developed the authentic steps to serve her theatrical purpose — enlarging a small slide until it went halfway across the stage, or blowing a little jump up into an enormous arc. Some Highland dance movements translated easily, for example, into the battements and port de bras of ballet. When she added new movements, such as contemporary lifts, they were consistent with the original dances.

The cast was headed by David Brooks, Marion Bell, and Pamela

Britton, all of whom were relatively unknown. The small but pivotal part of Harry Beaton, the man who tries to leave Brigadoon, could have been created with James Mitchell, who played the role, in mind. Mitchell's finest moments came during the sword dance, which had historically been performed before a battle. In it, the warrior steps at great speed, on his toes, in and out of the blades of crossed swords on the ground. If his foot touches a sword, it means he will not survive the battle. Mitchell performed the rapid crossed-footwork and the high-cutting double and triple beats with stunning precision and grace; but what lifted his performance to another level was his passion. He *was* the dark, brooding, intense Harry Beaton. To expand his role, Agnes created the character of Maggie, who loves Beaton. Lidija Franklin, a Latvian with dramatic flair and a strong but delicate technique, played Maggie.

Mitchell had assisted with Agnes's *Carousel* rehearsals while he was still appearing in *Bloomer Girl,* and he was her assistant on *Brigadoon.* "The term 'assistant choreographer' is a misnomer," Mitchell said. "To be Agnes's assistant meant sitting beside her at all times. Bringing her a lot of coffee. Being asked to try something for her, so she'd see it on my body — or if she was working with a woman in a pas de deux, I would be the woman's partner. Being a sounding board — did I like this or that, did I think it worked? Rehearsing what she had done, so she could then come back and see it learned and performed. And holding her hand in the rehearsal hall, so she wasn't entirely alone. When she was very low, very troubled because the work was not going well, she'd go off and hibernate for an hour or a day and have a long think about things.

"Her rehearsals were *always* behind closed doors. *Nobody* was allowed in — not directors, producers, composers. She didn't want them to see anything in progress because they'd have *no idea* what the finished version would be like. As her assistant, I enforced that rule a lot: 'No, you can't see Agnes, I'm sorry, she's busy.'"[2]

Mitchell's talent, good looks, and sexual magnetism inspired love, lust, and a certain amount of spite among dancers of both sexes, but he was simply too decent and gentlemanly to make any real enemies. He was interesting company, knowledgeable about music and art and literature. With Agnes, he was a calming influence, the quiet voice of reason.

If he sensed that she was about to create a scene, he could say, "Let's take a break," take her off privately, and give her the perspective she needed. Walter, she said, was "the North Pole to my compass" — but Walter maintained a deliberate distance between himself and her work.[3] In that crucial dimension of her life, Mitchell was her closest confidant. It was an open secret that she adored him. Fifteen years after *Brigadoon,* she would still refer to him as "the core of my heart."[4]

In the dances, Agnes made sure that each singer and dancer wore an appropriate tartan and had a particular identity and activity. In the first dance, for example — a market scene in the village square, involving nearly the entire cast — one girl sold flowers, another carried a water bucket, a ribbon salesman plied his wares, assorted young people played courting games, and a blowsy fishmonger performed comical grand jetés.

Brigadoon's dances were even more integral to the gestalt of the show than *Oklahoma!*'s had been, or *Carousel*'s — in fact, the entire show seemed to be choreographed, so skillfully did Agnes and Robert Lewis grease the transitions from dialogue to music and dance, and back again. In staging the big musical numbers, Agnes led into them by intensifying ordinary movements, such as walking, with pantomime, then almost imperceptibly transforming them into constantly changing groupings, directions, and designs. Some patterns had the intricacy, though not the symmetry, of a kaleidoscope ("Through practice," Agnes wrote, "I have learned to project a whole composition in rough outline mentally and to know exactly how the dancers will look at any given moment moving in counterpoint in as many as five groups").[5] When the number was over, the actors held the audience's attention by executing some strong action, given to them by Lewis, while gradually resuming the dynamics of ordinary speech.

It is impossible to evaluate what choreography can contribute to a musical. "A good dance," James Mitchell observed, "can illustrate the emotional progression of a show more directly and specifically than the music and words. The composers saw that as taking the guts of the show away from them. They weren't always pleased when the choreography became as important as the other elements."[6] Agnes's suggestions went far beyond choreography on every show she did. It was she who persuaded Alan Lerner, who would have dispensed with dance entirely in his shows if it were feasible, to replace the superfluous dialogue that ended the first act with the sword dance. At its climax, Harry Beaton kisses his beloved passionately and then announces to the shocked townsfolk, "I'm leaving Brigadoon. The miracle is over." It was one of the most dramatic moments of the show.

According to Trude Rittman, rehearsal pianist on *Brigadoon,* "Alan and Fritz didn't trust Agnes. They thought, 'She is so much involved in the balletic aspects, she doesn't have the whole show in mind.' On every show, it was always a struggle for her. Rarely did she get what she needed—not just for herself but for costumes, for whatever she needed for her dance! We used to say that we had to be *doubly* as good as men in order to make it in the male-dominated theatrical world. It was marvelous that we had each other to exchange our private jokes and comments about all these men for whom we worked. We used to talk about how ridiculous Lerner and Loewe sometimes were with their women. Incredible! Fighting over girls, fighting over divorced women. Always a crisis. They loved each other, couldn't work with anyone else, but then they *hated* each other. Agnes was very often much stronger than these two men together. She would fight for her rights, and the creative aspects of certain things. They always felt, 'She's going overboard and ruining our show! It's not *her* show, it's *our* show!' Nobody won; they compromised."[7]

In the end, the show's cloying plot was redeemed by the music and movement: the chase, with Mitchell fighting, dodging, and running perilously along the branches of a great tree; the farcical postwedding number, with dancers assuming various poses of intoxication until the last man left standing teeters into a slow, turning fall; and "Come to Me, Bend to Me," in which Jeannie and her friends—typical shy, frolicsome de Mille virgins—dreamily pack her trousseau. The movement was modern, but parts of the dance reminded some critics of *Les Sylphides.* One wrote, "In the deep back falls and mild contractions of this dance, occurring in formations that have an aspect of rural ritual, modern dance is once again made easily acceptable."[8]

The stark, somber funeral dance, accompanied by the blood-curdling sound of bagpipes, lasted only three minutes, but they were stunning minutes. Harry Beaton's body is carried in and laid on the stage. Maggie enters, barefoot, bends over the body and exchanges her black shawl for Beaton's bloody tartan, which she displays accusingly to the villagers. She places the plaid on her head, throws one end over her shoulder, and paces inside a circle formed by the villagers; she is tight, tense, and proud — stiff-legged, body rigid, pounding her body like a drum with her fists, throwing her head back in anguish. As she passes each villager, that person's head drops in response. Agnes's notes were precise:

> Facing front, [Maggie] stamps her right foot four times as though knocking on a grave. Four small hornpipe rocking steps. Some repetition . . . slides to floor, uses contraction to get up . . . [She marks the rectangle that is the grave], pointing downward with right index and forefinger extended, body bent forward while she takes quick small steps backward . . . There's a low, pleading run around stage, clockwise, always facing front and slowly opening arms . . . everyone else rises as she passes . . . At end she buries face in right arm, bent over as weeping, and stamps right foot in a semicircle, left to right four times. Repeat. Run in clockwise direction to Harry's body and kneel, grieving across his body. On second half of bar, face front swinging clenched hands up over head — head back. Slowly lower hands, leaving right hand over eyes, left across stomach, and turn to left and exit.[9]

Three men then carry Harry's body off, accompanied by pipes and funereal drumbeats.

Brigadoon underwent only minor revisions out of town and opened at the Ziegfeld Theater in New York on March 13, 1947. Few musicals had ever received such unanimous critical praise for its songs, sets, staging, and performers — for everything, in fact, except the silly libretto. Most reviewers agreed that whenever the plot sagged, the dances revived it. Howard Barnes, writing in the *New York Herald-Tribune,* called the dancing "inspired . . . the key to the compelling quality of the entertainment."[10] The dances, Margaret Lloyd wrote in the *Christian Science Monitor,* bridged "the difficult gap between fantasy and realism. You cannot help suspending disbelief in a people suspended in time when by their dancing they prove they are alive . . . As sheer design, apart from their intrinsic relation to the action, the dances are a joy."[11] *Life* magazine ran three pages of color photos of the dances, declaring, "*Brigadoon*'s real brilliance lies in its Scottish dances directed by Agnes de Mille."[12]

After *Carousel,* John Mason Brown wrote in the *Saturday Review,* there were those who "believed they knew the mixture of rustic innocence and sophisticated pantomime, the attitudinizing, the gesturing, the head-wavings, the stretchings, the caperings, and in general the turnings of a chorus into a ballet which they had once hailed — and rightly prized — as the mark of Miss de Mille's originality." But in *Brigadoon,* said Brown, Agnes had "mastered a new language" and created dances that were "among the finest to have been seen on an American stage."[13]

On March 22, the *New York Times* published a dissenting opinion by Brooks Atkinson, who complained that Agnes used clichés, "shopworn remainders from the Isadora school. When the maidens join hands in a circle and start spinning they might be treading grapes, illustrating a Parthenon frieze or expressing joy."[14] It was the kind of remark that would ordinarily have infuriated Agnes, but her attention was elsewhere. Five days earlier, her mother had died.

Anna had had two warning heart attacks, the second in 1946. While Agnes was in Philadelphia with *Brigadoon,* stretched to the snapping point between show, husband, and child, Anna had had a stroke. When Agnes returned to New York she found her mother, barely able to speak, working on her nearly completed biography of Henry George — the culmination of fifteen years' work. Agnes, who had read the manuscript and felt that it could be improved by adding some personal details about George's family life, sat beside her mother's hospital bed and coaxed her into reminiscing about her childhood.* For the rest of her life, she would reproach herself for being unable to comfort her mother when she was dying. "I wasn't outgoing and loving," she said. "I couldn't do those primitive

* Agnes later added the reminiscences and wrote an introduction to the book. Published in 1950, *Henry George, Citizen of the World* has a clear, fluid style, but is more hagiography than biography.

things, take her in my arms and hold her. I couldn't *give* myself that much, because she'd *take* me."[15] Proximity to that force field was dangerous; intimacy could be a disaster.

Anna de Mille's death grip on her loved ones cannot be exaggerated. Asked a routine question about her marital status by a hospital admitting clerk, she had replied, twenty years after her divorce, "My husband's living with another woman." The mystified clerk asked, "Do you mean he's married again?" "You could call it that," Anna said.[16] A week before she died, she noted her wedding anniversary in her diary. She was, Agnes said, "undivorceable." Even from the grave, she continued to issue directives. In a memo attached to her will, she instructed her daughters to give her a simple funeral ("a cheap wooden coffin and little pomp and ceremony") and added, "Don't let an undertaker put anything over on you just because you may be emotionally upset."

Anna had instilled in Agnes a sense of obligation that she could never discharge. Her help had been real, and immeasurable. But Agnes had also succeeded in spite of the encumbrance of her mother's sacrifices. Even after she finally extricated herself from the cobweb of Anna's love, her mother expected unrestricted access to her life. Anna had a key to the apartment, which had been her own but now belonged to Agnes and Walter. "We'd be having dinner, and suddenly she'd be standing in the dining room door, sometimes with a guest! Walter was frantic, he stopped coming home to dinner. I said, 'Mother, you must ring the bell!' She said, 'But I'm not coming into your *bedroom!*' I had to tell her, 'It's our house!'"[17]

Agnes had been a dutiful daughter, but she had reserved her love for her father — in her mind, an unforgivable sin. Her mother's death sent her into a tailspin of guilt and its offspring, remorse. Obsessively, she wrote to dozens of her mother's relatives and friends, eulogizing Anna's life and recounting the details of her death. To Warren Leonard, married and living in California, she wrote, "You know how deeply rooted she was in my life . . . [A]ll I've done or succeeded in was made possible by her efforts and sacrifices. I wish there had been no tension between us. I wish I had been able better to share the great happiness that I've known in the last few years . . . I left very much undone [that] I regret with anguish."[18]

In April, Walter took her to Bermuda for a rest. That summer, she was to direct Rodgers and Hammerstein's next show. She had grave misgivings about both the script and the score; but she was the first woman and the first dance director, as choreographers were then designated on Broadway, ever invited to direct a major musical. If she turned it down, she believed she might not get another chance. In July, looking thin and weary, she was on hand with Rodgers, Hammerstein, Theresa Helburn, and Lawrence Langner to audition hundreds of actors and more than a thousand singers and dancers for what would be, by Rodgers and Hammerstein's standards, their first failure.

twenty-seven

Allegro

In the four years since *Oklahoma!,* nostalgia had contributed to the success of a half dozen musicals: *Bloomer Girl, Carousel, Up in Central Park* (Sigmund Romberg with Herbert and Dorothy Fields), *Annie Get Your Gun* (Irving Berlin), and the biggest musical hit of the 1947–48 season (due in large part to Jerome Robbins's choreography), Jule Styne's *High Button Shoes,* which opened on October 9, 1947. *Allegro* would open, anticlimactically, on the tenth. "*Allegro* had some marvelous things in it," Agnes said, "but they were like healthy patches in a diseased person."[1]

In a country where an artist is not valued for a body of work but is expected to set new records every time out, the pressure on Rodgers and Hammerstein after *Oklahoma!* and *Carousel* virtually guaranteed disappointment. Hammerstein, who had so skillfully adapted *Show Boat, Liliom,* and *Green Grow the Lilacs,* now attempted his first original book. It told the story of Joe Taylor, a doctor, from his birth through his childhood, adolescence, college days, and marriage to a woman who nags him into exchanging his ideals for money and status. In the last scene he sees the error of his materialistic ways and goes home to be a simple small-town doctor like his father.

When Rodgers worked with Lorenz Hart, his melodies matched the

jazzy rhythms and slightly acerbic taste of Hart's lyrics — which matched, in turn, the mood during the Great Depression. Rodgers and Hammerstein's songs reflected the lyricist's sunny disposition as well as the country's resuscitated optimism. They were pure vanilla — the flavor, according to ice cream manufacturers, that outsells all others in America. But their shows took on an increasingly moralistic and self-righteous tone; good conquered evil, and love conquered all. *Carousel*'s "You'll Never Walk Alone" is an inspirational hymn. "Soliloquy," in which Billy Bigelow envisions a son "as tall and as tough as a tree" and a daughter "pink and white as peaches and cream," perfectly embodies the sexual stereotypes of its day. *Allegro*'s "A Fellow Needs a Girl" sent the same message: "A fellow needs a girl to sit by his side at the end of a weary day/To sit by his side, and listen to him talk, and agree with the things he'll say."

Allegro's staging was as heavy as its message. An omniscient chorus, always onstage, spoke and sang directly to the actors and the audience — bridging the episodic scenes, commenting on the action, and conveying the thoughts of characters living and dead. The device had worked for the Greeks and, more recently, in *Strange Interlude* and *Our Town,* but it had never been tried in a musical. Instead of a conventional set, locales were suggested by lighting, platforms, and projections of photographic images on a huge screen that served as backdrop. Forty stagehands were required to shift sixty sets and an elaborate system of curtains, which changed from opaque to transparent according to the colors, angles, and intensities of the lighting (there were a record-breaking five hundred light cues). Props, furniture, and actors rode on and off the stage on a semicircular track, behind which were three levels of moving platforms. On this obstacle course of a stage, Agnes was expected to orchestrate words, music, movement, dance, costumes, decor, and lighting, while manipulating forty-one principals and almost a hundred more dancers, singers, soloists, and members of the chorus, many of whom (excluding the dancers) had neither training nor experience in movement.

Agnes seemed uniquely qualified for the job. In 1947, she was the best-known choreographer in the world; not even the great Balanchine had anything approaching her celebrity. She was knowledgeable about music, movement, costumes, sets, lighting, and stage managing. Although she had complained bitterly, during her recital career, about having to do it all herself, she claimed that, as a result, "there was nothing technical that could daunt or bewilder me . . . The theater was my tool."[2] But *Allegro* was a leviathan of a show, on a scale exceeding the grasp of any individual.

Rehearsals took place in three separate locations, for principals, singers, and dancers (not until *West Side Story*, ten years later, would performers be required to sing, dance, and act). If anyone could have found a way to attend all three simultaneously, it would have been Agnes; but as not even she could suspend the laws of physics, the rehearsals at which she was not present were supervised by her assistant, Dania Krupska, and by Oscar Hammerstein.

When a show was in rehearsal, Agnes saw little of her husband and even less of her child. She did not work at home — except in her head, before dawn. She had breakfast in a drugstore, away from the telephone and other interruptions, making notes while she ate. Mornings were for dance rehearsals, afternoons for the chorus. After that, to avoid interruption, she sometimes took a room at the Algonquin Hotel and worked there through dinner, returning to the theater to rehearse the actors until ten or eleven. When she got home, she made notes for the housekeeper about the next day before going to bed, usually with a headache.

Allegro's choreography alone was a herculean assignment, for the dances would provide a stylized frame for the show. In them, the hero learned to walk, fell in love, went astray in the wrong tempo, then got back on the beat — all in the style of the various time periods, beginning in 1905. The children's dances were performed by adults in children's clothes; as there were no children onstage as a reference point, the illusion worked. From her recent observations of Jonathan's first unsteady steps, Agnes fashioned "One Foot, Other Foot," which captured the suspense of maintaining balance and made the ironic point that we learn to walk in order to keep from falling down. There were also glimpses of something darker. As the children played games at recess, the music suddenly changed, and they huddled together for a moment that Agnes called The Weather. "They didn't know what they were frightened of, but they were terrified. It was real animal fear of whatever you wanted to read into it — war, drugs, crime, whatever. Then they broke up, but this thing haunted them, always."[3] The buoyant, sweeping dances captured the essence of childhood so faithfully that Gloria Wills, who sang the show's hit song ("So Far"), recalled, "Years later, when I had children, I kept seeing that number — the dancers in little short dresses, full of joy and the wonder of life. So beautiful, so exciting!"[4]

In the college sequence, a group of flapper-era students danced with comic awkwardness under the supervision of eagle-eyed chaperones; the scene then faded into fantasy, with the chaperones dead and the students, in evening dress, effortlessly achieving floating elevations and high lifts in a graceful ballroom adagio style.

In Act Two, the plot thinned to the point where only the dances held the show together. The most memorable of them expressed the essence of a familiar experience — in this case, the inanity of a cocktail party. Butlers and maids circulated with trays among the guests, who chattered "Yatata yatata yatata yatata yatata yatata yata," their heads bobbing rapidly up and down. Their voices gradually softened to a rhythmic background, over which individuals emphatically proclaimed nonsense words (Broccoli! Balderdash! Darling! Angel!) to the other guests. The movements were quick, the gestures nervous, the guests milling around until they were crushed together in a tight, claustrophobic circle. The repeated refrain was

> The years of a life are quickly gone,
> But the talk talk talk goes on and on and on and on and on,
> The prattle and the tattle,
> The gab and the gush,
> The chatter and the patter
> And the twaddle and the tush go on and on and on and on and on!

Agnes could manipulate a crowd of people on a stage so that the audience was simultaneously aware of the mob and of its individual members, each of whom had some distinguishing movement or gesture or expression. When the dancers had to act, her instructions were simple and direct ("Don't mug," she told them, "and don't muddy it up — don't shrug your shoulders and do three things at once").[5] And with the right actor at the right time, she could perform magic. Rufus Smith, who played the hero's football coach, said, "Never again in my life will I experience what it's like to stop a show cold, by doing exactly what she taught me: 'Never be big until it's time, and put off the time. Let the audience dangle in the wind, turning slowly.'"[6]

Agnes knew what would work theatrically, but she was better equipped to direct bodies than minds. Like the movie actors she had observed in her youth, she worked from externals, relying heavily on gesture and expression to convey emotion. But with the advent of what became known as the Stanislavsky Method, actors had begun to think in terms of motivation and subtext and to draw on their inner resources and experience. With their psyches as well as their bodies exposed, they needed more reassurance than any dancer, the embodiment of discipline, would dream of expecting. As James Mitchell, a dancer who was also an actor, observed, "Agnes didn't work as well with actors as with dancers, because the dancer is absolutely blank, and relies totally on the choreographer; he needs to be told *exactly* when and where to move. The actor has read the script, and has preconceived notions of how he'll play his part. Actors don't want to be told, 'Take five steps over there and stop, and then four steps this way.'"[7]

On *Allegro,* Agnes swam upstream against the sheer size of the show and against management's refusal to give her the authority that a director needs. When there were disagreements about casting, she rarely prevailed. She was not consulted about who should design the costumes and sets, but was merely informed that Lucinda Ballard and Jo Mielziner had been hired. It was, she believed, a matter of gender. "A male director is given a rather wide latitude," she said. "Let a woman put one foot amiss and everyone is ready to jump down her throat."[8]

Like its counterparts in the larger society, the almost exclusively male theatrical establishment viewed strong women with confusion and fear. Faced with the eternal women's dilemma — how to exercise power without alienating men — Agnes sought a champion. In her clashes with Rouben Mamoulian during *Oklahoma!,* Richard Rodgers had stepped into the breach. Oscar Hammerstein, a natural mediator, was a more lasting source of support. Not unreasonably, Agnes expected to be treated professionally as an equal, with the respect automatically accorded a man. At the same time, she wanted the reassurance, consideration, and protection of a powerful man. In a letter to Walter after *Carousel*'s New Haven opening, she related how she had told Hammerstein, "'I've things to say so stringent about my work that I don't know whether my pride will permit me to stand up in a meeting with Mamoulian and the Guild Board and say them.' He smiled and put his hand on my shoulder. 'You watch out what you say. You're talking about the woman I love.'"[9] She reported the incident proudly; a surrogate father had bestowed his approval.

Hammerstein considered Agnes's dances for *Allegro* some of the most brilliant he ever saw, but they could not make up for the weak score and the preachy, plodding book (someone suggested *Lento* as a more appropriate title for the show). Agnes's solution was to add more dances. Hammerstein's was to fix the unfixable book. He rewrote and rewrote, until Agnes could no longer keep up with the new scenes, songs, and dances. At that point, three weeks before the out-of-town opening, Hammerstein took over the direction (retaining much of what Agnes had done) and Rodgers the staging of the songs, leaving Agnes to concentrate on the choreography. In one of her most elaborate ballets, the doctor wandered in agony through a wilderness of suffering humanity. Rodgers, saying "It will wound the audience" ("I hope so," said Agnes), cut it. In its place, he ordered the heavily symbolic "Allegro" ballet, intended to show the madness of the urban rat race. The dancers, wearing Daliesque costumes with organs sewn on, moved frantically up and down, forward and back, turning and running and leaping dangerously on and off platforms, up and down steps, trying to avoid the treadmill; "If you didn't watch yourself," said one dancer, "you could get killed."[10]

In New Haven and Boston, the atmosphere was as tense as in the ballet. It was always hoped that a show would gain strength during its out-of-town engagement; the pressure concentrates the mind, and nonessentials may be pared away. But *Allegro*'s flaws were intrinsic. For all its technical splendor, it had no one to root for. Its hero was an idealized American small town — populated by good people, in melodramatic contrast to the neurotic, corrupt city folk. Joe Taylor was two-dimensional and dull. The dialogue was saccharine to the point of embarrassing the actors who had to speak it. Gloria Wills recalled her fiancé saying, after hearing the line "Give me a hanky. Thanky" at the dress rehearsal, "Honey, you're in a stiff. The show is a bomb."[11]

When *Allegro* opened at the Majestic Theatre in New York, Agnes stood at the back of the house, as was her custom at openings — mouthing every word, mirroring every emotion expressed on the stage, and seemingly about to go into an agitated dance of her own. She thought some of her choreography "strained."[12] But the show was by then beyond her or anyone's help. Reviews were sharply divided, but "pretentious" was the consensus. In *Theatre Arts,* Cecil Smith pronounced the show "acceptable only as an exercise in stagecraft, not as a work of art." The score was "sodden"; the story "piles cliché upon bromide and stock character upon contrived situation. . . . *Allegro* fails where *Our Town* succeeded, in discovering the ways by which the commonplace may be transmuted into the universal. . . . Joseph Taylor, Jr.'s life has little or nothing to tell us about our own lives." But Smith applauded "the ease and flawless design with which Miss de Mille brings mobility to these non-dancing [speaking and singing choruses]. . . . She deserves the Theatre Guild's appreciation for enabling the production to absorb these apparently indigestible lumps of massed humanity without calling attention either to her own mechanisms or to the shortcomings of the script. . . . No previous musical has approached *Allegro* in consistency of movement, expertness of timing and shapeliness of visual patterns."[13]

John Martin, still the country's most powerful dance critic, agreed. "*Allegro* has definitely made history," he wrote. De Mille "gave form and substance to material with little of either . . . [she] gives fragmentary scenes a unified progression of developments, like phrases in a composition, neatly and skillfully joined by transitions of which one is scarcely aware. . . . The general effect is of superb dominion, spatially and dramatically."[14]

Agnes was praised by *Dance Magazine* for creating "the illusion of space and depth far beyond the confines of the proscenium," and by the *New Republic* for giving audiences "a dancer's idea of what a musical play should be like . . . [de Mille] floats the play on the light, glittering feet of expert dancers."[15] According to Oscar Hammerstein's biographer, her great contribution was "a consistency of visual pattern, a frame of movement and rhythm, a continuity of design."[16]

She had made the elephant dance, but it was still an elephant. *New York PM*'s Louis Kronenberger called the show "an out-and-out failure . . . a hundred clichés of American thinking and emotion marched by in procession, on a very vast, very unhomey, very trick-lighted stage . . . The really strange thing [is] not that it's bad but that it's boring."[17] George Jean Nathan pronounced it "an awful letdown from its authors' previous works."[18] Nevertheless, *Allegro* ran for nine months on Broadway and toured for another thirty. Inexplicably, it also won Donaldson awards for its book, lyrics, and score.

Richard Rodgers considered the show a failure and allocated an unfair share of the blame to Agnes. "She is supreme as a choreographer," he would write in his autobiography, "but to our dismay we found that she was unprepared to take on the additional chores of directing the dialogue and staging the musical numbers."[19] Unmentioned are the weaknesses in the book and the score, and the unmanageable size of the production.

To Agnes, her father's was still the opinion that mattered most. "When my father saw *Allegro*," she recalled forty-five years later, "he said, 'that's a *very* good job, Agnes. I'm *very* proud of you.' And he said to Walter across the lunch table, 'We can be *very* proud of her.'"[20]

twenty-eight

Lizzie Borden, C'est Moi

In the cutthroat world of concert management, Walter Prude was known for his taste, sensitivity, and integrity. His clients, including such luminaries as Isaac Stern, Marian Anderson, Roberta Peters, Jan Peerce, and Andrés Segovia, adored him. His boss, Sol Hurok, had brought some of the finest musicians and dancers in the world to the United States. Hurok, an uneducated immigrant who operated largely on hunches and chutzpah, ruled his office with a heavy paternalistic hand, playing his employees off against one another with Machiavellian skill. They stayed because in the concert management business, Hurok had no competition.

Walter was the WASP in the Hurok office, the yin to Hurok's yang. "Hurok may have been jealous of the way Walter carried himself and was accepted," said Isaac Stern. "He would love to have been a reincarnation of Walter. He provided that ambience: class."[1] The care and feeding of delicate egos was part of Walter's job, but he had no intention of pampering anyone on his own time. At work he might go white with anger, but his control never faltered. At home, he showed his temper. He had moods. He was a hard-core pessimist and a hard-nosed perfectionist; coming from Walter, "not too bad" was high praise. Dancing did not interest him particularly, with the exception of Martha Graham's, and

while he respected Agnes's work, his lack of enthusiasm for it grated on her most sensitive nerve.

"William and Walter shared a kind of sardonic humor," said Mary Hunter Wolf, who knew both men well. "Like William, Walter withheld his approval. He put out very little, except in very special relationships. He mocked himself — he mocked the world, including Agnes's crises and her work, which he did not take seriously enough to suit her. He knew that she was an artist, but he rather enjoyed letting her know that to him it was a minor art form, lacking the mythic quality of Martha's."[2]

Walter's intelligence, sophistication, and wit would not have saved him from being obliterated by the power of Agnes's personality. But he was also contrary, stubbornly independent, and, in his understated way, as self-centered and strong-willed as his wife. Agnes wanted a man who would dominate her — an impossible task. Walter won that game because he refused to play it. His game was teasing, along the lines of "I only married you because I thought I'd be killed in the war."[3] "They would spar," recalled Agnes's niece, "*all* the time. He would tease her to death; I've seen her near tears. And then he'd say, 'Oh, Puddy,' or whatever little love words he had, and pat her. I know they had rough times together, I remember oblique references by my mother. But she was always his bride, even when they were fighting."[4]

Oliver Smith said, "Walter was not a milquetoast, he was Agnes's equivalent. He had a certain finesse that she didn't have. It's not true that he rarely liked her work — a little of that was teasing. He was extremely proud of her. But Agnes is a very demanding person, she eats up the air. Walter had to maintain his own identity. There was a certain struggle, a certain friction about that."[5]

From the year of her marriage through the rest of her life, Agnes had letterhead printed for three different identities: Agnes de Mille (choreographer), Agnes George de Mille (keeper of Henry George's flame), and Mrs. Walter F. Prude (wife and mother).* Juggling those hats without occasionally dropping at least one of them was beyond even Agnes's prodigious dedication, discipline, and energy.

The mentality of the time was not congenial to "career women" — a code phrase for an unnatural creature, sexually repressed, if not perverted — and no woman had a bigger career than Agnes. Ambition that was admired in a man was considered aberrant in a woman. The composer Morton Gould, Agnes's collaborator on her next ballet, said, "When my wife wanted to get a degree, people said, 'What will people think? Mrs. Morton Gould, working?'"[6] If a working wife had children, she was doubly damned, as a reflection on her husband's assumed inability to provide for his family, and as a negligent mother. If she made more money than her husband, as Agnes did for years, it was unlikely that the marriage could withstand the pressure. After *Bloomer Girl* Agnes had bought herself a mink coat, but Walter's pride was hurt when she wore it.

For Agnes, there was an even greater pressure, which she described years later in a letter meant to ease her friend Rebecca West's distress over her husband's infidelity. The letter addressed the dilemma that plagued West and Agnes and every other woman who wanted what men took for granted: a career and a lasting marriage. West's husband, Agnes wrote, got something from his mistress that his wife could not provide: inferiority. "That you didn't feel superior, that you craved his support and

* A fourth letterhead, for Agnes de Mille Prude, served a double purpose.

cherishing, that you felt weak and needful and dependent in many ways makes no matter. You are a person of towering mind and incandescent force — feminine too and fragile — no matter. You are creative — and I have yet to meet the man who can accept with grace and comfort creativity in his wife. Men can't. They want to. But they feel dwarfed and obligated — and no matter the depth of their devotion they tend to seek comfort and reassurance in lesser cronies or doxies . . . Men can't stand the continual reminder of power and they — in spite of their hearts — take up with transient and regrettable comforters. I don't know of an exception to this except Robert Browning." Her reassurance to West, and undoubtedly to herself, was "He may have been absent and remiss and annoying but he did love you. And he was very proud to share his life with you." She understood, she said, "where the anguish lay — my God, I've lived with it. Walter has girls — some I know about. I'm pretty acute. None of them his equal or mine. He tires and comes back — or rather, he never really leaves. . . . That's how it is, darling. Gifted women pay. There are compensations."[7] Elsewhere she would write that the husband of a creative artist resents her work because it "renders her at times independent emotionally . . . [the wife] must never for one moment let him think that her work is important compared with his, or his interests or even his hobbies. . . . He will develop the classic symptom of women's frustration, the black, bitter headache, and . . . partial or total impotence . . . he may in the end leave her."[8]

Agnes was proud of Walter's prestigious position with Hurok, and she served his ego in her fashion — trying not to work when he was at home, waiting until he was asleep to put her ear to the muffled speaker of her phonograph, with her music spread out on the floor around her. When she exploded with exasperation, he ignored her, knowing that her temper was mostly bombast and rhetoric. His displeasure was icy. Casual observers thought them totally unsuited — Agnes with her histrionic Shakespearean style, Walter more Oscar Wildean — but in private, she deferred to him as to no one else, and their friends recognized how his cool complemented her heat. "Walter's withdrawn attitude, holding himself aside emotionally, wasn't continuous," said Harold Taylor, Jonathan's godfather, "but at times it was frustrating. What made the marriage work was Agnes's determination, and the completeness of her love for Walter. And a sense of duty, almost, on Walter's part — a commitment to behaving as he knew a gentleman should behave."[9]

For practical as well as psychological reasons (Agnes understood, however grudgingly, Walter's need for autonomy), the Prudes moved in separate orbits and socialized, for the most part, with their respective professional colleagues. When they entertained, their orbits overlapped. They were gracious, considerate hosts. Alcohol and social intercourse were inseparable, the cocktail hour sacrosanct. Splendid meals were presented on a table that glittered in candlelight; some of the china and crystal and silver, lovingly collected over the years, was museum quality. Agnes took great pleasure in choosing the linens, arranging the flowers, and setting the table; "Every lettuce leaf on the table was important," recalled Kitty Carlisle Hart.[10] Agnes enjoyed holding forth and was spellbinding when she did so, but she was also genuinely interested in her guests, a highly accomplished crowd who cumulatively represented the arts and letters of their day. The elite salon resembled that of Agnes's Hollywood childhood — without the movies.

Agnes threw a big party every year on Christmas Eve, to celebrate the holiday and Walter's birthday. It was always crowded and colorful — the lighted trees, the presents, women in marvelous gowns, laughter and gossip and stimulating ideas, and music played and sung, often by world-class talents such as Leonard Warren or Isaac Stern, who happened to be friends of the Prudes.

Walter liked to flirt, even with guests in his own home, knowing that it drove Agnes wild ("And how are you, my spavined beauty?" was her greeting to a dancer whose motives she distrusted). "She used to point at the windows above restaurants," Dania Krupska recalled, "and tell me, 'You know, there are bedrooms up there, Walter takes so-and-so there all the time.' I would tell her it was a fantasy."[11] If he did have affairs — and there is no solid evidence that he did — he was discreet. Agnes's mother had forced the issue of her husband's infidelity, and lost. Agnes would issue no ultimatums; she would honor the pledge she had made in a wartime letter to Walter. She loved him, she had written, "in a way I never dreamed of loving any human. Without question. With fresh delight at every encounter. With pride. With deepest gratitude to life that I found a friend so true, so comforting, so challenging, so absolute. Honey, it's for life with me."[12] But it was never easy.

The object of her most intense jealousy was Mae Frohman, the smart, personable divorcée who ran the Hurok office. Every day after work, Walter walked the few blocks from the office in Rockefeller Center to Frohman's apartment. Martin Feinstein, another Hurok employee who was present, said, "Mae was all business in the office; otherwise, she was fun. We had dry martinis while we discussed the problems of the day — the attractions and the artists, and politics — and relaxed. When Walter and I got a little high on martinis, we would sit down at the piano and improvise what we called 'modern music' — four hands, banging away. We stayed til around seven o'clock. Walter always seemed to have time. He went home for dinner but frequently he went out with us afterwards, to a concert. Mae and Walter were very close, but I never even *thought* that they were having an affair."[13]

Walter's relationship with Mae Frohman was the subject of considerable gossip and speculation, but if adultery took place it was probably symbolic, not literal. In much the same way that James Mitchell shared the part of Agnes's life from which Walter was, albeit voluntarily, excluded, Mae was Walter's intimate in the part of his life that was closed to his wife, with whom he refused to discuss his work. Agnes sublimated her desire to murder Mae Frohman in her art, thus enriching what is generally acknowledged to be her masterpiece: *Fall River Legend.*

The idea of creating a ballet about Lizzie Borden, the New England Sunday school teacher who was accused of hacking her parents to death with an axe in 1892, had first been suggested to Agnes by Edward Sheldon, a playwright whose theatricality and tragic situation were reminiscent of Ramon Reed's. Although bedridden and blinded by osteoarthritis, Sheldon collaborated *in camera* with writers and actors of the caliber of Thornton Wilder and Lillian Gish, who revered him and sought his advice. In his elegant bedroom, where he lay with a black satin mask covering his face, professional actors performed full-length plays. He knew Agnes and her family situation well enough to wire, when *Rodeo* opened, CONGRATULATIONS UPON YOUR SUCCESS LAST NIGHT HOPE IT WILL LEAD TO

GREAT THINGS WHAT ABOUT MISS BORDEN HOW WOULD IT BE IF PARENTS WERE CRUEL CIRCUS CLOWN AND LADY LION TAMER OR VAUDEVILLE COMEDIENNES WHO TURNED LIZZIE INTO SLAVEY AND REFUSED TO LET HER DANCE WHICH IS HER AMBITION ALL THIS WOULD FURNISH CHANCES FOR LOTS OF DANCING AND PUT IT IN MEDIUM OF BALLET.[14]

Agnes had been sufficiently intrigued by the idea to take *The Trial of Lizzie Borden,* Edmund Pearson's definitive account of the case, along as reading material on her honeymoon. Since then she had choreographed five Broadway shows but only one ballet, *Tally-Ho,* and she wanted to strengthen her reputation as a serious (as opposed to Broadway) choreographer. *Fall River Legend* would be a psychological exploration of "the passions that lead to a violent resolution of the oppressions and turmoils that can beset an ordinary life."[15]

Agnes had always had a penchant for the macabre. When the snake devoured the frog at Merriewold, she had watched, unblinking. At the time of her appendectomy, she related with delight having found unexpected delicacies in a hospital icebox: "an eye, a fibroid uturus [*sic*], a piece of fatty tissue, and something from an autopsy."[16] Squeamishness was apparently unknown to her; after finding a nest of mice at Merriewold, she wrote, "Five newly-born, pink transparent pulsating bodies. Drowned them."[17] So it is not surprising that she found the story of Lizzie Borden, with its Grand Guignol aspects, appealing.

The central characters in the real-life Borden tragedy were the wealthy but miserly father, his second wife, and his daughter, Lizzie, a forty-two-year-old spinster. Although Lizzie was the only suspect in the crime and was shown to have both opportunity and motive (hatred and greed), the evidence against her was circumstantial, and the jury found her innocent.

Filtered through Agnes's psyche and talent, reportage became art. As she worked on the piece, she identified more and more with her heroine, who suffers from grief over her mother's death, sexual frustration, disillusion with her father, and resentment of her stepmother. "The inner Lizzie," she wrote, "turned out to be me."[18] On the surface, the repressed New England murderess seems the antithesis of the Cowgirl. But under the skin they were both misfits, yearning for approval and love and suffering from alienation. Both *Rodeo* and *Fall River Legend* contain scenes in which the heroine watches, alone and outside, while happy young couples dance. The Cowgirl, created when Agnes was in love and thought all things possible, finds a way to win. Lizzie is doomed from the curtain's rise.

A crucial change in the plot was suggested by the composer, Morton Gould, who pointed out that acquittal music and choreography were not dramatic. Agnes, who had already decided that Lizzie was guilty, exercised balletic license and convicted her. In the Prologue, Lizzie, identified only as the Accused, stands at the foot of the gallows as the jury foreman solemnly reads the description of the crime and the verdict. The audience then sees, in a series of flashbacks, her idealized childhood, her mother's death, her father's weakness, and the malignant stepmother who tells her suitor (the Pastor) that she is crazy, thus destroying her hope of love and precipitating the tragedy. The murders take place offstage; afterward, Lizzie dances with her dead mother in a poignant dream sequence in front of a bloody backdrop. In the finale she is condemned to death; as the curtain falls, she is once again alone, looking up at the gallows.

Lucia Chase, who commissioned *Fall River Legend* for Ballet Theatre, would eventually play the Stepmother. It was appropriate casting, for Agnes had been the company's stepchild since its inception. Chase was its mother (and banker); Oliver Smith (codirector from 1945) was its father; Antony Tudor, its artistic director and only staff choreographer, was its favorite son. Although Tudor's job would not have suited Agnes any more than she would have suited it, it rankled that she had never been offered a staff position. In 1944 she had called her relationship with the company "diseased";[19] the following year she had referred to the company's "interior evil" and Tudor's "sadism."[20] In 1946, she was a member of Ballet Theatre's artistic committee, along with Chase, Smith, Tudor, Aaron Copland, and Jerome Robbins. She was recuperating from Jonathan's birth when the company planned its European debut, and she asked the dancer Muriel Bentley to look after her ballets (*Tally-Ho* and *Three Virgins and a Devil*) on the tour. Bentley reported that rehearsal was insufficient and the opening performance bad. "As usual," she wrote, "your not being here has given them a great chance to toss your ballets around."[21] Furious, Agnes wrote to Oliver Smith: "If the only way to ensure adequate and careful rehearsal is to be present and scream and shout and throw tantrums then there's no advantage in my serving Ballet Theatre above any other company."[22] Both Smith and Chase replied promptly with concern, apologies, explanations, and promises to do better. They had already discussed *Fall River Legend* with Agnes, and wanted it very much. Placated, Agnes signed a contract.

In his score, Morton Gould made judicious use of loud, ominous dissonance; at other points he evoked hymns and the popular tunes of the period. Gould had a special feeling for Americana — and for Agnes. "I worked with other choreographers," he said, "who would say, 'You're violating my idea! I can't work with this music!' But with Agnes, all my recollections are positive. She was very eloquent; she would say something, and I would sit down and play. She sometimes had the harried, hassled look of someone in transit creatively, who is always cooking. She could be lusty, even bawdy, but she always had quality. Class. Even today, she always makes me feel slightly guilty, I don't know about what! She seems to be at such a higher level than I am, I always hope I'm behaving right."[23]

To convey the stifling atmosphere of the Bordens' New England House, Oliver Smith designed an ingenious set: the open frame of a tall house with doors, windows, a visible parlor, and a portion of a stairway, all on movable platforms. Turned around, it is a church. At the beginning and end of the ballet, the set splits apart and a section of the house becomes, with striking symbolism, the gallows. The platforms are manipulated by the dancers in full view of the audience — an unconventional and theatrically effective device.

The dance movement in *Fall River Legend* is economical and at times lyrical, with emotionally charged lifts, but the drama is conveyed primarily through pantomime. Each character has a signature gesture that is borrowed by other characters for purposes of comment and identification. When Lizzie speaks hopefully to the Pastor, she uses the gestures her dead mother used with her father. When she holds the axe, she reprises gestures she used with the Pastor. "I don't think out my best gestures," Agnes said. "I become that person and I do it. It comes from levels way down."[24] From the beginning, when Lizzie clasps and unclasps her hands as the sentence is read, the gestures are human, ordinary, and explicit. When the townspeople talk, heads move and hands flutter. When

Lizzie and her about-to-be victims rock in their chairs on the porch to monotonous, discordant music, the picture is classic American Gothic. One of the most striking gestures in all Agnes's work belongs to the Stepmother: each time she whispers her lies about Lizzie, she slowly, almost elegantly, rubs her cheek with the back of two fingers of her left hand, eerily expressing her malevolence.

Movements that portray intense emotions are exaggerated, distorted, and stark. Among the many unforgettable images are Lizzie's slow, grinding rotation of her hips, indicating her repressed hatred of her stepmother — who at one point perches on a man's hip like a vulture on a tree, for a better view of Lizzie's anguish. To claim her father as her own, not her stepmother's, Lizzie runs across the stage and jumps, knees tucked under her, onto his back. Later she clings to the Pastor's arm and leg as he tries to leave her. Her pathetic attempt to look out a window before the Stepmother draws the curtains underlines her desperation.

Even the props serve the story. The audience knows that Lizzie's mother is dead when her neighbors wrap a black apron around her. The dead mother's scarf is appropriated by the Stepmother, then reclaimed by Lizzie — her only assertive act until the murder. But the truly sensational prop is the axe.

The real Bordens were murdered with a hatchet, but Agnes's Lizzie uses a long-handled axe. When she innocently carries it out to the woodpile, her parents mistake her intention; they jump up from their chairs, frightened, and her shoulders shake with hysterical laughter. Later, in despair, she focuses on the axe, its blade buried in a tree stump. Mesmerized, thrilled, and repelled by what it represents, she runs her hands slowly over the phallic handle and repeatedly approaches it, recoils, and falls, tormented, to her full length.

Having sinned, though only in her thoughts, Lizzie receives absolution from the Pastor and is welcomed by his congregation at a prayer meeting. She dances a tender pas de deux with the Pastor and then a joyous, quasi folk dance with the members of the congregation. A normal life seems, for a moment, possible — until the Stepmother enters and whispers into the Pastor's ear that Lizzie is crazy. Lizzie's reaction *is* crazy; she writhes on the ground, then moves as though in a trance. When the Bordens go home, Lizzie carries the axe into the house; the parents jump up, terrified, Lizzie covers her face with her free hand, and the stage goes dark. When the lights go up again, the backdrop shows the parlor dripping with gore, its rocking chairs overturned.

Fall River Legend was in large part the result of Agnes's years in Freudian analysis, trying to work out her relationship with her parents. In Lizzie's dream dance with her beloved mother after the murder, she shakes her head compulsively, brushing tears ("of blood," Agnes said) from her eyes. Expecting her mother's approval, she gets her wrist slapped for having bloodied her petticoat. "When [Lizzie] knows she is damned," Agnes wrote, "a transference takes place. Since she has murdered, she becomes the adult and she picks up her mother in her arms to comfort her like a baby. She has become in fact the mother figure. . . . The murderess, Lizzie, cradles her mother with infinite unavailing love until they drift apart into mists of forgetfulness."[25] She may as well have written *Lizzie Borden, c'est moi.*

The next scene opens in chilling silence. Under a violent red sky, townspeople run onto the stage and stand motionless, staring at the house. The Accused comes into view inside, in shock. She opens the door and runs downstage with a silent scream, signified by the staccato cupped hand movements that Agnes had borrowed from Martha Graham for *Oklahoma!,* and accompanied by sudden crashing, dissonant chords — a hair-raising moment. In the final scene, the Pastor tries to comfort her but then leaves her alone under the gallows. Nora Kaye, for whom the role was created, played it for hysteria; other Lizzies have awaited their fate with resignation.

Nora Kaye had joined Ballet Theatre in its first season as a member of the corps de ballet, but she soon established herself in the works of Antony Tudor as a dramatic ballerina par excellence. Kaye was short, dark-haired, with features that were too strong to be beautiful. She had broad shoulders, a short torso, long, slender arms and legs, a technique of steel, and a remarkable ability to project emotion. If not for her high, nasal New York accent, which could have been the prototype for the Judy Holliday character in *Born Yesterday,* Nora Kaye might have become one of the great actresses of her time; instead, she was known as the Duse of the Dance. As Lizzie, she projected a quality of foreboding that deepened and darkened the ballet.

Kaye's parents were Russian Jews, her background worlds away from Lizzie Borden's — but she was also undergoing analysis, and she had an intellectual as well as an instinctive understanding of the ballet. "There is an episode," she wrote in a newspaper article, "in which Lizzie appears to be thwarted at every turn. The balletic movements are closed in, tight, the shoulders are not quite free. The line itself may not be broken but the phrasing is. However, when Lizzie dreams of her life as she would live it, the academic steps become freer in attack, the shoulders lift, flow is present. I believe that every movement, gestural or pure balletic, must serve the characterisation. For this reason [the role] is as demanding as a purely classical role."[26]

Kaye was ill on the opening night of *Fall River Legend,* and Alicia Alonso danced, brilliantly, in her place. But from Kaye's first performance in the role, it was hers; her interpretation was the benchmark for all the others.

Agnes was not able to work with the dancers who would perform *Fall River Legend* until three weeks before it was to open in New York — because, she said, she would not leave her family to accompany the company while it was on tour. Jonathan, already undersized, had begun to lose weight, and the winter of 1947–48 was a succession of crises, sleepless nights, hospitalizations, consultations with specialists, and discouraging prognoses. In any event, it was Agnes's custom to do the preliminary creative work with the dancers with whom she felt most secure, with the understanding that if they were not right for her current project, she would use them when she could. They then taught the movement to the dancers who would perform it — in this case, Ballet Theatre's personnel when they returned from the road. It was not an ideal arrangement.

During those three pressurized weeks, nineteen other ballets, many of them new, were in rehearsal, and a dozen choreographers competed for the time of the exhausted dancers. Agnes complained that Tudor, who traveled with the dancers, had had time to rehearse them on the road. But there was never enough time for Tudor, whose working pace was glacial. He got what he wanted by threatening to withdraw his ballet — and meaning it. Agnes's threats were empty; to her, withdrawing a ballet was tantamount to infanticide. Her tactic was persistence, which sometimes backfired. "We all poked fun at Agnes," said a member of the company, "because she was, a lot of the time, a very laughable character — her intensity, and her abrasiveness."[27] Morton Gould listened to her endless complaints about Lucia Chase until he lost patience and told her, "We have a world premiere coming up; short of fascism taking over the United States, don't call me until after the opening!"[28]

Tudor's work had been a mainstay of Ballet Theatre's repertory and reputation since *Pillar of Fire* premiered in 1942, and he was a major influence in the contemporary ballet scene. But in the larger world, he was unknown. He had choreographed two Broadway shows, neither of them memorable. In 1948, although no one could have known it at the time, his most productive period was over. His personal life had been in disarray since Hugh Laing, his longtime lover and muse, had married Diana Adams (the marriage would be brief; Tudor's relationship with Laing would resume and continue until his death). His new work, the monumental but flawed *Shadow of the Wind,* opened on April 14, 1948, and vanished forever after six performances. So when *Fall River Legend* opened on April 23 to mixed but generally positive reviews, Tudor, whose work also had a strong Freudian flavor, was in no mood to be gracious. He had always viewed Agnes's success much as Agnes viewed Cecil's, with envy and contempt. Now he publicly accused Agnes of plagiarism, driving another nail into the coffin containing their friendship.

In the *New York Times,* John Martin pronounced *Fall River Legend* "the revelation of a woman's soul . . . beautifully consistent, an ingenious and intuitive melodrama that not only makes the pulses beat rapidly but draws tears more than once." The Accused, he said, is "such a part as actresses dream of and seldom achieve . . . perhaps the greatest dramatic role in the entire repertoire. . . . Good, spellbinding, tear-pulling, hackle-raising drama, decidedly unusual in the world of the ballet."[29] At the other end of the critical spectrum, Cecil Smith wrote that Kaye's portrayal "surpasses the material itself, which is utilitarian rather than original and inspired."[30] But as Agnes herself would point out nearly thirty years later, "Even critics who hate *Fall River Legend* are quiet when Lizzie picks up that axe and walks into the house . . . it gets them every time."[31]

t w e n t y - n i n e

Gentlemen Prefer Blondes

In October 1948, the two-and-a-half year-old Jonathan was operated on at Children's Hospital in Boston, and the malfunctioning section of his intestines was removed. From the hospital he was moved to a convalescent home in Boston, where he remained for months. Agnes made the six-hour train journey to Boston on Sunday nights and spent Mondays, her day off, with her son. During the rest of the week she rehearsed the road company of *Allegro* and staged an opera.

Of all the theatrical endeavors in which Agnes was involved, opera offered the broadest scope for her sense of drama and visual effect, her musicality, and her feeling for movement. *The Rape of Lucretia* would be her only opportunity to direct one. The music was by Benjamin Britten; the book, by Ronald Duncan, was a modern treatment of a sixth-century legend. Britten, Duncan, and John Piper, the set designer, were English, and the opera had premiered in England in 1946.

The plot had enough love, lust, jealousy, violence, and death for one of Cecil's movies. The virtuous Lucretia is the only woman in Rome who has remained faithful to her husband while the men are at war. The rapist, Tarquinius, commits his evil deed on a dare. Although her husband

refuses to blame the victim, the innocent Lucretia blames herself and commits suicide.

The script called for just eight singers, including Robert Rounseville, Marguerite Piazza, Brenda Lewis, Emile Renan, Giorgio Tozzi (in his first leading role), and Adelaide Bishop. "Agnes told us she was exhausted from taking Jonathan to Boston for treatments," said Bishop, "but she didn't seem so to us. It was *we* who were exhausted, by her energy. She was meticulously prepared; she got the best out of you, even though you may have felt you were being beaten to a bloody pulp. One sensed that she had a *will* that stood out like embossing."[1]

Agnes departed from the operatic convention of having a singer complete a gesture and then simply wait for the music to end. Kitty Carlisle Hart, who had sung on Broadway but never in opera, played Lucretia. "Agnes used movement for dramatic effect," Hart said, "so that every move was timed with exact notes in the music. She asked us to do things that no opera director would ever ask us to do. She took no notice of singers' insistence on standing still to sing high notes — the fact that you might have a high C coming up, or that you had to deliver your B flat at the end of the aria. We had to accommodate the singing to the acting. Instead of sedately walking around the stage while we sang, we were *acting, moving, performing!* We were *thrilled* to do these things! There was one moment when Tarquinius was kneeling and I tried to run past him; Agnes had me fall backwards over his shoulder and he rose, draped me over his shoulder — both of us still singing! — took me to the bed and threw me on the bed. That was quite a feat for two singers, but we did it!" In the script, the rape scene was little more than a footnote. Agnes's version, according to Kitty Hart, was "the longest rape scene in history — it went on for about fifteen minutes. At one point I stood on the bed, holding his sword as though I would cut him in two."[2]

The Rape of Lucretia opened on December 29, 1948, at the Ziegfeld Theater. Audiences that arrived expecting sex left disappointed, for it was really a ritualistic, symbolic, rather religious piece — too highbrow for the Broadway crowd, too low for opera purists. Critics slammed the libretto, but most of them praised the staging. *New York Times* critic Olin Downes wrote one of the most favorable reviews, but reversed himself ten days later. "The scales fell from our eyes, and the wax from our ears," he wrote; "we were taken in by a brilliant production of as arrant a piece of musico-dramatic twaddle as has been visited upon the public for years." Lest any reader mistake his meaning, he went on to call *The Rape of Lucretia* "a pretentious farrago, clothed in the appearance of intellectuality and sophistication."[3] The show closed the next night, after twenty-three performances.

Agnes still took class almost daily, although her public performances were rare. In 1949, she saw her analyst two or three times a week, choreographed a Broadway musical, planned her next ballet, organized and performed in a star-studded benefit for the Henry George School, and ran her household. It was not in her nature to put her career second to anything — but if anything rivaled it in importance, it was Jonathan. Every time she did a show, which meant working sixteen-hour days and spending weeks out of town, it seemed to her that Jonathan forgot her.

In her spare time, still driven by her mother's injunction to "do something," Agnes worked on her autobiography. She had made herself into a dancer, but she was a born storyteller, and language was her natural element. At the age of ten, she had written in her diary as a writer writes, intoxicated with language, arranging words to make life make sense. In her youth she wrote poems and short stories, and at twenty-five she published an article, "Acrobatics in the New Choreography," in *Theater-Guild Magazine.* Over the next fifteen years she had written profusely, mostly in the form of letters to her mother and Walter. After *Oklahoma!,* publishers heard her knowledgeable and entertaining speaking style on the radio and began hounding her to write a book.

During her pregnancy, she began writing her memoirs. She wrote in longhand, in composition books and on hotel stationery, napkins, and scraps of paper. She wrote on buses and trains, in subways and drugstores and dressing rooms, even in doctors' offices and hospital waiting rooms. In 1946 she tentatively showed some pages to an editor friend, who assured her, "You are a writer. I'm so glad that the hesitations and uncertainties you felt about it do not show in the writing, which seems utterly easy, straightforward and clear."[4] Without telling Walter, she continued to write, in bits and pieces, what would become *Dance to the Piper.* But in the fall of 1949, work on the book had to be fitted in around rehearsals of *Gentleman Prefer Blondes.*

ထ

It was Oliver Smith's idea to make a musical about Lorelei Lee, the ditsy flapper whose transatlantic search for a sugar daddy had been chronicled by Anita Loos in her 1924 novel.* Smith, who would design and coproduce the show, was well on his way to becoming the dean of theatrical design; in addition to *Brigadoon,* his Broadway credits included *On the Town, Billion Dollar Baby, High Button Shoes, Look, Ma, I'm Dancin',* and *Miss Liberty.* The other members of the creative team also had solid track records: composer Jule Styne, lyricist Leo Robin, librettists Joseph Fields and Anita Loos, and costume designer Miles White. The director was John C. Wilson, possibly the last of the producer-directors who really knew and loved the theater. Wilson had produced the shows of Noël Coward, Cole Porter, and Alfred Lunt and Lynn Fontanne; he had

* The book had also been the basis of a play and a silent movie.

produced *and* directed *Bloomer Girl,* during which Agnes had come to like and respect him. Except for his sexual preference, he was exactly her type: a tall, handsome, urbane, dignified, and amusing gentleman who wore beautiful clothes and used a long cigarette holder, like a character in a Coward play.

Gentlemen Prefer Blondes was to be a glitzy version of the 1920s-style musical comedies that it satirized. A promising young choreographer named Gower Champion had just staged *Lend an Ear,* a clever revue that spoofed the same period and style, and most of the members of the *Blondes* production team wanted Champion to choreograph their show. Oliver Smith pulled rank; dance was his field, he was co-director of Ballet Theatre, and he wanted Agnes. Everyone else, including Agnes, thought she was wrong for it, but Smith prevailed, and Agnes was ultimately persuaded by the most lucrative terms: $2,000 a week, plus two percent of the gross box office receipts.

The wild card in the show was a tall, twenty-eight-year-old platinum blond with big eyes and a funny voice that veered from little-girl squeak to husky baritone, on whose unproven talents the venture would live or die. Carol Channing had been performing for a decade, but she had received little notice until *Lend an Ear,* in which she played "this huge girl who thought she was cute and little. All the other girls were dainty, cute little flappers up to my shoulder, and we all had cloche hats on. Anita Loos and Jule Styne came to see it, and Jule said he went home afterward and wrote my 'Battle Hymn of the Republic': 'Diamonds Are a Girl's Best Friend.' And Anita said, 'That's my Lorelei!'"

Yvonne Adair and Jack McCauley had featured roles, but the show belonged to Channing. "It was a *ludicrous* piece of casting," she recalled. "I'm six-foot-one in heels, and Lorelei was a *little* girl — the cutest, most babyish flapper of the twenties, five-feet-two, eyes of blue. But Anita Loos said, 'I don't *want* the prettiest little girl in town, I want a comedienne's comment on it.' And Agnes thought that was just great! She said, 'That just makes the satire all the more pointed!' She knew I had a fix on the character, and she was willing to go along with it. Lorelei had the brain of a pea, but she also had the brain of the president of General Motors. She brought a bit of virginity to every man she met — and for every bit of virginity, she got a diamond. Dumb like a fox. She was really a little ho-ar, but with a Girl Scout quality."

Agnes staged Channing's two big comic numbers, "Diamonds Are a Girl's Best Friend" and "A Little Girl from Little Rock," in which, said Channing, "Leo Robin's fantastic lyrics told the story of a barefoot bumpkin from the foot of the Ozarks who became one of the richest women in the world. Agnes had the *nerve* to let me stand stock stone still and let those lyrics sink in. When we did 'Diamonds,' Agnes said, 'This is a standup comedy routine — I'm supposed to choreograph that? You can't!' We had to hold thirty-two musicians in midair, so the laughs wouldn't cover up the punch lines. Agnes said, 'Just stand still. Don't move.' Every other choreographer I've known doesn't understand how powerful that can be. They'll say, 'How long are you just gonna stand there and not do anything?' I would say, 'But I'm acting!' And they'd say, 'Well, aren't you gonna move an arm or a leg or something, so there won't be a stage wait?'

"In the 'Little Rock' number, when I sang 'Like the one who done me wrong,' Agnes put a little bump in to show that Lorelei enjoyed every minute of being done wrong. We couldn't do a forward bump in those days; we had to do a sideways bump, and that was wonderfully funny. Agnes said, 'How does Lorelei walk? Now do it backward, and that'll be your exit.' John C. Wilson said, 'Take that walk out, Carol, we don't want you to walk that way, it's overdone!' And I remember Agnes yelling out from the black depths of the theater where I couldn't see her, '*Why not?* My God, that's what's so funny! It's a cartoon character!'

"Agnes would stand there with that wonderful look on her face and say, '*Give* me the character!' She'd let it *sift* right into her. She said, 'Try skipping.' So we tried it, and I skipped so dainty, as dainty as I possibly could, and tried to be a weenie, weenie girl. She was like a little girl at the zoo with me — push the elephant and see what it does. Sometimes she sat in the audience with my father during rehearsal. She was so enthusiastic, she'd say, 'Look at that!' and she'd swat him on the knee. I would just *talk,* and Agnes would laugh her head off! My first starring part, and she believed in me."[5]

Agnes had talked John C. Wilson out of cutting her Civil War number from *Bloomer Girl*, but she was overruled when it came to some of her favorite numbers for *Blondes*. Most painful was a fiasco involving Muriel Bentley, a Ballet Theatre soloist whose comedic and dramatic talents Agnes had used to great advantage in *Tally-Ho* and *Fall River Legend*. Agnes had turned Ballet Theatre dancers into Broadway stars in the past, and she intended to do the same for Bentley, in the same way: by building up her role until she became an actual character in the script. It had worked in previous shows because of the excellence of both the choreography and the dancers — Joan McCracken in *Oklahoma!*, Pearl Lang, Annabelle Lyon, and Peter Birch in *Carousel*, Lidija Franklin in *Brigadoon*. But although the show-stopping numbers that featured those dancers sometimes advanced the plot, they tended to shift the audience's attention to an entirely new subplot revolving around an unfamiliar character. It was a dangerous tactic; even when her contributions improved the show, the authors' appreciation was tinged with resentment. In *Blondes*, it blew up in her face.

Before rehearsals officially began, Muriel Bentley underwent seven weeks of strenuous preparation. Her big number was a variation on a concert piece Agnes had done with Warren Leonard — a burlesque of an adagio number, popular in the nightclubs of the 1920s. It required some violent acrobatics, and Agnes arranged for Bentley and her male partners to learn the technique from an expert. According to one of the men, "Muriel was black and blue from being thrown through the air, twelve to fifteen feet, halfway across the stage. You can just smell from the beginning what's going to be cut. We smelled it."[6] The men may have smelled it, but Bentley smelled only the imagined fragrance of impending Broadway stardom.

Without consulting Anita Loos, Agnes wrote lines for Bentley and her partner, Peter Birch, to speak. When Loos found out, she exploded. Agnes called in Oscar Hammerstein to back her up, but to her surprise, he agreed with Loos, pointing out that the lines were not only irrelevant to the rest of the play, they set up a new romantic situation in a show that already had three love interests. Agnes cut the lines, but there was a more serious problem. With the exception of Oliver Smith, nobody on the creative team had wanted Muriel Bentley in the first place. Agnes had forced her on them, as she had forced other unconventional-looking dancers (like herself) on other producers. This time, she had overplayed her hand. Bentley had great presence and she was a beautiful dancer, but her face was a character face, handsome and dark and "ethnic," the code word of the day for Jewish. Agnes had miscast her as a vivacious, playfully sexy nightclub entertainer. And Bentley was not comfortable in the unfamiliar milieu of Broadway, where jazz and tap and modern dance were the lingua franca. She needed to get looser and softer; instead, she tightened up. Levin and Loos and Wilson disliked her number, and liked her even less. "They didn't think Muriel was sexy," said Oliver Smith. "She didn't meet their standards of pulchritude. I don't think they wanted the dancing to ever get serious. Agnes wanted a certain serious quality in it. There always was that tug of war. None of them knew anything about dancing — they never went to the ballet, they didn't know anything about modern dance."[7] Instructed to get rid of the dancer and the dance, Agnes had no recourse. In Philadelphia, she broke the news to the shell-shocked Bentley, whose confidence and career never fully recovered from the trauma.

Bentley was replaced by Anita Alvarez — a tiny, pert modern dancer who had been a big hit in *Finian's Rainbow*. Agnes devised a new number for her, "Mamie Is Mimi" — a jazzy nightclub routine in which she kicked off her shoes and wiggled and danced on a flight of steps while two tall, elegant black men in white tails and top hats tapped their hearts out. They were Honi Coles and Cholly Atkins, an established vaudeville team whose livelihood had, ironically, dried up when *Oklahoma!* had ended the vogue for tap dancing in movie and stage musicals. For *Blondes,* they adapted one of their own routines to Jule Styne's tune. "Agnes added her choreography to our choreography," said Coles, "and it swung!"[8]

Agnes greatly admired the artistry of Coles and Atkins, but she made no secret of her belief that the show itself was a vulgar enterprise and that, artistically, she was slumming. When Jule Styne requested that she choreograph the "Sunshine" number "in one," with the whole chorus at the very front of the stage, her reply, Styne related with disgust, was "Oh, I think that's just so *vaudevillian!*"[9] She did do the number, so well that it was a highlight of the show, but her attitude was unchanged. "*Blondes* made me a fortune," she said, "and my father said, 'as long as you know how bad it is, that's all right.'"[10]

Jule Styne's volatility matched his formidable talent. According to Carol Channing, "Jule's credo in life is 'The one that yells the loudest is the one that wins. I will commit suicide if you don't do what I want!'"[11] Oliver Smith, possibly breaking his own record for understatement, said, "Jule has a very excitable nature. He wasn't a great fan of Agnes's work."[12] Like any powerful personality, Agnes had her disciples and her detractors, and Styne expressed the collective opinion of the latter group. "Agnes never thinks about how good the show is," he declared. "She thinks about how good Agnes de Mille is. She was a Take Charge. She mixed in on direction, she mixed in on a lotta areas. . . . Not meaning to hurt, but just flaunting her know-how. She wrote dialogue for the show without consulting anybody! It had nothing to do with the show! It's *her ball game* when she's the choreographer! And you better damn well know it! *Agnes de Mille* — you have to say both words! Agnes can only remember what she wants to remember. Anything that's wrong with Agnes, she don't wanna remember. A lot of people in the theater respected Agnes, but they didn't like her."

Styne claimed to admire her professionalism, but her manner put him off. "Agnes always let you know that there were a lotta things you wouldn't understand if she told you," he said. "She had an authoritative way of speaking — the Grande Dame has walked into the room. Queen Mary. Everybody saying Oh Agnes, darling! That's the only side of her I ever saw." Styne, whose lack of tact rivaled Agnes's, declared, "de Mille's execution never amazed me. She used *all* styles and called it hers. Her dances were the wrong dances for that show. The show had a jazz score. *Blondes* was a hit in spite of Agnes."[13] But even Styne liked the ballet that Agnes staged in the Bois de Boulogne. In the park were nursemaids with babies, governesses, children playing with hoops, all cooing like doves, in harmony, to Hugh Martin's arrangement of a simple melody. Against this background, a tourist and a taxi driver danced and pantomimed a charming duet. Walter Terry wrote, "The most affecting dance number in the show had nothing whatever to do with the plot but as an isolated pas de deux, this dance of an American girl with a Parisian taxi driver represented Miss de Mille's choreographic direction at its best." He praised the ensemble sequences, "particularly the second-act curtain raiser with its view of a group of legs rising in 'releve' along with the curtain," but thought that the other dances "ranged, choreographically, from the adequate to the pleasant. In 'Mamie,' I couldn't decide whether [Alvarez] was supposed to be straightforwardly provocative in her dancing or concerned with satirizing dancing of the 'hot' school, and I am inclined to believe that neither Miss de Mille nor Miss Alvarez was sure."[14]

Other critics rendered harsher judgments; John Martin deemed it Agnes's "least successful job."[15] But the show's good spirits and fun and, most of all, Carol Channing, made it a runaway hit, and Agnes was already looking ahead. Cole Porter's *Kiss Me, Kate,* about to begin its second year on Broadway, promised to be the biggest success of Porter's career, and he wanted Agnes to direct his next show.

thirty

Dance to the Piper

For Cole Porter, *Out of This World* was a relatively brief footnote between *Kiss Me, Kate* and his next hit, *Can-Can.* For Agnes, it was all too reminiscent of past defeats.

Her *Allegro* experience had not lessened her desire to establish herself as a director, and a show with music and lyrics by Cole Porter, on the ever-popular theme of "what-happens-when-a-god-turns-himself-into-a-mortal," seemed promising. As it turned out, there were two insurmountable problems. The first, not uncommon and often fatal in the theater, was the book. A half dozen doctors, including Agnes, worked to save it — but although the beauty of the production was worthy of the gods, the script reflected only human imperfections. The second problem was that Porter and Arnold St. Subber, a co-producer, hired Hanya Holm to stage the dances.

Choreographer Holm had worked with Mary Wigman in Germany before moving to New York to open a Wigman School, and where, six years later, she briefly had her own company. She was considered one of the great teachers of modern dance, but Broadway was not her métier. Nevertheless, she had done a fine job with *Kiss Me, Kate,* and Porter quite naturally wanted to use her again.

Agnes respected Holm's concert work and wanted to give her the kind of protection from management that she herself had never enjoyed. But *Kate* had made the two women rivals. Their temperaments were antithetical, and the Germanic Holm did not appreciate Agnes's autocratic manner or her sense of humor. "It's hard to imagine them in the same room," said one of the producers, "let alone working on the same show!"[1]

As director, Agnes focused her attention on the staging. "She used movement to link certain things together," said choreographer Bella Lewitzky, a dancer in the show. "She staged movement scenes with *great* dexterity and brilliance — I watched her work absolute miracles with sweeping movements of chorus, dancers, and principals, and she would do it like on the moment. She could take eighty-two people on the stage and make stage formations that were absolutely magical. She could sweep everybody in the cast — it's just a wonder she never used the stagehands — into a finale that brought the house to its feet."[2]

World required a great many dances, and Holm, who worked very slowly, soon fell behind schedule. Informed that Holm had not yet set any of the songs, Agnes set some herself, which Holm did not appreciate. Meanwhile, the show was sinking under the weight of its script. Every week it became clearer to all concerned that not even a god could save it.

If Walter did not always take Agnes's complaints as seriously as she might have wished, he could be protective and supportive when she was in real trouble. During the hysteria leading up to the out-of-town opening, he dropped in on a technical rehearsal that had been interrupted by an onstage argument between Agnes and Lemuel Ayers, the designer and coproducer. Ayers was crouched at the base of a pedestal on which stood the handsome George Jongeyans (known as George Yumyum), who played Jupiter. Ayers was insisting that Jongeyans stay on the pedestal during a scene with the heroine. "He can't stay up there!" Agnes protested. "He's yards higher than she is, he's shouting straight down her throat, it's too awkward! I can't have Jupiter crouch or kneel or sit on the pedestal and dangle his feet. What the hell do you want me to do?"

Ayers said, "I'm protecting you from your own bad taste."[3] As the argument escalated, Ayers grew more insulting. Witnesses were surprised, said Dania Krupska, who was one of them, when "Walter jumped up from his seat and ran down the aisle and *really* let Lem Ayers have it. I thought he was going to punch him. Walter was always so smooth, he would never yell, but this time, he spoke *very* loudly and strongly: '*Don't you dare talk to my wife, Agnes de Mille, that way!*' And something like, 'Why don't you stop admiring Mr. Yumyum's balls'—but he said it deliciously—'and get on with the rehearsal?'"[4]

In November 1950, the show managed to open in Philadelphia. The dancer Glen Tetley, aware of Agnes's distress, invited her to have dinner with him. "It was snowing. She took my arm and we went upstairs into this very noisy, wonderful Greek restaurant and ordered, and she started to tell me what I'd surmised, that things weren't going well. All of a sudden she said, 'I'll be right back,' looking stricken. She jumped up and ran out and I was very worried, so I followed her. I found her leaning against the building; she had been violently ill, all because of the emotional stress of the show.

"The next day, the entire company was called for rehearsal. When we got there, Agnes was inside one of the rehearsal studios, alone, with the door locked. I could hear her inside, playing Scarlatti, playing it and playing it and playing it, as I had never heard it played. We were fifteen, twenty minutes into the rehearsal and finally the door opened and Agnes came out with the tears streaming down her face and her head thrown back and just said quietly, 'I've been fired.'"[5]

"It was not Agnes's fault," said St. Subber, who had fought to get Agnes on the show. "It was mine and Cole's. I think I fired her. I felt stupid; I said something like, 'It's not working, Agnes.' I think she *knew* it was coming, and *wanted* to be let go. What was onstage was a mess. My mess, not hers. Nobody could fix it."[6]

The new director was George Abbott, then sixty-three and at the peak of his career. Abbott was brisk, unemotional, businesslike; fast pacing was his specialty. He kept most of Agnes's work (the program read, "Entire production staged by Agnes de Mille"), but he cut it down, speeded it up, and eliminated much of its charm. When the show got to Boston, the nervous producers asked Agnes to come up and help with the big numbers she had staged; but when she got there, Abbott let her know she was not welcome. *Out of This World* ran four months in New York — against such formidable competition as *Call Me Madam, Guys and Dolls,* and *The King and I* — and was quickly forgotten. Agnes attended a performance and afterward went backstage to thank the dancers. "Hanya was there," she recalled. "I cut her dead from that moment on." A beat. "She got used to it."[7]

Before she left Boston, Agnes had phoned the office of Edward Weeks, a senior editor with the Boston-based *Atlantic* and its publishing affiliate, Little, Brown. Weeks had bought and edited (but not yet published) a chapter of *Dance to the Piper* for serialization in the magazine, and he had demonstrated his ability to restrain what she called "my natural tendency to gush and splash — he just took the blue pencil and made comments in my manuscript like, 'Ouch!'"[8] At this first meeting, they got on so well that she decided to have him edit — and Little, Brown publish — her book.

Weeks was a skilled midwife, kindly and firm. "I dumped an unclean and disordered bunch of manuscript in your lap," Agnes would recall. "Patiently you housecleaned, sorted, and tidied, while I went into megrim after megrim, had the vapors, doubted, foresaw disaster, Cassandra-ed, and performed a lengthy literary sit-down strike. . . . You came into [Jonathan's] hospital rooms to help me with the work, into nurseries, into dance studios, into theaters . . . into the innermost recesses of my heart."[9]

ꝏ

Dance to the Piper is a selective account of the first thirty-seven years of Agnes's life, ending on a high note with *Oklahoma!* and her engagement to Walter. It begins with disarming candor:

> This is the story of an American dancer, a spoiled egocentric wealthy girl, who learned with difficulty to become a worker, to set and meet standards, to brace a Victorian sensibility to contemporary roughhousing, and who, with happy good fortune, participated by the side of great colleagues in a renaissance of the most ancient and magical of the arts.[10]

As a record of the dance revolution in which Agnes participated, set in the context of a broad historical perspective and told in language that requires no prior knowledge of its subject, the book has no equal. With authority, wisdom, and wry humor, it conveys how dancing feels to the performer and looks to the observer. It simultaneously glorifies and demystifies ballet, describing in precise detail the agony behind the artifice. But Agnes was more than a dancer, and *Piper* is more than a dancer's book. It speaks to every artist who struggles — against family, against "bosses," against her own doubts and fears and limitations. Long before the existence of an organized women's movement, *Dance to the Piper* presented a credible heroine with whom any creative and ambitious woman could identify.

Character is style as well as fate, and Agnes was as chatty, incisive, and occasionally indignant on the page as in life, although far more discreet. Her opinions were unequivocal and provocative. "If there was one institution that blocked the progress of dancing in America more than any other, it was the Metropolitan Opera."[11] "Dancing seems to be practiced largely by the downright perverted and deranged."[12] In a thoughtful chapter on the relationship of dancing to both sex and the Christian Church, she explained why dancing from the nineteenth century became the only art given over mainly "into the keeping of fanatical women and emasculated men."[13]

She was too literal-minded to write fiction, but she had no qualms about embellishing the facts for the sake of a good story. When there was dramatic mileage to be gained by exaggerating her tribulations (which also served the purpose of building up her achievements), she seized it. At Edward Weeks's request, she telescoped the years of failure — reducing, for example, the many trips abroad to two. Her insights about others are sometimes profound, but self-revelation is minimal; a reader would conclude, for example, that at the age of thirty-seven she was still a virgin. But this was 1951, when sex was still considered a private affair.

Agnes's writing has the clarity, vitality, originality, and unexpected transitions, e.g., from humor to tartness to poignancy, of her dances. As a narrator, her weaknesses are self-pity ("Who's persecuting you now, dear?") and self-glorification, both of which Edward Weeks made her tone down. Her ability to laugh at herself is her saving grace. And when the subject is not herself, she captures its essence — as with the Hollywood landscape of her youth:

> The hills rose suddenly, untamed, pre-Spanish, coarse with desert weed and wild tearing sagebrush, riven with flood, blind with dust storm, formed and burnt in an endless sun, and hard and promising that the future was as unknown and terrible as the past, that there was enough strength and brutal promise in the land to stir the earth underfoot until the windows rattled.[14]

When the subject is dancers — training, practicing, rehearsing, touring, performing — they twirl and leap and sweat on the page. Her descriptions of Pavlova, Argentina, Isadora, Graham, Rambert, Toumanova, Maracci, Shearer, and Tudor are filled with perspicacity and wonder. Two such passages describe Pavlova, on the stage and behind it:

> She was small, about five feet. She wore a size one and a half slipper, but her feet and hands were large in proportion to her height. Her hand could cover her whole face. Her trunk was small and stripped of all anatomy but the ciphers of adolescence, her arms and legs relatively long, the neck extraordinarily long and mobile. All her gestures were liquid and possessed of an inner rhythm that flowed to inevitable completion with the finality of architecture or music. Her arms seemed to lift not from the elbow or the

arm socket, but from the base of the spine. Her legs seemed to function from the waist. When she bent her head her whole spine moved and the motion was completed the length of the arm through the elongation of her slender hand and the quivering reaching fingers. I believe there has never been a foot like hers, slender, delicate and of such an astonishing aggressiveness when arched as to suggest the ultimate in human vitality. Without in any way being sensual, being, in fact, almost sexless, she suggested all exhilaration, gaiety and delight.[15]

In her dressing room, Agnes wrote, Pavlova

> spoke in light, twittering sounds and her dark eyes flashed incessantly with enormous alertness and inner excitement. Her clawlike hands played nervously with the pearls at her throat. They were the veined hands of an old woman or of an instrumentalist. I noticed her insteps jutting up under the straps of her buttoned slippers. The rocky arch was like a bird claw. There seemed to be no flesh on the foot; it was all bone and tendon. The toe was clubby, broadened and coarse. Her little thin shoulders lifted from the gathered peasant blouse. What was gross had been burnt and wasted off her. She had kept no part of her body that was not useful to her art, and there was about her the tragic aura of absolute decision. The high pale brow, her front against the world, the somber eyes, the mobile lips shut with humorous tolerance on God knows what tumult and violence caged within the little skull, marked her as one apart. She had the fascination of a martyr.[16]

There are equally incisive sketches of some of the giants and supporting players in dance, movies, and theater over a period of three decades. About professional colleagues, Agnes was fair-minded and generous. She sent copies of the manuscript to a dozen of her subjects for their comments. Douglass Montgomery, of whom she wrote glowingly, scolded her for using him as "grist to de Mille" and for treating her parents with what he considered was undeserved harshness. After observing that her "lifelong penchant for dramatizing yourself — for seldom seeing anything in the world around you except in its relationship or influence upon you — your true talent, from girlhood, to extract (or slightly twist) an entertaining essence out of most any topic you touched — your born and ever since polished taste and respect for words . . . have paid off in a worldly . . . and artistic sense," he reminded her that "long, long ago you once told me that, because of our talents, we were ever in the positions of being 'guests' in our own homes . . . I propose to you . . . that sometimes those for whom we care (or, at least, who care or have cared for us) deserve to be in the position of guests in *our* lives. . . . You were dealing with the living, dearie."[17]

About her mother, she was supremely ambivalent; after every negative word, she sprang to Anna's defense. She was hardest on her fallen idols, William and Cecil. William, who had always encouraged Agnes to write, now saw himself portrayed as the "villain" of her book for not having supported her early dance efforts and for causing the divorce that had left Anna "a broken woman." His film career was over and his own autobiography, *Hollywood Saga,* had not been particularly successful — but he was not about to be portrayed as a has-been. He icily informed Agnes that "the picture of my being fired from the studios [his contract had not been renewed] makes me an object of pity — and to say I later joined the university where I made a reputation as 'lecturer and coach' is a bit rough. When I take charge of a stage and put on a whole production, I am still a director, my dear, not a 'coach.'" He also objected to her reference to Clara as the "current" Mrs. de Mille, "as if she were one of a constantly changing series."[18]

William's anger was tempered by his residual guilt, but Clara recognized the mark of a serpent's tooth when she saw it, and said so. "You have both by commission and omission been unfair, disloyal and in some places dishonest," she wrote. "The implication is that [William] started to decline after he left your mother and you. He may not have been so financially successful, but you know (and have repeatedly said) that he was happier and better adjusted than at any time you had known him." She pointed out that William had "kept sending you $400 a month long after he could afford it . . . the impression you give is that you were left practically with no 'de Mille money' and no one to help you out other than your mother. Haven't you forgotten that all that you got from your mother was de Mille money? That one of the reasons your father could not help you later was because he had settled almost all he had saved on your mother? . . . You mentioned that you had had a 'generous allowance,' but this rather got lost in later accounts of your near-starvation . . . I am at a loss to understand," she concluded reproachfully, "why you felt it necessary to omit completely the fact that on numerous occasions you lived in your father's home . . . Nor can I understand why in erecting a monument to your mother, you found it necessary to distort facts about your father."

Clara also objected to Agnes's self-dramatization at the expense of "the living, dearie," and cited the evidence. At Agnes's first Hollywood recital, for example, "There may have been some curiosity about a meeting between your parents [the first since their divorce], but certainly hundreds did *not* turn out to watch them in relation to you. Like any parent, your father was somewhat nervous, but certainly neither 'rigid' nor 'paralyzed with nerves.'" At the Los Angeles opening of *Rodeo,* William "was in no way 'humbled' nor 'diffidently' waiting for you. Stooped he has always been, but from bad posture and not humility. What he actually said was: 'My dear, I am very proud of you.' . . . He has never in my hearing used the Victorian form of address, 'My daughter.'"[19]

Cecil's comments ran to six single-spaced pages of indignation. He had always been magnanimous to his niece, as he could well afford to be. After her wedding, to which she pointedly did not invite him, he gave her a party. After *Cleopatra* there were years of coolness between them, but he had praised her extravagantly for *Oklahoma!* In 1944 she had given a reporter a version of the *Cleopatra* debacle in which Cecil came off as a pompous, arrogant vulgarian who pandered to the taste of the masses. When her comments were published in *Collier's,* she apologized abjectly to her uncle, claiming misquotation; his response was three dozen red roses across the footlights at the opening of *Tally-Ho,* with a card reading "Colliers come, Colliers go, We go on forever. Luck and love, Uncle Ce."

But Agnes's scars from *Cleopatra* had not healed — perhaps because she could not resist picking at them — and *Piper* was an irresistible opportunity to get her own back. Armed with insider information, she aimed at Cecil's most vulnerable spot: his public image. In the manuscript, one of the most powerful men in the world saw himself depicted, in a tone that mixed pride with contempt, as the epitome of achievement in the family, but also as William's kid brother. His response showed the same attention to detail that he gave to his movies (and Agnes to her ballets).

He flatly denied Agnes's account of the early, pre-Hollywood business failures in which William had staked him. On a more personal level, Agnes intended to tell the world that he owned three hundred-odd English tailored shirts and nearly as many neckties. "I have never counted my shirts," he wrote, explaining that when they began to wear out, "my excellent shirt-maker cuts the tails off to make new collars and cuffs. When the replaced collars and cuffs become too badly frayed, the family sends them to what is termed the 'shirt morgue' at my ranch where they work out their last days in rough work of tree surgery, wood chopping, clearing fire trails, etc." His ties, he explained loftily, "were acquired over some fifty odd years — many of them Christmas and birthday gifts, yet unworn, and many of them knitted by some gentle souls . . . as a sincere expression of appreciation of some of my work." He also took exception to Agnes's description of the elaborate Christmas morning ritual of unwrapping piles of "tribute" from his employees, claiming, "I do my staff the courtesy and justice of accepting their gifts in the same spirit of friendship and affection that I send mine to them." (Ironically, her niece recalled Christmases in Agnes's apartment after *Oklahoma!* when, "with the whole of New York and Hollywood at her feet, her professional gifts covered half of the living room. It was really lurid.")[20]

He protested that Agnes's description of "an Inquisitorial type of procedure" in his office was based solely on fictional accounts by journalists. But he was most deeply stung by her reference to money as "a passion and a premise" in his life; attuned to gesture, she made her point by repeatedly mentioning his habit of jingling the twenty-dollar gold pieces he always kept in his pocket. "Your paragraphs on my attitude toward religion and mankind that follow so closely your above expression on the subject of money being a God in your Aunt Constance's home," Cecil wrote (one can feel his jaw clenching), "tend to present me to the public as a charlatan . . . if that is your opinion, I presume you have a right to state it." In conclusion, he noted that it was "a bit difficult for me to be sympathetic to having the private lives of our families laid on the public operating table, but if you feel that the public will better understand your struggles, failures and successes, I shall try to accustom myself to this trend and wish you all success."[21]

Agnes stood her ground. "Everything I wrote," she replied, "was from personal observation and my memory has been proven to be unusually accurate." Her recollections had been corroborated by her father, her sister, and Cecil's professional colleagues. Defending her portrait of Cecil, she inadvertently described herself. "Both you and Pop talk with enormous theatrical exaggeration, in sweeping hyperbole and sardonic superlatives that are very funny but could be . . . misleading in cold print to the uninitiated. It is the clashing and contradiction in your characters that makes you both exciting." She respected his dedication to his work, but "at the same time I think you are greatly ambitious, and wish money and power as a symbol of achievement." She had described him, she explained slyly, "not as you are now, grown wise and gentle and tempered by life, but as you appeared thirty-five years ago to a ten-year-old girl. Every reader . . . comments on the fact that you come out not only a great man in your field . . . but kind and benevolent, and extremely colorful."[22] But with the same hubris that had sabotaged her on *Cleopatra,* she described Cecil's objections to her father as "so vague and picayune, I am hoping he will forget them . . . Many people have complained I have . . . flattered him."[23]

For all her bravado, she was careful not to go too far; Cecil was, after all, still alive. After his death, everything that was deleted from *Piper,* including her unexpurgated version of *Cleopatra,* would find its way into print.

William and Cecil both had the grace to praise Agnes's writing, and their objections may even have given her a certain satisfaction; she made some token changes to pacify them, but they had, after all, had to ask. Walter, on the other hand, told her not to publish the book.

Incredibly, during the years that the book was in progress, she and Walter had never discussed it. He had seen her working and said nothing. In his youth, he had wanted to be a writer — but although he had talent, he was as merciless a critic of his own work as of everyone else's, and he lacked what Agnes called "my terrible persistence."[24] Her career was already a source of tension between them, and she worried about the effect of a second one on his ego. So she was silent as well. As she had waited for her father to show an interest in her dancing, she waited for

Walter's attention. Finally, when the edited galleys arrived, she insisted that he read them. Halfway through, he informed her that the writing was not good and that her outspokenness would turn everyone she knew against her. He also pointed out that she already had a career and didn't need another one.

Craig Barton, Walter's boyhood friend from Texas and now manager of Martha Graham's company, had once advised Agnes not to take Walter's criticisms personally. "His one aim, since his teens," Barton told her, "has been to reduce. I'm not sure he even wants to, but it is his devil and he is possessed with it. . . . It is about his insatiable inner needs and his heartbreaking underestimation of his marvelous capacities. He does not love us less, but we must stuff our ears or our sensibilities with cotton and evaluate clearly."[25] For Agnes, that was not possible. Stricken, she told Edward Weeks she wanted to repay the advance and withdraw the book. Weeks explained that his company's investment in the book during the eighteen-month editing process far exceeded the $4,000 advance and suggested that Walter suspend judgment until he finished reading. In the end, Walter approved.

Dance to the Piper was published in January 1952. John Martin praised with faint damns, commending the book for its honesty but likening its theme to that of Agnes's early recital pieces ("the story of a woman with a purpose, who is continually being slapped down, who suffers and suffers and suffers").[26] Most reviewers, however, recognized a classic, and said so. Within weeks, the book was a best-seller.

Surgery had removed the chronic threat to Jonathan's life, but he was still subject to gastroenteritis — intestinal infections severe enough to require hospitalization, particularly in cold weather. Doctors prescribed a warm climate in the winter to build up his strength and resistance, so for several years he spent the coldest months in Florida, with a nurse or with Lily, the housekeeper. In the winter of 1951, he spent two weeks in Children's Hospital, where Agnes slept in a bed beside him for five nights. When he was released, she took him to Jamaica for a month — her first substantial chunk of time alone with him — and gratefully watched him thrive, swimming and climbing trees like a normal child.

For once she was free of worry and guilt, and jealousy of Lily, to whom Jonathan seemed more attached than to herself.

Out of This World had been an unfortunate hiccup, a temporary setback. Agnes's next show, Lerner and Loewe's *Paint Your Wagon,* would contain what she considered her best work on Broadway. She stood now at the top of several professions. Acclaimed for her work in ballet, in the theater, and as an author, with an adored husband and a child whose survival was no longer in doubt, she was as close as any woman could come to having it all. But the same drive that had taken her to the top also ensured that no top could ever be high enough and no achievement ever, except very briefly, enough.

thirty-one

Paint Your Wagon

Paint Your Wagon was only a modest success, but it was in many ways Agnes's favorite of all her shows. Its setting was the California gold rush, which perfectly suited her style. She had a score that she loved, the dancers she wanted, Trude Rittman as her right arm, her favorite set and costume designers (Oliver Smith and Elizabeth Montgomery) and a congenial company consisting almost entirely of handsome, bearded men.

Alan Lerner's book focused on the romance between a miner and a prospector's daughter, the only woman in town. According to Mavis Ray, Agnes's assistant on the show, "At the first read-through, someone said, 'There's not much room for the dances, where are the dances going to go?' And Agnes said, 'I'm *clawing* holes in the script to insert the dances!'"[1] The young director, Daniel Mann, had just begun his career (with Tennessee Williams's *The Rose Tattoo*) and had no previous experience with musicals, so it made sense for Agnes to stage all the musical numbers. The script was so weak, and Agnes's claws so sharp, that the dances would dominate the show.

Paint Your Wagon gave Agnes an opportunity to create a featured role for James Mitchell. *Brigadoon* had established Mitchell as one of the top male dancers on Broadway and brought him to Hollywood's attention.

Since then, he had acted and danced in movies and had toured as a guest artist with Ballet Theatre in Europe and South America, dancing leading roles in *Rodeo, Fall River Legend,* and some of Tudor's ballets. He preferred acting to dancing, but when Agnes needed him, she exercised her considerable persuasiveness. Another member of the cast recalled that when Mitchell warmed up backstage before the show, "I could hear the bones and the ligaments popping, little clicks and clacks dancers make as they begin to stretch — and under his breath Jim was muttering, 'God Damn Agnes de Mille! God Damn Agnes de Mille!'"[2]

In her staging of the first song, "They Call the Wind Maria," Agnes captured a striking mood of men without women. Mitchell paced restlessly, thumping the palm of one hand rhythmically with the clenched fist of the other, and one-by-one all the men joined in, pacing back and forth in shifting patterns like caged animals — building to a climax, then slowing and ending, as they began, with natural movement. At the end of the act, a coachload of prostitutes on the mining town circuit arrived (by then, the audience was as glad to see them as the miners were). Accompanied only by a long, suspenseful sting on the violins, each woman in her fancy dress emerged from the coach and walked, in her own individual style, up to one of the awestruck miners. The reactions of the men heightened the sexual tension. "What do you like?" Agnes had asked them. "Blonde, brunette, redhead? You'll sell your claim and all the gold from it just to touch her, just to be with her." When the last woman was in place, one man reached out and touched the silk on her gown. She took his hand and put his arm around her, the dancing started, and all hell broke loose.

In Agnes's scenario, James Mitchell played a miner who fell in love with an itinerant prostitute. His partner was Gemze de Lappe, whose association with Agnes's work would outlast that of any other dancer. Gemze had had a big success as the Dream Laurey in the London company of *Oklahoma!* and had been featured in *The King and I.* She was twenty-nine — a petite, green-eyed brunette with high cheekbones, a wiry and wonderfully limber body, and a quality of wistful vulnerability that Agnes used to great advantage. Her technique was strong, both balletic and modern, encompassing the free movement of the Isadora Duncan school and also the acting skills she had learned in the character ballets of Michel Fokine, in whose company she had made her professional debut at the age of nine. Her jumps seemed effortless; Agnes described her as "a combination of India rubber and gunpowder."[3] And like all of Agnes's favorite dancers, she projected extraordinary energy and *thoughts* on the stage, even when standing still.

The chemistry between Mitchell and de Lappe was compelling. "We *breathed* together," de Lappe recalled, and her leaps and his lifts electrified the audience. Their two duets were quite similar in movement but entirely different in feeling. The first is urgent and sexual, almost a rape. The other is subtle, poignant, and tender, transformed by love. Agnes considered them the most erotic dances she ever choreographed. "Watching Agnes watch Gemze and Jimmy dance," said one of the dancers, "made me uncomfortable. Agnes had some kind of fantasy going, something deeply personal. You felt, 'I shouldn't be watching this, it's voyeurism.'"[4]

For the second act, Agnes staged a rowdy dance-hall fandango that featured "a much dirtier than usual can-can dance, done by a great beefy woman in hoop skirts."[5] The woman was Mary Burr — a dark, dramatic dancer who had performed in ballets (including Tudor's and de Mille's) and on Broadway. Burr was sensational in a demoniacal eight-minute solo that she and Agnes had created on a hot August night. Agnes had brought a drummer along, and as the drummer drummed, Burr recalled, "Agnes said, 'Just improvise. Do what you love to do most.' I thought, 'Mary, this is it — once in a lifetime — go for it!' So I did everything I did best, that I loved most to dance. When I finished, there were pools of water all over the floor. And Agnes said, 'That's great! We'll keep it in!'"

In the dance-hall scene, Burr descended the stairs wearing a sensational dress that weighed sixty pounds, including its four-tiered hoopskirt. She looked over the men, clasped her hands in front of her diaphragm, and beckoned with one finger to a terrified miner who eventually joined her in a wild dance in which she threw her legs over him, ripped off her skirt, and whipped him into a frenzy until he tore off the rest of her costume. Practically nude, she whirled, leaped, kicked above her head, and performed fifty-nine fouettés. "At the end," Burr said, "it was Agnes's idea to have everyone just dance themselves crazy until they all fell down dead, exhausted. I was the only one left standing, and I sat on top of them."[6] If Alan Lerner feared that the number might overpower his book and lyrics, it is not surprising.

Although one reviewer would describe the show as "Sex Life of the Miners, With Song," the sex on the stage was innocent and romantic compared with what went on behind the scenes. "Sex was rampant," said director Daniel Mann; "even the goat got knocked up. I wish to Christ that some of that energy would have gone into the play."[7] According to Dania Krupska, "Everybody went wacko in *Wagon.* You couldn't walk into a dark room in a hotel or at a party without interrupting something." Krupska and the singer Ted Thurston, whose affair during the show led to an enduring marriage, attributed the atmosphere to Agnes.

Agnes's youthful conflict about sex — her fears and her longings — resulted, in adulthood, in paradoxical personas. Anna de Mille's daughter had the rigid backbone and prim manners and rather high-pitched, slightly affected speech of a Victorian virgin who had mislaid her bustle and fan. But the girl who had embraced tree trunks and felt the sap move inside them was mother to a sensuous woman. "She would demonstrate a little walk across the stage," said Krupska, "and *immediately* the nostrils of all the men were *flaring!*"[8] "Agnes permeated that whole company with sex," Thurston said. "Everyone was ablaze."[9]

Throughout her adult life, Agnes had a deep need to prove that although she was not beautiful by her uncle's standards, she was sexually desirable. *Dance to the Piper* includes a portion of a wartime letter to Walter that read, "If only this were real measles, I'd have a brand-new skin all over me and when you saw me in that you'd die — brand new all over, pale, translucent, pink, like a baby's stomach."[10] The quote informed her readers that despite all the self-deprecating humor in the book, she was capable of exciting a man.

Agnes valued her women friends, but she needed "virile" men to validate her femininity, and during the preparation of *Wagon* she reveled in their company. "The men all adored her," Ted Thurston recalled. "She was great with men. There was a quality of a timorous little something — she'd look up at all those big bearded fellows, rough-looking — she *loved* that!" According to Krupska, "Fritzie [Loewe] was sexually very *hot* for Agnes. He was after her like a hound dog; he used to rhapsodize about how all her musks and her flavors, the scents of her body, drove him *crazy*. He would stand next to her, *breathing*. She would get those red splotches on her face that she always got when she was upset. 'Oh *Fritzie,*' she would say, 'Get away!' Like a dog." One evening Agnes was having dinner with eight or nine of the men when she saw Loewe come into the restaurant, looking for her. Pleading, "Don't let him see me!" she lay across the men's laps, and they covered her with the tablecloth — a ploy that worked until Loewe asked, "Has anyone seen Agnes?" and she began to laugh.

When working, Agnes was so focused that Daniel Mann likened her to a fighter entering the ring, ready for combat. When Mann stepped into the ring with her, the outcome was surprising. The actors in *Wagon* sang and danced, and the dancers acted and sang — an emerging trend in musicals — so Agnes and Mann were allotted separate times to work with the cast. "Agnes kept taking more time, more time, more time," Mann said. "Finally one day I walked into her rehearsal and I said, 'Thank you, Agnes! That's it!' She looked rather shocked. I said, 'The show is not about your dancing, the show *includes* your dancing, so you'll be kind enough now to end your rehearsal.'"[11] She complied, but the atmosphere between them remained edgy.

As an emotional outlet, Mann, who had been a jazz musician, sometimes arrived early for rehearsal in order to improvise on the piano. One morning when he was doing so, Agnes walked in. "She stood there and listened. Finally she said, 'You're very angry, aren't you?' I said, 'Well, we're working together and this is my first musical, and I want and need all the help and care and concern that'll make it a better show, so for us to have this kind of relationship is ridiculous!' She said, 'I'd like to talk to you about that. Why don't we have dinner tonight?' So we went out to dinner. And during dinner she said, 'You know, Danny, you're reputed to have a lot of heart. But let me tell you something. Life . . . enters . . . here' — and she pointed between her legs — 'and this is where it's released. And that's what it's all about.' I said, 'Yes, but wouldn't it be wonderful if it were connected to the heart?' From that moment on, we were friends."[12]

At forty-six, Agnes was gripped by a "midlife madness," a consequence of a lifetime of largely unfulfilled sexual yearnings.[13] She once surprised Gemze de Lappe by remarking that when their cat was in heat, "Walter said something like, 'Is that the way you feel sometimes?' and Agnes said, 'That's the way I feel a lot of the time!'" Her feelings for Mitchell were, said de Lappe, "a nonsecret that was not talked about"; talk was unnecessary, for she put them on the stage for the world to see.[14]

James Mitchell's face and form and air of mystery made him the object of many people's fantasies, but it was his contention that "the only thing I was really interested in was going on the stage and doing the work. I wasn't interested in Agnes other than as a friend, or in Gemze other than as someone to pick up and put down — up and down, up and down, up and down and catch. But Agnes didn't like me getting too friendly with Gemze, or with anyone else."

Mitchell said, "Agnes enslaved people. She knew her power, and that people would do for her. People considered it a privilege to do for her."[15] She could take away, and she could give; she loved to give Mitchell lavish presents — a piece of luggage, a gold chain from Tiffany's, a special book. During *Bloomer Girl,* when he was unable to pay his rent, she had surprised him with a gift of $500.

During eight long, grueling weeks in Philadelphia and Boston, *Wagon* was almost completely rewritten and some of Agnes's favorite dances were cut. "Agnes and I would sit in her hotel room in Philadelphia," Dania Krupska recalled, "just looking at each other by the hour. She would be drinking Scotch out of the bottle—which meant she was *very* upset."[16] In New York, most reviewers liked the score, loved the dances, and thought the script rambling and repetitious ("a lumbering stage-coach").[17] "*Paint Your Wagon* is the wrong advice," observed *Time*'s reviewer. "It should be: Grease your wagon wheels."[18] "*Paint Your Wagon* is filled with talented people," wrote Walter Kerr, "but a lot of the time they have to get out and push."[19]

Unanimous accolades went to Agnes, whom Kerr pronounced "the real heroine" of the show. "With the barest glance from James Mitchell, the simplest gesture from Gemze de Lappe, the spark we have been waiting for all evening is thrown off, the stage ignites . . . [de Mille] gives the show that honest and moving quality which the authors have everywhere aimed at and rarely achieved."[20] The *Chicago Tribune*'s Claudia Cassidy wrote that Mitchell's "Maria" dance "told you more about men imprisoned by avarice, their own or others' to whom they are enslaved, than a dozen chapters of Mr. Lerner's dull book."[21]

Agnes reported to her stepmother that as a result of such reviews, "the author hauled me into the theatre the following day and ordered me to cut the dances. I was verily tart in my reply. If he pressed, I shall simply leave town."[22] He did not press. But when *Brigadoon* and *Paint Your Wagon* were filmed, Agnes's services were not requested.* And when Lerner and Loewe did their next show together, they hired Hanya Holm to choreograph it. The show was *My Fair Lady,* one of the biggest hits of all time.

* Gene Kelly choreographed *Brigadoon,* and no one would accept blame for the dances in *Paint Your Wagon.*

t h i r t y - t w o

Harvest

Agnes would do six more Broadway shows, but *Paint Your Wagon* was the beginning of the end of the kind of Broadway musicals she had helped to create, and she no longer had a corner on the market of what remained. By 1952, Jerome Robbins, Hanya Holm, Helen Tamiris, Anna Sokolow, and Michael Kidd had danced through the door Agnes opened for serious choreographers on Broadway. Her most formidable rival, as she saw it, was Robbins, who was thirteen years her junior; his *Fancy Free* (1944), which evolved into the hit musical *On the Town,* had been the first important American ballet after *Rodeo.* Of the two enormous hits with which Rodgers and Hammerstein had followed *Allegro, South Pacific* (1949) had only one dance number, which was staged by Jerome Robbins, and *The King and I* (1951), which Agnes had very much wanted to do, was also choreographed by Robbins. Agnes had road companies and revivals to rehearse, but no compelling offers of new shows.

The timing was fortuitous, however, for she was temporarily fed up with Broadway. Its financial resources were vast compared to those of a ballet company, but it was also fraught with frustrations. "To do something exquisitely lyrical in a musical," Agnes said, "you have to stop everything, quiet the audience, and say, 'This is totally different.' It can be

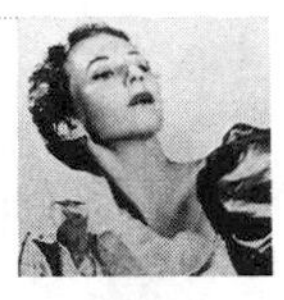

done, but directors and backers don't think it can."[1] Five weeks of rehearsal before opening out of town were ample for singers and actors, but not for a choreographer, whose dances often had to incorporate singers and actors of all sizes, some with the flexibility of a rock. The dances had to fit the style of the songs and story, and the sets tended to flatten dance patterns into two dimensions. Show costumes covered bodies and inhibited movement (Miles White, who designed the costumes for *Oklahoma!*, *Bloomer Girl*, and *Carousel*, always added extra buttons and braid and trim, knowing that Agnes would need something to remove after the dress rehearsal). Most dances were limited to three or four minutes, and more than half of them would be cut, for reasons that had nothing to do with their quality. And choreographing a show meant fourteen-to-sixteen-hour workdays, during which Agnes rarely saw her son unless the housekeeper brought him to rehearsals, where he would sit quietly and watch for hours.

As the only child of a father who was remote and an adoring mother whose attention was often elsewhere and whose presence could be overwhelming, Jonathan's formative years were complicated by more than his chronic health problems. To one contemporary, the daughter of his godfather, "Their home seemed quite formal to me — not a children's environment. There was no screaming, no hiding under the piano. Jonathan had a bunk bed but there was nowhere you could leave your Legos out, or maybe even *have* Legos. You wouldn't know there was a kid around."[2] When he was four, Agnes had dismissed his beloved Lily (for requesting what the Prudes thought was an unwarranted raise), and hired Anna Horvath, a superb cook and "a serious hugger," to whom he would eventually become even more attached than to Lily.[3] But Lily had been the most consistent person in his life since infancy, and after her departure he developed what his mother called "little nervous ailments" — car sickness, enuresis, disinterest in food.[4]

Agnes was very much aware of her son's emotional needs, and of her inability to fill all of them. His attendance at the Friends School was a partial antidote to the only-child syndrome; in addition to high academic standards, it had small classes that approximated surrogate families and provided some close and enduring friendships. During Jonathan's sixth winter, Agnes wrenched herself away from New York at the height of the ballet season and took the child to Jamaica again. This time they stayed in a borrowed villa (equipped with eleven servants) and had "wonderful times going on picnics *à deux* and traveling around in the little car I rented. He ran about all day half naked, swam whenever he felt like it. . . . I am reading him 'Treasure Island' and 'The Jungle Books.' . . . He is really very sweet — totally unmusical but with a wonderful feeling for words."[5]

They spent the summer at Merriewold, where Jonathan had friendships that he renewed each year. Except for the addition of electricity, indoor plumbing, and a cottage to accommodate a constant stream of guests, little had changed since Agnes's childhood. Walter commuted on weekends, as her father had once done. "I have dedicated this summer to family quiet and healing up some bad emotional ravellings," she told Michael Hertz, "and Walter has tried to cooperate in every way. . . . [I] have been scrupulous about never leaving [Jonathan] for any chore whatever if he just wanted me around."[6] The child would not be completely well for several more years, but that summer was the turning point, and from then on he grew gradually stronger.

In the fall, Agnes went back to work — not on a show, but on a major ballet, *The Harvest According.* With a ballet company — in this case, Ballet Theatre — she had the advantages of fine dancers (who were accustomed to working together as a unit), great music, a symphony orchestra, forty minutes of stage time, and a bare stage, with nothing to hamper movement. What was missing was money.

Broadway subsidized Agnes's ballet habit. In 1950, one of her best years, she had earned over $125,000, the bulk of which came from *Gentlemen Prefer Blondes* and the hugely successful London production of *Carousel.* That year, royalties from her ballets totaled $1,400. For creating *Fall River Legend,* she was paid $1,500, plus a $30 royalty for each performance; for rehearsing it with the company she received $10 per hour. For appearing as guest artist in her ballets, her top fee was $100.

A solvent ballet company is a contradiction in terms — a truism that accounts for disputes over amounts of money so small as to be laughable if they were not pathetic. Agnes's sense of fairness began with herself, and any real or imagined threat to her position or pocketbook strengthened her fearsome tenacity. Her correspondence with Sergei Denham during the nine-year period in which the Ballet Russe de Monte Carlo had the exclusive right to perform *Rodeo* is a litany of complaints about overdue royalties, unacceptable casting, inadequate performances, and undesirable programming. Given the plethora of problems in any ballet company, that was business as usual. Agnes took it personally, and she was never one to cut her losses. Her letters to Denham were righteous, urgent, and peppered with threats to withdraw the ballet or to cancel a guest performance in it. Denham protested that there was no pleasing her, that she was almost always too busy to rehearse the company. Denham's account of a chance meeting that took place between them in a restaurant captures both of their characters as succinctly as one of Agnes's stage gestures: "I showered you with compliments on your young looks," he wrote, "and you asked me 'Now, what do you want of me?'" When she demanded complimentary tickets, he replied, "My dear, I am quite sure that you will not be ruined by putting out the extra $9–$12 . . .

To give complimentary tickets would set a precedent and would not be fair to our rank and file . . . if you insist, I will pay for the tickets myself which will be my gift to you in lieu of flowers. You might know that I purchased with my own money a box for Mr. Copland but he was nice enough to conduct without charging a penny either for rehearsal or performing."[7]

In 1948, Denham's office canceled a *Rodeo* rehearsal but neglected to notify Agnes, who showed up to conduct it. For an entire year, she dunned Denham for the twenty dollars she claimed he owed her for the rehearsal that never took place. She finally informed "Dear Sergei Ivanovich" that if she was not paid, "I shall find it expedient not to have any further dealings whatsoever with your organization."[8] Denham scrawled "What a cheap scandal" in the margin of her letter — and paid the twenty dollars. His final word on the subject was "I can well imagine what a row you would raise if a department store insisted on payment of a charge of which you had no record."[9]

In 1950, Ballet Theatre acquired the exclusive right to perform *Rodeo* — by then a recognized classic and the most frequently performed of all American ballets — and introduced it to eight countries on its European tour.[10] The following spring, Agnes danced the Cowgirl at the Metropolitan Opera House, with John Kriza and James Mitchell. That she was then forty-six, ten years older than when she created the role, did not go unmentioned by the critics. John Martin said it with sarcasm ("She may not be a mere slip of a child any longer, but she is a fine performer"), and the *Musical Courier*'s Rosalyn Krokover, while acknowledging that the audience cheered and applauded, was downright spiteful ("Miss de Mille was never exactly a lightweight and now she has a good bit to carry around. The awful truth is that onstage she looked more like a woman out of a Hokinson cartoon than she did the young Cowgirl").[11] *The New Yorker*'s Douglas Watt wrote, "She tired visibly in the long role, but her acting was first-rate, and I wouldn't have missed her performance for the world."[12]

Agnes could never resist comparing other interpretations of the Cowgirl with her own, and inevitably found them wanting.* Her contractual

* Her favorites were Dorothy Etheridge, Jenny Workman, Bonnie Wyckoff, and Christine Sarry.

right to approve the casting of her ballets was an ongoing source of contention with Lucia Chase. "Over the years, at her behest," said Chase, "we have allowed ourselves to be persuaded to engage a series of charming and talented comediennes from the Broadway musical stage, without whom, in Agnes' view, '*Rodeo* could not possibly be performed.' There were times when we were able to persuade Agnes to permit a regular member of the company to dance the role, principally on tour in smaller cities. We and the critics, along with the public, found these to be admirable Cowgirls, and in time Agnes was won over to them — so much that when they left the company, she insisted they be brought back as guest artists, as there was no one in the company capable of performing the role."[13]

It is hard to imagine a more striking example of irresistible force meeting immovable object than the forty-year war between Agnes de Mille and Lucia Chase. Lucia, a small brunette who was not above using girlish helplessness to get her way, was Agnes's senior by eight years. She had not started to study dancing seriously until she was thirty-six, after her husband died and left her with two small children and seven million dollars. Although Agnes lacked Lucia's society background — the concept of Agnes as debutante boggles the imagination — both came from privileged families that stressed education, family, manners, and excellence. Neither Lucia nor Agnes was beautiful, and both had become dancers in spite of the wrong bodies and late starts. Onstage together in *Judgment of Paris* and *Three Virgins and a Devil,* they were hilarious.

In 1945, Mary Burr had sometimes found herself taking Vladimir Dokoudovsky's ballet class with the two most powerful women in the ballet world. "Agnes and Lucia were middle-aged and flabby then," she recalled, "but they sort of dominated the class, which at one time or other had all the great dancers in it — Alicia [Alonso], Nora [Kaye], Igor Youskevitch, Mary Ellen Moylan, [Alicia] Markova, Maria Tallchief, Johnny Kriza. Agnes wore a revealing costume — a low-cut leotard, little ruffled skirts, pink fishnet tights, and black ballet slippers on her tiny feet. It was the day of the snood — she'd wear a black snood with this frizzy red hair, with a bow. She was very vociferous, pushing herself to the front in class. Agnes was the most fiercely determined person I've ever seen in my life — determined to live in the now, to be in that class, to do what she had to do. She was totally involved. People laughed at her but I just thought, God, what guts!"[14]

"Agnes and Lucia both played God to a lot of people's careers," said Melissa Hayden, "but Lucia could lie straight to your face with those blue eyes of hers and convince herself, even when you knew she was lying. She knew how to push Agnes's buttons."[15] Eliot Feld, who ultimately left Ballet Theatre to form his own company, said, "Lucia walked with little mincing steps, but her progress was as inexorable as a glacier. She was all about expediency. She wanted a ballet company, and she did those things that in her judgment would make it survive."[16] Codirector Oliver Smith oversaw artistic matters, but the power remained with Chase, who supported the company with her personal fortune as it lurched from one financial crisis to the next. By 1951, Lincoln Kirstein's New York City Ballet was comfortably ensconced at City Center while Ballet Theatre still spent most of its time on exhausting tours, renting the Metropolitan Opera House for its short New York season.

When Chase planned a program, she had to consider balance, temperaments, the limits of the dancers' physical endurance, the audience's patience, and the time stagehands needed to do their jobs. In addition to choreographers and dancers, she had to deal with unions, agents, publicists, board members, and committees. Agnes had a grudging admiration for Chase's New England character and determination, and she understood that what was best for the company was not always best for her ballets; nevertheless, she frequently accused Lucia of sabotaging her work. Whatever the legitimacy of her complaints, Sergei Denham was right; there was no pleasing her.

ꝏ

The theme of *The Harvest According* (from Walt Whitman's, "Life is the tillage/and death is the harvest according") is the cycle of life, as experienced by Everywoman (Agnes).* The ballet is a trilogy, its unifying form "the circle of womanhood and birth, the ring of the female principle, which is the oldest symbol of iconography, the circle of children's games,

* Agnes had first used the harvest metaphor in *Harvest Reel,* and in a wartime letter to Walter (December 8, 1944) she had asked plaintively, "When, when, when can we *harvest* our love? This sowing goes on overlong, it seems."

the circle of the folk dance, impregnable, immaculate, the perfect round of communal love."[17] Each section is an expansion of a Broadway ballet: the (aborted) childbirth dance in *Carousel,* the children's games in *Allegro,* and the funeral dance in *Bloomer Girl.* In place of the original Broadway music, Agnes used portions of an opera and a cello concerto by Virgil Thomson, and his arrangements of familiar hymns and folk tunes. Watercolor backdrops by Lem Ayers represented hills, sea, sky, and clouds.

In the birth sequence, the women conveyed apprehension, agony, release, and joy through Grahamesque contractions, bends, and sweeps toward the ground. The children's scene contained spectacular cartwheels and headstands, as well as intricate leaps and lifts and a good deal of pointe work. The final sequence incorporated square dance patterns, circling and revolving, representing the continuity of the cycle. Agnes's amalgamation of ballet, modern dance, and Broadway once again alienated purists of all persuasions, in the audience and also on the stage.

Ballet Theatre's classically trained dancers were proud of their ability to do anything from a timestep to *Les Sylphides.* Agnes demanded both more and less. She asked them "to leap from prone positions, to faint backwards until their shoulders brushed the resin on the floor-boards, to run around on their knee-caps, to writhe and twist in spasms that lay well outside the usual range of swan queens . . . The tiptoeing girls now tread the earth as though the flesh of their heels feel the live ground down thru rubble and rock to seed. Corps de ballet dancers . . . now permit themselves to be human women and just to stand . . . with tears in their eyes waiting for their men to return from war. They think about war and their men and not about the direction of their toes."[18]

In the relatively small company of forty-two dancers, stars lived in a bubble, protected from the outside world and from much of what went on inside the company. They were addressed formally as Mister and Miss, and members of the corps were not allowed to walk down the hallway outside their dressing rooms. The stars were the crème de la crème; when required to learn their roles from Agnes's coterie of dancers, on whom she had constructed the work, the crème soured. "Agnes always caused turmoil in the company," principal dancer Ruth Ann Koesun observed, "because she had the attitude that nobody in Ballet Theatre could do it as well as her little dancers, who were mostly not as well trained as we were. . . . If you didn't do it exactly as she had set it on her little acolyte, she was very upset. She would say, 'Gemze, show Nora what I want done in this scene!' Gemze de Lappe teaching Nora Kaye? That makes you feel second rate. I resented being taught my part by a little dancer who has probably disappeared into oblivion."[19]

When Agnes forced Lucia to hire one of "her" dancers, insisting that no one in the company was as qualified to dance the lead in one of her ballets (e.g., Gemze de Lappe in *The Harvest According*), resentments intensified. Maria Karnilova said, "We didn't want to do Agnes's little comedy bits . . . Her dances were more about energy than beauty. She never was one of us."[20] Karnilova and her colleagues would not accept Agnes's work on its own terms; they insisted on comparing it — unfavorably — with that of Antony Tudor. They took their cue from Tudor, who had been Ballet Theatre's resident icon until 1950, and whose influence lingered on. To Tudor, "popular art" was an oxymoron; Agnes's work was overrated, her commercial success unforgivable. But even Tudor had to admit that that success had been responsible, directly and indirectly, for countless jobs, some lasting years, for trained dancers on Broadway.

Agnes's persecution mentality meshed neatly with the pathology of the ballet world, in which only the strongest characters can withstand the strain of the work and the likelihood of an early, involuntary retirement. Intrigue and rivalries raged between individuals and groups; at Broadway auditions, modern dancers and ballet dancers sat on opposite sides of the stage, glaring at each other. During his brief marriage to Nora Kaye, Isaac Stern was introduced to a world in which "pettiness and jealousy were basic to the profession. Relationships were tenuous, haphazard, ambiguous. People lived with their bodies, not their minds. A body is the instrument that you use. And you treat it like a third person! I was a little taken aback by the utter giving to this God of the body."[21]

A dancer's work is unending and pays off, at best, in a few evanescent moments of glory. Wedded to their vocation from an early age, often undereducated and necessarily narcissistic, dancers (called "boys and girls") are often treated like children and behave accordingly. Maturity comes hard, if it comes at all. Masochism is a given; one's body receives no mercy.

The relationship between choreographer and dancer is fraught with emotional as well as physical perils. The same vulnerability that enables a dancer to move an audience renders her (or him) defenseless in the pressurized rehearsal hall, where every emotion is magnified. Agnes had a wicked tongue; Tudor's was worse, but *his* "acolytes" defended him. "Tudor could say things to make your skin crawl," said Ruth Ann Koesun, "but it was to bring something out of you, I don't think it was personal."[22] Tudor manipulated not only the bodies but the psyches of women dancers, stripping away their personalities, bullying them to get to what was underneath, to find their weaknesses and exploit them. But his ballets served the dancers, who forgave him his cruelty for the sake of his genius. That Agnes used the dancers to serve the story did not endear her to those who wished to show off their hard-won classical technique. To them, simple movement, enriched with emotion, was not enough; a request to run, skip, or walk was the equivalent of asking a thoroughbred racehorse to pull a carriage through Central Park. They were not interested in what might be achieved theatrically with the "vernacular steps" that Agnes believed "rest the mind and are familiar and comforting."[23]

If a dancer playing the Cowgirl understood Agnes's injunction to "stand absolutely still and just *be* there" when she gazes adoringly at the Wrangler, she could hold the moment, and the audience's concentration. Bambi Linn, whose stillness could convey more emotion than some dancers' grand jetés, said, "Standing still is about the hardest thing you can do. You're holding your breath trying to hold the mood, hoping that the audience will understand what's going on, and you have no steps, nothing to fill *in* for you, to give it *body*. If you give me that kind of freedom, I love it! But most dancers aren't secure unless they've got that little bit of footwork going on. With someone like Nora [Kaye], it was annoying that she wasn't given more."[24]

Tudor's dancers were accustomed to being told precisely how to move and look; the story and the emotion were built into the choreography, so that acting would have been superfluous. Agnes's method, which she called creative rehearsing, was to give her dancers rhythms and gestures and steps, but to leave space for improvisation. "She might say, 'Do something that goes from there to there and you look like a piece of seaweed fastened onto a rock,'" one dancer recalled. "Someone would try something, and she would mold it into what she wanted."[25] If some dancers felt like privileged collaborators when she incorporated their ideas, others felt exploited. Unlike Tudor, she was generous with praise when the dancers pleased her — but if she took a dislike to a dancer, whether or not for good reason, "she could throw some acid remarks that could reduce you to ashes, in front of other people. 'You really shouldn't be dancing at all!' Crushing. It was hard on everyone."[26] She could demolish a dancer with a look. The rudeness to which she had been subjected during her years of apprenticeship had not led her to behave differently when the roles were reversed.

Although the fate of a new Ballet Theatre work rested largely on its reception in New York (a maddening but unavoidable fact that is much the same in the 1990s), its choreographer rarely was allowed more than two frenzied dress rehearsals onstage before the crucial premiere. Even if the work is successful, tastes change, the public constantly demands new works, and few last more than one or two seasons. *The Harvest According* opened on October 1, 1952. "It will bewilder many, bore some, and move others to tears," the *New York Post*'s critic predicted, and reviews ranged from "a great new ballet" to "an interesting failure."[27] The most common complaint was the disparate styles, the combination of abstraction and realism. "At times it touches the heights of epic grandeur," wrote the *Christian Science Monitor*'s Margaret Lloyd, "at others it recedes to musical comedy shallows."[28] At the end of the season it vanished, unsung and unfilmed, into limbo.

With the ballet world proving as frustrating as Broadway, Agnes changed direction again. She would form her own company and take it on the road.

thirty-three

Not Swan Lake

The Agnes de Mille Dance Theatre "is not *Swan Lake,*" Agnes told an interviewer, "but it is real dance theatre."[1] The program, billed as "from Bach to Broadway," was a sampling of her early concert pieces and Broadway ballets. Dances from *Brigadoon* and *Paint Your Wagon* became suites, each with a new scenario that told a complete story. Also included was Anna Sokolow's *Lecture and Demonstration on the Evolution of Ragtime* narrated by the performers.

It was to be a return to the territory Agnes had covered as a hopeful young and then not-so-young dancer, first with Adolph Bolm and then with Sybil Shearer, Joe Anthony, and the rest of her little troupe before the war. She intended to "go over the old tracks in good style" with a company of nineteen dancers, some of whom sang, and an orchestra of thirteen musicians, augmented with pickup string players in the big cities.[2] In four months they would cover 36,000 miles, playing mostly one-nighters — coast to coast, south to Texas and north to Vancouver, traveling by bus to 126 cities.

Walter predicted financial disaster — but Walter was always predicting disaster. Then Sol Hurok decided that his organization would handle the company, thereby causing considerable uproar in the Prude

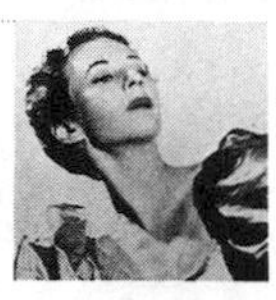

household. Agnes had disliked Hurok since 1929, when she had asked him to manage her and he had refused. Nor had he endeared himself to her by shouting loudly, when watching her dance at a rehearsal of *Tally-Ho,* "This is *booooring!*"[3] The immigrant Hurok, ignorant of social niceties and proper syntax, brought out the snob in Agnes George de Mille, as she still liked to sign herself. "He was a peasant," she said. "A midget. He had no taste except about food, no aesthetic sense; he spoke of 'the bal-lot.'"[4] On the two previous occasions when he *had* wanted to manage her, after *Rodeo* and *Oklahoma!,* she had had the satisfaction of turning him down. But he was Walter's employer, and he was determined to manage this tour. A series of meetings took place between Hurok's lawyer and Agnes's representative, Mortimer Becker. "We're negotiating hammer and tongs," Becker said, "and Walter was either sitting there or was told about it afterwards. Then I'd get phone calls from Agnes asking about points I'd made — why did she need this, why that? I told my boss, 'I make points during the day but I lose them when Walter goes home.' My boss spoke to Agnes, then told me, 'As long as he's got her in bed, you're in trouble.' I never did get a good deal for her — she made me give up some things I had gained!"[5]

Unlike Tudor, Balanchine, Robbins, and Graham, Agnes had never had a company of dancers with whom she could work with any continuity. Now, using her own money and with no "bosses" to answer to, she could hire her favorites, with whom she could use a kind of shorthand. The nucleus consisted of Gemze de Lappe, James Mitchell, the dramatic Lidija Franklin, the comedic Loren Hightower and Virginia Bosler, the Highland dancer James Jamieson, and the handsome, sexy Casimir Kokich. Danny Daniels, a self-described whizbang tap dancer of the Fred Astaire school, would demonstrate his specialty. Elizabeth Montgomery and Peggy Clark would design the costumes and scenery.

The company rehearsed for a month in Martha Graham's studio. Agnes was always at her best in the rehearsal hall; however much she sweated and struggled, she was focused and happy there. She sat in a chair, knees wide apart with her skirt hanging between them, leaning forward, holding a coffee cup and burning "with the concentration of an acetylene torch."[6] When she got up to demonstrate, her hair sprouted wildly in every direction and her tiny hands were always in motion; her face reflected everything she saw and felt. In the midst of intense activity she would suddenly stop and go blank, like a child's windup toy—one dancer called it her fish-out-of-water pose. She was refueling, waiting while her mind processed her intuition. When things went well, she could giggle like a schoolgirl with delight. "Often she was frustrated," Loren Hightower recalled, "because she didn't have the movement to fulfill what she had in her head. But she would stick it out and have you do the same things, over and over and over. You just *knew* she was stuck, but she would never say so. She was short-tempered when that happened, and the tension could be *painful*."[7] But "When it was right," said Virginia Bosler, "she was triumphant! You felt like a real collaborator. The kick wasn't just someone saying "Well done," but *"YES, THAT'S IT!"*[8]

After the opening in Baltimore on October 12, 1953, Agnes left James Mitchell in charge of the company and returned to New York to prepare a new show: *The Girl in Pink Tights*.

The culture was changing. Television had arrived, and rock and roll. As a result of the Cold War, the H-bomb, the Korean War, and Senator Joseph McCarthy, postwar optimism was eroding. Escapism was welcome — but *The Girl in Pink Tights* was nothing *but* escapism.

The shopworn story of how a stranded French dance company merged with a blood-and-thunder stock company in 1866, thus creating the first real American musical comedy, was based on the actual events leading up to *The Black Crook,* which Agnes had choreographed with Warren Leonard in 1929. In its favor, the show had the French ballerina Renée Jeanmaire, affectionately called Zizi. Known in the United States primarily as Danny Kaye's co-star in the film *Hans Christian Andersen,* Zizi was a seductive pixie who could sing, dance, and entrance an audience — but although her personal notices for *The Girl in Pink Tights* were sensational, not even she could redeem the show. The score needed major work, but the composer, Sigmund Romberg, was unavailable, having died after writing the music, and additional material was unsuccessfully patched in. Shepard Traube, the director-producer, had been successful with melodramas and comedies but had no experience with musicals, let alone an extravaganza with seventeen scenes, each more elaborate than the last. To George Jean Nathan, one of its kinder reviewers, it was "a drab, bastard mixture of ballet and burlesque."[9]

Jerome Chodorov, who wrote the book (with Joe Fields), remembers the show as "a painful blur. I've gone into rehearsal with worse books in my time and saved them," said Chodorov, who rewrote *The Girl in Pink Tights* twelve times, "but most musical failures are because of egos, and this one was Traube's. He felt overwhelmed, and got more and more hysterical. What was needed was a cool head, a very tough guy at the helm. With a hysterical director it just fell apart. It was a shambles. Agnes tried to direct some scenes, but that didn't work too well."[10] Friction intensified after rehearsals shut down for a crucial week because the star was ill. According to stage manager Bill Ross, "Shep was on uppers and downers. It wasn't coming together, and everyone could see that. Zizi loved Agnes — she called her On-yess — but only trusted her so far as a choreographer. She would squeal with delight at things Agnes would create, but she would not go that extra mile."[11]

Agnes rehearsed the women in the daytime and the men at night; everyone marveled at her stamina. Her attention was divided between the show and her company, which she occasionally caught up with on the road. When she did, the dancers bombarded her with complaints. The tour was grueling; traveling four hundred miles a day and playing up to six shows a week, they sometimes slept on the bus and had no time to eat before going onstage. "Once we had a sort of official meeting," Loren Hightower recalled. "Agnes sat on the table, fingering her silk scarf that had pearls sewed to the edge. She said, 'What you tell me is terrible, but . . .' and her tone changed, using her acting skill, 'there is one worse way of spending your youth, which is not dancing. And that is how I spent mine.' We were grateful for the job, but most of us weren't all that young, and we wished we were doing better."[12]

In January 1954, just two weeks before *Tights* was to open in New Haven, Agnes left Dania Krupska in charge of rehearsals and flew to California, to dance with her company in San Francisco and Los Angeles. In her hometown, with her father in the audience, she performed two of her classic recital pieces. Members of the company who were unfamiliar with her pre-*Rodeo* career were pleasantly surprised. "She was very funny," said Loren Hightower, "and also pathetic and sad. In *Ballet Class* and *The Parvenues,* the things that went on in her face, in her eyes — I stood there with tears in my eyes every time she did it."[13]

Tights limped from New Haven to Philadelphia, where Agnes conducted "a mournful rehearsal" at which she tried to inspire the dancers with Joseph Conrad's thoughts on the art of seamanship — the necessity of a dedication to technique, and the honor of labor, tradition, pride, and the love of a perfected skill.[14] But the finest sailor cannot keep a sieve afloat, and *The Girl in Pink Tights,* which Walter Kerr called "relentlessly uninspired," sank after fifteen weeks in New York.[15] Reviews for Agnes's dances, highlighted by a luscious pas de deux (between Renée Jeanmaire and Alexandre Kalioujny of the Paris Opéra Ballet) and a burlesque Bacchanale with the obligatory satyrs and nymphs, were mixed.

The Agnes de Mille Dance Theatre completed its tour in June and disbanded. Audiences had been largely enthusiastic; the company paid its expenses and made a modest profit for the Hurok organization. Walter had been right; Agnes never recouped her investment of $35,000. But as a retrospective of a career still in progress, it had demonstrated the range, the strengths, and the weaknesses of Agnes's work. Some critics complained that not only was it not *Swan Lake,* it wasn't even ballet — it was variety. Others pronounced it variety, and loved it. It was ballet, all right, made palatable to a mass audience by a sugar coating of character and story. Her movement vocabulary was small, but she used it resourcefully, developing variations on steps as composers develop a theme. Movement was not an end in itself, but a means; the end was to reveal character and to tell a story.

It is as easy as it is unfair to criticize Agnes for not being Tudor — or Balanchine, or Graham. The prolific Balanchine, creator of more than two hundred major works (plus dances for films and Broadway), extended and streamlined the vocabulary of classical ballet. His ballets were clean in line and movement, meticulous in technique, inventive, musical, and plotless. Graham invented a new language that would outlive its creator. Agnes was eclectic, a borrower; what she had was an astute sense of theater, and a personal style. Balanchine's dances dazzled. Graham's were mythic. De Mille's were human.

A Georgia critic grumbled that the Dance Theatre program was too much "Golden West" and had made him feel as though he'd sat through four consecutive performances of *Rodeo,* "which, like fruit cake, is best in small doses."[16] Agnes could be even harder on herself. Standing next to Daniel Mann at the back of the theater during an out-of-town performance of *Paint Your Wagon,* "she was kinda fidgety," Mann said, "and not terribly happy about what she was seeing. Finally she looked at me and she said, 'Goddammit, I look at this and I see that I've been doing the same thing, the same kind of choreography, all my life!'"[17] But she could also argue, with irrefutable logic, that "the great repeated constantly. How do we, for instance, recognize Bach in any two measures of his music? Obviously because it sounds precisely like him and no one else."[18]

The recurring theme in her choreography (and in *Dance to the Piper*) was prefigured in her childhood: paradise lost and the futile attempt to regain it. Her preoccupations were nature, love, sex, and death. But although her dances could be passionate and even violent (in her *Carousel* scenario, she had the "brutal" carnival men "knock the women around with real cruelty and the women rather like it"), they were rarely sexy, at least not in comparison with those of Jack Cole or Jerome Robbins, for she could not resist the temptation to go for a laugh. "Somehow I seem always to break lyric developments with a joke," she told dance critic Walter Terry, "as though I distrusted the development of emotion."[19] She did it consistently when dealing with sex, for she had more confidence in her comedic skills than in her sexual power (she once astonished a colleague with the non sequitur, "Every time a man left me, he left laughing. They should put that on my tombstone: 'At least they laughed'").[20] *Oklahoma!*'s whorehouse, populated with Jud's "postcard girls," really *is* a postcard. But Agnes's work was a step on the ladder that Bob Fosse would climb — or descend, depending on one's point of view — to put realistic sex on the Broadway stage (beginning with *Pajama Game* in 1954).

In Agnes's dances, love and sex were irreconcilable. Her pas de deux were tender, romantic dreams, but she admitted to "an almost Henry Jamesian inability [to allow] the hero and heroine to come together happily," and the lovers were more likely to find frustration than fulfillment.[21] Her female characters — the innocent children, adolescent misfits, repressed virgins, jubilant pioneers, and audacious whores — all represent parts of herself, actual or imagined. They either long for sex or they exploit it.

Balanchine's ballerinas played the traditional role of beautiful, fragile, dreamlike creatures who live to be pursued or awakened with a kiss. Graham's female characters are threatening and powerful. Agnes's women are strong, often distinguished by a certain stance — feet planted and head defiant — but they are also vulnerable. Always, and most tellingly in the lifts, her women are women and her men are "real" men — cowboys, miners, loggers — with never a hint of sexual ambiguity. The ultimate power is male; the ultimate goal, love and marriage. Yet her most fully realized woman character, the mother in *The Harvest According,* has no man.

She had grown up surrounded by women; men were the idealized "other." "My heroines are part of me and my heroes are part of what I'd like to know," she told a *Newsweek* reporter."[22] Her choreography for men was strong but sparse. James Mitchell, who danced the best of her male roles (in *Rodeo, Brigadoon, Fall River Legend,* and *Paint Your Wagon*), observed, "The men were all passionate, caring, loving, gentle; the women can be trollops and tramps. My character in *Paint Your Wagon* was stalwart and gentle, in relationship to the rough and tough other men. The woman was a whore, so she had to go off, leaving the man stranded. In *Fall River Legend,* the Pastor is gentle, willing to enter into a relationship; the heroine is a murderess. The women have the flaws; the men don't have any flaws. Even the villains are romantic."[23]

All choreographers have special idioms in their work, as in everyday life, as inexplicable as a preference for coffee or tea. They are the ingredients of style that make parody possible. Agnes was known for movements that were derived not from dancing but from acting. She liked her dancers to walk, to run, and to jump. She had a fondness for pas de basque, for "bells," and the movement known as "falling off a log." Hands were semaphores for emotions; often they seemed to be pushing waves away, or screwing in overhead lightbulbs, or simply fluttering with joy. The quivering hands in *Oklahoma!* reminded her of birds in the air and Laurey's heart, fluttering with happiness. Hands reached out — pleading, seeking, inviting. Clenched, they created tension and excitement, often beating with small, rapid gestures on the chest. In the depth of her agony, Lizzie Borden beat upon her body with her fists.

Classical technique was the foundation of Agnes's work, but she had learned from Martha Graham that nonclassical movement was also acceptable — that truth was as important as beauty. But Graham's work tended to be universal, abstract, and anguished. Agnes's work was specific, literal, and celebratory. Like Graham, Agnes used the floor a great deal, especially for lifts that began with the woman on the floor. When her women are struck by strong emotions, they frequently faint, to be suddenly swept up by a male rescuer — or they seem to fly, as the music builds, into the man's arms. In a variation of Graham's contraction-and-release, Agnes might have a dancer assume an extended position, perhaps an arabesque, and then curl herself into a ball or a coil, sometimes falling to the floor, to convey pain. "I am continually using falling patterns," she wrote — "the falling to earth, the swooning back, the resurrection, the running away always to return to a focal point."[24] She used pointe work, which the moderns eschewed, sparingly, as punctuation.

She disliked symmetrical forms, except for the circle; she was partial to lean, angular movements and diagonal patterns, with dancers entering at one corner and leaving at the opposite. As she contrasted tension and comedy for dramatic effect, she contrasted movement and stillness — usually a woman, or trio of women, motionless, surrounded by moving figures or groups that suggested, she said, the passing of life. A motif she had used repeatedly since 1927 (in *Jenny Loved a Soldier,* a precursor of her Civil War ballet) was that of a woman waiting, alone, until a man eventually entered upstage, behind her. It mirrored her image of herself, waiting for her father, and affected her so strongly that she had to consciously remind herself not to use it too often.

The Agnes de Mille Dance Theatre had presented an overview of the first half of Agnes's career as an artist. The second half would begin with the resurrection of the childhood dream that had foundered but not died on the shoals of *Cleopatra:* a career in the movies.

thirty-four

Oklahoma in Hollywood

Agnes's ambition was a locomotive on which she was sometimes the engineer and sometimes a passenger, but Hollywood had always been one of its destinations. After *Oklahoma!,* she had turned down movie offers in order to stay in New York, in case Walter got leave from the Army. After the war, there were no offers — until Rodgers and Hammerstein, who had acquired the rights to *Oklahoma!* from the Theatre Guild, were ready to produce a $7 million movie version.* The job would mean a six-month separation from Walter, but when the offer came, there was no question of turning it down.

Rodgers and Hammerstein formed their own production company and rented space on the MGM lot, intending to make a movie that would match, perhaps even top, the success of the stage production. It starred two young unknowns, Shirley Jones and Gordon MacRae, with Rod Steiger as the villainous Jud. The Austrian-born director, Fred Zinnemann, had won an Academy Award for his last picture, *From Here to Eternity,* but had never directed a musical. Oliver Smith designed the sets,

* As of 1954, the most expensive movie ever made.

and the exterior scenes were shot against the background of the vast Arizona landscape (standing in for that of Oklahoma).

In June 1954, Agnes and eight-year-old Jonathan were installed in an old-fashioned movie-star's house, equipped with swimming pool and houseboy, in the Hollywood foothills. Noting that it was difficult to find good dancers in California ("You'd better rest," a studio dresser told a dancer, "you're perspiring!"), Agnes had sent Rodgers and Hammerstein a list of twelve people she wanted to import from New York, rating them on looks, charm, presence, comedy sense, and dancing. Hoping to preempt Rodgers's objection to Mavis Ray, "a slightly faded beauty, i.e. 34" whom she thought would make an excellent madam of the "postcard" whores, she asked, "Don't you think there were some women of 34 in Oklahoma at that time?" — a point that Rodgers and the producer, Arthur Hornblow Jr., undoubtedly found irrelevant.[1] With the exception of Gemze de Lappe, who had been Agnes's first choice to play the dream Laurey (the part went to Bambi Linn, who looked more like Shirley Jones), Agnes got everyone she wanted. According to a possibly apocryphal story, when Hornblow insisted that she augment the group with some MGM beauties, she got her revenge by putting one of them in a dress that matched the wallpaper and rendered her invisible.

In addition to the dream ballet, Agnes choreographed three big dance numbers: "Many a New Day," "The Farmer and the Cowman," and "Everything's Up to Date in Kansas City," which was shot on location at a real railroad station in Arizona, near the Mexican border. For three weeks in the middle of the Arizona summer, Agnes rose every day at 5:30 and was driven in a limousine from her motel in Nogales to the set, fifty miles away. Also in the limousine was Jay Blackton, the musical director. "We would *dish!*," Blackton recalled. "Agnes had something to say about movement throughout the show, not just her dances, and she had comments about everybody. Poor Dick Rodgers got the worst of it. She never felt that he allowed her to share in the glory of *Oklahoma!*" Blackton theorized that Agnes needed to be unhappy in order to create, like the grain of sand that forces the oyster to produce a pearl. "I think it was natural for her to beef," he said, "and she could beef like hell!"[2]

Understandably, most choreographers are unwilling to show their work until it is ready; nervous producers have been known to demand changes and cuts in a work in progress that they might embrace without reservation in its finished form. Agnes had written in *Dance to the Piper* of waiving her rule about closed rehearsals for "people like Rodgers and Hammerstein . . . who have understanding of the creative process and who have, moreover, a sense of courtesy."[3] But when she rehearsed the dances for the movie, she barred the bosses. Rodgers, who hated to have anyone listen while he composed, was enraged; in his autobiography, he would accuse Agnes of being "the most temperamental person associated with the project. On one occasion," he wrote, "she had the door locked on a sound stage during a dance rehearsal and made Arthur [Hornblow] and me — both her employers — wait outside until she deigned to let us in."[4]

On the periphery of all this activity was Jonathan, who was an extra in the movie (as Agnes had played extra parts in her father's movies). At lunchtime Agnes was observed reading *Dr. Dolittle* or otherwise trying to amuse the boy. One day he was seen searching rather frantically for her and told not to worry. "Wouldn't *you* worry," he said vehemently, "if *your* mother had disappeared?"[5]

Everyone close to Agnes on the picture noticed that she seemed to be under tremendous stress, to the point of fainting on the set one day. Elmer Bernstein, the rehearsal pianist, attributed her anxiety to a lack of support from Rodgers and Hammerstein. "Rodgers was very dictatorial, steely, and self-important. His tunes are like his personality. They're head tunes, a kind of brilliant musical intellect at work — compared with the tunes of Jerome Kern, what I call heart tunes. Rodgers was the bête noir and Oscar was the loved one, the good cop. That was very useful for both of them." Bernstein considered Agnes "a victim of Richard Rodgers's macho attitude toward women, and also a victim of the stratification of Hollywood in those days. In that class system, the choreographer would be *way* down — and Agnes was also a woman, and therefore an inferior being. My feeling is that she felt beleaguered and knew she was fighting a losing battle — that for whatever reason, it wasn't working out the way she had hoped. I think it may have been particularly burdensome for her that Hollywood was her home, and she was a stranger in her home."[6]

In a sense, Agnes had always been a stranger in Hollywood; her parents had been in the town but not, unlike Cecil, of it. Now, she had other reasons for concern. Theater was her medium; she visualized in terms of the stage, and she could not accommodate to the fact that the audience could see only what the camera saw. Furthermore, moviemaking was no longer the process she had observed when she and the industry were young. It was no longer financially feasible, for example, to shoot thirty or forty takes of a production number, using a full crew. The studio seemed to Agnes "an enormous factory," an obstacle course of "mechanics" that limited instead of expanded her options.[7] Unfortunately for all concerned, said Oliver Smith, "She thought she knew all about it, and she didn't have an eye for the camera at all! And you couldn't instruct Agnes de Mille, at her age of life and with her success — talking about having grown up as Cecil B. De Mille's niece, and her father writing movies — about the camera!"[8]

Oklahoma! was the first film to be shot in Todd-AO, a process so complicated that it quickly became a footnote in film history. Named for Mike Todd, who financed it, and the American Optical Company, which developed it, Todd-AO was meant to create the same feeling of audience participation as Cinerama, but without the visible seams. The 70-mm cameras were expensive and cumbersome, and every scene had to be shot a second time, in 35-mm Cinemascope, so that theaters that were not equipped to project the wide-frame version could also show the movie.

Whatever the size of the screen, a choreographer must constantly choose between long shots, which sacrifice detail, and close-ups, which sacrifice the overview and can distort the picture. Agnes wanted both; she wanted to show faces, and to show dancers jetéing across the camera like birds flying across the prairie. But the broad sweep of her choreography that was so thrilling on the stage was lost on the screen. James Mitchell, who played Curly in the dream ballet, pointed out that although there were long runs and wonderful lifts, "Agnes never got a shot of us coming together so you could see both our faces. She got Bambi running presumably toward me, then me from the back, running, and then a cut to the lift almost accomplished. So you never saw the whole thing."[9]

The dream ballet was filmed on a 54,000-square-foot soundstage and employed thirty-two dancers. According to Bambi Linn, "Agnes was bull-headed. Robert Surtees [the cinematographer] would put her on the boom and she'd fly up in the air and he'd say, 'See what we can do? We can do this, we can do that.' And she'd say, 'No, I don't like it that way!' They had this huge ninety-degree scrim so that the camera could just swing around, and she didn't use it. She staged the ballet like it was for a proscenium arch, and it didn't work! Surtees and Zinnemann finally convinced her that the camera had to come in and go around and *do* things, and they scrapped that whole first version. I think they did it about twenty-five times before they finally got the version you see on the screen. It took a long time to get through to her, and money was just flying out the window."[10]

Walter joined his wife and son for a month, but Agnes worked long hours, and the company was a family (a dysfunctional one) to which Walter did not belong. She flew to New York to be with him for three long weekends, but the strain of the work went with her. To Elmer Bernstein's surprise, "She talked a lot about always having trouble with her relationships with men. The subtext of everything she said about herself was that she didn't consider herself attractive. I thought she was one of the more attractive people I've ever known!"[11]

Not everyone thought Agnes attractive. Nearing fifty, her hair was graying, her figure thickening; a year later she would have a face-lift. Except on public occasions, her clothes were hopeless. "If I had walked onto a set and not known who she was," Loren Hightower mused, "I'd have thought, 'What is this housewife doing in the theater?'"[12] But no one could deny the fact that she was an exciting woman. She laughed a lot when she talked — a giggly, girlish laugh — and gestured emphatically with her small, capable hands. When the conversation was stimulating, her eyes brightened and darted about, and her face flushed. She still had the energy of a teenager and, for someone who thought herself unattractive, an unexpected sexual chutzpah. On the set, she often wore a wraparound denim skirt that was not always wrapped securely. One day, a dancer got up the nerve to tell her that her rear was exposed when she put her hands in her pockets. She shrugged, put her hands in her pockets, and sashayed away.

She spoke nostalgically to Elmer Bernstein of her early days in California — of her father, whose health was failing, with great affection, and of her uncle with some bitterness. Bernstein, who also worked with Cecil, observed that both uncle and niece had "the same kind of steel, the same professional drive and determination, and *amazing* minds. But they were very different people. C. B. — I never would have called him C. B. to his face — was perfectly ready to give the public what it wanted. Agnes hoped the public would like the things she believed in, but she was gonna do them anyway."[13] Cecil was always Mr. De Mille. Agnes was Agnes; James Mitchell even called her Aggie-poo.

The underlying cause of Agnes's distress was the same arrogance that had sabotaged her work on *Romeo and Juliet* and *Cleopatra.* In a preproduction memo to Rodgers and Hammerstein, a studio executive had stated that the dance numbers must be "subordinate to the story and to the pace of the picture as a whole. Any attempt to overemphasize them or to make them stand out independently by lengthening them would destroy the flow of the story and distract the attention of the audience."[14] Instructed to make the dances shorter than in the stage version, Agnes made them longer, believing that their quality would change the bosses' minds. She deliberately choreographed so that the dances could not be cut without reorchestrating the music, gambling that Rodgers would not take such a drastic step. She miscalculated; even Oscar Hammerstein was furious about what she had done. Extraneous characters that she had invented were excised, along with much of the choreography's fluidity and nuance and the quiet moments that provided dramatic contrast. Most of the dances seem abrupt, frenetic, unbalanced. Ignoring her own culpability, Agnes lamented that some of her finest work had been "mutilated" and "butchered."

In the theater, *Oklahoma!*'s artifice was its charm. The movie had the same weightless story and stylized dances, but the settings were realistic — real barns, real cornfields, real vistas of plains — and the widescreen process worked against the more touching scenes (one reviewer complained that Laurey's rendition of "Out of My Dreams" was marred by "a colossal close-up in which the heroine's left nostril alone is large enough to park a jeep in").[15] Under the weight of the clashing styles, the cumbersome technology, and the hand of a director whose forte was drama, the soufflé collapsed.

Reviews were generally positive, but some reviewers called the movie static, old-fashioned, and, at 143 minutes, too long. Others thought that the dances seemed shopworn, "as though they have been a little too thoroughly through de Mille."[16] "All that is lacking," Arthur Knight wrote in *Dance Magazine,* "is invention, and imagination, and a little daring."[17] But the dream ballet, which escaped severe cutting, was widely praised. The six-track, state-of-the-art sound was glorious. And forty years after its release, audiences still enjoy *Oklahoma!*'s fresh young stars, its breathtaking vistas of prairie and sky, and the songs that are imprinted on its collective memory.

For Agnes, who left Hollywood feeling "whipped and dejected," the final blow came the following year, when Rodgers and Hammerstein announced plans to film *Carousel* — with dances choreographed by Rod Alexander.[18] "My career with Rodgers and Hammerstein has turned rancid," she told Michael Hertz when she heard the news. "Everything I ever did for them has been exploited and dirtied up."[19] Bambi Linn, who worked with Alexander, said, "Rodgers was furious with Agnes because she had taken up so much time and money with her ballet in *Oklahoma!* And I think he and Hammerstein were petrified that if they allowed her to do *Carousel,* the ballet would take over the movie. They weren't going to allow that. Consequently, the choreography is nothing special, and the movie has faded away into nothing."[20]

In the spring of 1955, William de Mille died of cancer. The father who had ignited Agnes's ambition ("I'd rather love you for what you do than because you're mine"), the father she never stopped trying to please, was the grain of sand in the oyster. Her mother's injunction was Do something!; her father's was Do something great! At the height of her success, she was still compelled to write, "Pop . . . was very proud of me because I was the first dancer ever to direct a big musical *(Allegro)* and he thought I did it very well."[21]

William de Mille is remembered less for his movies and plays than for founding the drama department at the University of Southern California, where he taught the craft of dramatic writing. After his death, Agnes wrote to a onetime student protégé of his: "All the fatherly love and attention which he found himself unable to give us during our growing up and my early professional struggles, he was free to lavish on his students."[22] Her father was the template for the unattainable man who appears in her work in many guises, beginning with the Tyrolean boy (Warren Leonard) in *May Day.*

In Agnes's "The Glitter and the Gold," a ballet that exists only in the form of rough notes, the adolescent heroine has two father figures: the lover of her dominating mother (he awakens the daughter with a kiss), and an actual father who is more interested in sports and in "talking, talking, talking," than in his family, and who at one point gets drunk and dances orgiastically with the maids. The girl is an heiress; she has incestuous uncles and aunts. She dances alone, in a garden — "waiting, waiting, expecting"; a real lover appears and they dance a pas de deux of "innocent" love, but as in Tudor's *Lilac Garden,* the girl is pledged to "The Man She Must Marry." After the wedding, which takes place in the family mansion, the mother is spurned by her lover and left alone to "slowly die of attrition, fixed in her glory like a fly in amber."[23]

It requires no psychological insight to recognize the members of Agnes's family (the girl even wears a white dress), to speculate that the heiress's inheritance could be her family's famous name, or to observe that the address of the family mansion, described as "If Piranesi lived in the 1880s and on cocaine, he would design this," could be De Mille Drive.

The same elements, rearranged as in a psychological kaleidoscope, appear in Agnes's 1956 ballet *The Rib of Eve.* The protagonist is no longer a girl but a middle-aged woman, gripped by what appears to be Agnes's "midlife madness." The husband could be modeled on any of the three central men in Agnes's life: William, Walter, or James Mitchell, who danced the role.

Like the Prince in *Tally-Ho,* Eve's husband ignores his frustrated wife. She retaliates by flirting outrageously with the male guests at a series of parties. But where *Tally-Ho* has a plot, and understandable characters and humor, *Eve* is a confusing mishmash of Freudian symbolism that in its various versions includes mirrors (dancers are obsessed with mirrors), murder, masks, cages, severed body parts ("When she kisses a young man, she detaches an eye or an ear or an arm and hangs them like fetishes on her dress"), a chastity belt, and an analyst's couch. Men dance with men, women dance with the furniture. When a young man kisses Eve, "walls crash down."

As a portrait of marriage-as-power-struggle, *The Rib of Eve* reflected Agnes's perception of her marriage in its thirteenth year. She and Walter were happiest on holiday together — at Merriewold or, on rare occasions, abroad, when Agnes Prude displaced Agnes de Mille. At home, he was jealous of her career, she of real or imaginary rivals. Mae Frohman, however, was no longer an issue. While *The Rib of Eve* was in rehearsal, she died of cancer.

In the penultimate scene of the ballet, Eve hurls herself against her husband "in a series of frantic maneuvers to dominate, but instead of giving way like foam as the guests invariably do, he stands like rock and she very nearly bashes her head in on him." There ensues a passionate pas de deux, after which Eve is momentarily content. But ultimately, unable to hold her husband's undivided attention, she breaks down. In the end, they die — he of exhaustion, she "of boredom and loneliness." The guests place their bodies in cages, and "the woman slowly extends her hand to meet her husband's. The clasped hands are snatched like a curio by a guest and hung on the ceiling. The armless helpless woman inclines yearningly toward the armless ruined man," and the final image is of the two bodies, "always apart and imprisoned, always straining, yearning and forever forbidden to touch."[24]

The nightmarish *Rib of Eve* would be Agnes's most disturbing and least successful dream ballet.

Evangelist for Dance

In spite of its impressive repertory and roster of stars, Ballet Theatre was in 1955 still primarily a touring company with no permanent home; it merely rented the Metropolitan Opera House for its New York season. As it lurched from one financial crisis to the next, Agnes, as a governing trustee, was expected to solicit funds from foundations and other potential donors. At the same time, she was forever dunning the company for her royalties — a demeaning and usually unproductive exercise.*

In Lucia Chase, she continued to battle an "absolutely wonderful stubbornness" that matched her own.[1] Agnes's letters to Chase, pitched in a haughty key, were punctuated with threats to withdraw her work if her demands concerning casting, rehearsal time, and programming were not met. For example:

> Through most roundabout channels, I learned that you do not intend to do *Harvest According* on the American Composers' Night. Don't you think it

---

* The royalty on her ballets averaged $20 per performance. On the rare occasions when she danced in *Three Virgins and a Devil* or *Rodeo* or, on even rarer occasions, *Judgment of Paris,* she was paid $75 per performance. Her fee for choreographing *The Rib of Eve* was $2,000.

> would be courteous if someone in the office notified me about this directly and gave some of the reasons for the change of mind? Inasmuch as it seems very likely that I will withdraw *Rodeo* from the Spring season because of the casting problems, I shall be rather poorly represented in your repertoire and this is disappointing to me.[2]

Lucia replied,

> I knew when I saw the Special Delivery (or even without it) it was bad news . . . If you are planning to withdraw *[Rodeo]* it would be considerate to say so soon or is that too much to ask. It has not been easy to set the programs for 28 ballets in 24 performances and please everybody.[3]

The problem was resolved when Lucia signed James Mitchell for the season. His roles would include the Wrangler in *Rodeo,* the Pastor in *Fall River Legend,* and the Husband, opposite Nora Kaye, in *The Rib of Eve.*

In celebration of its fifteenth anniversary, Ballet Theatre reprised its most popular works — among them, Agnes's *Three Virgins and a Devil, Rodeo,* and *Fall River Legend* — and mounted a new production of *Tally-Ho.*

The *Rib of Eve* and Antony Tudor's *Offenbach in the Underworld,* were the company's only new works of the season.

The Rib of Eve premiered on April 25, 1956, with music by Morton Gould, sets by Oliver Smith, and costumes by Irene Sharaff. The ballet was praised for its patterns and its dancing, especially the pas de deux by Mitchell and Kaye, but its meaning was incomprehensible. The Wife, described in the scenario as "brilliant, radiant, successful and frenetic" came across as merely vain and self-obsessed, and the audience had no reason to care what happened to her. The dances were derivative, most noticeably of the *Allegro* ballet. The reviews were among the worst of Agnes's career. Frances Herridge was gentle ("She seems on the verge of saying something significant about women's nature that never gets said").[4] Miles Kastendieck was dismissive ("It appears outdated").[5] Robert Coleman was disdainful ("A waste of talent"), and John Martin was scathing ("The choreography is coarse-grained, fidgety and unintelligible").[6] Louis Biancolli was evenhanded: "What one saw was a succession of group flights across the stage, one or two very strenuous duets, a set of intricate body-twisters for Nora Kaye, and a few very attractive but oddly timed lapses into classic ballet . . . It went wrong in trying too hard to be too many things and in the end being very little at all — a very spare rib indeed."[7] *Eve* lasted just one season in the repertory.

Agnes's next ballet lasted one night. *Sebastian,* with music and libretto by Gian-Carlo Menotti, was part of an experimental series called Ballet Theatre Previews, presented at the Phoenix Theatre in the spring of 1957. The series consisted of seven new works by a group of choreographers that included Herbert Ross, Kenneth MacMillan, and Erik Bruhn. Sets, costumes, and rehearsal time were minimal, and everyone felt the strain.

In the melodramatic *Sebastian,* two sisters try to destroy the courtesan with whom their brother, a prince, is in love, by stabbing an effigy of her.* Her black slave, Sebastian, is also in love with her; he substitutes his body for the effigy, which is behind a curtain, and is stabbed to death. Agnes moved the setting from fourteenth-century Venice to the Renaissance and substituted a jealous wife for the sisters.

---

* *Sebastian* was originally choreographed by Edward Caton in 1944.

Agnes always claimed that Nora Kaye, who played the wife, sabotaged the ballet. Darrell Notara, who danced the role of the Prince, said, "Nora had done nothing but leads until then. In *Sebastian,* Lupe [Serrano] danced the lead [the Courtesan]. That's where the ego problems started." During rehearsals, Kaye made it clear that she would rather have been somewhere else, and her attitude clouded the atmosphere. "Choreographers like Agnes need input from the artist," Notara said, "and there's certainly nothing wrong with that. You get a lot of great work, if you have a dancer who's committed and wanting to contribute. Agnes got unhappy if she had dancers who stood like, 'Okay, what do you want me to do?' And Nora did that in *Sebastian.*"[8]

Nothing can be more infuriating to a choreographer than a sulky dancer — but Agnes, who banned corps members from the rehearsal hall for the smallest infractions, seemed almost intimidated by stars. Her eyes might flash with anger, but only for an instant; then she would sniff, perhaps make a joke, and go on. According to Gemze de Lappe, who frequently assisted her, "Agnes expected people to behave well, and she never could understand why they didn't. With Nora or Lupe [Serrano] or Sallie [Wilson], she was never able to say, 'Shape up, I don't like your attitude!' You'd know that she was very unhappy, which is of course not pleasant for anybody, and she'd say terrible things when they'd staggered out of the room — 'No talent!' 'Can't act!' — but not, 'Look, if you really don't want to be in this ballet, why don't you say so? Either be helpful and do it as well as you possibly can, or I'll have to find somebody to replace you.' Because they *did* sabotage, just by being negative, not trying to do their best."[9]

Sebastian opened and closed on May 28, 1957. After the performance, while Agnes was telling Herbert Ross, "That bitch has just fouled up my whole work!" Kaye was telling Glen Tetley, "'I got out there and I couldn't remember a thing, so I just made up Agnes de Mille!' Agnes was acting as though she'd been crucified," Tetley said, "and Nora was giggling."[10] Kaye might have improved the ballet by dancing her role with conviction, but there is no reason to believe that she could have saved it. In its only favorable review, *Sebastian* was praised for capturing, "via pageantry and pantomime, the intrigue, superstition, and religious faith of Venice, circa 1590."[11] Nine years would elapse before Ballet Theatre would introduce another de Mille ballet.

During Ballet Theatre's 1956 European tour (at which time the company's name was officially changed to American Ballet Theatre), Agnes fulfilled an old ambition: to dance the Cowgirl on the stage of the Opera House in Covent Garden.

She was fifty years old, and had not danced the role since 1948. Ignoring Walter's advice ("Don't do it. You've had enough. You're past it"), she lost ten pounds, and got the dancer Enrique Martinez, who knew the ballet well, to coach her.[12] "Agnes said, 'Give me hell,'" Martinez recalled. "'Anything you want to say, say it. Anything you want to make me do, I'll do it. I want to give a good performance.' She forced me to demand from her what I'd seen *her* demand."[13] Therese Horner, with whom Agnes stayed during the rehearsal period, remembers her collapsing into bed so wearily each night that the linens remained wrinkle-free.

Agnes gave, as always, an electrifying performance. The reviews were ecstatic, belated reparations from the city she had left in defeat in 1938. It was an appropriate coda to her performing career. "I didn't think of it as my dramatic farewell to dancing," she said. "There was no heart-wrenching, 'I'm-going-to-put-on-toe-shoes-for-the-last-time.'"[14] The shape and direction of her career were changing. She was working on a sequel to *Dance to the Piper* and building a lecture career. In 1951, Harold Taylor, the young president of Sarah Lawrence College, had invited her to speak at the dedication of the school's Art Center.* She subsequently joined the distinguished roster of Sarah Lawrence Board members (including Archibald MacLeish, Marshall Field, and the author Catherine Drinker Bowen, with whom she formed a lasting friendship), and she spoke at other colleges about the arts in general and dance in particular. In 1956, the lectures culminated in two memorable television shows that made her a household face.

Omnibus was an educational series, sponsored by the Ford Founda-

* In 1930 she had delivered a series of radio lectures on modern dance, geared for colleges.

tion, that survived, miraculously, for five seasons in network television's Sunday afternoon "cultural ghetto." Leonard Bernstein had popularized serious music on *Omnibus,* and attorney Joseph Welch had brought the Constitution to life for the upper-middlebrow audience. In 1952 and 1953, *Omnibus* had televised *Rodeo* and *Three Virgins and a Devil* (discreetly renamed *Three Maidens and the Devil,* with Agnes dancing her original role), two of the first complete ballets ever shown on television. Agnes's programs, "The Art of Ballet" and "The Art of Choreography," outlined the history of dance and the choreographer's role in it, illustrated with excerpts from her own and other choreographers' work.* What made them exceptional was Agnes's exhaustive knowledge of the subject, her contagious enthusiasm for it, and her ability to obey her own dictum: Never bore.

Too vain to wear glasses and unable to read cue cards without them, she memorized the hour-long script — and then wrung her hands nervously lest she forget her lines. She wore a conservative black dress and pearls, and spoke in a rather high-pitched voice, with an accent that was part mid-Atlantic, part theatrical. She addressed her audience without condescension. "This is a class," she began. "This is the barre. . . . This is the way the practice has always begun, for two hundred and fifty years." She explained that the purpose of ballet was "to lift up the hearts of those who watch." Her dancers showed how movements developed into different styles in various parts of the world. They demonstrated the techniques of the great dancers of each era, with Agnes herself recreating a performance by Marie Camargo, the great artist of early eighteenth-century ballet. Commenting on the action, she explained the relationship of emotion to movement, distinguished between execution and performing, and spoke almost worshipfully of the dedication of dancers (when she compared a ballerina to a five-star general in the army, no viewer could miss the point). To rebut the stereotype of the effeminate male dancer, she showed the dances of African and Scottish warriors. At the end of the second show she asked, "Why do we care so dreadfully?

* Broadcast on February 26, 1956, and December 30, 1956, they ran forty and fifty-eight minutes in length.

In order to communicate. With whomever will listen. To say what lies behind language." In less than two hours, she had immeasurably enlightened and expanded the audience for dance.

Because *Omnibus* was live, each segment had to flow into the next. John Butler, one of the first choreographers to use the new medium effectively, advised on camera angles and helped to avoid mistakes that were common in television's early days, such as cutting off the heads or the feet of the dancers. "She had a chip on her shoulder," Butler recalled, "that everyone was out to do her in until they had proved themselves. She would hardly speak to Robert Saudek [the producer], except to fight with him about what should be in the program. She would have kept Charlie Dubin [the director] out of her rehearsals if Jim Mitchell hadn't explained to her that this was live television, and the director had to know everything that went on."[15] After a heart-stopping moment when Agnes dried up and had to be thrown a line, Butler ran across the room as soon as she was off camera and kissed her hands, to give her courage.

No one before or since has been such a persuasive evangelist for dance. Accolades came from reviewers and balletomanes, but also from the newly converted — taxi drivers, construction workers, and shop clerks. Walter Terry called her "something of a sorceress, as are all great performers. . . . She deserves medals, laurel wreaths, a gold statue of Terpsichore."[16] After the disappointments of *Sebastian, The Rib of Eve,* and the *Oklahoma!* movie, the success was delicious. Even the dance establishment, which had always looked down its nose at Agnes, finally acknowledged her contribution to American dance. In 1956, Joseph Welch presented her with an award on behalf of *Dance Magazine.* "Millions of people awoke the morning of February 26, 1956," he said, "possessing either no knowledge of the ballet or at best a dim perception of this ancient, beautiful art. That night those same millions fell asleep with their lives enriched and their hearts gladdened. . . . They had looked at *Omnibus* and seen Miss de Mille's 'The Art of Ballet.'"[17]

"The Art of Choreography" was chosen as one of the two American television programs to be shown at the 1958 Brussels World Fair ("Bernstein on Bach" was the other). It still exists on kinescope, as does the companion "Art of Ballet"; both would be worthy additions to the curricula of every high school in the country.

Agnes made her final appearance on *Omnibus* in 1957, sharing the stage with Joseph Welch, who had represented the Army during the Army-McCarthy hearings in 1954. Welch's dignified outrage at Senator McCarthy's demagogue tactics had made him a folk hero of the day — and like all great courtroom lawyers, he was enough of a ham to enjoy his celebrity. He had grown up in Massachusetts — Lizzie Borden country — and when Agnes discovered that he was as fascinated with the murder as she was, she organized a program about the case. It would consist of a discussion of the crime, reenactments of the morning of the murder and the trial, and a full-length performance of *Fall River Legend,* with Nora Kaye as the Accused.[18]

Agnes respected Welch's New England character and enjoyed his plain, dry humor, and the two formed a warm friendship. "My feeling for you is so fond and admiring," she wrote to him, "as to be positively sticky."[19] He wrote, "I consider my life sweetened by knowing you."[20] The two now-famous television personalities visited Fall River together to view the scene of the crime and interview the few remaining souls who had secondhand knowledge of the case. They rented the actual hatchet, paying $250 for a twenty-second close-up that was wasted on the viewers, who were unaware of its grisly authenticity. They even used the actual plaster casts of the victims' skulls that had been presented as evidence at the original trial (one of the dancers remembers Agnes thoughtfully fitting her fingers into the cracks).

Fall River Legend was Agnes's most successful adaptation of her choreography for the screen. With John Butler again advising her on camera angles, she maintained the sweep of the action and used close-ups to emphasize the dramatic details: the expressions on Lizzie's face, her hand reaching for the axe, her stepmother's vicious whispering to the Pastor. "For the third time," Walter Terry wrote, "Miss de Mille has done a wonderful job . . . in bringing the excitement and the dignity and the urgency of dance to television."[21]

thirty-six

Just Living

Much as Agnes loved her husband and son, her ambition all but consumed her. In 1958, she was pursuing careers in choreography, writing, and lecturing, while doing her best to meet Walter's and Jonathan's demands. "I haven't yet found the solution to the problem of being a woman and an artist," she said. "I answer it the best way I can just by living."[1]

At twelve, Jonathan was an extremely bright child, with the rather querulous quality of children who have been sickly as infants and in early childhood. His facility with language would eventually rival that of both his parents, and he shared his mother's fascination with history. Agnes was loving, but often physically unavailable. Walter was emotionally unavailable; he seemed indifferent to his son, and there was tension between them. "Walter and Jonathan were like strangers," a family friend declared. "They were like two dogs sniffing around each other."[2] His godfather, Harold Taylor, recalled, "When Jonathan was ten or eleven he needed somebody he trusted to talk to about his father and mother, and he would talk to me. He isolated himself inside the family, partly in self-protection. He *felt* isolated — with his mother inventing new dances and his father booking acts, there wasn't really enough time for him. Walter never wanted to take on the duties of a father, and Agnes was concerned

that Jonathan didn't get enough parental time — 'face time' was the phrase that Jonathan used."[3]

Agnes's formal analysis was over, but in stressful times she still sought professional guidance. In the 1950s, she switched from Florence Powdermaker to Richard Frank, whom she would consult from time to time over the next thirty years. She took Jonathan to Dr. Frank for an evaluation, which revealed little more than that the boy yearned for an ordinary life. His ambition, he said, was to be an average man with a good income. His mother could not resist cracking, "No average man has crossed our threshold in years."[4]

Agnes had been away from Broadway for four years, during which she had done a movie, two ballets, three television shows, numerous lectures, and a prolific amount of writing. She had traveled with Walter when they could arrange it — usually to Bermuda or the Caribbean in the spring, and on two memorable month-long trips to Europe and one to the Far East. On those rare occasions (with Jonathan ensconced at camp or at Merriewold with Anna), they relaxed and simply enjoyed their favorite company — each other.

Every summer Agnes spent at least a month at Merriewold, and as many weekends as she could manage. She and Walter drove there in separate cars, partly because her habit of stopping to pick wildflowers made him impatient, but also to accommodate their independent itineraries. Merriewold was her lifelong refuge; "It teaches me the verities," she said, "and puts me in proportion."[5] At Merriewold, she ate at her parents' dining room table and slept in their brass bed. The garden was restorative, even though the wildlife consumed most of what she planted. She adored day lilies; so did the deer. For a time, she and Walter surrounded the plants every evening with a jerry-built fortification of barbed wire, old floorboards, and rocking chairs, under which they had to crawl on their stomachs to get to the front porch. Plastic bags proved more practical, and were a partial solution; Agnes covered the plants with them at night and removed them in the morning. But the deer kept on eating. Agnes kept on planting.

Walter would never love Merriewold as Agnes did, but he grew to like it; he enjoyed the tennis (so did Agnes, who still played a mean game, but it pleased her that Walter was better) and the bar in the clubhouse on Saturday nights. In the community of about forty-five families, Agnes was one of two celebrities (George Abbott was the other); she once danced a bit of *Rodeo* as part of a clubhouse entertainment, wearing her Cowgirl costume and stamping her feet with abandon on the wooden floor. When asked to exhibit her memorabilia in the clubhouse or speak about Merriewold's past, she always obliged. But she was usually a presence in absentia, preferring drinks with a more selective gathering on her front porch. There were midnight swims in the lake, sometimes au naturel. In the daytime, Jonathan and his friends swam or sailed little boats. The boy loved the place as his mother had done; but "there was a time," he recalled, "when I presented Mom with the proposition that life would be simpler if she would just come down to the lake like the other mothers and knit, or whatever it was they did."[6] That was never a possibility.

In 1957 Agnes completed the sequel to *Dance to the Piper, And Promenade Home.** *Piper* had been a Literary Guild selection and a Reader's Digest

* Published in October 1958.

condensation, and was published in five languages; nevertheless, Agnes complained that it wasn't sufficiently advertised, wasn't a Book-of-the-Month Club selection, and she blamed its inevitable slide off the best-seller list on the publisher's "lethargic" promotion.[7] Two years after publication, Edward Weeks grew impatient. "Don't growl at us under your sweet breath," the editor admonished her. "Don't think we are curmudgeons or casuals if the sale is on the slim side."[8]

"And promenade home" is the final call of every American square dance; it means "return to your base." To Agnes, it had two additional connotations: Walter's return from the war, and acquiring a home of her own. The book tells the story of her courtship and marriage and wartime separation from Walter, all in counterpoint to her career. In *Piper,* Walter was identified only as "a soldier" or "WP." Here, although he is the pivotal character, he remains a shadowy figure.

And Promenade Home details the preparation of *One Touch of Venus, Bloomer Girl,* and *Carousel.* It contains vivid portraits of Mary Martin, Martha Graham, Jerome Robbins, Trude Rittman, Bambi Linn, Sono Osato, Diana Adams, Kay Kendall, Elia Kazan, Sol Hurok, and others. Whatever her private feelings, Agnes was generally generous and fair in her written assessments. To write without rancor about Rodgers and Hammerstein was a challenge, and she rose to the occasion:

> It is hard in a few pages to sketch these complex, contradictory, fascinating, passionate and gifted men who played such an overwhelming role in my life and of whom I grew so fond, so grateful to for so much, with whom, in fact, I fell in love, yet who, for all the rich and fruitful hours spent together, the miles traveled, the honors and horrors shared, were bent on preserving what in the end could not be shared. For over the years they became more and more concerned with what tragically and inevitably must raise barriers between their ambition and all collaborators.[9]

And Promenade Home is better organized and more economically written than *Dance to the Piper.* Its references range from Henry James to Coleridge, Beethoven, Schubert, Brahms, Shakespeare, and Anne Lindbergh. On the subject of failure, Agnes was philosophical:

> We may be grateful that very seldom are circumstances propitious and that the work fights through hard and slow. The moment one knows how, one begins to die a little. Living is a form of not being sure, of not knowing what next or how. And the artist before all others never entirely knows. He guesses. And he may be wrong . . . One leaps in the dark.[10]

The real failure, she wrote, was in *not* taking the risks, *not* trying. "Far better than succeeding regularly is a good tough falling-short of a challenge," she concluded — advice that would sustain her through unimaginable challenges that lay ahead.[11]

The chapter titled "Rhythm in My Blood" is a shrewd analysis of personal style — for example,

> Whereas Balanchine's rhythmic sense is spatial and linked to the music, Robbins's is independent. I, on the other hand, am totally derivative and lean and grow on melody. I cannot move without melody. May there not here be revealed a subtle sexual distinction? The men work free and on their own; the woman must wait for the lead.[12]

And Promenade Home presents paradoxical images of Agnes, all of them valid. She saw herself as one of a sisterhood of war brides "waiting for the lead," i.e., their soldiers' return — yet she was also a well-connected member of the privileged class who had taken initiatives, pulled strings, and broken rules in order to get to Walter in London during the war. The third factor in an equation that would never balance was her role as an artist. In the book and on the lecture circuit, the family-career dilemma was a recurring theme. "If women are happier to be engaged in creative work," she told women's groups across the country, "they will be better wives and mothers and everybody will profit."[13]

Like most sequels, *And Promenade Home* did not match the commercial success of its predecessor, but it was well received critically, especially by female reviewers. "What emerges best," Phyllis McGinley wrote, "is the picture of herself — a brave, thorny, opinionated, great-hearted woman, attempting and achieving the nearly-impossible. Surely she deserves that special trophy, that privilege reserved for the few feminine talents able successfully to combine marriage and a career — the right to have her cake and eat it."[14]

Male artists were spared such conflicts, and it is not surprising that the "superdirectors" who followed the trail Agnes had blazed were exclusively men. If *Allegro* had been a hit, Agnes might have become a superdirector in spite of her sex. Instead, she had paved the way for Jerome Robbins to choreograph and direct *Peter Pan* in 1954, and for Michael Kidd to do the same with *Li'l Abner* in 1956. A year later Robbins conceived, directed, and choreographed *West Side Story,* in which the dancing was not merely integrated with the show's other elements, but integral to the entire show. *Brigadoon* without Agnes's dances is enfeebled. *West Side Story* without Robbins's dances is impossible. Robbins thus became the most powerful superdirector on Broadway.

Robbins and Kidd and their successors — Bob Fosse, Michael Bennett, Gower Champion — would become the auteurs of the musical stage. Agnes would never possess that kind of clout. During the 1958–59 season she returned to Broadway with two shows, but not as director. The first, *Goldilocks,* was a takeoff on the early days of moviemaking, complete with pirate fights à la Douglas Fairbanks, soldiers and Indians; the heroine clutches her baby as bullets and arrows fly. The leading character, a flamboyant director, bore a distinct resemblance to Cecil B. De Mille. How could Agnes resist?

Goldilocks was written and directed by Walter Kerr, a respected New York theater critic who had begun his career as an academic and whose hands-on theatrical background had been almost entirely limited to a university setting. His coauthor and wife, Jean Kerr, was the author of the humorous and best-selling book *Please Don't Eat the Daisies* and of the play *King of Hearts. Goldilocks* had lyrics by the Kerrs and Joan Ford, and music by Leroy Anderson, known for "The Typewriter Song" and "The Syncopated Clock." Elaine Stritch, the female star, was a many-splendored performer, but her abrasive quality was wrong for the part and completely overpowered her costar, Barry Sullivan. Stritch, who had a drinking problem, was unpredictable and uncooperative, objecting to much of what she was asked to do.

"The show needed a tough son-of-a-bitch," Walter Kerr said. "I was the director; I should have been it." He has no recollection of criticizing anything Agnes did. "If she wanted the whole stage, she got it. I think my admiration of her made me negligent in that sense. I'd been away from directing for too long. I'd been reviewing for seven, eight years. I'd forgotten the procedures. I blew it!"[15]

At a preview in Philadelphia, the Kerrs paced the long corridor behind the Erlanger Theater in flop agony, muttering as they passed each other, "Why isn't it working? Why aren't they laughing?" The answer came in notices such as, "Big, expensive, formless, unintegrated, filled with startling non sequiturs and musical comedy clichés."[16] The Kerrs took the show apart, cutting and rearranging. They replaced Barry Sullivan with Don Ameche. Stritch stayed. "We did make improvements," Kerr reflected in hindsight. "There were more laughs, and the songs sounded better. Maybe we improved it twenty percent. But if it was only twenty percent successful to begin with, what have you got?"[17]

They moved on to Boston, where Noël Coward saw the show and described it in his diary as "One of the most idiotic, formless, amateur productions I have ever seen. The music is entirely dull, the lyrics overburdened with effort and the book non-existent. The production is grandiose and fabulously expensive. . . . Aggie de Mille's ballets are not really good enough, and the cast, with the exception of Elaine Stritch, is lamentable. . . . How does an eminent critic of [Kerr's] calibre have the impertinence to dish out such inept, amateurish nonsense?"[18]

Reviewing *Goldilocks* for *Dance Magazine,* Leo Lerman thought it contained some of Agnes's best work:

> She consistently and triumphantly translates into vigorous dance terms the musical's period, its original intentions. She opens the show with a recreation of a typical 1913 musical's finale. Here is sprightly use made of that old standby, the locomotive step, of acrobatic dancing, of contortionist skill. There is much skirt waving and fluttering . . . Nothing much happens until the next de Mille staged number, 'Who's Been Sitting in My Chair?,' danced by Donald Barton in a wonderful black bear suit, and by Elaine Stritch . . . [de Mille] is careful to exploit to the full the bear's sweet clumsiness and the star's tough sweetness, but she does it with great taste and restraint. In 'The

> Pussy Foot' . . . [de Mille] abstracts the turkey trot, the bunny hug, the cakewalk, other dance forms popular in 1913. Over all is her essentially balletic point of view — her use of the *pas de chat* is brilliantly effective in this number. She uses her dancers' bodies as though they were capable of any movement she could devise for them, and — surprise — they are. It is all subtle, staccato and beautifully sustained.[19]

Agnes was nominated for a Tony, but the only award for the show went to Pat Stanley, the featured dancer, who gave Agnes much of the credit. Stanley was the kind of performer on whom Agnes could work minor miracles. She had a Joan McCracken quality, sexy and droll, and she could act; she had stopped the show in a funny-poignant dream ballet (a lonely girl dreams of being the belle of a ball). "I was totally unafraid of flinging myself about," Stanley said. "I loved running through space and leaping, my elevation was wonderful. Agnes *mined* me. She loved my fearlessness and abandon and joyousness, and she blended that with her own imagination and skills. On bad days, I still remember her precise words during a rehearsal out of town. She was making some changes that were needed. She was sitting in the pit, and when we finished she just looked up at me and said, 'You turn everything you touch into gold.' I *felt* golden when she said that. She actualized that part of me. I would have done *anything* for her."[20]

Although *Goldilocks* ran only twenty weeks in New York, it had been in many ways a labor of love. Agnes's next show lasted just sixteen performances in New York, and it was all labor.

Juno was Joseph Stein's adaptation of Sean O'Casey's modern classic *Juno and the Paycock,* about a woman who struggles to keep her family together during the Irish troubles of 1921. Stein and Marc Blitzstein, who wrote the music and lyrics, viewed the show as a bitter melodrama. The director, Vincent Donehue (whom Agnes considered "an absolute boob") took a sentimental approach, more suited to *The Sound of Music,* which he would direct the following year.[21] He miscast Shirley Booth, who never wanted to play an unsympathetic character, as Juno. "Donehue wanted Juno to be a warmer, sweeter, gentler character than she was in O'Casey's play," said Joseph Stein. "With a weak director going in the wrong direction, things started falling apart."[22]

Agnes instructed her dancers in the mores and culture of Ireland (taking a Georgist view of the Irish situation, she blamed the troubles on the absentee landowners). She hired two Irish dancing experts to teach the dancers authentic step dances (based on the Irish clog), which she then integrated with the classical idiom and molded to the theatrical needs of the play.* The featured dancer was Tommy Rall, a strong and versatile performer who somewhat resembled James Mitchell and had recently danced the Champion Roper in Ballet Theatre's *Rodeo.* Agnes created a twelve-minute dance for a scene in which Rall realizes that the IRA are coming to arrest him for informing on his friend. The dance, one of Agnes's most powerful pieces of work, was called a "haunt." It was pure emotion — terror, grief, rage, defiance, self-hatred, and despair. As the tension mounted, the music and Rall's feet moved faster and faster until he seemed about to explode with grief and rage.

The clog dances provided a thematic structure for the big production numbers. In a clog dance, the upper body is virtually motionless, arms hanging loose, face expressionless with eyes straight ahead, legs relaxed. Emotion — anger, primarily — is expressed by steps that shoot out from below the knee in complicated rhythms, the feet beating a tattoo on the ground. For a classical dancer such as Glen Tetley, the clog dance was almost impossible. "I was not having any luck with it," he said, "and one day Agnes said, 'I'm going to give you something you *can* do.' She had found the oldest Irish dance, which is called the slip jig. It's done in soft shoes; everything is very smooth and slips and slides across the floor, and you don't make any sound at all. It's balletic, all done in the air. It takes very big elevation and extension, and both of those I had. Vincent Donehue, who was just an absolute son-of-a-bitch, wanted to cut as much dancing as possible. When I would do it in rehearsals he would put his head down, or he would turn his back. I would say, 'Agnes, this is not staying in!' She would say, 'It is! I want it!' I said, 'Okay, I will do it with my utmost being.'" Dancing the slip jig, Tetley was a feather on a

* Loosened up and syncopated by American blacks, clog dancing became the basis for tap dancing.

trampoline, a heart-stopping moment in the show. "I'll always be grateful to Agnes," he said, "for being so supportive."[23]

Agnes was in need of some support herself, but it was not forthcoming. When Blitzstein saw her work in progress he tore it apart, calling it slick and superficial. He was not the first composer to complain that her familiar idiom distracted from the play. Having built a reputation on a recognizable style, she was now expected to provide something completely different.

Out-of-town tryouts were extended for two interminable months (in Washington, D.C., and in Boston) and were miserable for all concerned. Psychologically, "out-of-town" is always the same place: an insulated, hysterical world of round-the-clock labor. Sometimes the pressure actually promotes creativity. With *Juno,* it merely promoted paranoia. Agnes felt beleaguered by Donehue and by Blitzstein, whom she described as "small and furtive, with a rodent quality." As the dancers struggled to get the difficult clog dances right, she broke out in blotches and hives from frustration. She said, "I remember walking around the White House thinking, Other men have suffered, they were strong, I must be strong, too."[24] Twice she resigned, and twice reconsidered.

In Washington, reviews were so bad and attendance so low that the producer replaced Vincent Donehue with José Ferrer. According to Agnes's dancers, Ferrer undermined Agnes behind her back. "He would say in a very lordly way, 'Well, we'll let madame have, shall we say, twenty minutes to see if she can fix it — if not, *I'll* fix it.' To her face he'd say, 'Agnes, my *love!* My *love!*'"[25] But Agnes was always susceptible to a man she perceived as her champion, and Ferrer endeared himself to her by defending her against an increasingly obstructive Shirley Booth.

Booth knew she was wrong for the part, felt that her career was on the line, and made no secret of her unhappiness. During rehearsals, she made such pronouncements as "You need me more than I need you" and "I've gotta get outa this turkey!" Repeatedly, she threatened to quit. "Shirley was sassy and raw and mean," Agnes said. "One day she said something like, 'You have changed your mind three times. Make up your mind what you want me to do!' Very bitchily. Joe Ferrer slammed his book down on the desk and said 'I haven't signed a contract yet and the sun is shining in California, and if you talk to Miss de Mille again like that, I'll leave!'"[26]

Together, Agnes and Ferrer worked out an expository prologue that showed the British soldiers' violence and cruelty to the Irish; in pantomime, it captured the fury and hatred of the original play. "It was too late to do more," Ferrer said. "Marc was difficult and petulant. He had been brutalized by the critics. Leonard Bernstein had told him it was the worst score he'd ever heard, and Lillian Hellman said the show stank. By the time I arrived on the scene, he had dried up. When I asked for new material, he broke down and cried. The book was marvelous, but it needed at least two new songs, which Marc was no longer capable of writing, and leads with good voices."[27] Melvyn Douglas, Booth's co-star, was a fine actor but could not sing.

In Boston, an exhausted Agnes — "her eyes bleary, her face puffy" — told an interviewer, "This show has been the roughest I've ever had." Her ballets, he reported, "have fallen, risen, vanished and reappeared like Saturday night brawlers in an Irish pub."[28] She could neither save the show nor leave it. "When we came to the Winter Garden in New York," Glen Tetley recalled, "the feeling was that *Juno* was not going to be long there. One night after the show I heard, on the darkened stage, someone sobbing. It was coming out of the Dublin set. There was Agnes, down in the corner, sobbing her heart out. She said, 'Oh, Glen, help me — don't go away, don't leave me.' I asked if she'd like to have a drink and she said yes, she most certainly would. Agnes couldn't drink at all, and I think maybe she'd already had one. We went across Seventh Ave to a restaurant that had a bar and sat down. Agnes had one, two and three drinks. She told me things about Lucia, things about Martha, things about her own early life, things about her early relationship with Walter. She just poured her heart out!"[29]

"*Juno* was a very bad show," Joseph Stein said, "with some wonderful things in it. Oliver Smith's sets, Irene Sharaff's costumes. The first act finale got a standing ovation almost every performance."[30] Stage manager Lynn Austin said, "Agnes brought to that show an incredible sense of Irish spirit. She got the dancers and, through them, the audience, to understand what it was like to be Irish."[31]

Immediately after the show closed, Agnes arranged to have the dances recorded on film, lest they vanish forever. "Agnes clung to everything," Trude Rittman said. "I had a way of tearing up things I had written and she was always diving into the wastebasket to retrieve them, saying, 'Don't do that!' Something I threw out could be just right next week, or in another show. She was like a good housewife who has stuff in the icebox that could come in handy at a certain time."[32] Thirty years later, she would reconstitute the dances from *Juno*.

thirty-seven

"Echoes and Extensions"*

On December 6, 1959, Agnes made the most controversial appearance of her life. *Small World* was a popular half-hour weekly television program hosted by broadcast journalist Edward R. Murrow, who mediated discussions between guests of opposing persuasions on a variety of subjects. The gimmick was that the guests were filmed live in different parts of the world and brought together in the control room, en route to the viewers' television screens.

It was the fifties, and therefore unremarkable that Murrow would introduce "our first all-lady symposium": actress Simone Signoret, in Paris; gossip columnist Hedda Hopper, in Hollywood; and Agnes de Mille, in her New York apartment. The subject was "politics in the arts" — a code phrase for witch-hunts, the blacklist, freedom of speech. It was a setup, conceived by Murrow and his producer, Fred Friendly. Against the politically sophisticated Signoret and de Mille, the reactionary Hopper never had a chance.

Signoret's husband, Yves Montand, sat beside her. Walter, who always avoided being photographed publicly with his wife, was not pres-

* "You move, ringed with echoes and extensions." (*To a Young Dancer,* p. 31).

ent, but Agnes had James Mitchell on hand — off camera — for moral support. Hopper, who could destroy a career with her pen, began by defending gossip about the courtships, marriages, and divorces of celebrities. "I put gossip," she said proudly, "in the same category as news." Agnes rolled her eyes heavenward and said, "I think it's touching that the American people take such a deep interest in the basic facts of life." Murrow, loving it, plunged ahead. "Is there any reason why a performer's political affiliations should hurt or help his career?" he asked. "Only if his belief is doing harm to his country," Hopper said, fluttering her false eyelashes, and called for stronger laws against subversion. She continued in that vein while the camera cut to Signoret and Murrow, watching with bemusement, and to Agnes, who shook her head disdainfully and looked as though she smelled a nasty odor. She was so incensed by Hopper's smug righteousness that, between shots, the makeup man had to cover the red blotches that blossomed on her forehead and neck. Afterward, she had a nosebleed — her frequent reaction to stress.

Agnes could improvise brilliantly but she never worked without a net, and James Mitchell had arrived before the show to find the dining room table covered with open volumes and notes. When Hopper paused for breath, Agnes was ready. "Lord [Josiah] Wedgwood said to my mother — he was a very great liberal in Parliament, you know — 'The English have committed every crime in the calendar . . . but there was always a man on his feet on the floor in the House denouncing the iniquity' . . . If ever we try to suppress our own voices just so people who are less informed will get a glossy picture of us, we are lost. We have given up our big freedom."

Hopper faltered. "And what is that?" she asked.

"Our big freedom," Agnes said, her voice charged with emotion, "is the ability to protest freely among ourselves. Not to subvert, not to betray — to protest and to criticize freely among ourselves, in whatever medium we choose to use. Don't you agree? I'm sure you agree, Hedda dear." Looking as though she had been skewered by her own hatpin, Hopper could only say, "You have shut me up completely. I'm dry."

If the event had been a prizefight, the referee would have stopped it at that point. But after a commercial, Agnes continued: "The preservation of liberty and civil rights is vital to any country anywhere. . . . When creative freedom is stifled anywhere . . . totalitarianism walks right in the country." Hopper would not concede defeat. "I see that I'm in a nest of liberals here!" she fumed, and pledged to fight "to my dying breath against Communism." Agnes looked pained. "You say you believe in freedom of speech, but not for people who disagree with you. I'm not afraid of the American people turning Communist, not for one minute. Justice Holmes said he was agin' anyone who was agin' free thought. He was very specific — not just free thought for those who agree with us, but freedom even of thoughts we hate. I'm against trial and condemnation and sentencing by people not qualified by our laws to do that."

At a time when the country was still suffering from the trauma inflicted by Senator McCarthy, Agnes's impassioned statements hit a nerve. She received nearly two hundred letters, overwhelmingly positive (except for a few along the lines of "I hope you drop dead soon and are buried in Russia"), all of which she acknowledged personally.[1] To a fan in California, she wrote, "Thank you for thinking I am pretty. That puts you in a very, very small but I think choice group."[2]

Small World galvanized Agnes's lecture career; suddenly she was speaking to overflow audiences across the country for "great, thwacking sums" ($750 to $1,000).[3] She broadened her subject, addressing why the arts are essential and why symphonies, opera, ballet, and great dramatic repertory companies need private and public support. "They are designed to last and expected to pay off long hence, with immortality," she explained. "They never have been asked to foot the bills as they went along."[4] She developed a text that she would deliver, with minor variations, for the next thirty years. "There has never been great art without great patronage" was her theme. A greater danger than the H-bomb, she said, was "a corruption of the spirit, the idea that you get by with whatever you can and charge the most you are able that is our doom." Theater, as she described it, was a sort of communal sex — "a fusion, a shared excitement, a shared explosion of perception . . . a flame point passing back and forth, an enlarging of both sides beyond what either could experience alone." She concluded, "We can have such a theater as Russia can never envisage, because we are free. Let them get to the moon. Let us go into the hearts of men."[5] Audiences invariably rose to their feet, cheering.

In 1960, Agnes delivered a stirring testimonial for Ballet Theatre, now known as American Ballet Theatre (ABT), at its twentieth-anniversary celebration. The company had recently been resuscitated after an enforced eighteen-month layoff. "Because of what it has done," Agnes said, "and will, if permitted, do, uniquely, Ballet Theatre deserves to be cherished with all our enthusiasm." "If permitted" meant if Lucia Chase relinquished her power and allowed the company to be run like a business, instead of a fiefdom. But as long as Chase paid the bills — by now totaling an estimated $3 to $5 million dollars per year — she intended to call the tune.

Between Agnes and Lucia lay a boneyard of contention that was no longer negotiable. When ABT went on tour overseas that spring, Agnes tried to prevent them from performing *Rodeo* and *Fall River Legend,* on the grounds that neither had been properly cast or sufficiently rehearsed. Chase overruled her, and *Fall River Legend* was so well received in Cuba that a U.S. government official wrote, "This is considered by the State Department as a ray of cheerful light amid the gloom of our political relations with Cuba at the present moment."[6] From Italy, Chase wrote, "Contrary to your expectations, *Rodeo* is having great success, and I do not think anyone else would consider it (or *Fall River*) in a mutilated or second-rate form.'"[7] And from Bulgaria: "[*Rodeo* has] had the warmest reception here in Bulgaria, in Sofia and Plovdiv. . . . I am sorry you cannot see us here — it might take away some of your bitterness which is most distressing and depressing to me and to all of us who have tried to do our best for you. We are not ashamed of the results — I do not believe you need worry for your name. . . . Please try to cheer up."[8]

The anniversary season, underrehearsed and lacking in new works of quality or interest, was a critical and box office disaster. That summer, ABT was to perform *Rodeo, Fall River Legend,* and *Tally-Ho* on an unprecedented State Department-sponsored tour of the Soviet Union. At the eleventh hour, officials pronounced *Fall River Legend* "too macabre" — a decision for which Chase could not be blamed. But Lucia then canceled *Tally-Ho,* after Agnes had spent two and a half months revising the final section, with which she had never been satisfied. Chase's explanations were financial and logistical, her apologies profuse. Agnes would not be appeased. In the fall she resigned from ABT's governing board and turned her attention elsewhere.

∞

Agnes was now devoting more time to lecturing and writing. She still did much of her writing in drugstores, while eating breakfast or drinking cup after cup of black coffee. She wrote in pencil; a secretary typed and endlessly retyped, instructed by notes that Agnes taped to the pages. In 1960, she was working on two books, both of which she was uniquely qualified to write.

To a Young Dancer is a practical and succinct handbook of advice about teachers, auditions, performing, discipline, and practicalities to consider before choosing a career in dance. The book required little research beyond questionnaires, sent to sixty-seven colleges (Agnes based harsh conclusions about their inadequate level of dance instruction on the results). An assistant provided a list of contemporary repertory and a list

Martha Graham and her disciple, 1945. (Agnes de Mille Collection, New York Public Library)

Robert Pagent and Bambi Linn in the 1950 production of *Carousel.* (Courtesy Robert Pagent)

Tally-Ho rehearsal, 1946, three days before Jonathan's birth, with John Kriza, Janet Reed, and Diana Adams. (Courtesy Agnes de Mille)

Agnes, Walter, and Jonathan, 1947. (Courtesy Agnes de Mille)

Agnes with producer Lawrence Langner, Richard Rodgers, and Oscar Hammerstein—"the Bosses"—at *Allegro* rehearsal. (Agnes de Mille Collection, New York Public Library)

The sensational *Brigadoon* sword dance, with James Mitchell and company. (Agnes de Mille Collection, New York Public Library)

Fall River Legend—Nora Kaye as the murderess Lizzie Borden with Peter Gladke as the weak father and Lucia Chase as the malevolent stepmother. (Lido)

Gemze de Lappe, Agnes, and James Mitchell rehearsing *Paint Your Wagon*. (Courtesy James Mitchell)

Gemze de Lappe and James Mitchell in *Paint Your Wagon,* 1951. (Courtesy Gemze de Lappe)

Mary Burr's cancan dance in *Paint Your Wagon.* (Photofest)

Shirley Jones's Laurey and the girls in *Oklahoma!*'s "Out of My Dreams" (Photofest)

Agnes and Jonathan on location for *Oklahoma!* in Nogales, 1954. (Courtesy Eleanor Fairchild)

The Prudes on Christmas Eve, 1956. (Courtesy Agnes de Mille)

Rehearsing a 1956 television production of *Bloomer Girl*. (Photofest)

Agnes and Walter in 1975, shortly before the stroke. (Agnes de Mille Collection, New York Public Library)

At a 1977 dress rehearsal for "Conversations About the Dance," Agnes's paralyzed right foot and the fiberglass brace she considered so ugly were concealed. The photo was used on a promotional pamphlet for the centenary edition of *Progress and Poverty.* (Vladmir Sladon)

Agnes and Walter in 1987, when "she was living by inches and he was dying by inches." (*top:* Beryl Towbin; *bottom:* Courtesy Agnes de Mille)

Amanda McKerrow, Victor Barbee, and Roger Van Fleteren as the Maiden, the Lover, and the Other, 1992. (Courtesy American Ballet Theatre)

of available films for rental. Without patronizing her young readers, Agnes told them everything she wished someone had told her in her late teens about both the disadvantages and the satisfactions of the profession. Regarding the latter, she wrote,

> Performing . . . means this: To step out on the great stages of the world, before thousands of rapt and hopeful people, into pristine space, trained and able comrades on either hand, a symphony orchestra at your feet, a carpet of music spread under you each night, to flash and soar — you the ordinary one — to ride violins and trumpets. . . . You are out of yourself — larger and more potent, more beautiful. You are for minutes heroic. This is power. This is glory on earth. And it is yours nightly.[9]

As Walter Kerr pointed out, the book "has nearly as much to say about moral character and the creative temperament as it does about which dance school to attend and which to avoid. . . . *To a Young Dancer* speaks to more than young dancers."[10] It was an invaluable resource for an audience that was not, sadly, large enough to keep it in print.

The Book of the Dance, initiated in 1957 by Golden Books, was originally envisioned as a glossy picture book, with Agnes's *Omnibus* narration as its text. Over the next six years, it evolved into a cultural history, covering seven thousand years of theatrical, social, and ritual dancing. Two years into the project, Agnes called its growth "almost malignant. It has taken over the house, my life, and my brain. . . . My dreadful fear is that it's . . . just a dull text book. The area covered is so enormous, its scope has exceeded so far what I had originally intended, I am beset by terror that I have spread the text so thin it has lost all pungency. The analysis of the relationship between dance and costumes, dance and armor, dance and social customs, dance and religion, are wholly mine, as is the comparison between the eastern and western forms of gesture, but the more I studied the more I realized I didn't know, and I kept stuffing facts into the chinks."[11]

In 1960, the book had become "this God-damned history which is *monumental.*"[12] Agnes did most of the massive research herself and rewrote the entire manuscript four times. She wanted the book to have a certain look and worked closely with the art director to select four hundred opulent illustrations of paintings, drawings, sculpture, engravings, and photos, ranging from Egyptian tombs to action shots of Watusi dancers in Africa.

The Book of the Dance is the product of a lifetime of experience, study, and observation.* A section on Ritual and Social Dance describes dances of war, fertility, hunting, and courtship, from primitive societies to Balanchine's abstractions, and goes on to explain the development of dance in Eastern and Western cultures, beginning with the Middle Ages. A long section on the history of theater and ballet is followed by biographies and appraisals of important dancers and choreographers, from the seventeenth century through revolutionaries Duncan and Graham. Based largely on interviews she conducted herself, Agnes analyzed the work methods of leading contemporary choreographers. She listed the principal ballets of influential choreographers, including herself. But in the body of the text, her references to her own contributions are so cursory that one reviewer called attention to "a serious lacuna. Where is one Agnes de Mille, whose *Rodeo* brought American folkways to the ballet stage; whose choreography in *Oklahoma!* changed the face of American musical comedy? Her name appears only from time to time at the end of a list."[13]

Agnes gave even shorter shrift to some of her contemporaries; Ruth Page, Hanya Holm, and Helen Tamiris, for example, are barely mentioned, for she believed that their work would not last. But Jerome Robbins received extravagant praise as "the most forceful and characteristic voice for the American urban or jazz form" and the most important influence on the younger generation of artists here and abroad. She applauded his dancing, his choreography, and his wit; his fusion of dance and drama in *West Side Story* had created, she wrote, "virtually a new balletic form." She noted that he had made "historic strides in dance photography, an art in itself," and had received the first Academy Award ever given for choreography[14] — something Agnes would dearly love to have won herself.

Agnes and Robbins had been friends since he made his solo debut in the original production of *Three Virgins and a Devil.* As a sort of devil's apprentice, he had watched the proceedings, twirled a red carnation, and

* *The Book of the Dance* earned Agnes about $1,000 — half what she had paid for the typing.

grinned. Agnes loved his humor, inventiveness, and style; she called his *Fancy Free* "the finest first work I have ever seen in the theater."[15] But when some of her dancers left *One Touch of Venus* to go into Robbins's *On the Town,* their relationship grew prickly. Then four of *Bloomer Girl*'s dancers, including James Mitchell and Joan McCracken, left the show to go into Robbins's *Billion Dollar Baby.* Agnes, who was working in London at the time, accused Robbins of "raiding" her show. Mitchell had her blessing if the move would help his career, she told Robbins in a letter, "but I don't think it is quite ethical to tease the chorus boys away at a time when they are so dreadfully difficult to replace, and when I am far from the scene . . . I cannot bear to think of you and me playing at this cut-throat game, and caring not a damn what hurt we do to one another's works or reputations. Out of friendship and mutual respect I think we should not raid one another's shows unless we can better the lot of the individual dancer. . . . I do burn up to learn that a good piece of my chorus has skipped out to join your chorus, and at precisely the moment when the leading dancer is leaving."[16]

Agnes had disapproved strongly when Robbins named names before the House Un-American Activities Committee, but her admiration for his work was unchanged. But Robbins, instead of acknowledging the bouquets in *The Book of the Dance,* complained that it presented its author's viewpoints as facts. Agnes answered emphatically: "The facts can be found in any encyclopedia, but the essence of criticism is enthusiasm — that is, prejudice. They are inextricable. It is impossible to take a long view or a detached view, and as long as my name is on the book, it means that a highly opinionated woman is speaking."[17]

The Book of the Dance, wrote *Dance Observer*'s reviewer, "may be the crowning laurel in Agnes de Mille's highly distinguished literary career. . . . It merits the widest possible readership."[18] Richard L. Coe, writing in the *Washington Post,* called it "as handsome a 'popular' book on the dance as ever you're likely to see" and expressed amazement "that no foundation or grouping of same has offered to back a permanent de Mille company. We flock to such from abroad but do nothing about creating any folk group of our own."[19]

In fact, Agnes had been soliciting friends and foundations for years, hoping to form a national folk theater, a "Heritage Theater," with singing, dancing, and acting. In a *New York Times* article, she wrote, with slight exaggeration, "All other countries have such theaters (the Moiseyev, the Bayanihan, the Folklorico of Mexico, the Feux Follets of Canada, Inbal of Israel). We alone do not."[20] She obtained tax-exempt status, put together a modest prospectus ("I am not wasting money on printing"), and recruited a board of directors. She needed substantial funding for research, conferences with folk dance specialists, training programs, and rehearsals. But although she had her mother's habit of keeping accounts to the penny, even to the price of Jonathan's orange juice at the Friends School, finances were not her element. Nor would she delegate fund-raising to a professional. Instead, she wrote beseeching letters to friends, colleagues, and wealthy individuals who crossed her path. To Fritz Loewe, she wrote, "There will be almost no money in it for me, but I have reached a place in life when doing what I believe in means the most."[21] She was crushed when the Ford Foundation answered her request for a $100,000 grant with a boilerplate "in-view-of-the-limited-number-of-grants-available" rejection.[22] For the rest of her life, she would crusade for government support of the arts.

thirty-eight

Fairy Godmother

In December 1961, a year after John F. Kennedy was elected President, the show that would become a sentimental symbol of his administration opened on Broadway. *Camelot,* by Alan Lerner and Fritz Loewe, was choreographed by Hanya Holm.

The country was sliding from Oscar Hammerstein's cockeyed optimism into a decade of social and political turmoil. In the musical theater, Hammerstein's death in 1960, of cancer, seemed symbolic. Agnes had considered Oscar "a sort of older brother . . . one of the chief influences in my adult life"; they had shared an upbeat, folkloric vision of America, and their most popular work reflected that spirit.[1] Agnes credited Hammerstein more than anyone else for her participation in *Oklahoma!, Carousel,* and *Allegro.* Their friendship had fractured during the filming of *Oklahoma!*; but in a condolence letter to Dorothy Hammerstein, Agnes wrote, "He is an absolutely indestructible piece of our lives, and I am grateful for every minute I had with him. . . . Girls and boys are going to be talking with Oscar's words, with Oscar's point of view, long hence, and never be aware whom they quote. He is the air they breathe, their memories."[2]

Agnes spent six weeks at Merriewold during the summer of 1961.

"The summer has been wet and cold," she wrote to her old friend Therese Langfield Horner, "but now it's turning beautiful, all the lilies and what's left of my roses are out. And now I must leave. The radio said that the heat in the city yesterday was 99 degrees — with humidity that's killing. There will be no air-cooling in my rehearsal hall, or bedroom. Hey! Hey! So I leave this sea of ferns and depart."[3] (Agnes actually considered humid weather perfect for dancing; the humidity, she said, limbers the bones.)

The reason for her departure was *Kwamina,* one of two shows of the 1961–62 Broadway season that dealt with interracial love stories, then a controversial topic in the theater. In Richard Rodgers's *No Strings,* the woman is black, the man white. In *Kwamina,* a London-educated African doctor falls in love with the daughter of white missionaries when he returns to his tribal village.

Kwamina was the first solo effort of composer Richard Adler after the premature death of his partner, Jerry Ross, with whom he had written *Pajama Game* and *Damn Yankees.* Playwright Robert Alan Arthur wrote the book, and Robert Lewis, with whom Agnes had worked so felicitously on *Brigadoon,* directed. Agnes staged *Kwamina*'s dances and musical numbers — all seventeen of them — and her favorite designer, Elizabeth Montgomery, designed the costumes.

Agnes's adviser on African customs, attitudes, manners, movement, and music was Alfred Opoku, from Ghana. Gemze de Lappe, who assisted Agnes, recalled, "Mr. Opoku would arrive at the little studio in the back of Ballet Arts with his drummers, and he would start around the floor with Agnes following him and I was following Agnes and we would just follow, imitating this man, for a couple of hours. It was really strange movement for both of us; we just persisted."[4] To dance arranger John Morris, working with Agnes for the first time, her work method was a revelation. "Agnes steeped herself in the African dance vocabulary until she made it her own. And then she just pulled it out, like words that she had been taught in a foreign language, and put it together in a most amazing way, so it had a structure and form. She used the African vocabulary, but it was much more than editing."[5]

The result was inventive and exciting, blazing with energy. Accompanied by wild drumming that elevated the blood pressure of the audience as well as that of the cast, muscular, near-naked men performed spear dances, ceremonial dances, and a macabre funeral procession. In the long and at times terrifying "Fetish" scene, as described by *Dance Magazine*'s Leo Lerman, "Miss de Mille used sustained and frenetic (but severely disciplined) Afro-dance movement (enormous jumps and leaps, multiple beating with the feet upon the stage floor, sudden horizontal movements). This scene also depended on massing abrupt flares of light and abrupt bursts of darkness, through which Miss de Mille sent her dancers careening in tightly packed, circular, twisting masses."[6]

Wedding rituals were Agnes's specialty, and *Kwamina*'s was arguably the most exquisite of her career. When the curtain rose on the second act, the stage shimmered and quivered with the anticipation of women who were instructed to "feel as though their hands were trailing in water, and to have a feeling like hummingbirds in their throats."[7] Their movements, combined with costumes, lighting, and music resembling the sound of an African bush piano, created images that were sexual and poetic and stunning.

Kwamina's rehearsal period was only slightly less acrimonious than *Juno*'s. Sally Ann Howes, the female lead, had followed Julie Andrews as Eliza Doolittle in *My Fair Lady;* this would be her first opportunity to create a Broadway role. Composer Adler, who was married to Howes at the time, intended that it would make her a star. But Adler would not allow Terry Carter, who played Kwamina, to kiss Ms Howes at any time during the action of the play, an incongruity pointed out by every reviewer. "Miscegenation," one wrote, "is handled so gingerly that you scarcely know whether it is happening or not."[8]

Rehearsals in Toronto, the show's tryout venue, were interrupted by recriminations, threats of lawsuits, and open quarreling. Adler fought with everyone; at one point, the producer, Alfred de Liagre, had to break up a fistfight between composer and librettist. In that rancid atmosphere, the company proceeded to Boston and then to New York, where the show opened on October 23, 1961.

Kwamina was praised for its good intentions and its dances, and panned for its book. "Sinuously quivering shoulders and hypnotically swiveling hips make the stage thrum with barbaric force and sensual splendor," *Time*'s reviewer hyperventilated, "but the dances are less show builders than clock stoppers. Between them, the wordy worthy talk ticks on."[9] The *Christian Science Monitor*'s reviewer was more specific: "The pyrotechnical ways [with which de Mille] represents the drive to freedom could make even the Declaration of Independence seem mere meagre verbalizing. The point is precisely this: the rest of the musical must pay for Miss de Mille's brilliance. . . . As a kind of superbly popularized Afro-American dance suite, *Kwamina* has its separate triumph and, in the end, defeats itself."[10]

The show closed after a month, but Agnes won a Tony award — tying with Joe Layton, who choreographed and directed *No Strings*. As a postmortem, Walter Terry wrote, "One of America's great choreographers turned her attention to a distant continent . . . and gave us a stirring view of hearts — fighting, tender, fierce, frightened, hopeful — through her mirror of dance."[11]

At about the time that Agnes lost the last of her patience with Lucia Chase, a regional ballet company in Manitoba, Canada, invited her to choreograph a ballet for them. To their great surprise, she accepted.

The Royal Winnipeg Ballet was relatively unknown in the United States, but like Ballet Theatre, which it predated by two years, it was one of the first ballet companies to develop an eclectic repertory. Unlike Ballet Theatre, it was supported by public as well as private funds. Arnold Spohr, its artistic director from 1958, was a flamboyant former premier danseur who spoke seven languages, had a background in music as well as in dance, and demanded total commitment from his dancers.

Agnes had never been to that part of the world; she envisioned Winnipeg as the rim of the Arctic, a culture of fur trading and trappers. "She arrived on one of our coldest nights of the year," Spohr recalled, "maybe forty below; she was stunned with the cold. All the Board members had drinks with her at the hotel, and her frigidity was not just because of the weather. She was reserved, standing tall — charming but not *too* much so, waiting for anybody to let her down."[12] But having scored the coup of getting the prestigious Agnes de Mille to their provincial town, the arts community received her like royalty. "I felt as though they'd given me Manitoba," she said. "It was a lovely feeling. I'd never had it here."[13]

At the first rehearsal, Agnes was surprised to find a group of handsome people who could act as well as dance. To Therese Langfield Horner she wrote, "They are far from here, roughly 2,000 miles, but that's only four hours by jet, and I find them so terribly touching and exciting, jumping like mad out there on the prairies . . . they remind me of our earlier struggles with Tudor and company, except that they are well-captained and there is no viciousness."[14]

Using music by Frederick Loewe and Trude Rittman, she reworked her *Brigadoon* suite and renamed it *Bitter Weird,* "weird" meaning fate in Celtic. In her scenario, two men love the same woman; she marries one of them, and the rejectee crashes the wedding and murders his rival. "Agnes rehearsed with us for about six weeks," said Spohr. "She whipped us to get her ballets right, but she gave us her love and support. We were like her adopted company. She captivated the dancers with her stories, she inspired them with her standard of greatness. I waited on her hand and foot. I gave her extra time when she needed it, and I *listened* to her. How many choreographers get that anywhere?" Spohr understood comedy and timing, and the deceptive simplicity of Agnes's work. "It's much harder than it looks," he said, "because it's *so* simple that you can't cover anything up."[15] He took such scrupulous care of her work that when she returned for the opening, she was surprised to find that the performance had actually improved during her absence.

Reviews of the premiere on March 9, 1962, were studded with superlatives. According to the *Winnipeg Free Press,* "At some point during the eight bravo-studded curtain calls which left no doubt that the lady from the south had just put the world's frostiest audience into her pocket and melted its heart, trim, tiny Agnes de Mille walked onto the Playhouse stage to receive her due and her flowers."[16]

Bitter Weird was more a revival than an original work, but it was excellent entertainment. Agnes had tailored the roles to the personalities of the dancers, with one exception. James Clouser, who danced the role of the murdered lover in a subsequent season, said, "The problem was that none of us were Jimmy Mitchell. She used two other men, and then she used me. I think she thought I didn't have enough sexual undertones for that role. She told me, 'I have no choice, I have to put you on.' In rehearsal, when it came to where I bring a bunch of heather to the woman and do a solo, she said to the company, 'Would you please leave, this is going to be very difficult.' They left. She said, 'James, you are a wonderful lyrical dancer, but you do not have the authority for this part.' And then she proceeded to teach it to me. I'll never forget that rehearsal. We worked on my entrance for an hour and a half. 'Enter and take three steps and then pause for two seconds. No. Take two steps and pause for three seconds.' She worked and reworked and reworked it. The whole process was devastating to my confidence but it was very educational for me, what I learned about the importance of timing.

"We all called her Agony," Clouser said, unaware that Louis Horst had bestowed the nickname on her in her youth. "She had a thing about wanting to be accepted as an equal to the men with whom she worked. But when she got frustrated, she pulled out the tears, she reverted to the most feminine wiles. I saw her do that in Winnipeg and later in New York, during a revival of *Brigadoon* with Edward Villella."[17]

Agnes became quite devoted to the Royal Winnipeg Ballet, and her stature would propel them onto the international stage. "Agnes became our fairy godmother," Arnold Spohr said. "She opened the dance world to us."[18]

Agnes spent much of the summer of 1962 fighting a David-and-Goliath battle against the monolithic League of New York Producers. Wielding slingshots alongside her were choreographers Michael Kidd and Danny Daniels, director Philip Burton, and Erwin Feldman, a high-powered labor lawyer. At issue was the right of choreographers and stage directors to engage in collective bargaining.

Agnes equated the craft unions that represented the nonperforming side of the theater with highway robbers. It outraged her that truckers and carpenters and stagehands earned more than the dancers, thereby driving production costs to prohibitive levels. But when she was the employer, her interests collided; she fought for her dancers' rights, but felt entitled to suspend them when she felt it necessary. She made a point of paying the dancers on whom she worked out material — not much, but what she felt she could afford — but she pushed them beyond the time limits eventually set by their union. Out of loyalty and the hope that it would lead to paying work, they complied. This was not unfamiliar in the dance world. But to a member of the *Juno* company, Agnes was "the prototype of the person for whom they had to make rules regarding breaks and hours worked. She never stopped. She had a nice fat sandwich brought in and sat eating it and drinking a malted while the dancers sweated."[19]

In Agnes's mind, however, she remained one of the workers, victimized by greedy management. "Every night my dances play to sold-out houses and ovations," she had written to her mother during the run of *Nymph Errant* in 1933, "and I do not get one penny royalty." There followed a series of bad contracts, some of which were her own fault. Agnes expected people to behave according to her moral standards. When they did not, she accused them of exploitation. Rodgers and Hammerstein took the brunt of her resentment. In *And Promenade Home* and in subsequent books and interviews, she went public with her grievances, the most bitter of which concerned *Oklahoma!*

In the hundreds of subsidiary productions of *Oklahoma!* — touring companies, stock companies, amateur productions, and most foreign productions — Agnes's work was usually reproduced by a dancer who had done the show. Even when the steps were different, the concept and the scenario of the ballet, organic to the show, was Agnes's. But according to a contract that was standard at the time, Agnes's dances, which constituted twenty-six minutes of *Oklahoma!*, belonged to the Theatre Guild. As the authors, producers, and investors added up their profits, Agnes earned no royalties at all.

In 1951, when Rodgers and Hammerstein acquired the rights to *Oklahoma!* from the Theatre Guild for a reported $851,000, Agnes had asked them to rectify the Guild's original injustice and to acknowledge her contribution in dollars. They refused, claiming that they could not set such a precedent. They did pay her handsomely for restaging her dances for certain important revivals, and for the movie ($1,700 a week for nine months). But in 1955, when the movie was released, *Oklahoma!* had been onstage somewhere for twelve years. It had played in the United States, Canada, Europe, Australia, New Zealand, and South Africa, to an estimated total audience of thirty million people. Out of a total gross of $100 million, its backers had earned a 2500 percent return on their investments.[20]

With the exception of *Brigadoon* (for which she was paid a royalty after 1963, when she threatened a lawsuit), Agnes's strongest contracts were for her least successful shows, such as *The Girl in Pink Tights* and *Goldilocks*. "I never got in the position of owning the piece until I began doing shows that really weren't any good," she said bitterly. "They gave me lots of things then, whole hunks of the show and residuals, whatever I wanted. What difference did it make? The show didn't run and nobody ever, ever revived it."[21]

Composers, playwrights, lyricists, librettists, actors, and Broadway dancers all had unions to protect them. Choreographers had no union, no bargaining power, no copyrights, no defense against plagiarism, and no share in the secondary rights, including movies and television, where the real money is to be made. Historically, authors and composers shared 60 percent of the profits from those productions, the rest going to the show's producers and investors.

Agnes had argued for years for the recognition and remedy of the choreographer's plight. Her energy, her overdeveloped sense of injustice, and her stature on the national stage made her a logical spokesperson for the cause.* In the 1940s, she and Antony Tudor and Eugene Loring had tried unsuccessfully to get the American Guild of Musical Artists (AGMA) to represent choreographers. In 1948, she and Michael Kidd, Helen Tamiris, and Jerome Robbins, acting on behalf of over fifty colleagues, were refused membership in Actors Equity, which represented Broadway dancers, on the grounds that Equity was not set up to police choreographers' royalties and copyrights. (Adding injury to insult, Equity's rules made the cost of filming dances, which existed in those prenotation days only in the "muscle memory" of the dancers, prohibitive.)

While Robbins and Kidd resolved matters for themselves by producing, directing, and choreographing their own shows, Agnes continued her attempts to organize. In 1959, she learned that Shepard Traube, with whom she had worked on *The Girl in Pink Tights,* wanted to organize a union for theatrical directors. Choreographers and directors competed for power, prestige, and percentages, but they shared the problem of having to negotiate every deal according to what the traffic would bear. Contending that both groups worked on musicals, Agnes persuaded Traube to include choreographers in what became the Society of Stage Directors and Choreographers (SSDC).

In 1962, the threat of a strike brought representatives of the League of New York Producers, notorious for their flagrant violations of contracts, to the bargaining table. Three- and four-hour shouting matches took place four times a week, with Agnes occasionally banging her hand on the table and demanding that the producers clean up their language. The League finally agreed to recognize the SSDC's legitimacy, but only on the condition that the crucial issue of subsidiary rights would not be raised for twenty years. Agnes and certain other choreographers and directors would continue to negotiate for those rights as before, on an indi-

* She stated her case in speeches, in magazine articles, and in *And Promenade Home.* In 1961 she addressed the Congressional Subcommittee on Education and Labor on "Economic Conditions in the Performing Arts," emphasizing the problems of choreographers. Other speakers included Ralph Bellamy, Dore Schary, and Leopold Stokowski.

vidual basis. But a beachhead had been established. Inexorably, the troops would advance.

Shepard Traube, who had initiated SSDC, was elected its first president. His successor was Agnes's onetime partner, Joe Anthony, now an established director whose credits included the play and the movie of N. Richard Nash's *The Rainmaker.* In the summer of 1963, twenty-three years after their affair had ended so badly, Agnes and Joe Anthony embarked upon a new venture: a musical version of *The Rainmaker,* entitled *110 in the Shade.*

t h i r t y - n i n e

Out of Step

According to dance critic Arthur Todd, "The best Broadway choreography of the 1962–63 season thus far was on view at New York City Center in the revivals of the twenty-year-old *Oklahoma!* and the sixteen-year-old *Brigadoon.* The superb dance numbers . . . demonstrate to a new generation of theatre-goers the lasting influence and imprint stamped indelibly on the American musical theatre format by Agnes de Mille. . . . The choreography in both works was always there for a reason: chiefly, to further the action, to illuminate the characters and, most important, to say things that could not be completely expressed in either word or music. . . . Mr. [Edward] Villella's dancing and Miss de Mille's choreography won screaming ovations at every performance."[1]

The revivals underscored the growing obsolescence of shows with big singing and dancing choruses. The best of the last would be dominated creatively by director Harold Prince (*Cabaret*) and superdirectors Jerome Robbins (*Fiddler on the Roof*), Bob Fosse (*Sweet Charity*), and Gower Champion (*Hello, Dolly!*); at the end of the decade, *A Chorus Line* would become the prototype of the more economical "concept musical." But Agnes was not ready for obsolescence. Her hair was gray but her energy was prodigious, and *110 in the Shade* had the kind of heroine with

whom she had always identified: another plain Lizzie who is terrified of becoming an old maid. This Lizzie is not driven to murder; she is awakened and transformed by a charismatic con man (played by Robert Horton) who seduces her, after selling his rainmaking powers to her drought-stricken town. Whereupon the drought ends, in Lizzie and in the earth.

N. Richard Nash had written a tight book, and he and the composer and the lyricist, Tom Jones and Harvey Schmidt (they had recently collaborated on *The Fantasticks*), originally planned only minimal dancing. "We had to try to chip away at the play just to get the *songs* in," Schmidt said. "If you got interested in the story you wanted to keep on with the story."[2] But Joe Anthony believed that Agnes could make a great contribution, and he prevailed. "We had one major discussion with Agnes way up front," said Nash. "She told us, 'I don't know what you need me for, this stands on its own and needs very little dancing.' Then she went off with her dancers. None of us was permitted to see her work in progress. And long dances were inevitably created."[3] "Agnes had this history of going off on her own," Tom Jones noted. "In *Oklahoma!* they were up a creek and she went off on her own and *solved* those problems with that dream ballet. She saved shows that way over and over again. Then she'd go around saying, 'They didn't pay me anything, they exploited me.' Agnes loves to be the victim. It's her joy. So this, as it turned out, was another contribution to that."[4]

Agnes's first words to the relatively unknown actress who played Lizzie were "You must be Miss Swenson. I've never seen you before, I've no idea whether you are gifted or not." But Agnes became, said Inga Swenson, "a great, *great* champion of mine. She told me, I'm sure out of sweetness and not truth, that I was the best dancer in the show! Which was patently absurd, 'cause there were *great* dancers in the show. But she had a reason for telling me that, and it worked! I felt wonderful about myself!"

For a number called "Raunchy," designed to show that the proper Lizzie yearns (like Agnes) to be sexy, Agnes had Swenson strip without taking her clothes off. "I worked with a tablecloth — stuffed it down the front of my dress, moved it back and forth behind my fanny, dropped it as though I was stepping out of my dress. She had me shimmy, all that outrageous stuff that works for someone like me because of the incongruity. The nice person doing dirty stuff doesn't look dirty, just funny." Swenson's character carried the show. "It was a *huge* part," she said, "and even though I was very young, I was tired all the time. One day at lunchtime I was lying half asleep on an old couch in the rehearsal hall and someone came over and tucked a big beach towel around me. It was Agnes. It was such a Mom kind of thing to do, something you do automatically for someone you love. I was crazy about her."[5]

In Lesley Ann Warren, who at sixteen had not yet shed her baby fat, Agnes recognized potential that astonished even Lesley. "Agnes helped me to be so incredibly powerful in that show," Warren said. "She gave me body language that looked like I was squirming with repressed sexuality at all times. She choreographed a duet for Scooter Teague and myself that had beautiful, lyrical lifts. I'd never done lifts, and every time Scooter would lift me, my spine would just collapse. Agnes would say, 'What are you doing with that spaghetti spine?'"[6] Warren learned adagio so well that the number stopped the show every night.

The other musical numbers, as opposed to the big dances, were staged with Agnes's usual flair. But when her creative juices began to flow, she could not deny them. Knowing that "most authors are afraid I'll take the show in my teeth and run away," she proceeded to do precisely that.[7] When Nash, Jones, and Schmidt were finally allowed to see what was far too much of a good thing, their hearts sank. "*Cut* a dance of Agnes de Mille's?" Nash asked. "Who would do that? Certainly not Richard Nash, who bit his nails when someone in the audience began to talk during a pause. Agnes was a person of enormous reputation, a legend! We were *so* impressed that she even deigned to *do* our show! And she had more *balls* than all the rest of us put together!" Only the producer had the ruthlessness that was required. "David Merrick," Nash said, "would cut his *mother* out of the show!"[8]

Merrick was known for turning rehearsal rooms into battlefields strewn with lacerated egos. Harvey Schmidt recalled Merrick's first meeting with Agnes: "He kissed Agnes's hand and said, 'Oh Miss de Mille, it's such an honor to have you in this show.' ["At that point," Tom Jones interjected, "what you should do is put your hand on your wallet."] I remember her saying, 'Mr Merrick, I worked for my uncle, Cecil B. De Mille, and nothing you can do to me can be worse than what he did.'"[9]

The complex logistics of a musical show call for a commander in chief, or a unified team of commanders who understand all the elements — actors, singers, dancers, chorus, musicians, designers, and technicians — and their relationships to one another and to the show as a whole. A clear vision of structure and form, and the power to implement it, is essential. Usually the director is in charge; by default the author; or, ideally, a coalition of the two. "We were sort of stumbling around," Tom Jones said, "waiting for it to become clear who was in charge. Everybody was in their own department doing their thing, coming from different directions. It was our first Broadway show — *we* had no power. It was more of a power *vacuum* than contending powers." Compounding the problem, as Jones explained it, "David Merrick had a philosophy that creative people are too kind to each other, whereas the critics are *not* kind. He wanted people to be tearing and ripping at each other and questioning, as it is in his perception of the real world. So he deliberately created an atmosphere of anger and hysteria."[10]

Stage manager Bill Ross, a survivor of many Merrick productions, said, "Merrick can go on for forty-five minutes spewing forth filth at a person. He did that to Joe."[11] Anthony was a gifted director of plays, but had previously directed only one musical. A tense, anxious chain-smoker, his reaction to confrontation, especially if the combatants were Merrick and Agnes, was to flee. "It was a shabby page in my life," he said. "I was told, 'A dance can't go on for thirty-five minutes! All she gets is fifteen! Cut it!' I said, 'Agnes, you'll have to take out so many minutes of that dance.' It was the only time I ever saw her weep. She said, 'I'm leaving, Joe — you are exploiting my material.' I think she was terribly hurt that I didn't fight for her work. I can't remember whether or not the request was valid — but if it *was* her fault, I might have found a better way to spare her ego. I think that spoiled our relationship and I feel ashamed of it."[12]

Anthony saw his behavior as cowardly; to Agnes, it was vengeful. "Before I agreed to do the show I said to Joe, 'There's been a great deal between us — love and violent resentment, tumult and difficult times, a struggle of wills. You finally broke loose with a great deal of cruelty, but you had to be cruel. Are you going to be able to not take out any hidden resentments on me?' He said, 'Absolutely!' Well, he couldn't."[13] More than once, she threatened to quit. But her contract contained a hard-won royalty clause, and by leaving she would forfeit her percentage of the box office receipts — so she stayed.

"When things are not going well out of town," Tom Jones said, "David Merrick asserts himself by having hysterics, firing people, and just going bananas."[14] In Philadelphia, things went badly. Harvey Schmidt recalled "a horrifying moment after one performance when the curtain had just come down. Merrick had called a meeting and while waiting for everyone to gather, he sat in a chair backwards on the stage in front of the dancers, rocking back and forth and chanting, 'Agnes de Mille is over the hill!' over and over again. Agnes wasn't on the stage, but she was somewhere in the theater, back in the dressing rooms. It was one of the most chilling moments I've ever seen."[15]

According to Richard Nash, "Agnes's attitude was, 'Let's stop the show long enough to appreciate this dance.' She took everything personally, and in the end she felt betrayed by all of us. I constantly heaped praises on her with respect to what she had done with Lizzie. But that was not enough." Comparing Agnes with other choreographers with whom he worked, Nash said, "Gower Champion let you watch him work from start to finish; he was perfectly willing to scrap whole numbers. Michael Kidd didn't let you in while working in the early stages, but at some point he did let you in, asked for criticism, and changed it to fit. Agnes was totally different."[16]

Throughout the last week in Boston, Agnes cut Nash dead. "It's no [worse] than always," she wrote to Mary Green, "except my situation is complicated with friendship and loyalty. I'm not free to rage . . . And I'm living on sedations (I have a blood pressure problem these days — result of fifty years of bad temper. Half a century of unabated rage does something to the arteries)."[17] All but one of her dances had either been excised or cut to the bone. Her dance arranger, William Goldenberg, recalled, "During the two-week run in Boston there were hardly any dances left, and there was nothing for Agnes and I to do. We got so tired of seeing the show and what wasn't being done, we looked for things to do in Boston, especially during matinees. We did wonderful things. She introduced me to the Isabella Stewart Gardner Museum. She had many friends on Beacon Hill who were writers, lecturers, poets, historians — movers and shakers in the literary world, people I'd never heard of — and we would go and visit them. I'd sit quietly and sip my tea while Agnes discussed some aspect of Thomas Paine's writings with them, or the American Revolution. One afternoon, I introduced her to S. S. Pierce, the famous purveyor of foodstuffs — an enormous, beautiful department store of canned goods, gourmet items, early American things like Indian pudding, chowder, all those wonderful recipes that you can't find any more. She loaded up a shopping cart with Christmas gifts for all her friends. The matinee of *110 in the Shade* is going on, and Agnes is taking out her aggression on these canned goods until I can barely push the cart!"[18]

110 in the Shade ran for a year on Broadway, vindicating Agnes's decision not to relinquish her claim on her royalties. "I stood the humiliation in order to keep my rights and it's paying off," she wrote to Edward Weeks, "but my blood pressure is pretty high and I have to be a good girl."[19] Like her mother, Agnes suffered for years from hypertension headaches — in her case exacerbated by alcohol, for which she had notoriously little tolerance ("smell of the cork," Walter used to say). Under extreme stress, she was subject to attacks of dizziness and vertigo, and nosebleeds that were at times so severe as to require emergency medical treatment. But she also had the energy and the training to "Do something!" so energetically that a doctor once remarked, "Fifty minutes after you're officially pronounced dead, they're going to have to send a man in with a gun to quiet the limbs. You won't stop."[20] When she was exhausted, she was able to catnap on a rehearsal room floor and wake up ten minutes later, refreshed.

Only at Merriewold, or on a rare vacation, could she reduce speed from gallop to canter — and only there had she ever been able to spend significant time with her son. Jonathan was a studious boy who saw himself as "withdrawn but not necessarily unhappy."[21] In 1964, the summer before he was to go off to college, Agnes took him to London for ten days — as a gift to herself, she said, for he was witty and she delighted in his company. Until then their travels together had been limited to Jamaica and, in 1961, Mexico, where he and a friend had snorkeled and dived in Acapulco Bay, and they had visited pyramids near Mexico City. To her great relief, he had grown to average height and weight; in features and coloring, he still resembled his mother, who bragged at every opportunity about his proficiency as a scholar, swimmer, and sailor.

The trip was a chance to show London off to him, and to show him off to her old friends in London. She had remembered them all faithfully throughout the war (except for the treacherous, in her mind, Charlotte Bidmead) with food parcels and had brought them nylons and other gifts on her first postwar visit, when *Oklahoma!* opened there in 1947. "She was tremendously kind," Therese Langfield Horner recalled, "to people who had nothing at all to offer her. She sent me weekly magazines when I was ill with tuberculosis for four years, and she continued to send me *The New Yorker* for forty-four years. She invited Nora Stevenson — this shabby, poor old woman who had been her rehearsal pianist — to stay at the Ritz for a week. And she got her some clothes, and lovely hampers of food, and a television set. As a thank you for being Nora, and having worked for Agnes for so little money."[22]

Without a child, Agnes could not have considered herself a complete woman. But Jonathan's significance in her life went far beyond that. Agnes loved as her mother had done, intensely and completely, and her loved ones had to guard against becoming satellites, subject only to her will. Walter had always protected his autonomy, and Jonathan was learning to do the same. He still longed for normalcy; his mother's celebrity made him uncomfortable, and some of his friends were astonished when they discovered, after knowing him for some time, that she was Agnes de Mille.

In September, Jonathan left for Amherst College, in Massachusetts. "There were a few hours of blasting loneliness after he'd gone," Agnes told Therese Langfield Horner. "I felt absolutely evacuated, and lay awake all night thinking of the opportunities I'd missed with him. Well, my life wasn't simple, and that's a fact. He'll never know how hard some of it was or what he meant to me."[23]

Ordinary mortals would have had a hard time merely keeping up with Agnes's lecture dates, which had gradually become the primary source of her income. The strain of preparation often caused her to break out in a violent rash before she spoke; nevertheless, in one month she delivered eighteen lectures and fourteen seminars, most of them at colleges, from Denver through the Midwest to the Northeast. "My lecture fee is twice what I was paid for *Rodeo,*" she liked to point out, enjoying the irony. "I arrive, put on a dress, talk for an hour (without notes) and earn much more than I do for creating a ballet. It's insanity."[24] An acquaintance who happened to be in Detroit shortly after the 1965 riots heard that Agnes was addressing a women's group there, and dropped in to hear her. "Nobody else could get away with lecturing an audience of privileged Grosse Pointe women about black history and their contribution to the arts, culture, and dance," he said. "She really told it like it was, and that took great courage. She just spun my head and took my heart away."[25]

In 1965 Agnes was elected president of the Society of Stage Directors and Choreographers, thus becoming the first woman president of a national labor union. It was not a pro forma position; she chaired the board meetings where grievances were dealt with and policy hammered out, and played an active role in recruitment and arbitration. That year she also returned to television to narrate "The Best of the Bolshoi." She was a dedicated board member of the Henry George School and the Committee to Save the Met, and an adviser to the North Carolina School of the Arts. She was also working on several writing projects that were in various stages of completion. An ongoing project was a "lyric history of the United States," a sort of cavalcade of American history, as related largely through dances, songs, jokes, superstitions, and other material in the public domain. In her search, Agnes tracked down personal letters and diaries, and accumulated an enormous amount of data on clothing, laws, recipes, household remedies, customs, and music.

Over the years she recruited a series of collaborators, beginning with her dear friend Catherine Drinker Bowen, the biographer whose subjects included Oliver Wendell Holmes, John Adams, and the Constitution itself. "Kitty" Bowen, to whom Agnes had been introduced by Harold Taylor in the late fifties, was one of the select group of women (Rebecca West, Carmelita Maracci, Mary Hunter Wolf, Therese Langfield Horner, and Michael Hertz) whose friendship Agnes treasured, even though their meetings were infrequent. Bowen was a kindred spirit by virtue of her ancestors — a long line of distinguished Philadelphia Quakers — and her passion for music and for American history. Like Agnes, she believed herself plain, especially in comparison with a beautiful sister, and had built an illustrious career against long odds. Bowen made a valiant effort to work on the script, but finally begged off on the grounds that the Bryn Mawr libraries, not the theater, was where she belonged. Disappointed, Agnes nevertheless assured her that "nothing, Kitty, could mar our friendship except a total disintegration of your character, which is impossible to conceive, or the fact that you might get on to mine, which is likely, but you have a forgiving heart and that saves us."[26]

She turned next to the playwright Horton Foote, who did "mountains of research. What she started with was pristine," he said. "It had a nice little Agnes style to it. Slightly ironic, then suddenly very much like paying homage in a profound way. Regarding the English settlers, she said something like 'The sounds they heard here for the first time were not the sounds they were used to — not nightingales.' But the historic quotes leaned toward oratory, and they were deadly. And it all became so vast."[27] The problem, never resolved, was that the episodic nature of the material was antithetical to dramatic tension. Eventually she would obtain a $10,000 grant from the National Endowment for the Arts and would seek help from Leonard Bernstein, Morton Gould, playwrights Arthur Laurents, Jerry Lawrence, and Robert Lee, lyricist E. Y. Harburg, poet Richard Wilbur, and Thornton Wilder, all of whom wished her luck and politely declined.

Sick of Broadway and sensing that Broadway might soon be sick of her, Agnes renewed her attempts to form a Heritage folk theater. "They are putting a house and a car at my disposal," she wrote to a friend when the Mexican government invited her to advise them on their national ballet, "and paying for the whole trip. Isn't it ironic? All I want to do is work in my own country, with my own people."[28] She advised James Clouser, the young dancer-choreographer, to make the most of having the Royal Winnipeg Ballet to work with. "I, as an old battered professional, tell you . . . you have no conception how frustrating, broken, unfruitful and heart-wearying it can be not having dancers to work with, nor rehearsal space, nor music. . . . Even now I, with all my resources and with what reputation I have, cannot hold a troup [*sic*] together for a week without the expenditure of many hundreds of dollars. A month of rehearsals would be quite beyond my ability to pay."[29]

With little to show for her efforts, she continued to appeal for money from individuals and foundations. "My pride has disappeared," she wrote to a member of her board of directors. "I am just greedy now."[30] When Richard Rodgers advised her, "Don't look for anything too substantial as the [Rodgers and Hammerstein] Foundation is not a very wealthy one," she was furious but not surprised.[31] Then, as though to demonstrate that her pride was not only dead but had decomposed, she solicited the De Mille Trust, established after Cecil's death in 1959. The response was a check for $250, with a standard letter explaining that the trust received a large volume of requests. Agnes returned the check with a note, its tone similar to that of the one telling her uncle that she could get better terms from a pawnbroker. "Two hundred and fifty dollars will not go very far in the American theater today, as you know; it can work material good in some charity — so I am returning it to you as I believe you will know where to send it for the most fruitful results." Thanking them politely for their prompt reply, she concluded, "In this peculiar business it's always helpful to know exactly where one stands."[32]

Agnes bewailed the fact that potential contributors "will buy a set of shows or an orchestration but they won't just put money vaguely into my hands and leave it to my professional discretion how to disburse the sums."[33] She was constitutionally incapable of dealing with the foundation mentality, with its insistence on accountability, i.e., how every dollar would be spent. She likened her situation to "the old pre-War London days . . . Things never seem to get better on this front. After a lifetime, never any security to do the work one believes in."[34]

In 1963, the Ford Foundation awarded the bulk of grants totaling $7.75 million to companies and schools dominated by George Balanchine and his protégés, with Balanchine and Lincoln Kirstein to administer the funds. A furor erupted in the dance world. Walter Terry, expressing the majority opinion, protested the "flagrant favoritism" of the "shockingly one-sided grant" and called it "nothing short of a scandal."[35] Agnes, who had been turned down three times by the Ford Foundation, was enraged. In a letter to Terry she called Kirstein "a con-man in the great historic sense. He would have done well with the Medicis. . . . This episode comes under the heading of a national disgrace . . . the equivalent of the railroad and oil [cartel] monopoly of the nineteenth century."[36] To Edward Weeks, she offered an article on the subject for publication in *The Atlantic,* saying, "I will be able to write like Zola because I feel that mad."[37] Her quarrel was not with Balanchine, whose work she respected, nor even with Kirstein, whom she despised, but with the Ford Foundation. "It is immaterial," she wrote in a draft of an unmailed letter, "whether or not Balanchine is the best living ballet choreographer or one of the best. The point I am trying to make is that he is single not plural; that his tastes are exclusive; that he prefers imitators to rivals; that he is assuming a position of power and influence unknown even to choreographers under the Csars; that he is being encouraged to imprint his viewpoint on every area of American dance."[38]

Without a company of her own, she continued to work irregularly with others. With *Bitter Weird* now a staple of its repertory, the Royal Winnipeg Ballet opened its 1964 season with another de Mille work — not a ballet, but a forty-five-minute lecture-demonstration based on the *Omnibus* "Art of Choreography" television program. One of the dancers explained that the problem with *The Rehearsal,* as it was called, "was that you never saw a complete theatrical work. But you learned a lot about the rehearsal process, and about Agnes. She had a line that dancing is all about touching another human being, to make real contact with another person — that if we are lucky enough to do that once or twice in our lives, we're successful. I felt very sorry for her when she said that — for what it revealed about her, that she felt that way at that age."[39]

To her friend Bella Lewitzky, Agnes wrote, "Honey, I'm a riot. They wired me up for sound and I panicked them — great big belly laughs and an ovation at the end."[40] But as Walter Terry pointed out, "There is, of course, only one Agnes de Mille. Her wit, her bite, her fabulous timing in delivery of lines, her dedication to dance and her stage presence seem almost essential to *The Rehearsal* in its exposure of the frustrations and agonies to which the choreographer is subject, and the discoveries and ecstasies which are his reward."[41] As had so often been the case in Agnes's work, *The Rehearsal* came with an inherent and insurmountable obstacle. As it required her presence, and as her availability was limited, *The Rehearsal* had only a dozen performances.

forty

Strip-Mining

Agnes was no stranger to the homes of the rich and powerful; she had taken tea with Eleanor Roosevelt and dined at the White House with the Trumans and, later, the Eisenhowers (despite having made some campaign speeches for Ike's opponent, Adlai Stevenson). But she particularly esteemed the Kennedys because they were the first First Couple in living memory to publicly embrace and encourage musicians, writers, artists, and intellectuals. In 1962, at a dinner for André Malraux, the French minister of culture, Agnes was seated at the President's table with Mrs. Kennedy, Norman Cousins, Edmund Wilson, Geraldine Page, Andrew Wyeth, Mrs. Elia Kazan, Charles Lindbergh, and Mrs. Malraux. Thornton Wilder table-hopped, embracing his friends and exclaiming, "They let us in, darlings! We're here! We're inside!" The following spring, Agnes returned to the White House to watch proudly as the cast of the acclaimed revival of *Brigadoon* performed her dances in the East Room.

President Kennedy had promised to get the country moving again, but his assassination accelerated moves in unimagined directions. America's complacency, pumped up by victories in two world wars, was eroding. An ever-colder Cold War, hot wars in the Middle East, the Bay of Pigs, protest movements, and the Vietnam War were darkening the mood

of an increasingly cynical populace. But in 1965, the newly created National Council on the Arts and Humanities was a beacon of idealism.

The council was the result of the first legislation in the nation's history to endorse and support the arts. Its advisory panel, appointed by President Johnson and chaired by theatrical producer Roger Stevens, glittered with twenty-four representatives of all the arts, from architecture to weaving. Among them were Isaac Stern, Leonard Bernstein, David Brinkley, John Steinbeck, George Stevens, Rene Davencourt of the Museum of Modern Art, architect William Pereira, Eleanor Lambert of the fashion world, and Gregory Peck. Lobbying for dance were Oliver Smith and Agnes de Mille. "We were a bunch of roaring egomaniacs," she said, but "we tabled our special enthusiasms and thought in generous and embracing terms." She had her own committee of sixteen advisers from all over the country; they could and sometimes did outvote her.

"I remember Agnes as being quite determined and serious, not larky," said Gregory Peck. "She gave us to believe that dance was important to the cultural climate, to the quality of life, as an avenue of expression for young artists. We were frankly an elitist group, brimming over with concern for the arts in America. At our first meeting we asked, 'What are we supposed to do?' Bernstein said, 'It's simple: we're going to give the American public the best in everything, across the board.' We had $5 million to distribute for the whole country, in all of the arts. It was peanuts! Someone reminded us of Congressman Gross, well-named, from Iowa, who had stood up on his hind legs in the House and said, 'Taxpayers' money to toe dancers over my dead body.' And the very first grant we made was to toe dancers.

"We got together four times a year at a conference center which had once been a mansion, overlooking the Hudson. We would pitch our tent there for three days, eat together and talk and socialize and work. There were meetings in other cities, as well. In between meetings we all were scouting, trying to decide where to make the money count. My wife and I visited regional theatres, at our own expense, and came back and reported on what they were doing. Everyone advocated for their own cause, and everything eventually went to a vote. Debates were passionate but good-natured, because we all wanted the same thing: to prove to Congressman Gross and other Neanderthals that the taxpayers' money was *not* going to be wasted. That art was *good* for the United States. We all liked to use a line about how the city of Hamburg alone gave $8 million to its opera. And here we had $5 million for *all* art disciplines!"[1]

The grant to toe dancers took the form of matching funds for the chronically desperate American Ballet Theatre. The company was a prime example of the statement in a 1965 Rockefeller Report on the arts in America that "from the standpoint of finance, administration, and organization, the dance world is close to chaos."[2] Even Lucia Chase's "asbestos optimism," Agnes's apt description, was faltering.[3] ABT had discovered and fostered more dancers, designers, and choreographers than any other company. It had toured more than any other company in history, performing in forty-four countries, but still had no home of its own. After a three-year absence from New York, it would celebrate its twenty-fifth anniversary season at the New York State Theater at Lincoln Center.

The State Theater would become the permanent home of Lincoln Kirstein's New York City Ballet, the company with which ABT necessarily competed for audiences. In that sense they were rivals, but their characters were complementary. Kirstein's organization was devoted to

Balanchine's work and the classical ballet style. ABT was about diversity; classical ballet was just one of the strings on its bow. In this ambitious season it would present twenty-three ballets by eighteen choreographers, including Antony Tudor and Jerome Robbins. Agnes would be represented by *Fall River Legend,* a new version of *The Frail Quarry,* and two new works — the largest number of works by any choreographer. She had worked out a deal with Lucia: in lieu of a fee for creating and rehearsing her new ballets, she would retain the rights, orchestrations, and costumes for her company, if and when it materialized.

As the season approached, the war between Lucia and Agnes resumed. "If there is any contemplation of putting [*Fall River Legend*] on in its present state without at least two days of rehearsal with me," Agnes warned, "I will sever all connections with Ballet Theatre and countermand all plans for the twenty-fifth anniversary season."[4] Agnes could be supremely thoughtful and controlled, but she was also an actress, capable of putting on what Oliver Smith recognized as "a whale of a show."[5] A dancer recalled, "We'd be in rehearsal and there would be Agnes in the anteroom of Ballet Theatre's studio, having one of her tantrums — holding her umbrella up in her little tiny fist and shaking it. 'I'm calling the NEA, going to Washington! You're not going to get your grant this year! You won't have a season!'"[6]

Joseph Carow, whose thankless job it was to schedule rehearsals, said, "There were days when we rehearsed all morning with Agnes, with Jerry in the afternoon, and in the evening with Tudor. Agnes was blunt as a sledgehammer. Jerry was like a cutlass, slashing. Tudor was like a rapier — he just ran you through, emotionally. Jerry said, 'I want all six hours, or *Les Noces* will not go on!' Lucia said, 'Give him whatever he wants.' Agnes and Tudor were beside themselves!"[7]

The program on March 17, 1965, consisted of Balanchine's *Theme and Variations,* Lichine's *Graduation Ball,* and Agnes's *Wind in the Mountains.* The twenty-five-minute ballet, set to Laurence Rosenthal's arrangements of folk tunes, consists of a series of country scenes structured on the seasons, both climatic and in the heart of the heroine (another of Agnes's shy girls who suffer from unrequited love). When she cries, there is spring rain and umbrellas. When she is abandoned, there is winter snow and ice skating — and a Champion Roper–type boy who comforts her.

There are also some flashy solo turns, a tap dancing traveling man, and an *Our Town*ish folk philosopher who provides a colloquial commentary. At the end, everyone square-dances in a big circle. Critics likened the ballet, with its stock de Mille characters and its kinder, gentler time, to Grandma Moses or "a sort of sophisticated Currier and Ives calendar."[8]

Agnes was caught in the trap that awaits any American artist who produces an original landmark work: she was always expected to top, or at least match, her best work. Her idiom — Americana — was a rich vein, but narrow. She could still produce nuggets, purer than the fool's gold of her imitators — but now she was strip-mining. *Wind in the Mountains* was received politely, but most of the praise was grudging, and the word "corny" flashed conspicuously between the lines. "In *Rodeo* it was cowboys," wrote Douglas Watt, "here it is skaters."[9] After one more season, *Wind in the Mountains* would drift out of ABT's repertory.

Agnes's other new work, an adaptation of a sixteenth-century Scottish folk ballad, was serious and controversial. In *The Four Marys* (a common name for servant women in the South), a servant in the antebellum South is seduced by her mistress's lover; she bears a child, drowns it, and is condemned to death. With the Civil Rights movement nearing its peak, the subject could not have been more timely.

As there were no black women in the company, Agnes brought in her own: Cleo Quitman, Glory Van Scott, and, in her New York debut, Judith Jamison. The primary Mary was Carmen de Lavallade, a strikingly beautiful modern dancer of African, Indian, and Caucasian descent who had made a stunning Broadway debut in *House of Flowers*. Making it clear that her offer was prompted by Carmen's talent, not her race, Agnes offered her the lead in *The Frail Quarry* as well. "I appreciate that Agnes did not bring me in only because she needed a 'black' dancer," de Lavallade said. "That hurts a lot when you know you can do other things. I thought Agnes was very brave to do that. If you go through the history of the City Ballet, as far as *lead* dancers, there have only been black *men*. In ABT there might have been one token man — if there was a lady, she was so fair that you couldn't tell. Mr. John Martin wrote that people of color did not have the bodies, the feet or the legs, their hips were too big. That is the way people thought."[10]

In their portrayal of illicit lust, De Lavallade and Paul Sutherland, who danced the role of the cad, projected a powerful chemistry; and for all its melodramatic gloom and doom, *The Four Marys* held and, at moments, chilled the audience. Recalling the ending, Glory Van Scott said, "When we all turned and went upstage and the bell started to toll, signifying the gallows, we turned back to the audience and came downstage with our arms raised. We were all very tall, we looked like giants; it was as though we were saying, 'You are killing her, but we are still here, we will always be here.' With the bells tolling we kept moving forward, like a wave, as the curtain came down. The audience was left gasping."[11] But although its reception was respectful, *The Four Marys* had a predictably brief run with ABT, which did not have the dancers to perform it.

Neither Agnes nor the critics were happy with *The Frail Quarry* in its new incarnation. But *Fall River Legend,* with Sallie Wilson as the murderess, was one of the season's hits. Wilson, then thirty-three, had been a principal dancer with ABT for four years. "Agnes was the first one who envisioned me in a great role," she said. "I love her for having had confidence in me before I had confidence in me." In addition to an outstanding classical technique, Wilson had the dramatic presence that Agnes always looked for. She became a disciple of Antony Tudor, and danced, famously, in his ballets. Comparing his working method with Agnes's, she said, "Tudor played mind games on you, he let you struggle. Agnes didn't play games. She was so *clear* — she inspired you or she yelled at you, it was right there. The best thing she ever said to me was, 'Sallie, please try to overact.' And I thought, Good, I can let go. I was being tasteful, instead of coming quite out."[12] Wilson's interpretation was quieter than Nora Kaye's, but it was also more touching. "[She] did not have Kaye's classic delivery nor her doomed drive," Agnes wrote, "but she had something kinder and frailer. She performed at the other end of the scale."[13] Wilson would dance the role longer than anyone else — more than a hundred times in eleven years.

In 1966, when the Vietnam War had heightened tensions between the United States and the Soviet Union, the State Department sponsored a second ABT tour behind the Iron Curtain. They would appear in Moscow, Leningrad, and Minsk; and this time, *Fall River Legend* would be on the program. Choreographers were not invited. Using all her clout, Agnes became the exception.

The trip began with a crashing discord. Agnes had fought to get *Rodeo* positioned second on the program, where she believed it worked to its best advantage. According to dancer Scott Douglas (and, in a slightly different version, Agnes herself), "No sooner had the Aeroflot flight taken off than Lucia turned to Agnes, sitting next to her, and said, 'Agnes dear, I have some terrible news — *Rodeo* is going to be last on the program.'" Chase claimed that the Russians had made the change arbitrarily, and said they had already printed the programs. "It caused a major brouhaha," Douglas said. "We got off the plane in Paris and Agnes said, 'Do you know what that woman did to me? The minute the wheels got off the ground she informed me that my ballet would *not* be where it is supposed to be on the program! And I immediately got a nosebleed and bled all the way across the ocean!' Later on I said to Lucia, 'I understand you gave Agnes a nosebleed last night.' She said, 'Gave her a nosebleed? She *picked* it until it bled!' Their relationship was like that."[14]

The issue turned out to be moot, for the Russian audiences had no idea what a rodeo was; they did not understand that the dancers were on horseback, and were offended by gestures that drew laughs in America, e.g., the Cowgirl thumbing her nose. But "*Fall River Legend*," said Sallie Wilson, who danced the lead, "just socked 'em in the eye, and they were overwhelmed."

In 1970, *Dance Perspectives*, a quarterly with a relatively small circulation, devoted an entire issue — fifty-six pages — to Agnes's account of the tour. "Russian Journals" contains some of her best writing but, like some of her best dances, reached a minuscule audience. It is vintage Agnes, through the looking glass. Her observation of detail is precise, her juxtapositions funny and fresh. One grand palace was "too much, too many styles. One feels here a touch of William Randolph Hearst." The taxi drivers "feel about their brakes as they feel about Lenin — unquestioning faith." The Russian peas "could be used to weigh scales." Two brief passages illustrate the slapstick clown and the blueblood patrician that coexisted in her personality. In her Moscow hotel: "I've run out of toilet paper. I can pantomime most needs, and I can pantomime this one, but I do not choose to." After visiting Tolstoy's home: "I gazed at the desk with emotion because it was undoubtedly here that he wrote the letters to my grandfather, Henry George."

Her reportage was careful and fair, crediting the Soviets for their accomplishments but also exposing their bureaucratic stupidity. "Russian Journals" concludes with her return to the Soviet Union in 1969 as a judge of the first International Ballet Competition, and ends on a sarcastic note that Edward Weeks, had he edited it, would probably have asked her to reconsider. Although the United States had reached the moon, she wrote, the government's arts budget remained "woefully inadequate. No matter. We can always import. Russia will pick up the tab. And our native artists can learn to be maintenance men or IBM operators for whom there is certainly need. Artists, especially dancers, are bright and adaptable and these trades pay well."[15]

f o r t y - o n e

"Bored Thou Never Wert"

When Senator Jacob Javits presented Agnes with the 1966 Capezio Dance Award, he cited her accomplishments as a dancer, choreographer, writer, crusader, and more: "a generative catalyst of determination, courage and vision who has enriched, enlivened and enlarged the horizons of the American dance and the American theatre."[1] Ironically, the honor came at a time when Agnes was a legend without a job.

According to Charlie Baker, her agent from 1950, "No one questioned Agnes's talent, but her greatest virtue was her most serious handicap: she couldn't keep her mouth shut. Ego-driven men have very slim egos, and when it came her time to put in her two cents, they would shake. The producer of *Kwamina* was Alfred de Liagre — he was my client and a close friend of mine. After the show closed, I asked him, 'Would you hire her to work with you again?' He said, 'Absolutely not.' It had nothing to do with her contribution — it was her vocabulary! When people in show business are in trouble, and we always are, a lot of invective goes around, we scream and yell. But Agnes finds a word that you take to your grave." De Liagre told Baker, "I'll never shave again without looking in the mirror and thinking of what she said about me." He never could bring himself to tell Baker what she had said.

"Deals fell apart," Baker explained, "because she wanted an author percentage and subsidiary rights for her contribution at a time when there was no precedent for that. She turned things down if she thought they were cheap or badly thought out. Neither of us made a lot of money from her work. Ever."[2]

In the twenty-five years since *Rodeo,* critics had called Agnes everything from a revolutionary genius to "the Edna Ferber of the dance."[3] John Martin's enthusiasm for her work had waxed and waned, but he had the background to see it in context and he appreciated her contribution. The *New York Herald-Tribune*'s Walter Terry was a rarity in that he had practiced what he critiqued (as an amateur), and he was Agnes's most consistent champion. Both he and Martin were analytical; Martin was more objective, Terry more constructive. The dancers considered Terry a friend, Martin an observer.

In 1965, the *New York Times* hired Clive Barnes as its first-string dance critic. He was soon appointed theater critic, as well, thus becoming the most powerful critic in the world. "There have been prejudiced and vitriolic critics before," Agnes observed, "but never one with such power."[4] For once, her claims of persecution were justified. Barnes, who was

British, had a strong bias in favor of choreography that was classical or British, preferably both. "*Rodeo* is what Agnes can do," he told Harold Taylor, "the rest is imitation."[5] Of *The Rehearsal,* he wrote: "If one could have believed either in Miss de Mille's agony or in the value of what was being created, or even if one could have been amused by her abundant light relief or mordant wit, it might have been mildly diverting."[6] He dismissed *Fall River Legend* as "a melodramatic, sentimental mound of some substance with the consistency of, say, Jello, or, perhaps, blancmange." If Truman Capote's *In Cold Blood* was a nonfiction novel, Barnes wrote, "then Miss de Mille, anticipating him, has achieved, in effect, the noncreative-dance ballet."[7]

Barnes's gratuitous slams were a red flag to potential employers who did not want to risk a bad review in the *New York Times.* Choreographer Brian MacDonald recalled a weekend at Merriewold after one of Barnes's attacks. "Agnes resented it very deeply—that after John Martin, who had some understanding of her work, here was this English twit reviewing both dance *and* drama in a very smartass and offhand way. I remember her sitting on the porch in tears. It's always surprising to find a very strong person, whom you think could *deflect* the slings and arrows of outrageous fortune, in fact being as sensitive as we all are. But our artistry is *based* on our sensitivity! If we're insensitive to the world, we're not artists!"[8]

Agnes planned to spend the summer of 1966 in Hollywood choreographing a movie of *Bloomer Girl,* to be directed by George Cukor, with whom she had worked on *Romeo and Juliet* so long ago. But while in Puerto Vallarta with Walter—a vacation combined with a business trip for Hurok—she learned that the deal had collapsed. (Walter, she said, was relieved; for all his autonomy, he preferred her to be in New York.) She then accepted a job she would not have considered a few years earlier: a road company revival of *Where's Charley?,* directed by Cyril Ritchard. It was the first time she had choreographed a show that was originally done by someone else (in this case, George Balanchine). The show had a good cast, the costumes and scenery were sumptuous, and Agnes was quite pleased with her dances. But although the opening got brilliant reviews, attendance was poor, for the producer had no money left for advertising or publicity. After two week-long engagements, the producer went bankrupt and the show closed, with Agnes still owed her $3,000 fee.

Agnes's relationship with ABT was yielding diminishing returns on both sides. In the twenty years since the premiere of *Fall River Legend,* ABT had premiered five de Mille ballets: *The Harvest According, The Rib of Eve, Sebastian, Wind in the Mountains,* and *The Four Marys.* All were created in an angst-ridden atmosphere and quickly slipped out of the repertory. With ABT again on the verge of extinction, Agnes took a new ballet to the young, New York-based Harkness Ballet.

Golden Age was set backstage at the Paris Opéra of the mid-nineteenth century. In an overripe scenario worthy of Belasco, an aging prima ballerina allies herself for purely practical reasons with a rich aristocrat, causing the young man who loves her to kill himself. She sinks into the grave to join him, as her rival dances off with the noble lord. Subsidiary characters are the sexually exploited dancers and their wealthy "protectors." The dancing superimposed Agnes's style onto a pastiche of classical works, so that the ballet consisted of some dance history, a bit of sex, and a sure sense of theater. In one scene, the stage turned so that the audience saw both the desperate ballerina onstage and the young girl in the wings, duplicating her steps. In her usual fashion, Agnes alternated satire with pity for the fading star.

Golden Age had an old-fashioned romantic charm, but the operative word was old-fashioned, particularly relative to the rest of the Harkness repertory. Brian MacDonald, then artistic director of the Harkness Ballet, noted, "At that time we had quite a few works by John Butler, by myself, by Norman Walker. The ballets we were doing were very much influenced by the sixties and San Francisco and flower people, and a kind of liberation that was happening. Other choreographers were beginning to use rock groups in their work. A story about the Paris Opéra in the past, no matter how nifty it sounds, seemed curiously out of sync with the times."[9]

Agnes took class daily along with Rebekah Harkness, the company's patron, as she had done with Lucia Chase. She was sixty-two — "puffing and blowing," ballet master David Howard recalled, "but she would *never*

ever let Rebekah know she was in trouble." She needed the workout to vent her frustration with the dancers, whose lack of discipline dismayed her. During rehearsals they stood around looking bored, talking, and chewing gum. When she relegated some principals to the corps, they abandoned what little courtesy they had shown her.

According to David Howard, "Agnes blamed the dancers, but you're only as good as the piece, and it was not good. And the dancers resented having crap thrown at them and being expected to consider it high art because it was Agnes de Mille's. She was not the easiest person in the world to work with. She screamed at me once when I opened the door of her rehearsal room. The company had to give her hours and hours and hours and hours of time. Agnes brought her people in to demonstrate how it should be done. She thought they were the best in the world — and *we* felt they were *inferior!*"[10]

When *Golden Age* premiered in New York, Clive Barnes accused Agnes of stealing the idea from Tudor's *Gala Performance, La Gloire,* and *Offenbach in Hades [sic],* and of producing a work with "not one ounce of originality." The idea "might have been interesting, especially if choreographed by Mr. Tudor himself. But as choreographed by Miss de Mille, the interest evaporates like empty breath on an idle window pane. . . . [T]he emptiness of the ballet, the conventionality of its choreography — often the ensembles look like those for a bad musical that died on the road back in the forties — and the thinness of the well-worn theme hardly provide the dancers with the rosiest of opportunities. . . . The horses involved in the Charge of the Light Brigade must have had much of the same uncomplicated charm."[11]

Barnes's spiteful review prompted condolence calls from Jerome Robbins, Anton Dolin, and Martha Graham, who sent three dozen roses. It *was* a shopworn idea — ballets that send up the ballet go back at least as far as Diaghilev — but the only choreographer from whom Agnes had borrowed was herself. *Golden Age* incorporated three of her recital pieces with virtually no changes: *Ballet Class* and *The Bumble Bee in the Garden,* both of which predated her acquaintance with Tudor, and *Gala Farewell,* which she created in 1939, after leaving London, and before seeing Tudor's *Gala Performance.* She had never seen *La Gloire,* and the only resemblances between *Golden Age* and *Offenbach in the Underworld* are the costumes and period. In a rebuttal to Barnes, Winthrop Sargeant asserted in *The New Yorker* that *Golden Age* "has a right to be judged on its own merits — some amusing as well as striking dancing [and] some wonderful bits of parody ballet. . . . It has Miss de Mille's customary theatrical touch, her dagger-like approach to feminine psychology, and her keen wit."[12]

The Royal Winnipeg Ballet would later perform *Golden Age* with some success. But by misunderstanding Agnes's intentions, distorting the image of her work, and pronouncing her worthless as an artist, Barnes had undermined Agnes's confidence and inflicted real damage on her career at a time when her options were narrowing. A company of her own seemed more than ever the answer, but without proper fund-raising help, which she claimed she could not afford, it was more dream than reality. On the lecture circuit she was more popular than ever, earning up to $1,500 per date. (As a commencement speaker, she was unexcelled. "What is the use of freedom of conscience," she rhetorically asked the 1967 graduating class at Western Michigan University, "if we have no conscience; freedom of speech, if we've nothing to say; freedom of action, if we are afraid to move; freedom of religion, if we are incapable of faith; freedom from want, if we lack pride in our work; freedom from disease, if we find no joy, no meaning in life?")[13] She choreographed well-received City Center revivals of *Oklahoma!* and *Carousel,* and restaged the latter with the Volksoper company in Vienna. She wrote some short stories, but they were heavy-handed and humorless; magazine editors who had bought her articles, many of which were excerpted from her books, rejected her fiction as being "too special."

In a 1960 letter to Joseph Welch, Agnes had written, "I still think the most interesting points about the [Borden] case are not whether or not she did it, because I firmly believe she did, but why she did it, how she did it, how she got away with it, and the appalling view into Fall River life which the case affords. I feel like an anthropologist about that household. It horrifies and fascinates me, more before the murder than after. I still intend to do something about it."[14]

The result was *Lizzie Borden, A Dance of Death,* published in 1968. The first third of the book deals with the crime, the characters, and why Agnes believed Lizzie was guilty. The middle section explains, to the extent that any creative act can be explicated, how she transformed historical facts into art. The final section describes rehearsals and performance, and includes perceptive portraits of Nora Kaye, Jerome Robbins, Oliver Smith, Antony Tudor, and Lucia Chase. Out of honesty and her sense of drama, Agnes even quoted from Barnes's contemptuous review. For once, the jacket copy did not exaggerate: "No other woman can write about the breathless anticipation, the agonizing, bone-jarring work, the fear of failure and the glory of triumph which are intrinsic parts of ballet, as can Agnes de Mille." By simultaneously participating in and observing events, she had accomplished a feat akin to performing surgery on herself.

While the book was in progress, Agnes learned that another author, Victoria Lincoln, had grown up next door to the Borden house and remembered Lizzie. To her everlasting regret, she sent Lincoln her manuscript, asking for comments and factual corrections. Lincoln proceeded to write her own book on the subject, leaning heavily on Agnes's research and even lifting whole sentences from her manuscript, and then managed to get her book published first. "She got the book clubs and all the TV appearances," Agnes told a friend. "[T]he episode has forced my book to struggle under quite unfair disadvantages. Oh, well, fortunes of war!"[15] She was less philosophical about the fact that Clive Barnes's review for the *Times* "was so vicious they would not set it up in type — therefore, no *Times* review. . . . Since this is the only nationally read book review section, it naturally damaged the sales to quite an extent."[16]

In 1968, when college campuses were rife with dissension over the Vietnam War, Jonathan was a senior at Amherst, where he followed his conscience on protest marches and hunger strikes. He was anxious about the draft — as was Agnes, who agreed with his position. Walter, who never spoke of his war experience, seemed to disagree. After much agonizing, Jonathan arrived unexpectedly at his father's office one day and announced that if he were called he would refuse to serve, whether that meant going to Canada or to jail. To his immense relief, Walter, still without stating his own opinion on the issue, offered his total support for whatever consequences ensued.

After two more years of uncertainty — during which Jonathan graduated, had a breakdown, underwent psychoanalysis, and taught in a public school near Cambridge — the draft board classified him 1-Y because of his medical history, ensuring that he would be called only in the event of a national emergency. He then accepted a fellowship in history at Harvard.

In 1973, Oliver Smith hosted a big party at his home in Brooklyn Heights to celebrate the Prudes' silver wedding anniversary. At Agnes's request, Isaac Stern played the Norwegian music that had been played at their wedding, and Jan Peerce, Jerome Hines, and three other Hurok artists sang part of an opera that Walter had written in his youth. "After twenty-six years she still amazes me," Walter told Smith. "How she had the gall, the chutzpah, to ask notable artists to learn and rehearse and perform as a favor!"[17] His toast to his wife (after Shelley's "To a Skylark") was "Hail to thee, blithe spirit; Bored thou never wert."

What sounded glib was in fact the reason why their union, improbable as a hummingbird's flight, had survived. On a superficial level, observers who assumed that the tall, handsome Walter was Agnes's trophy husband were right. In a 1980 book about dance, her caption for a photo of herself is the non sequitur, "My husband carried this portrait through the war."[18] And at rehearsals, instead of the usual practice of clapping her hands to stop the proceedings, she habitually hit the mirror with the back of her left hand, her wedding ring clanging, "I'm married!" Walter was her proof of success as a woman. But they were also devoted friends who truly delighted in each other's company.

Nevertheless, the air between them was often turbulent. Walter's lack of enthusiasm for her work remained a sore point for Agnes. "His idea of a good musical show is *Otello* by Verdi," she told a reporter. "You can imagine what he thinks of what I do."[19] After viewing a production of Jean Kerr's *Please Don't Eat the Daisies,* she wrote to Kerr's husband, "There was nothing in it . . . to make you ashamed or wish that Jean could not write. That's in more ways than one a triumph."[20] According to Charlie Baker, Walter's friend and drinking buddy, "He *always* claimed he didn't like her work, and he never went to see it if he could avoid it. It was pure perversion. He gave other people the impression that he was very proud of her, but the last thing he was going to tell *her* was how proud he was."[21] James Mitchell theorized that Walter "might have learned that he couldn't speak frankly about her work, so he wouldn't go to see it. I once said I didn't like a piece she did for Ballet Theatre. It was in the outer lobby of the new Met. She bounced right up to me and said, 'What do you think?' I said, 'It doesn't work, Agnes.' It was as though I had driven a stake through her heart. She didn't speak to me for months. A long time later she said, 'Neither you nor Walter must ever find fault with my work. Don't tell me if you don't like it.' And since then I've said it's all gorgeous, no matter what she does. I think she felt that the two of us, no matter what, should stand with her."[22]

Agnes urged Walter to pursue his own aspirations to write, even prodding him into analysis to overcome his resistance. But the talking cure was not for Walter, and he soon gave it up. "Walter didn't know how good he was," Harold Taylor believed. "He was in the middle of the major cultural movements of this century. He told great anecdotes. I said, 'Why don't you write your memoirs of working with all this great talent?' He said he didn't write well enough."[23] But if his work was not creatively fulfilling, it did give him the satisfaction of being virtually indispensable to the finest musical talents in the world. Isaac Stern said, "Those clients for whom he felt a special affinity — Marian Anderson, Segovia, Jan Peerce, I, and Roberta Peters — were the artistic family to whom he gave special devotion. He gave us opportunities to perform under circumstances that made it possible for us to perform at our best. But he didn't care that much about the business. It was a sinecure. And it was a foil to Agnes's success. Being number two to Hurok was very important in the world of music."[24]

During the 1960s, Walter grew bored with concerts. "Even if I get there just before the final curtain," he said, "I know exactly what they've played and how well, and what I'll say: 'A magnificent concert!'"[25] The artists were not fooled. "He would come backstage with comments about concerts with alcohol on his breath and rain on his coat," Stern recalled, "clearly having just arrived."[26] Tennis remained Walter's passion, an outlet and an escape. At Merriewold, he played every day; in the city, three times a week at the Heights Casino in Brooklyn, with a congenial group of men that included broadcaster Edwin Newman, critic Leonard Probst, and businessman Ed Dietz, who became a close friend. "It was a warm, scintillating group," Dietz said. "Agnes didn't play tennis, but she would come and watch. Then we'd dress and go to dinner, at the club or at a nearby restaurant, and mix the beans. Saturday and Sunday mornings we had our Round Table group. It was always a sparkling experience, the equivalent of the Algonquin."[27]

Walter was a gentleman, but he was not a saint. Normally he measured every word (unlike Agnes, who flung hers at the world and let the chips fall, sometimes on her own head), but his temper could be explosive, and he was capable of sniping at Agnes to the point of insult while guests squirmed with embarrassment. On the subject of infidelity, Isaac Stern said, "All of us assumed that Walter had many dalliances, none of which were very deep. Because he wouldn't give of himself to that degree. If he didn't to Agnes or those closest to him, he certainly wouldn't to a casual encounter. With Agnes's schedule, Walter had a life apart from her that was completely free. And being as handsome and convivial as he was, he would take his comforts as they came along. They obviously weren't overly demanding of the other. I think they knew there was a limit, and beyond that it was dangerous territory."[28]

Dania Krupska's recollection of a midnight swim at Merriewold illuminates one aspect of the Prudes' multifaceted marriage. "It was Walter's idea for us all to go skinny dipping. The water was like warm beer and Agnes was doing sunfishes, with her bottom up. But Walter wouldn't get in the water. He stood on the shore, dressed nattily in his sweater, with a flashlight — flashing the light on us, laughing like mad at the whole crazy scene. It was the only time I ever saw him really animated, really enjoying himself."[29]

f o r t y - t w o

Indian Summer

By 1968, the wave of great musical shows — and, some would argue, talents — had dissipated. Production costs and ticket prices were roughly double what they had been ten years earlier. Broadway was suffering from the competition of television, the escalating Vietnam War, and the protest movements that were polarizing the country. The Great White Way held little appeal for the Woodstock generation, whose members cared more for visual and sound effects than for literate lyrics and librettos. *Hair*, the sensational musical of the previous season, had opened *off*-Broadway. As hippies celebrated the dawning of the Age of Aquarius with drugs and sex, Agnes agreed to direct and choreograph *Come Summer*, a sentimental paean to the nineteenth century. *Come Summer* would be the painful and ignominious end of her Broadway career.*

James Mitchell, her assistant director, said, "I can hardly talk about *Come Summer*." Agnes said, "I hate to even *think* about it." Her previous directorial experience had been frustrating at best, but *Allegro* and *Out of This World*, coming at a time when her career was in high gear, could be

* *1776*, which opened the same week, was also old-fashioned, and *was* a big success — but it had more wit, more sentiment (as opposed to sentimentality), and no dancing.

considered aberrations. Now she was sixty-three, and seventeen years had elapsed since her last hit.

Come Summer, adapted from Esther Forbes's *Rainbow on the Road,* was about an itinerant peddler of broadsides (the *National Enquirer* of its day) and his sidekick, who provided a romantic subplot. The score, the period (the 1830s), and the setting (the Connecticut River Valley) appealed to Agnes, and she was a great fan of Ray Bolger, who played the peddler. In interviews, Agnes strained to make the story sound contemporary, even drawing a parallel between the Bolger character and the hippies' rebellion against conformity. But the peddler was a victim of change; the hippies were creating it. *Hair* had rock music and nudity. *Come Summer* had a dream ballet. And in the sixties, nostalgia was a thing of the past.

On the first day of rehearsals, Bolger, whose part was written as the second lead, informed the cast, "Remember, I'm the star."[1] He insisted that his role dominate that of leading man David Cryer, thus making the already incoherent book even more confusing. Like *Allegro* and *Out of This World, Come Summer* was a huge, expensive show with complicated technical effects. At one point it had twenty-seven musical numbers, including reprises. By Agnes's estimate, between December 3 and mid-March she rehearsed the equivalent of four shows, with no time to get any of them right. She set the scenes and Mitchell rehearsed them while she directed the dances.

"She couldn't get beyond the terrible, terrible book," James Mitchell said, "and rather a mediocre score. She did her best to yank it out of its doldrums with choreography. When they were unable to fix the book, they of course fired the director. In Boston they brought in Burt Shevelove, who was also unable to fix the book." Shevelove lasted five days, during which Agnes was barred from the theater and forbidden to speak to the actors. When he left, the producers asked Agnes to come back, but only to choreograph. James Mitchell was asked to direct. He refused, but "when they put in new material, I did stage it and get it on its feet, and I asked Agnes to come and look at it. And she wouldn't do it. She was terribly humiliated; she'd been demoted and told that she couldn't fix it. It was probably her worst disaster."[2]

The program gives Agnes directorial credit for *Come Summer*, but in retrospect neither she nor anyone else could say who directed the show. Before the opening night performance in New York, Agnes went backstage, dressed to the teeth, and told the dancers, "I will be there watching. I am going to be buried tonight by Clive Barnes. But you've worked hard, you're ready for an opening, and I want you to do the most brilliant opening night you've ever done."[3] She was wrong about Barnes. "Apart from the book, lyrics and music," he wrote, "*Come Summer* is not all that bad. . . . Agnes de Mille's staging is beautifully stylish; it has a class that the show does not even aspire to. It has the best dancers and the best dancing on Broadway."[4] But after seven performances, *Come Summer* was gone.

But for *Come Summer*, Agnes might have left Broadway before it left her. Fortunately, there was no time to brood; her energies were demanded elsewhere. In 1970, in addition to her full schedule of speaking engagements, she addressed the Maine House of Representatives, a governor's conference on the arts, and the House Select Subcommittee on Education, urging government support for the arts. "What better investment can a country make than in the talents of its truly gifted?" she asked the legislators, and then shocked them with statistics on how little money dancers and choreographers earned.

In 1964, the state of North Carolina had sponsored a competition to determine what city would be the home of the state's new School of the Arts. Agnes was on the panel of judges that chose Winston-Salem, a community that prided itself in its culture. When the school became a reality, Agnes was an adviser to its School of Dance.*

She developed a friendship with Philip Hanes, a wealthy North Carolinian who admired her work, and apprised him of her tribulations. "I have no company to work on," she wrote, "and all my rehearsals are with unemployed dancers who leave me the moment they smell bread and butter. At this stage of my life it seems hard."[5] Hanes offered to underwrite the score for a new ballet to be created at the school, with students dancing all but the leading roles. Agnes would have at her disposal the latest equipment and facilities, and her pick of the most talented students, who would work for college credit rather than union scale. She could visit the school periodically to set movement, and a faculty member would rehearse the students in her absence.

The arrangement pleased everyone. The administration was thrilled to have the prestige of Agnes's name; classes were disrupted, rehearsal time extended, whatever she needed was given priority and, when possible, anticipated. She was paid a token amount for her time, but waived her royalties. The cost, including music, costumes, and sets designed by professionals but built at the school, was about $40,000 — one-sixth of what it would be in New York. And Agnes could invite people from ABT and other companies to view a ballet that they might want to pick up, without exposing the work to the New York press.

In its period, costumes, and movements, the new ballet, *A Rose for Miss Emily* (based on William Faulkner's short story) bore a family resemblance to *Oklahoma!, Carousel,* and *Bloomer Girl* — but the eponymous heroine's closest relative is Lizzie Borden. Like *Fall River Legend, A Rose for Miss Emily* is a theatrical melodrama with a solid structure and handsome sets. Both are about lonely, desperate spinsters who murder people

* The North Carolina School of the Arts became affiliated with the University of North Carolina in 1973.

they love — and hate — in their own homes. Emily's victim is her lover, who makes the fatal mistake of showing an interest in other women. She strangles him with a scarf, hides his body in her house, and becomes a recluse. When the ballet starts, she is old and alone, taunted by neighboring children; the corpse lies on a chaise, covered with a lace wedding veil and dead rose petals, unseen by the audience. About eight minutes into the ballet, as Emily dances in a reverie, the corpse suddenly sits up (as does the audience), and the crucial events of Emily's life are reenacted. At the climax, believing that the man is about to leave her, Emily runs across the stage and leaps onto his back, wrapping her legs around him; violent lifts and throws build to the murder, after which she drags his body to the chaise and covers it. Like Lizzie, Emily dances with the ghosts of her past selves and observes happy couples going off together; and as in *Fall River Legend,* the reactions of curious neighbors who discover the gruesome remains after Emily dies telegraph the horror to the audience.

Agnes worked out the principal parts on David Evans and Gemze de Lappe, who starred in the North Carolina production. Composer Alan Hovhaness, who had worked with Martha Graham, wrote the music, and Christina Giannini's decor emanated claustrophobia and decay. Lucia Chase then decided that *A Rose for Miss Emily* would be a good vehicle for Sallie Wilson, and acquired it for ABT's forthcoming season.

Nearly twenty years earlier, when Gemze de Lappe had danced the leading role in *The Harvest According,* Agnes had insisted that Lucia make her a member of Ballet Theatre. Gemze was quite happy there, and some critics even considered her performance as Lizzie Borden superior to Nora Kaye's. But when *The Harvest According* was dropped from the repertory, Agnes wanted Gemze to leave Ballet Theatre and tour with the Agnes de Mille Dance Theatre. And when Agnes wanted someone, according to another dancer who more than once succumbed to her persuasive powers, "She would talk to you with such an incredible amount of words, you were never aware of the moment when she had talked you into what you were determined never to do, and you were sitting there smiling!"[6] Gemze now found herself in the position of teaching the role of Emily, which had been created on her and which she had danced brilliantly, to Sallie Wilson, who would dance it with ABT. As compensation,

Lucia allowed Gemze to dance one performance. "She tore 55th Street right up — "Agnes reported, "sobbings in the wings and screaming out front."[7]

Agnes was never happy with the score; Hovhaness, who was half Armenian, used Armenian melodic and rhythmic patterns that were ill-suited for the Southern Gothic style. But reviewer Joseph Gale wrote that "de Mille's artistry becomes purer with the years. It is an artistry steeped in the skill of the short-story writer. She grasps the central core and permits only those embellishments that serve it. There is not an ounce of fat in any of her recent ballets, and each grows in power over the one before."[8] Other critics were not impressed. Anna Kisselgoff, Clive Barnes's colleague at the *Times,* pronounced the choreography weak and the story banal; others objected to the dream sequence's similarity to *Oklahoma!* and *Fall River Legend.* Barnes's judgment was that it should have been canceled. After ABT's spring tour, *A Rose for Miss Emily* was consigned to the limbo of lost dances.

Despite her disappointment in the sales of all her books since *Dance to the Piper,* Agnes continued to write. In the early 1970s, she updated and expanded portions of *The Book of the Dance* for a brochure on American dance that was translated into Russian and distributed by the United States Information Agency. She also completed a book based on her copious correspondence with her mother during her years in London — a period she had condensed into three chapters in *Dance to the Piper. Speak to Me, Dance with Me,* published in 1973, tells the truth, though not the whole truth, about her relationships with her mother, with Edgar Wind, and with Ramon Reed. She changed the names of a few minor characters and some details about herself — implying, for example, that she had been a virgin well after her affair with Warren Leonard, who goes unmentioned — but the book is essentially factual, and more than fair to Anna de Mille. Agnes's account of what she learned about her craft and how she evolved as a choreographer is instructive; her descriptions of the personalities and the work of Marie Rambert, Ninette de Valois, and Frederick Ashton, "a languid exquisite with one of the soundest gifts ballet has ever known," are superb.[9] Ashton, she wrote, had

> the kind of technique that develops the instruments which steer vessels, that grinds microscopes and telescopes, that balances watches. Even in his ornamental pieces, in the pure decoration that he puts so lavishly on the stage, one finds a craft like Cellini's, like Faberge's. Each dancer and each phrase is set as a master goldsmith sets a gem.[10]

Tudor, "the first totally new balletic voice of our time," dealt with life's "unfathomable mystery"; his work contained "tenderness, compassion, love and grief that may have been beyond the power of any other contemporary choreographer or stage director. . . . [E]ven though the great shock of his idiom has disappeared, the delight and the strength [of his ballets] remain."[11]

To the artist, everyone is potential material, and the cast of characters in Agnes's life was rich material indeed. With her uncle Cecil safely dead, she was free to include her account of the *Cleopatra* fiasco, which had been deleted from *Dance to the Piper* for legal reasons (the dead have no protection against libel). She deplored his dictatorial tactics and what were, by her lights, his crass values and unsophisticated tastes (Kipling, Wagner, Tchaikovsky), at the same time acknowledging her ambivalence toward her most famous relative, whose name she used with pride as often as with scorn. The book ends with an homage to Henry George: a history of the Single Tax movement, followed by a five-page statement of the philosophy in its founder's own words.

In 1971, a young editor at Doubleday named Kate Medina had approached Agnes with the idea of a biography of Martha Graham. Agnes declined, saying that she admired Graham too much to risk offending her by writing truthfully about her private life. Medina proposed that Doubleday would not publish the book while Graham, then nearing eighty, was alive.

Agnes was loyal to Edward Weeks, but she blamed Little, Brown at least in part for the fact that none of her other books had approached the success of *Dance to the Piper*. So when Weeks failed to match Doubleday's $8,000 advance, Agnes accepted Medina's offer and began a series of interviews with various Grahamites.

It was at about this time that Agnes encountered Clive Barnes, whom she had cut dead for six years, at a party in Virgil Thomson's apartment in the Chelsea Hotel. Barnes had recently called *Fall River Legend* "one of [ABT's] worst, and one of its most popular bad ballets . . . a blend of choreographic mannerisms from Antony Tudor and Martha Graham . . . fundamentally cheap and lurid."[12] But at Thomson's party, he greeted Agnes warmly, like a friend. Behind Barnes stood Walter, half expecting his wife to slap the omnipotent critic in the face, and signaling that she should behave. But Agnes's tongue was her weapon. "Mr. Barnes," she said, with a haughtiness that would have done credit to the Virgin Queen, "do you expect me to kiss your axe?" From then on, although Barnes never reversed himself about *Fall River Legend,* he found something positive to say about everything Agnes did.

In the early seventies, the eclectic or "crossover" choreography that was considered revolutionary when Agnes put a tap dance into *Rodeo* had become unremarkable. A job in ballet or on Broadway might require a dancer with training in classical, modern, and even jazz techniques; except for the most remarkably gifted, only the versatile survived. Jerome Robbins and talented younger choreographers, such as Eliot Feld and Robert Joffrey, were creating ballets that were informal and experimental. Balanchine, who was Agnes's age, was still active with his New York City Ballet. Graham, even older, was still the premier modern dance choreographer, but the next generation was represented by two former members of her company, Paul Taylor and Merce Cunningham, who founded their own companies to present their idiosyncratic styles. More radical groups had discovered what Agnes had practiced for decades: the power of simple nondance movement, such as walking and even standing still, to communicate their ideas. Agnes's work, with its traditional American forms and stories, was out of fashion, but she hoped that the approaching Bicentennial would bring it back. What could be a more appropriate addition to the country's self-congratulatory festivities than a celebration of American song and dance, presented from coast to coast by the Heritage Dance Theater, the company for which she had sought funding for so many years?

Throughout Agnes's career, the performing arts had been the purview of impresarios and entrepreneurs. But with the notable exception of the now octogenarian Sol Hurok, arts organizations were now controlled by boards of directors, run by businessmen, and subsidized by corporations, foundations, and the National Endowment for the Arts. Fund-raising was a full-time occupation for which artists had neither the time nor the temperament — a fact of life that Agnes continued to resist. "Agnes's ideas about fund-raising were on a par with Lucia's," said Harold Taylor, who served on the board of directors of both women's companies. "Like everything in her life, it came down to, in her mind, personal loyalty. If we needed $10,000 or $15,000, she would write to friends who had supported her in the past. That undercuts fund-raising efforts by the board."[13]

Through sheer perseverance, she obtained a $10,000 grant from the New York State Council on the Arts, and several other grants, totaling $111,500, from the Rockefeller Foundation.* The National Endowment for the Arts, on whose dance panel she had served, turned her down. Her friend Bella Lewitzky recalled Agnes's mood at this time. "She felt, and she had every right to feel, neglected by the dance world and by the Endowment. She was discounted and undervalued by everybody, and it set her in a very black, despairing mood."[14] Agnes appealed the decision, asking prominent friends to intercede on her behalf; Nancy Hanks, then director of the NEA, finally overruled the advisory panel's recommendation, and a $50,000 grant was approved.

Agnes decided to form her company out of the students in North Carolina, where she had had such a positive experience with *Emily.* In the fall of 1972, she made the first in a series of trips to Winston-Salem to build a company. She often stayed with Philip Hanes and his wife, who found her to be "a demanding and difficult person to host. She was fire and spit and lightning," Hanes said. "When she left, you were exhausted — but the memories were worth every minute of it. She was probably the tenderest person I've ever known, but she didn't want people to know that. She'd snap and fuss at me and make me feel like the country hick that in a way I am, but then I'd overhear her telling someone, 'He's the noblest man in the arts.'"[15]

A year later, she had a company of thirty-one dancers, most of whom

---

* The money was contingent on $20,000 in matching funds, which Agnes raised.

had never been on a professional stage before. She discovered their special talents, from playing the saxophone to riding a unicycle, and found ways to use them. She hired Gemze de Lappe, David Evans, and three other soloists to perform the leading roles. Professional designers went down periodically from New York to work with the students on costumes and simple, evocative sets.

The two programs of dances she assembled consisted entirely of her own dances, with two exceptions: a blues number by Katherine Dunham and a ragtime piece by Anna Sokolow. (Originally she had intended to present the work of other choreographers — but as they were not willing to waive their fees and royalties, as she did, the cost proved prohibitive.) She resurrected two big production numbers that had been cut from shows. *Texas Fourth,* salvaged from *110 in the Shade,* was a spoof of a small-town Independence Day parade in 1936. Teenagers performed exaggerated versions of the jitterbug, Charleston, and other popular dances of the day. Confederate veterans marched, boys clapped rhythms on their overall trousers, cheerleaders waved pompoms, acrobats flipped across the stage, children played kazoos, and a majorette twirled a baton. The unicyclist did his turn, and a honky-tonk piano rolled by on a float. "Loggers Song," cut from *Come Summer,* was an elaborate clog dance based on Irish and French folk steps reflecting the backgrounds of New England lumberjacks. The men skittered flatfooted across the stage as though riding logs downstream, walking and leaping with terrific energy, using their feet and a pole to guide them. There was also material from *A Rose for Miss Emily, The Four Marys,* and *Gold Rush. The Cherry Tree Carol,* which the students had performed on educational television, was a bucolic fourteenth-century folk ballad about the Holy Family, transferred to Appalachia around 1850, with dances built around the Virginia Reel.

Fifteen years after Hurok had sponsored the costly (for Agnes) tour of her Dance Theatre, Agnes swallowed her contempt and asked him to represent her again. The outcome would be the same, with Agnes again taking a loss, and Walter caught between conflicting loyalties to his boss and his wife. But Hurok was responsible for the Heritage company's only appearance in New York. The occasion was a gala celebration of the impresario's eighty-fifth birthday at the Metropolitan Opera House in May 1974. The dancers gave a rousing performance of excerpts from *Texas*

Fourth; young, fresh, and exuberant, they held their own on a program with Margot Fonteyn, Isaac Stern, Van Cliburn, and other luminaries. It was Hurok's last birthday; he would have a fatal heart attack while Agnes's company toured the Northeast the following spring.

In the fall of 1973 and again the following spring, the Heritage Dance Theatre performed in colleges and small auditoriums across the country — traveling by bus, making enormous jumps, rarely staying anywhere more than one night. Agnes joined them occasionally in major cities, returning to New York to make sure, among other things, that she could meet the $23,000 weekly payroll. In her absence, Gemze de Lappe and David Evans were in charge. "The Hurok office treated Agnes like dirt," Evans said. "The stagehands and propmen they hired to tour with her acted as though it was beneath them. They would half unpack the truck and not put out important pieces. They told me that the Hurok office really didn't want her, but felt compelled to do this because of her husband."[16]

Reviews ran the gamut, from "the entire evening is one of a glowing feeling of being glad to be American" to "the same vigorous, stagy use of American folk elements and the same soft-focus romanticizing of the past that Miss de Mille has been turning out since *Rodeo* and *Oklahoma!* Very skilfully worked stuff it is, but untouched by the many other currents of American dance in the past thirty years."[17] Albert Goldberg of the *Los Angeles Times* pronounced the dancing "undistinguished" and wrote, "After four weeks on the road the company is still in try-out condition."[18] Florida State University's chairman complained to the Hurok office, "Never has our own campus Dance Department presented a recital that was of as poor quality as this. It was, truly, appalling. I cannot see how Miss de Mille, whose name and work I almost revere, could have let her name be associated with this show, and I am astonished that Hurok would present it."[19] The canned music was dreadful, the male-female stereotypes seemed archaic in the era of women's liberation, and many spectators found the two-and-one-half-hour program tedious and repetitious.

For the second tour, Agnes consolidated the two programs into one and had the music rerecorded, greatly improving its quality. But she could not afford to pay salaries during the winter hiatus. Her dancers, whose "muscle memory" made them the involuntary archivists of her work, were no longer amateurs but dues-paying union members; when other work was offered, they could not afford to turn it down. Agnes, who had fought to establish her own union, now fought for exceptions to the rules of other labor organizations. Promised monies did not arrive on time, and the bureaucratic complexities of the National Endowment demanded attention and time. At one point, she had two weeks in which to raise $20,000 needed to make the spring tour viable. She had spent money set aside for taxes to pay bills, and now the taxes were due. It was almost as though she was compelled to recreate her recital days, counting pennies and flirting with bankruptcy. The spring tour, originally planned to last six weeks, ended after three, with a $23,425 loss.

While she had struggled to keep her company solvent and intact through the winter, Agnes worked out a new format for her speaking engagements: a lecture with film clips, tapes, and pianist David Baker. With her longtime friend Mary Meyer Green acting as road manager and amanuensis, she introduced it at Harvard's summer school. The response was so positive that she took it on the road as far as Honolulu, refining it along the way. In October 1974, she presented it in Washington, Boston, and six other cities in the Northeast, in conjunction with the Heritage program — her lecture on Friday night, the dances over the weekend. In its final version, "Conversations About the Dance" was an inspired fusion of Agnes's talents as researcher, writer, and entertainer, enhanced by her ability to explain dance in its social, religious, political, cultural, and historical contexts. She began with the thesis that dance is an extension of universal body language, and proceeded from gesture and mime to seventeenth-century galliards, eighteenth-century minuets, nineteenth-century American folk and ballroom dances, and the relationship of the Irish jig to African-American ragtime and tap. She peppered her text with aphorisms and one-liners; eighteenth-century girls danced in their corsets with "all the abandon of lobsters," and certain classic ballets had "princes with curious relationships to their mothers — or birds."

Using some of her Heritage dancers to demonstrate, she segued from the first European ballerinas (Fanny Elssler and Marie Taglioni) to Isadora Duncan (whose bare feet "caused more of a ruckus than bare genitals do today"), Martha Graham, Broadway, and contemporary disco dancing. "Young people do not dance with one another," she lamented. "They dance in spite of one another. Without discipline, manner, style, courtesy or plan. There is no communication." But she ended on an up note, predicting "We'll survive, with gallantry and boldness."

Two performances at Hunter College in New York were scheduled specifically to attract new sponsors for the Heritage company. To that end, Agnes augmented her "Conversations" with twenty-six dancers, including guest soloist Honi Coles, whose syncopated tribute to Bojangles provided a sensational ending for the first act. *Newsday*'s Byron Belt wrote that she "demonstrated for the umpteenth time that she is the wittiest, most articulate, insightful and ultimately poetically touching spokesperson the arts have in America today."[20] *Dance Magazine*'s Louis Pastore pronounced her a "national resource of the dance world."[21] Clive Barnes had been converted; "Combative and superbly armed with a bulldoggedness that would have done Churchill credit," he wrote, "de Mille is a brilliant fighter for dance causes. . . . She is also dazzling as a lecturer . . . terribly funny and beautifully articulate, yet still has a common touch that audiences identify with. . . . [T]he fact that I do not admire de Mille's work more does not mean that I admire de Mille herself any less." Barnes now considered Agnes "the nearest thing we have to an American Moiseyev; no one else knows the entire gambit of American dance and has the theatrical know-how to put the whole thing together. . . . [Heritage] is unlike any other American company. Let us get it in shape for the Bicentennial and show the world America dancing."[22]

forty-three

Paying the Piper

Early in 1975, the North Carolina School of the Arts honored Agnes with a bricks-and-mortar appreciation of what the chairman of the board expressed in a letter:

> You have allowed us to share your grand dreams, in which you have caught up these young artists, turning the stars on in them before our very eyes, and sending across the footlights your visions of an America that was hearts and flowers, sometimes mixed with bitter sorrow, but more often with a hearty guffaw.[1]

The dedicatory program for the Agnes de Mille Theater included readings from her books and a performance of *Three Virgins and a Devil* by former students. Agnes said, "I wish my father and grandfather were here."

Still lacking sufficient financial commitments from foundations and corporations, Agnes invited their representatives to a third "Conversation"

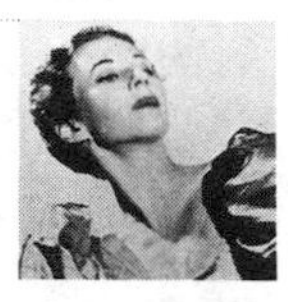

at Hunter College on May 15, 1975. An issue that she never addressed directly was the fact that the grants givers would see a show in which she was the centerpiece, while being asked to support the Heritage Dance Theater, which would appear without her most of the time. The question is moot, for the performance was canceled. Three hours before it was to begin, a blood vessel burst in Agnes's brain.

A lifetime of investing everything she had in everything she did had taken its toll on a vascular system that was genetically predisposed to hypertension. Agnes had taken medication for years, and had recently developed an alarming new symptom — brief memory lapses, twice during lectures — but she did not slow down. She was now in her seventieth year, the age at which her mother had suffered her fatal stroke.

A massive cerebral hemorrhage in the left hemisphere of her brain left the entire right side of her body paralyzed and without feeling. Her vision, speech, memory, and mobility were impaired — whether temporarily or permanently, no one could predict. Her condition was critical for weeks and she was hospitalized for three and a half months, during which smaller strokes and other complications ensued. Two operations were required to remove blood clots (in her right leg, and then in the carotid artery in her neck) — a serious risk for an already debilitated woman of her age.

When Agnes finally went home, her hair had faded from gray to white. Her sight had returned to normal, and her speech was much improved. But her right side remained worse than useless — dead weight, a drag on her left side — and she was right-handed. Physical therapists would help her to salvage what was salvageable, but life as she had lived it had ended, literally, in a heartbeat.

To lose control of one's body is calamitous for anyone, but perhaps most of all for a dancer. Agnes's body, like that of any dancer, had endured punishing discipline, but the habit of the barre had kept it strong for its age. At sixty-seven, she had danced her original role of the world-weary whore in *Judgment of Paris* (at a benefit for the New York Public Library's Dance Collection). Just four months before the stroke, at an anniversary gala for ABT, she had danced the first few bars of her original role in *Three Virgins and a Devil* before Sallie Wilson took over. In "Conversations" she had sashayed and waltzed and punctuated her text with expressive gestures. The stroke catapulted her into old age and infirmity; the body that had been her instrument became her prison. "There would be no more shortcuts," she observed ruefully. That was the least of it. Life would have an entirely different texture and tempo, and design. The simplest, most ordinary procedures — eating, bathing, dressing, getting from one room to the next — required forethought and assistance. To cross the street, let alone the city, was a major undertaking. "My trip to the bathroom in privacy and decency," she wrote after accomplishing this strenuous feat, "meant more to me than a rave notice in the *New York Times*."[2]

Agnes had always equated fatalism with spiritual laziness. Her code was stringent, her models heroic: her mother, for whom surrender was never an option; Henry George, who said, "You can't make the wind, but you can sail by it"; her other grandfather, Henry de Mille, who had sucked the infected matter from the throat of a child dying of diphtheria; Ramon Reed, who had endured what poet William Ernest Henley had called "the bludgeonings of chance" with transcendent grace; and Mrs.

Obie, who had counseled Agnes in London, "How it is dished out, so you must swallow it down." Doctors marveled at Agnes's courage, a word that belittles the effort. Friends were not surprised. "People use the word brave," Harold Taylor said, "but she was sort of cocky about everything."[3] After telling a reporter that she still hoped to regain the use of her right leg, she added, "but even if I don't, you can say I certainly used it when I had it, kiddo."[4]

Wearing a fiberglass brace, and risking serious injury if she fell, she practiced walking. She had a barre installed in her apartment, and worked at it daily with the same determination with which she had learned to dance. She relearned phone numbers and simple arithmetic — information that had been erased from her brain as from a blackboard. She learned to write, shakily but legibly, with her left hand. Told that she would never be able to rise on the toes of her right foot, her competitive spirit took over and she practiced what she had preached to young dancers: "Elevation is accomplished by thinking up and not down."[5] In six months she was doing eight wobbly relevés. By the end of the year she could walk, haltingly, with the brace and a cane. Her right side remained insensate; eventually she could make gross movements with her right arm, but only if she watched it. Learning her limitations, measuring her progress, she acquired "the inchworm's point of view."[6] When her doctor indicated that she should not expect to get measurably better, she dealt with the news as she had always dealt with unpleasantries: "I simply refused to consider it."[7]

Always acutely conscious of her appearance in public, Agnes now saw herself as a clumsy embarrassment to her elegant husband. Walter demurred; "This has been the making of me, my dear," he said. Strong and even devoted husbands have fled from a wife's chronic disability; that Walter did neither was a revelation to both him and his wife. Agnes, who had learned as a child that love was earned by accomplishments, discovered that Walter's love was based on something deeper and more durable. To Ed Dietz he confided, "I'm afraid I haven't been a very good husband, but all my life I've wondered what I would do without Agnes," then put his arm on Dietz's shoulder and wept.[8] "I don't want to live if she is gone," he told another friend.[9] The stroke stripped away jealousies, power struggles, all the defensive weaponry and emotional fortifications with which he and Agnes had protected themselves. In that sense, the last years of their marriage would be the best.

Agnes had seen little of her son since he had entered Amherst College, and she missed him. "It takes a family catastrophe to bring us together," she had written to a friend with inadvertent prescience.[10] Jonathan was now an astute, scholarly twenty-nine-year-old working on his doctoral thesis (ultimately published as *The Coming of the Industrial Order,* a study of factory conditions in rural Massachusetts before the Civil War) at Harvard. His mother's illness neutralized long-standing tensions between his parents and himself and united them in the common cause of Agnes's recovery. "There was a kind of outpouring of affection," Harold Taylor said. "All three got realigned."[11]

At the same time, Walter was coping with problems on another front. Sol Hurok — a man so secretive that he had not only sold his organization (to Tomorrow Entertainment) without telling his employees but had conducted the negotiations in Yiddish — had died without bequeathing even a token acknowledgment of Walter's twenty-eight years of loyal and effective service. Nor had he ever subscribed to the idea of a medical or pension plan for his employees. Walter was sixty-seven, but he had no wish to retire — nor did he feel, given Agnes's astronomical medical bills, that he could afford to. Instead, he joined a newly formed agency, ICM Artists Ltd., taking with him Isaac Stern, Pinchas Zukerman, Andrés Segovia, and some of his other prestigious artists; but for the first time since World War II, his future was uncertain.

That Agnes would continue to work while she had breath and her mental faculties was never in doubt; however diminished her physical capacity, she would push it to the limit. Renoir had continued to paint in his seventies, after arthritis rendered both legs useless and his brush had to be tied to his fingers; he then took up sculpting and, by guiding his assistant's hand with a long stick, created two masterpieces. Goya produced a totally new style and some of his best work in his late seventies, when he was completely deaf, and could not see to paint without several layers of spectacles and a magnifying glass. Agnes had the same urgent need to create, to communicate, and her output over the next eighteen years would be astounding.

"Dancer" was the identity she had most painstakingly constructed and to which she had clung long after her dancing career was over, but it was not her only identity. She was also a writer. The Graham biography, only barely begun, was a mountain she could not yet contemplate climbing. But she had another book in progress, for which she had already done most of the research. "She called me from the hospital," Kate Medina recalled, "asking would we be interested in this manuscript she had been working on for a long time. In our editorial meeting I said, 'I really don't know whether Agnes is going to do this book or not, but she has an absolute will to do it and to be fine.' So we sent her a contract. I remember her saying that she had the pile of papers on a table under a towel in the hospital, and that it represented the far shore — that when she couldn't work on it, she could look at it. It represented the future, something to work toward. And of course she finished that book."[12]

In the hospital, Agnes began working for the first time with a tape recorder, which she could barely manipulate with her left hand. Merely handling papers, pencils, scissors, and paper clips was a complex and frustrating exercise. The faithful Mary Meyer Green now functioned as secretary, transcribing the tapes onto pages with enough white space to allow for Agnes's barely decipherable changes. The result, achieved under the equivalent of battlefield conditions, contains some of Agnes's finest writing.

*Where the Wings Grow** is a memoir of Merriewold, where Agnes's wings grew. It had begun as the story of her Aunt Caroline, whose sister had married Henry George Jr. In 1884, the beautiful, cultured young Southern belle had become one of the first Americans to marry a Japanese. "She lost her citizenship to do it," Agnes said. "Think of the *courage!* She was ostracized by two cultures!"[13] Her husband, Jokichi Takamine, was an internationally known chemist, credited with discovering adrenaline. He had accumulated a fortune in fertilizers and pharmaceuticals, and was responsible for the gift of cherry trees from Japan to Washington, D.C. He also bought the exotic Japanese palace that was built for the 1904 St. Louis Exhibition, named it Sho-Foo-Den, and had it transported to the Merriewold woods for his family's summer home.

---

* The title refers to Martha Graham's instruction to a pupil to keep his shoulders straight because that was "where the wings grow."

Agnes and her cousins had been enchanted by the Takamines' wealth and elegance, their achievements and fame, their imperial lifestyle. "They were a family," Agnes wrote, "around which legends glittered."[14] The children were blissfully oblivious to what the glamorous image concealed: bigotry, greed, injustice, incestuous love, and violent death. The Takamines' story evolved into a layered memory book, with Agnes's adult understanding of characters and relationships superimposed on the impressions of the imaginative child who had chanted, "This is my land. I shall die for love of it if I am taken away. I am the queen of the forest."[15] Without glossing over the price that their Victorian values exacted on their husbands and children, it pays compassionate homage to Agnes's mother and aunts, righteous women who provided "a kind of perfect pitch to which all the members of their society referred."[16] And it relates, with wistful regret, how the ignorance and the repression that surrounded the subjects of sex, illegitimacy, alcoholism, insanity, adultery, and homosexuality forced them all into hypocritical denial.

Where the Wings Grow contains some exquisite writing about the pure joys and the inexplicable fears of childhood and adolescence, which Agnes had so often recreated in her dances. It shimmers with sensual imagery: the taste of fresh huckleberries, the smell of mildew, the sound of a woman's voice calling ("a kind of household musical signature. Each mother and aunt had her own little cadence which punctuated from time to time, like bird notes, the comfortable kitchen and household noises").[17] Sixty years after the fact, Agnes conjured up the image of her nine-year-old self "sitting on my chamber pot alone and saying, 'I shall never forget this moment.' And I didn't forget: the candle in its aureole, the feel of the china against my flesh, the overwhelming night silence, the noises of small animals."[18] It recaptures Eden:

> As we watched from the porch, the rain stung off the curving tin-tiled roofs and bounced in a haze from the red lacquered porch that gleamed in the reflected light of water. The tall, black, naked pine trunks glistened. On the bright moss, pink salamanders tried the soft wetness with their dainty cold toes. The great wooden gong, shaped like a fish, creaked overhead. The bronze porch lanterns sounded, knocking dully as though with muffled clappers. The smell of laurel, rhododendron, and pine came to us in great whiffs.

> The ground opened before us and breathed suddenly. The green of moss and grass was more brilliant. Leaves were glossy as metal. A mist of water-like perfume rose and hung over the uneven garden steps. And then on the instant, way below by the lake among the blue iris, a wild doe arched on stiffened forelegs, broke cover and bounded off through the bracken to the shelter of the deeper woods.[19]

It ends with the approach of autumn in 1914, with Agnes and the world on the brink of enormous, irrevocable changes.

> The sky was high blue and absolutely flat — flat as enamel — the gold trees cut out against it as though with scissors. Not a leaf stirred. In the reflected green and gold light of the deep afternoon there was a sudden green rush of fern, untouched yet by frost, still verdant, still sweet-smelling, and puffs — cushions of moss, green as Imperial satin. On this the rosy little mushrooms bloomed. Occasionally an acorn dropped, and silently, all through the windless air, the yellow leaves drifted down, golden, golden, falling forever. They made a sound like a pricking, a sort of tinkling. It was the sound of time.[20]

"It seems I am loved," Agnes wrote to a friend, "which I really didn't know about."[21] She seemed genuinely surprised by the outpouring of flowers and cards from friends all around the world as well as from people she scarcely remembered. One dancer with whom she had had no contact since 1944 wrote to say, "The attitude turn [in *Bloomer Girl*] that spiraled down to the floor in a billow of skirt and resolved up into a new strength has long been one of the most gorgeous, soul-satisfying turns I have ever done. . . . The coda with the lifts and the expanded pinwheel turn I thought would fling me out into the universe. . . . I can hardly sit still to think of it. . . . I want you to know that the goodness you gave to me with your dance stays with me, a bright glow that opens and lifts my heart."[22]

In the daytime she wore long Chinese tunics, with trousers to hide the brace. By the end of the year, she could walk around her apartment — haltingly, but without a cane. During the first half of 1976, again assisted by Mary Green, she returned to the lecture circuit, giving her arts speech in Washington, Indiana, Illinois, and Pennsylvania. She wanted to be active, and she wanted the income (her hospital bill, exclusive of physicians' fees, was $32,000). Her speech was deeper, thicker, slower than it had been. Dramatically rolling her *R*'s (a theatrical mannerism of her father's generation), marrying early-nineteenth- and late-twentieth-century language in a single sentence ("we are mugged in our parlors"), she was an even more compelling speaker than before.

In May she gave a speech in Easton, Maryland, where Margaret, now widowed, lived alone. Whatever their superficial differences, the sisters had always been fiercely loyal to each other. Now Margaret was undergoing chemotherapy that would prolong her life for a few years, but could not save it. Agnes was distraught; her beloved sister was dying, and she could do nothing. In 1978, when Margaret lost her battle, Agnes eulogized her candor and courage in a letter to Margaret's close friends. "I am bereft," she wrote. "Half of my memory is gone. Half of my life experience is gone. . . . I'll never hear her say, 'No, that wasn't quite right. It was this way.'"[23]

Ironically, as Margaret faded and Walter developed chronic cervical arthritis — literally, a pain in the neck — Agnes's professional star brightened. She already had an impressive collection of honors and awards, but her return from the brink of extinction had elevated her status from elder doyenne of dance to icon. She was designated a national treasure, and showered with tributes. She received a standing ovation whenever she was introduced, and another when she finished speaking. ("Were you overwhelmed with emotion?" a friend asked after one such occasion. "I'm a pro, darling," she replied. "It's my job.")[24] At public events she was more than ever the imperious grande dame, dressing exquisitely — often in fuschia, turquoise, and other bright colors that she had had to avoid when her hair was red. She favored décolleté necklines and ruffles and rich, textured fabrics: velvets, silk brocades, chiffons, taffetas, satins. Every outfit had its particular evening bag and its special jewelry, each piece heavy with her personal history. She would draft someone, usually a dancer, to pull her hair back and attach a false chignon and to make her up.

She was suddenly more prominent than she had been in years. The Bicentennial coincided with a renewed interest in the story ballets that had gone out of fashion in the fifties.* The Boston Ballet, the Cleveland Ballet, and other regional companies staged revivals of Agnes's work, and American Ballet Theatre announced a gala evening consisting of *Rodeo* and *Fall River Legend,* with Aaron Copland and Morton Gould conducting their scores, and the New York premiere of *Texas Fourth,* which now included the running set (the square dance accompanied only by clapping hands that she had used so effectively in *'49, Hell on Wheels, Rodeo,* and *Oklahoma!*) and a dream sequence, in which the ghost of a girl's mother demonstrates the decorous dancing of her day.

Vernon Lusby had often danced in Agnes's ballets, and he had set her works for ballet companies all over the world. Lusby rehearsed ABT's dancers in *Texas Fourth,* with Agnes supervising from her wheelchair. Her verbal imagery had always been original and precise (forty years after the fact, one of the original dance-hall girls in *Oklahoma!* recalled being told to shake her skirt like a rattlesnake), but up until the stroke she had also been able to demonstrate how the horses bucked in *Rodeo,* how the cowboys stood and walked and rode. What she had not been able to demonstrate, she had at least indicated with movement. Now she had to depend entirely on language. With Lusby and other dancers who had frequently worked with her, she could use a sort of verbal shorthand. But with new people, her frustration was palpable. At times her hands twitched, and she seemed about to jump out of her chair.

The gala, on the evening of July 8, 1976, was Agnes's first public appearance after the stroke and the occasion of one of the most emotional moments of her career. The curtain rose to reveal her alone onstage in a bright pink dress, holding tightly to a lectern but standing as straight as a general reviewing his troops. "Dear friends," she said, when the applause finally allowed her to be heard, "here I stand before you, although I thought never to stand again." The audience that had stood and cheered at the sight of her stood and cheered again, and wiped their eyes. Oliver Smith read a letter from President Ford that said in part, "You have placed an enduring and distinctly American imprint on the world of

* Agnes informed a reporter that every ballet company in the country wanted *Rodeo* that year, "'but I won't let them do it. If you see a regional company do a bad *Swan Lake* . . . you know it's a lousy performance, but you don't say Petipa didn't know what he was doing. But if people see my ballet done very badly, they say Agnes de Mille can't choreograph.'" (*New York Times,* July 4, 1976)

dance," and Mayor Abe Beame presented her with the Handel Medallion, New York City's highest award for artistic achievement.

The audience appreciated the color and vitality of *Texas Fourth,* but some critics faulted its length, repetitiousness, and lack of narrative structure. Clive Barnes dragged out his old accusation that Agnes borrowed from Graham and Tudor, but he praised her guts and her style, and called *Texas Fourth* "a happy explosion of Americana . . . good entertainment, and accessible to more than dance freaks."[25] Anna Kisselgoff, also writing in the *New York Times,* observed trenchantly, "A de Mille ballet is not defined by a particular movement technique or a style, since the style is changed to suit the subject. A ballet by Agnes de Mille is probably the only kind of contemporary ballet that can be instantly recognized by its attitude toward life. And that attitude is a humanist one."[26] Agnes's own assessment was characteristically severe: "The real bang-up fun came first," she said, "and then you went into heavy nostalgia, and it didn't hold."[27]

In October, Vernon Lusby staged *Rodeo* for the Joffrey Ballet, which would perform it in New York for the first time since 1972, when Christine Sarry had memorably danced the Cowgirl in ABT's production. Robert Joffrey understood that the ballet's emotions were timeless, if its how-to-get-a-man theme was not, and he intended to revive the original spirit of the thirty-five-year-old work. He had Oliver Smith and Kermit Love supervise the recreation of their original scenery and costumes, and delighted Agnes by giving her and Lusby as much time to teach it as though it were brand-new. On opening night, *Rodeo* was a triumph, but Agnes was not on hand to enjoy it. She was in New York Hospital recovering from a myocardial infarction, commonly known as coronary thrombosis or, more commonly, a heart attack. After three days in intensive care, she moved to a semiprivate room, where for two weeks she worked on *Where the Wings Grow,* surrounded by papers and taking so many phone calls from her agent and her editor that her roommate said, "Mrs. Prude, please! This is a hospital, not an office!"

The second of the four books that Agnes wrote after her stroke was *Reprieve.* With notes by neurologist Dr. Fred Plum adding technical accuracy, it documents the details of the stroke and its aftermath, and is an illustrious addition to the small but potent body of literature written by individuals who view the world from a wheelchair. *Reprieve* is a journal of life in a country whose inhabitants bear unbearable losses, indignities, and frustrations, but it has no trace of the self-pity that had occasionally crept into Agnes's previous autobiographical writing. "I did not say, 'Why me?'" she declared, "because the answer was so patently clear: 'Why not me?'"[28] Nor did she indulge her tendency to exaggerate molehills into mountains. This was real life, and the real prospect of death. "My brain," she wrote in one astonishing passage,

> my brain, my precious brain! A miraculous cauliflower in its bony case, marinating in my life juices, pulsing sentience, direction, aggression into its tentacles, into its moving fringes — this was the dynamo, now a broken toy, this clock, this *me,* ticking, ticking, wanting, asking, commanding, curious to see and be seen, to be unguarded, to be tended, still wanting, surprised always, urgent, unquiet, wanting.[29]

As she had dispensed advice to aspiring dancers, she now advised the able-bodied, informing them what behavior would and would not be welcomed by their afflicted friends and loved ones. She also had advice for the patients, such as "Don't always talk about yourself as in this book."[30] She still tended to view life through a lorgnette ("Your servants may not be quick. They probably do not know the house. . . . Don't bark out so many orders that they may be immobilized"), but the stroke did not affect her honesty or her humor.[31] "I have always liked being the center of attention and I have very frequently achieved this," she wrote. "Now I was a freak, but I was still the center."[32]

"*Piper* was your victory in your art," Edward Weeks wrote to her. "*Reprieve* is your victory in survival."[33]

forty-four

Phoenix

The performance of "Conversations" that was preempted by Agnes's stroke was the first she had ever missed in her life, and she was determined not only to make it up, but to improve it. Her goal now was to attract enough grant money to have the show filmed for public television. This time she would work with the Joffrey Ballet, augmented by as many of the original dancers who knew the works as she could round up. She added excerpts from *Rodeo* and a section of Jerome Robbins's *Interplay,* which the Joffrey company had permission to perform. There would be new costumes, new orchestrations, and a full orchestra. For a seventy-two-year-old woman who could barely walk without assistance to carry a two-hour show was a formidable undertaking, and there were real doubts that she would have the stamina to get through the evening. She was afraid of a mental lapse, or even another stroke. On the night of October 9, 1977, James Mitchell stood in the wings at City Center with a vial of nitroglycerine in his pocket and an extra script so that, if she should collapse, he could take over and the show would go on.

Wearing a crimson, off-the-shoulder gown, Agnes conducted the proceedings from a chair. If she lacked mobility, she still had her text,

her timing, her expressive face, and the conviction that what she was saying was of vital importance, and her command of the audience was unimpaired. "They laughed as though I was pushing buttons," she said, "and I suddenly realized I could not do wrong, that they were there to protect me . . . comforting me and supporting me." At the end, the company left her standing alone without a cane. She raised her left arm and willed the right one to follow, until both arms were outstretched above her head in an Evita-like pose. The ovation, she said, "was like ocean waves. I never have experienced anything like it."[1] Clive Barnes described the event as "the Goddess Terpsichore communing with one of her favorite prophets . . . a great evening in the theater — a show that illuminated dance and spoke up for civilization."[2] "Conversations About the Dance" was filmed for public television in Los Angeles in 1978, and broadcast nationally in 1980. The *Los Angeles Times* music critic pronounced Agnes "a model demonstration of defiance, against time . . . against infirmity . . . against lazy thinking. She was irreverent and naughty, candid and breezy, lofty and eloquent. She sighed, she cooed, she sputtered, she roared."[3] Had Agnes ever had the chance to film a series about world dance on its actual locations, the result would have been a priceless resource.

Agnes worked sporadically on her biography of Martha Graham, who, at eighty-three, was still active and seemingly immortal. Offered a $10,000 advance on a book based on what she had written for the USIA "Dance in America" brochure (which had only been distributed abroad), Agnes could not resist. She wrote the text and selected the copious illustrations; the book packager, Helena Obolensky, helped with the research. Because of staff changes at Macmillan, which was to publish the book, and because Agnes consistently missed deadlines, three editors eventually worked on *America Dances*. Agnes had as little interest in the production process as she had in music theory, and her attitude toward such details as galley proofs was cavalier to the point of contempt. She had always had a maddening habit of cutting up page proofs and returning them in pieces and out of sequence, with bits of paper taped over them containing illegible handwritten notes, and the fact that her words had been set in type did not deter her from endlessly rewriting. In the end, after two years of missed deadlines, there was no time to make final corrections. "They rushed it into print without my okay," Agnes explained to a reviewer who had pointed out numerous inaccuracies, "[with] bad printing, incorrect French, misnomers, wrong names under pictures. They were given to them correctly but it was a gigantic job and got mixed up."[4] Publication was followed by arguments over royalties and other monies due, which Agnes claimed were never paid.

During the last years of her life, there was considerable speculation among her friends about Agnes's financial situation. She was certainly not wealthy, but could she be as poor as she claimed? In the early seventies, she had donated all the films of her dances that she owned to the New York Public Library's Dance Collection and then, on the advice of her accountant, taken a $35,000 write-off on her tax return. But a recent law had made such donations tricky, and the government began an audit that dragged on for years. In the meantime, her accountant retired and left the state.

Investigators from the Internal Revenue Service questioned Genevieve Oswald, then curator of the Dance Collection, to put a dollar value on Agnes's films. Oswald was outraged by their ignorance. "They didn't know anything about dance or music. They would not have been embarrassed to admit that they didn't know who Picasso was. They said, 'Prove to us that she is an important artist, as important as Danny Kaye.' There was no feeling of their wanting to know what her films were really worth. At one point they were going to appraise the films by the number of feet. We made all kinds of lists; we tried to evaluate it in terms of content, artistic value, the cost of remaking or replacing the film. We gave them all kinds of documentation. We were fighting for de Mille but also for dance, its importance. Her dances had not been notated at that time, so these were the only records. And they were telling us that they had no value. They presumed her guilty and they were going to set her straight, teach her a lesson."

Eventually there was a hearing, at which Agnes was the only witness. Oswald was present, but not allowed to testify. "Agnes was strong and dignified on the stand," she said. "They did not treat her like a distinguished artist. She read letters from the National Endowment for the Arts into the record. They were not impressed, they were dismissive. They were rude and offhand when they interrogated her, without even making any concession to her age."[5] The deduction was disallowed, and at a time when her future earning power was uncertain, Agnes was informed that with fines and compound interest, she owed the government $182,000. "It was my fault in a way," she said, "because I took bad advice and hired a lawyer that I knew wasn't first-class."[6] She was forced to sell some investments and reassess her financial situation. But when Genevieve Oswald told her she thought the hearing had been rigged, Agnes replied that it was un-American to be so cynical about the system.

1979 was Agnes's busiest year since her stroke. Her lecture fee rose to a top of $2,500. She was guest of honor at a Carter White House dinner, after which some of her dances were performed. She continued to crusade for the cause of the Single Tax, and spoke at the centennial celebration of her grandfather's *Progress and Poverty* in Philadelphia. With Joan Mondale, actor James Earl Jones, opera singer Jerome Hines, and pollster Lou Harris, she testified at hearings of the Senate Subcommittee on Education, Arts and the Humanities on behalf of reauthorizing the National Endowment for the Arts. "If we want the best," she instructed the legislators, "you have to give the best. The United States pays $1.10 for every citizen for art annually. England pays $4. France pays $10. Little Denmark pays $20. . . . Suppose [Pope] Julius II had said to his painter, 'Hey Mike, that's enough, get a matching fund, a challenge grant'?"

The year ended with her name back in lights on Broadway, where a revival of *Oklahoma!* was a tremendous hit. In the wake of Vietnam and Watergate, with hostages in Iran and a recession at home ("People worry whether they can gas up to cross a state, let alone found one," wrote *Time*'s reviewer), the show carried a double dose of nostalgia: for the pioneering days in which it is set, and for the optimism and common purpose that had united the country when it opened in 1943.[7] Gemze de Lappe set the dances, and Agnes added the small but crucial finishing touches. Codirector William Hammerstein recalled, "Agnes could only move one arm, and she could barely walk. But when she waved that one arm it was the most eloquent arm wave I've ever seen, because it meant so many things, even what she wanted them to do with their legs. She could look at the picture onstage and have someone make one small movement — sit on a fence, or kneel, or anything, and it would bring it all alive."[8]

The show toured for a year before reaching New York. When it played Los Angeles, Martin Bernheimer wrote, "Some of us may even have forgotten how stylish and poignant de Mille's choreography actually is . . . [her] tippytoe Americana, injected with a little Freudian imagery and a lot of modern-dance introspection, may not be the profound theatrical device we used to think it was . . . but it is so beautifully created, so naturally fused in tone and mood and point, that it remains a thing of wonder."[9]

Oklahoma! had not been seen in New York since 1963, and its opening at the Palace was an event. After the curtain calls, the dancers introduced their counterparts from the original company who were in the audience and brought them to the stage. Then Agnes's name was announced. She walked with her cane from her aisle seat to the front of the house, but could not negotiate the ramp that led to the stage. David Evans, the lead dancer in the show, leaned toward her over the footlights and whispered "Trust me," and she put her arms around his neck. He picked her up as though she were a statue, lifting her onto the stage as the audience stood and screamed their delight. *The New Yorker*'s reviewer declared that the joyful songs and the vitality of the dancing "makes all the other musicals on Broadway sound jaded and strained."[10]

The 1980s would be a decade of accolades, beginning on December 5, 1980, with the nation's highest award for artists: the Kennedy Center Career Achievement Award. "She introduced gutsy American laughter into prim and proper classical ballet," said presenter Kitty Carlisle Hart. Jerome Robbins said, "She changed the history of dance in the United States," and Natalia Makarova read a congratulatory wire from Lucia Chase. Antony Tudor even delivered an uncharacteristically warm reminiscence of Agnes and belatedly credited her with his having joined Ballet Theatre. Flanked by Walter and Jonathan and the other distinguished honorees — Leontyne Price, Leonard Bernstein, Lynn Fontanne, and James Cagney — Agnes beamed while excerpts from her dances were performed.

In 1983, "A Memorable Evening of Dance honoring Agnes de Mille" featured selections from *Carousel* and *Brigadoon* (danced by Lee Theodore's American Dance Machine) as well as works by Gower Champion, Katherine Dunham, Tommy Tune, Patricia Birch, Donald Saddler, and Jack Cole, and there were elegiac tributes by Jerome Robbins, Natalia Makarova, James Mitchell, Tommy Tune, Lee Theodore, Donna McKechnie, Isaac Stern, and other notables. Director Josh Logan wrote, "What a glow the stage has when you are on it or when your brain and spirit are there in the dances you have made. . . . You are *echt theater*, Agnes! It comes out of your nostrils and sets us all on fire."[11] In 1984 she gave a series of lectures on the West Coast, where she was feted as befit the icon she had become. In 1986 she was awarded the National Medal of the Arts, along with Marian Anderson and Lewis Mumford, at the White House (at the luncheon that followed, she told President Reagan, "You're a much better actor now than when you were in the movies."). That year she also traveled to Los Angeles for the opening of an exhaustive exhibit entitled The De Mille Dynasty, a somewhat smaller version of which had been on display at Lincoln Center. A 1987 public television documentary — "Agnes: The Indomitable de Mille" — presented a factual, if one-sided view (Agnes's) of its subject, and won an Emmy.

Jonathan had married Rosemary Eberiel, a fellow graduate student at Harvard, and moved to Atlanta, where he taught history at Emory University. Their sons, David and Michael, were born in 1982 and 1987. Agnes was fond of her daughter-in-law, who taught French literature, and although geography prevented her from seeing much of her grandsons, whose presence she found "clamorous" (not surprising, considering her age and physical limitations), she often sent them presents and was inordinately proud of them.

Agnes and Walter maintained a scaled-down version of the lifestyle they had adopted in the forties — she with her Victorian manners and values, he with his ascots and tennis and cigarette holder and cocktails before dinner, asking, "How are you, Old Boy?" Their dinner parties were still glittering occasions, with old friends comprising the core of the guest list: James Mitchell, Stanley Simmons, Harold Taylor, Gemze de Lappe, Mary Green, Ed Dietz, Morton Gould, Robert Whitehead and his wife, Zoe Caldwell. "It was a sort of gemütlich gang," Mary Rodgers recalled, "always fun."[12] Agnes recruited young dancers to assist the cook and to serve. Robert Whitehead said, "It was like a salon. Agnes would be in a wonderful dress before the fireplace, it didn't matter how hot it was. And the beautiful table and beautiful, graceful ballet girls serving you. That was Agnes's lifeline, to create an evening."[13]

Walter had suffered from sinus problems (for which he took snuff) throughout his life (it invariably became acute sinusitis just in time for the annual Christmas Eve party), but his health had generally been good. By 1982, however, his cervical arthritis had worsened, despite traction and surgery, and he was in pain most of the time. He could no longer work or play tennis, or even raise his left arm. He spent his time reading mysteries, watching sports on television, and chain-smoking unfiltered Chesterfields, even after doctors diagnosed emphysema. His friend Ed Dietz tried to persuade him to stop smoking. "I lost," Dietz said, "and he lost. He was as strong and as willful as Agnes, and he was on a course to self-destruct."[14]

When they went to Merriewold, Walter insisted on driving their loaded-up station wagon, even though he wore an orthopedic collar that made it impossible to turn his head. Agnes and other passengers found the ride hair-raising, but she did not object. Then he could no longer drive at all, and Anderson Ferrell, a young dancer-turned-writer who had appeared in the 1979 *Oklahoma!,* took over the chore. Agnes had taken a liking to the engaging North Carolinian and had offered to let him live at Merriewold while he wrote his first novel. In exchange, he cooked for the Prudes when they were in residence. Ferrell recalled a morning at Merriewold when he and Walter came in from the garden and found Agnes sitting calmly on the floor in her bedroom. Around her was a clean circle on the rug; beside her was a pile of paper clips, pencils, and detritus. "I fell and couldn't make you hear me," she said, "so I decided to clean the rug."

"Walter preferred staying home and watching football on television to all the bother of going up to Merriewold," Ferrell said, "and Agnes would often stay in New York with him when she would rather have been in the country. On occasion Walter would go, groaning all the way. When he got there he would sit down on the lounge and stay there, half sitting, half lying, smoking. He and Agnes would argue about anything — his smoking, the news, the menu. He'd complain about the heat, his difficulty breathing, his cough, the pain. 'Oh mercy, mercy' — he must have said that a million times. But at Merriewold I sat on the porch steps and heard them talking upstairs, in the bedroom. He was Prudie or Puddy, she was Punk or Punkin. They were in love." One day Agnes got out of her wheelchair and sat on the ground in the garden, weeding, in the sun. She was wearing a straw hat, at a jaunty angle. Walter, watching with Ferrell from a distance, murmured, "There's my girl."[15]

When Walter could no longer walk the three blocks to sit on a bench in Washington Square Park, he took the sun sitting on the brass water hydrant outside the front door of their apartment building. Eventually, he hated to leave the apartment. Agnes, who had been grateful that she at least had no pain, now developed arthritis, and her right foot became so sensitive that she could hardly walk. Nevertheless, according to Anderson Ferrell, "Agnes did the bending. Walter found the phone irritating so she made restrictions about hours when people could call. She did her best to entertain him." She read poetry to him, which he had always enjoyed. She gave small dinner parties; he was still witty and debonair, the orthopedic collar notwithstanding. Then his shoulder would hunch as though in a spasm, and when he saw that it was noticed, he would suddenly excuse himself and disappear into the bedroom. He had morbid depressions. "Walter doesn't like me to leave the house," Agnes told a friend. "He doesn't like me to have people in. He doesn't like me to see people. Well, it just won't do. And, of course, I get stir crazy. I don't get out for days on end. . . . Last Wednesday night he stumbled over the rocking chair in the dark, fell and broke two ribs. . . . Oh, my God, what a life!"[16] But at Agnes's eightieth birthday party, Walter stunned his wife and their guests by raising his glass and declaring, "Amo Agnes, ergo sum."

In 1985, Agnes started work on a ballet called *The Informer,* an adaptation of the dances from the ill-fated *Juno,* but with a scenario based on John Ford's film and Liam O'Flaherty's novel. *The Informer* is a statement on a controversial political situation — a rarity in a ballet. Set during the "troubles" that had accompanied England's occupation of Northern Ireland in 1916 and were still very much in the news, it focuses not on who is right or wrong, but on the human cost. The central characters, all Irish nationalists, make up a romantic triangle: the Girl, the Young Fighter, and the Wounded Veteran, who betrays his rival to the British and is murdered in retribution.

Agnes asked composer John Morris, who had worked with her on *Kwamina,* to make sense of a jumble of pages of Celtic music, various bits of it arranged by Marc Blitzstein, Martha Johnson, and Trude Rittman. "You wouldn't believe the mess!" Morris said. "But there's a quality to her will that makes everything go down before it, and you know you can't fail her! She just takes for granted that you'll do it and it'll be wonderful. Like a general who expects his soldiers to be brave — to go over that hill and die if necessary!"[17] Morris finally managed to assemble the music; he wrote, rewrote, and patched, then had it reorchestrated to give it unity.

About three times a week, Agnes conducted workshop sessions at a rehearsal studio with eight dancers. She had always had to struggle to devise new choreography, and the best of it had come to her instinctively when she moved to music. Now she was forced to rely almost entirely on what she knew from experience would work. She began with the old film of the *Juno* dances. She hired an expert to teach Irish step dancing, a foreign language to the dancers. "In rehearsals she could be cruel to some of the girls," Dirk Lombard, her assistant, observed. "She'd say 'What are you doing? Haven't you ever had sex? Haven't you ever been with a man? You look like a clothespin!' Or, 'You're moving like an elephant!' Tact was something she didn't have time for. And people would take it, because it was Agnes de Mille. When she got mad at them she'd say indignantly, 'I'm paying them good money!' She paid ten dollars an hour — she thought it was great money but it wasn't, people only did it so they could work with her. They would've done it for free."[18]

The work proceeded intermittently for eighteen months, with no company committed to performing it. ABT had not presented a new de Mille ballet since 1966; but in 1979, its board had forced Lucia Chase into retirement and named Mikhail Baryshnikov as artistic director. He had admired Agnes's work since first seeing ABT perform it in Leningrad, and had loved the recent *Oklahoma!* revival. In 1983 he revived *Three Virgins and a Devil* and danced the Devil himself, brilliantly, with some coaching by Agnes. Four years later, she sold him *The Informer*.

The workshop group taught the ballet to ABT's dancers. Ballet master Terry Orr, who had been one of Agnes's favorite Champion Ropers in ABT's *Rodeo*, helped to convey her ideas to the dancers. The ballet was still malleable; "Agnes was very young in mind," Orr said, "very open to discussion. She'd ask me, 'Does it work?' If not, she'd want to know why not. Sometimes she woke up in the middle of the night with a fresh idea. Sometimes it took her three days to think of something new."[19] Orr understood her need for dramatic dancers and brought two natural actors in the company to her attention: Kathleen Moore, young and reed-like with waist-length red hair (Agnes had always been partial to red-heads), and Victor Barbee, dark and intense. According to Barbee, who played the Wounded Veteran, Agnes originally saw the Girl as the central character and his character as "just somebody for the Girl to dance with. I was looking for the key to the character and I kept saying, 'Why am I doing that?' She said, 'You think too much. Just do it.' But she kept adding more and more to the character, making it pivotal. This is when I found she was someone you could work with, as opposed to just work for. When Agnes started to trust that I was there to make that ballet as good as possible, even if I did something on my own, she'd consider it. As long as it works, she doesn't care how you get the effect. If it should be funny, it had better be funny — but if she trusts your instincts, she is rather open to the way you find that."[20]

In *The Informer* the corps de ballet, as the citizens of Dublin, move in dynamic, deceptively simple patterns and designs. Agnes created suspense by keeping the British soldiers offstage, indicating their menace by means of the dancers' gestures of fear and defiance, accompanied by military drums, church bells, and other orchestral sounds. But when she asked for dramatic gestures that she was unable to demonstrate, the dancers responded with the balletic ones they had been taught. "Do you think," she would ask hoarsely, "do you think you could simply dance? I cannot wake up the human being inside each one of you! Well, I will. You look like hard-boiled eggs. You can put your dancer faces back on when you do *Swan Lake*." They were teenagers who could easily have been her great-grandchildren; they had studied technique, but not acting. They had learned beauty; she wanted truth. To them she was an intimidating legend in a wheelchair, a tiny anachronism with a hawklike profile and wispy white hair usually topped by a hat that matched the season. Her face was remarkably smooth, and still flushed easily in anger; she held her chin defiantly high. When spoken to, she listened with tight lips and a poker face, without the signals of encouragement that accompany ordinary discourse. Then she might roll her blue eyes upward (exasperation), cover her mouth with a hand (mock shock), laugh explosively, or heave an enormous sigh. She was absolutely centered; her gaze, direct as a laser, seemed to penetrate the brain of anyone whose word she doubted. Although the dancers tried hard to please her, it was an excruciating exercise in frustration for all concerned. But those who persevered found the theatricality of her work a revelation, and discovered ways of expressing emotions beyond what the most dazzling pirouettes and fouettés could convey.

After six weeks of rehearsal the company left on tour, with Agnes planning to join them in Los Angeles, where *The Informer* was to premiere on March 15, 1988. But her health, and Walter's, prevented her going, and she did not see her ballet until two months later, in New York. *Ballet Review*'s critic noted, "At a time when few choreographers can put together a convincing narrative, move masses around the stage effectively, or come up with an imaginative pas de deux, she demonstrates how much skill in a dance work counts for."[21]

Although Agnes had remained remarkably active considering her disabilities, she nevertheless spent most of her time propped up on her bed, in a nightgown and bed jacket and bare feet (stockings were painful on her arthritic, now grotesquely twisted, toes). Her books and papers and telephone were close at hand and so, with increasing frequency, was Walter, propped up on the adjacent bed. Wearing his neck brace, pajama coat, gray flannel trousers, and slippers — and smoking, always smoking; he charmed the elevator attendant into bringing him cigarettes — he read mysteries and watched television. "We just lie here all the time like two old turtles," Agnes said. "We crawl toward each other like two handicapped crabs, to kiss each other good night." Needing less than a nurse but more than a housekeeper, they settled for the latter: Ivy Nevis, a Jamaican woman who adored Walter and tolerated Agnes. After Walter's death, Agnes discovered that he had kept a loaded pistol in his nightstand with which to protect them.

"Walter was dying by inches on one side of the bed," a friend said, "while Agnes was living by inches on the other."[22] When visitors came for tea, neither of their hosts could lift the pot to pour. But they were still entertaining, interested, and interesting. "Welcome to the golden years," Walter would say, gasping for breath. When his pain was severe he became silent and turned up the volume on the television. At five o'clock Agnes would put aside whatever she was doing and hobble to the rocking chair at the foot of his bed for drinks and hors d'oeuvres, and they would watch the news together.

"Nothing more now could happen to me," Agnes had written in *Reprieve,* "except extinction."[23] But now she lay awake at night listening to Walter cough and waiting for his next breath. In the summer of 1988 — Walter's seventy-ninth year — the eventuality that she refused to contemplate came to pass. On August 21, Walter was admitted to St. Vincent's Hospital, where, eight days later, he died.

He was eulogized at a public memorial, at the 92nd Street YMHA auditorium, as an honorable man with extraordinary elegance, integrity, wit, and dedication to quality. Harold Taylor spoke of how, after Agnes's stroke, "Walter's attentiveness and concern took on the character of a whole new marriage vow." Kate Medina characterized the Prudes as "such bulwarks of civilization as sometimes seemed almost single-handedly to hold up the standard of the English language, if not of the poor old western civilization itself." Robert Whitehead said, "He was always aware of our purposes and that sense of failure that haunts all of us and he saw what was ridiculous in it. He laughed at himself and he could make us laugh at ourselves." At Agnes's request, Zoe Caldwell read some of Walter's early poetry. Then Jonathan spoke of his fondest memories of his father: hearing him read nineteenth-century English novels aloud in the garden at Merriewold, and sharing "long precious twilights on the porch, the three of us sitting and talking and watching the sun pass its yellow, fading light down through the forest. Sometimes there was croquet in these quiet hours. And for a number of years there was a small troop of chipmunks which my father painstakingly seduced, first to come to his chair, then to eat peanuts, then finally, his great triumph, to sip martinis." Jonathan, an honorable man like his father, spoke the truth; as befits a eulogy, it was not the whole truth, but it was sincere.

Finally, Isaac Stern spoke of his manager's empathetic dedication to him, Arthur Rubinstein, Andrés Segovia, Marian Anderson, and other clients and then played, with pianist Emanuel Ax, a portion of Beethoven's "Spring" sonata.

A private ceremony took place at Merriewold. On a rainy September afternoon, Agnes, Jonathan, Oliver Smith, Harold Taylor, Mary Green, Ed Dietz, Anderson Ferrell, and a few Merriewold neighbors watched as a box containing Walter's ashes was placed in the ground on which the five-year-old Agnes had danced, under the oak tree that shades the house. A few people spoke about Walter. Then Agnes said, "I want to stand up," and she was helped to do so. In a shaky but ringing voice in the quiet woods, with Andy Ferrell holding an umbrella above her head, she said, "Walter darling, we've been married for forty-five years, and in all that time I was never bored."

"We all threw some dirt on the box," Ferrell said, "and then we went in and had drinks by the fire."[24]

f o r t y - f i v e

Decrescendo

Agnes's mind and spirit remained robust, but from the neck down, she was a wreck. After eight years of increasingly painful daily exercise with no discernible improvement, she had given it up ("I know it's lazy and I know it's cowardly, but I don't give a damn"), and her legs had become, she said, like celery.[1] She could totter precariously to the bathroom and get herself into and out of a car and even, refusing help and with an effort that was painful to watch, up the stairs to her bedroom at Merriewold; but she was essentially helpless. Ivy, the housekeeper, now slept in the maid's room during the week, and a substitute usually stayed with her on weekends; but on nights when no substitute was available, she was alone.

She worked, read, received visitors, watched television, and took her meals on her bed, often wearing the big, boxy shirts Walter had bought himself in the Philippines, and surrounded by what looked to the uninitiated eye like chaos. She had always had a kind of manic order that she now tried in vain to maintain. Every book, every piece of clothing and jewelry and paper had its proper place, but she had to rely on others, who tried but often failed to find and replace things where they belonged. Papers were the most difficult to keep track of. Her working files were plastic bags filled with papers, stuffed into bureau drawers.

Her history permeated the apartment — books, paintings, memorabilia, all the furnishings of a long life in the arts. A Piranesi print that had belonged to her parents hung above her bed; photos of Walter and Jonathan and his children were nearby. In the sitting room hung two portraits by the designer Elizabeth Montgomery: one of Agnes, looking young and flirtatious; the other of Martha Graham, looking enigmatic. On the piano was a framed photograph of Agnes in 1942, inscribed to Walter Prude. The upholstery was worn, the paint peeling from the walls; Agnes seemed not to notice. Only after chips of paint from the ceiling appeared in her food did she have the place painted.

She had once written, "I cling to my old loves with an absolutely vampire-like attachment."[2] Most of those old loves were now beyond reach. Of her professional colleagues, she had or soon would outlive Louis Horst, Antony Tudor, Hugh Laing, Marie Rambert, Joe Anthony, Aaron Copland, Oscar Hammerstein, Richard Rodgers, Rouben Mamoulian, Nora Kaye, Lucia Chase, George Balanchine, Charlie Baker, Elia Kazan, Alan Lerner, Frederick Loewe, Hanya Holm, Daniel Mann, John Butler, Edward Weeks, Joseph Welch, Honi Coles, Marc Blitzstein, José Ferrer, Ray Bolger, and an inexorably lengthening list of others. Friends, too, were going or gone: Michael Hertz, Catherine Drinker Bowen, Rebecca West, Carmelita Maracci, Harold Taylor, Mary Green, Ed Dietz. She coped, as she had always done, with wit. "Friends die," she said, "but so, thank God, do enemies." When a group of her remaining friends — choreographer Glen Tetley, singer Rufus Smith, designer Stanley Simmons, and dancers Evelyn Taylor, Scott Douglas, and Cassandra Phifer — gathered to drink, eat, and dish at her apartment one evening, the conversation turned to trashing a recently deceased choreographer. "Darlings," Agnes said, "when I die, you mustn't talk about me like this . . . for one week."

That Agnes was still able to accomplish more than most able-bodied people in their prime was possible only because she rationed her energy to make every calorie count. Mornings were for work: writing, rehearsing, correspondence, or other business. After lunch, she napped. Visitors were not so much invited as commanded to come for lunch, tea, cocktails, or dinner, and to bring a supply of current gossip. When they did, there could be much hilarity. But when in her victim mode, Agnes tended a poisonous garden of grudges, some of which reached back eighty years. Discussing her childhood for the "Agnes: The Indomitable de Mille" television documentary, she complained bitterly that "although every director in Hollywood had pictures of his children playing ball with the dogs or jumping in the swimming pool . . . not a foot was ever shot of Aggie de Mille dancing around doing her stuff."[3] James Mitchell, Mary Rodgers, and other old friends sometimes wearied of hearing her tales of persecution and moved quietly out of her life. But in months, or even years, they realized that the best of her more than made up for the worst, and returned to the fold.

Dusk was a miserable time; she watched the news on television, alone. She said little about the nights; but in *Reprieve,* writing of her sister's courage in her last years, she had imagined long nights "endured alone, with all their attendant dismays and regrets and bewilderments and emptiness. . . . Nobody to talk to, nobody's hand to touch."[4] When sleep eluded her, she read: biographies, mysteries, some new fiction, some classics. She reread most of Trollope, whose Victorian values and humor and iconoclasm matched her own. The stroke had affected her sense of smell and for that reason, as well as her immobility, she feared fire, and instructed Ivy, the housekeeper, never to lock the front door.

At a time when loneliness, grief, physical discomfort, and the unwanted intimacies imposed by disability were legitimate cause for complaint, Agony de Mille was silent. But Agnes was quite capable of banging her fist on a table and shouting "You must obey me!" when confronted with domestic ineptitude. Her relationship with her housekeeper was an ongoing tragicomedy of errors. Ivy was functionally illiterate, unable to read a shopping list or write down a telephone message. Frequently reminded that her best was not good enough, she grumbled, protested, and sought refuge in audible conversations with Jesus. Agnes claimed she could find no one better — at least, not for what she was willing to pay. Her financial frame of reference was decades out of date; the cost of living seemed to her hideously expensive, and she feared outliving her resources.

Work was the answer.

Agnes had completed her biography of Martha Graham in 1987, putting herself and her publisher in the ghoulish position of having to delay publication, according to their original agreement, until Graham died. She had had little contact with Martha since 1974, when she had made the mistake of assuming that if she credited Martha with having changed the history of dancing with her movement, she would not need permission to demonstrate her exercises in "Conversations About the Dance." When Graham found out, after the fact, she was furious. "To me it was like any great seminal discovery," Agnes said. "I think what angered Martha was that I had taken for granted that I could use them." They argued bitterly on the phone for two hours until "it got so ugly," Agnes said, "that I was ashamed for us both."[5] She ultimately had to delete the exercises, and they do not appear in the PBS film. After Agnes's stroke, Martha wrote, "You are having one hell-of-a-time . . . I know you will hold fast to your 'goddess-energy.'"[6] But when Agnes tried to pry information out of Graham for the biography, disingenuously claiming that she was writing about the early lives of women artists, Martha tersely informed her that she was writing her own book.

In 1986, Agnes delivered her support-for-the-arts speech in a lecture series at the Graham school. Mary Green recalled that afterward Agnes and Martha sat alone in a corner, "nose-to-nose, whispering to each other. Agnes was all in white, with frills at her wrist and neck. She was all askew, with her white hair frizzy around the edges and her face was flushed. And there was 'Madame Halston,' severe and sleek and groomed and brushed, in a skintight black dress, with her black gloves and her lacquered dyed hair — like an elegant raven with that profile, that makeup and that white skin. They were enchanting polarities in black-and-white."[7] According to Agnes, Graham spoke only of herself, except to ask after Walter's health. She promised to visit him, but never did. After his death, Agnes asked Martha to speak at his memorial service. Martha declined, and that was their final conversation.

While the *Martha* manuscript awaited its subject's demise, Agnes worked on three other books. One was to be the basis of a television series about the historical, cultural, psychological, and sociological meaning of costume and clothing. Her passion for costumes was possibly prenatal — the dresses her mother made for her, with painstaking perfection, are in the Museum of the City of New York — and she had always paid meticulous attention to the details of costumes and their specific cultural meanings. The project was dear to her heart — but when it was well under way, Jonathan informed her that he was writing a book on a similar subject. What would be a stretch for most history professors was not so surprising for Jonathan, considering his background, and he asked his mother to wait until he had published his book. She agreed, packed up what she had done, and stored it in the basement. If her success had somehow kept Walter from achieving his creative potential — an unprovable thesis, but one that had caused her some guilt — she would do nothing that might be considered to be in competition with her beloved son. Years later she observed of Jonathan's book, still in progress, "I didn't know it would be a lifetime work!"[8]

Walter's Book, privately printed, is a heartfelt, if hagiographic, testimonial to Agnes's husband and to her marriage. In a process both therapeutic and excruciatingly painful, she selected some of Walter's early poems and journal entries, photographs, excerpts from their wartime correspondence, and eulogies. She distributed copies of the handsome volume, boxed with an audiocassette of Walter's memorial service, to their friends.

Portrait Gallery, published in 1990, is a collection of sketches, some new and some exhumed. Agnes recycled her prose as thriftily as she did her choreography, and she had saved everything Edward Weeks had deleted from *Dance to the Piper* for fear of libel, "pending the day when all these lovely people are dead."[9] That day had arrived, and she rewrote and added to the old manuscript pages. Now she could state with impunity that Lee Shubert "would rather have lost a leg than a bargain — and he was rather more likely to," and that Sol Hurok confused "his primal instincts, greed and vanity, with discernment."[10] A chapter about Cecil and William and their families illustrates how Agnes, who was herself a mosaic of contradictions, could accept contradictions in others. She acknowledged Cecil's greatness — a matter of personal pride as well as historical fact — but for the first time she was publicly candid about his mistresses, his attitude toward sex ("an aging juvenile, glued to adolescent eroticism"), and his secret adoption of his brother's illegitimate son.[11] *Portrait Gallery* also contains new chapters about an assortment of people, famous and not, who interested Agnes: a despotic French cook she had employed, her spinster cousin Allie, Isadora Duncan, Alicia Markova, Carmelita Maracci, Katherine Dunham, Billy Rose. In all there are thirteen subjects, and a chapter on her childhood in New York City that recalls the pleasures of a privileged life when she and the century were young. "My greatest gift," she claimed, "is my memory."[12] If its accuracy was subject to her prejudices and her admitted habit of taking dramatic license, it was nevertheless a phenomenal memory, crammed with trenchant observations not only of people but of social and cultural history as well.

Martha Graham's death in the spring of 1991 (at the age of ninety-six) prompted a flood of tributes, none more moving than Agnes's in the *New York Times.* "So, she has gone," it began. "The lone figure, the standard bearer, the adventurer who dared the unexperienced. All our lives she has been there, out front, ahead." The eulogy ran a full page, and ended, "Uncompromising, unblemished, her theater stands as a generic force in the culture of our time."[13] Agnes's *Martha* was published in the fall.

Martha shows no trace of its author's age or infirmity; it has the same vitality and immediacy as *Dance to the Piper.* At 475 pages, it is Agnes's biggest and most ambitious book — and certainly the most extraordinary, if only for the circumstances in which she produced it. She dredged the memories of some two dozen people, taping the interviews and then having them transcribed. Mary Green and a secretary did the legwork, collecting necessary research material, but the heart of the book is Agnes's own knowledge and recollections. As an informed observer of Graham's art for sixty-three years, she was uniquely qualified to explain the forces that shaped it as well as its nature, evolution, and significance, all in the broadest possible context — e.g., "[T]he theater of Elizabethan times was a theater of words, and the theater of the eighteenth and nineteenth centuries was a theater of music and sound. The twentieth century is a theater of sight and visual image."[14] She could also assess with some authority the price that Graham the artist exacted from Graham the woman.

Agnes knew she had not written the definitive biography; that, she said, would have to await access to Graham's files, if they had not been destroyed. *Martha* contains some dissenting opinions, but it is largely, in fact doubly, subjective — Agnes on Agnes as well as Agnes on Martha — and as opulent, stimulating, gossipy, and full of inconsistencies as the two women themselves. Ever since her early introduction to Ruth St. Denis, Agnes had been fascinated by the relationship between the work and the men in the lives of great women artists. Her astute, sometimes controversial psychological insights about Graham's masochistic love relationships and her lack of a child prompted one reviewer to protest, "[S]he cannot see beyond her own conventional concept of what constitutes a good life (for a woman), so we must endure her dogged insistence that Graham was somehow 'deprived' by her 'sacrificing' the roles of wife and mother to that of artist."[15]

Agnes considered Martha a genius, but she often found the woman exasperating; and although she regarded her own work as frivolous and derivative compared to Martha's, it hurt her that Graham (who on at least one occasion privately referred to her as "the Barnum and Bailey of the dance world") agreed.[16] When Agnes's ballets premiered, Martha sent flowers and effusive notes, but rarely congratulated her afterward. Asked to comment on Agnes for this book, Graham called her a dear friend and a "demonically dedicated artist."[17] She commended her contribution to the musical theater and her early Degas studies, and conspicuously omitted any mention of her ballets.

Kate Medina had moved from Doubleday to Random House, and Agnes had followed her there. Medina was a patient and sensitive editor; her suggestions helped shape the chronology and narrative of the book and curbed Agnes's penchant for sarcasm, her bias against certain characters (notably Ted Shawn), her references to what readers might not understand, and anecdotes that were unrelated to the story. Agnes occasionally lapsed into biblical phrases and rhythms ("Martha rose from the dead, and verily she was changed now") and melodramatic hyperbole ("Martha's paranoia was growing. . . . She came to rely on the lethal energy of this working compost, this false, frantic excitement engendered by troubles. . . . Her life wisdom, the quietness of her soul, the loftiness of her ideas were put aside too often as she drank this fateful brew. She presided over it; in many ways she concocted it, like a witch's broth, and inhaled the hideous aroma. During this period, she often supped with Hecate").[18] But the book is a feast, rich with vivid, original descriptions of people, places, and dances. Some statements are startling, many are very funny. Of Ruth St. Denis, Agnes opined, "Taking . . . is the art of the really frigid woman."[19] Shawn's vanity "was like an exposed organ."[20] In Graham's 1984 *Rite of Spring,* with costumes by Halston, "the sacrificial victim appeared to die, not from cosmic necessity nor archetypal doom, but from a surfeit of yardage."[21] When Graham posed for a Blackglama mink ad with Nureyev and Margot Fonteyn and became, in her nineties, a fixture of the disco scene, "Martha was called 'tacky,'" Agnes wrote, "but given the fame of the people involved, surely it could be considered '*haute* tacky.'"[22]

Agnes's biography and Martha's autobiography, *Blood Memory,* were published almost simultaneously. Some reviewers faulted Agnes for her lack of objectivity, but most pronounced hers the better-written and more informative of the two books. *The New Yorker*'s Arlene Croce called it "a triumphantly unruly and truthful book, because, for all de Mille's settled opinions on what Graham stands for, her information and her insight keep flowing."[23] *Newsday*'s Elizabeth Kendall wrote, "This is more than a biography. It's the gallant bow of the Apollonian artist — the steady, unfiery yet at times inspired craftsman that de Mille has been as choreographer and writer — to the searing flame of the Dionysian one . . . In terms of quid pro quo, of a friendship based on equivalent give and take, Martha Graham didn't deserve such a book. But she got it."[24]

Agnes's disability limited but did not prevent her from going out to dinner or to a movie, or to grand events at which she spoke or was honored (Anderson Ferrell was a favorite escort). Neither illness nor age had dulled the edge of her abrasiveness. She could be wicked, announcing, as a friend wheeled her into a pleasant Italian restaurant, "This is where the Mafia launders their money" (the friend immediately turned and wheeled her out).[25] She could be brutal, telling the dancers who performed *Rodeo* as part of a tribute to her by the Cleveland Ballet that they were terrible. But she could also recognize her mistake and do her best to repair the damage, in that instance delaying her return to New York in order to apologize to the dancers, who she realized had only followed another choreographer's directions. She could even be diplomatic, as with a leading ballerina who wanted to dance the Cowgirl but lacked the comedic skill ("With your looks and your glamour," she said, "you would never work on this ranch, you'd own it inside of a week").

She was politically liberal, morally conservative, an altruistic egocentric. She was a patrician snob with a genetic sense of entitlement; and she was a populist, a small *d* democrat. She was honest and fair — except when she wasn't. On the subject of homosexuals, a category that included many of her dearest friends, she could be derisive and insulting. And not until 1991, when the Rodgers and Hammerstein Organization agreed to pay her a royalty for future productions of *Oklahoma!* and *Carousel* (with the understanding that she would, in exchange, help them to document her dances in the form of an instructional video), did she dismount from her Rodgers-and-Hammerstein-cheated-me hobbyhorse.

But the people she trusted also knew a softer Agnes — kind, empathetic, deeply appreciative of beauty, of anything "fine." Anderson Ferrell knew her as "a core of mush surrounded by steel."[26] When she saw that Ferrell shared her love of Merriewold, she deeded some of her acreage over to him. She continued to spend summer weekends there, when she was able to recruit people to drive, to cook, to dress her. Relatively recent young friends or sometimes employees whose company she enjoyed — Cassandra Phifer and her husband, stage manager Paul Moore, and dancers Denise Cogan and Diana Gonzalez — performed those tasks with singular sensitivity. Agnes loved to sit on the porch or in the garden, oblivious to the flies and mosquitoes and mildew and dirt. Jonathan came for a fortnight with his wife and children, giving Agnes the pleasure of seeing a fifth generation of her family in her beloved woods (the boys called her Owie, the name she had given herself as a child). Once or twice a year she made the trip to Atlanta to visit Jonathan and his family, but she asked few questions, made no demands, and did her best to spare him the sense of obligation that her mother had imposed.

Agnes knew that it was not always easy to be her friend ("I tend to use all those close to me as I use myself, relentlessly," she once wrote), but it could be infinitely rewarding.[27] Many people felt they were at their best in her presence — smarter, wittier, on the qui vive. She was unfailingly entertaining, sometimes at her own expense. She had always been able to make a three-syllable word sound like a four-letter word; and when she loosened the corset of her grande dame persona, the four-letter words that she did use had an incongruously dignified tone that enhanced their potency.

She expected total loyalty, and she returned it. "Agnes will be with you in the death camps," composer William Goldenberg said. "Agnes will pull you out of the ovens."[28] When a friend was in trouble, she opened her heart and, if necessary, her checkbook. Her epistolary arrogance could rival that of the Romanovs, but she also wrote some extraordinarily loving letters — as when she learned that Lisa Hewitt Harland, who had been so supportive during the difficult London years, was dying of cancer. Without mentioning Harland's illness, Agnes reached back forty years to recall "your thoughtfulness in providing a corner of the stove, a sofa, a cup of something hot, a cool hand, a laugh. . . . [You] made me believe that possibly circumstances would change and I would amount to something. . . . [H]ow I wish I could sit by you and talk a little! . . . How you have comforted and sustained me and lifted my spirits! . . . My whole time [in London] was warmed by you. . . . My arms are around you."[29]

Agnes loved fine things, and giving them had always been her sometimes extravagant pleasure. She had once told Therese Langfield Horner, "One of the good things about my having had some recognition is that I can do something for the people I think ought to have more and correct some of the matters fate fails to take care of."[30] At Christmas, close to a hundred friends, relatives, employees, and the children of friends received thoughtful presents ordered from catalogs, the shopping mall of the invalid: fancy shoe buckles for a dancer's tiny feet, an exquisite Renaissance vase for a designer, a wildly expensive perfume for a young actress's opening night, monogrammed silver cuff links for a rehearsal pianist, special bulbs for ballet master Terry Orr's garden, an imitation pewter plate for lighting designer Tom Skelton ("It isn't pewter, but it's beautiful, and you can put it in the oven!").[31] But in *Martha,* she wrote that Martha Graham "found it easier to be the generous one, which is in reality inverse selfishness and a form of pride."[32] She had discovered that it can be as worthy to receive as to give.

forty-six

The Other

In 1976, Agnes had written to Rebecca West that she was choreographing a new ballet, "which I thought was pretty good going because I couldn't demonstrate a single gesture." She added, "I suppose, Rebecca, from now on we can expect, just like landmark buildings, to keep dropping bricks and window sills and cornices and ornaments into the street and have people carefully pick them up and patch them back . . . the alternative I'm not quite ready to accept yet."[1]

The "new" ballet, *Summer,* was based largely on dances from the disastrous *Come Summer,* and Agnes had initially devised it in 1972. Set to "Der Tod und das Mädchen" (Death and the Maiden)* and other Schubert songs that she had loved since her childhood, its allegorical theme is based on an old German folktale about a young woman who is drawn to a mysterious stranger on her wedding day. *Summer* was first performed by the Boston Ballet a few months before Agnes's stroke, and in a revised form in 1977. Neither attempt, Agnes felt, was good enough. It was next performed as *A Bridegroom Called Death* by the Joffrey Ballet, and then in

* Andrée Howard had used the same music for her *Death and the Maiden* for Ballet Rambert in 1937 (restaged by Ballet Theatre in 1940).

1981, by the Richmond Ballet, as *Inconsequentials*. For that version, Agnes deleted the more serious sections and added some ballet burlesque that she had done with Warren Leonard. She tried repeatedly to sell it to ABT, but Lucia Chase and, later, Baryshnikov declined to put it on.

In 1989, Baryshnikov left ABT. Jane Hermann and Oliver Smith, the new codirectors, decided that the upcoming fiftieth anniversary season should include three de Mille ballets: *The Informer, Rodeo,* and a revival of *Fall River Legend,* which had been in mothballs since 1980.

Agnes approved the casting of all principal roles: Cynthia Gregory, a strong dramatic ballerina, was to dance Lizzie Borden for the first time, and Kathleen Moore, whom Agnes had liked in *The Informer,* would also dance the Cowgirl. Ballet master Terry Orr conducted rehearsals, consulting frequently with Agnes, who came in when the movements were set. She attended rehearsals over a two-month period at ABT's downtown rehearsal studio — a half hour from Agnes's apartment, by wheelchair. In all but the harshest winter weather, someone — usually Diana Gonzalez, her assistant — pushed her up Broadway to 18th Street. Negotiating the traffic around Union Square could be daunting, but Agnes sat bolt upright in her Queen Victoria persona — glaring, and holding her good arm straight out like a policeman. That the traffic ignored her did not deter her from trying.

She was now more familiar with the young ABT dancers, and they knew her better. Watching Kathy Moore perform the movements she had created half a century ago, Agnes murmured, "Nineteen-forty-two. Hollywood, California. The Russians said, 'This isn't dancing.' I said, 'I never said it was. Just do it.'" Her remarks to the dancers clarified the nonballetic movements that mystified many of them. "You ballet dancers spend your whole lives not doing anything naturally,' she told them. "I'm asking you to just be ordinary people." She established the motivation behind seemingly trivial movements — the Bordens fanning themselves with their hands, for example, because of the killing heat. (She could not resist describing the Borden's disgusting breakfast of spoiled meat. "Mr. Borden went out in the back yard and threw up. In the grass. Where they all walk." After a beat: "I adore that family.") Of the scene in which Lizzie's mother collapses: "Darling, please don't just sit down on your pretty little rump, arrange your skirt and just die. You look like you swallowed too much whipped cream. The pain grabs you like an *animal.* If you make meaningless gestures, it's bad choreography." To the timorous young man portraying the doctor who is summoned for the dying Mrs. Borden: "Don't hold back — you are the *doctor!* You would brush everybody aside! You can't have a doctor hang back. That's an interesting problem, but not what this is about. Go in the house as though you know what you're doing! The woman is dying and you go in there to help her. You are the only person with any command of the situation."

She explained to the young corps de ballet that even when a dancer was in a back corner, doing nothing and feeling invisible, "That 'nothing' that you do is *very* important. Without you, without the looks that you create, this ballet doesn't happen. The minute you let down, that's where the eye goes." At the end of rehearsals, when there was time, the company sat on the floor around her and listened, spellbound, while she told stories about incidents in her life that related to the emotions in the ballet. She also instructed them in the facts. *Fall River Legend,* she said, "is a true story and a naked ballet. There is no fancy dancing in it, but some of the dancing is very hard. The positions of the body, of the head, the way you move as men and women, that's the stuff of this ballet. It begins as ordinary New England life. People who settled in New England had *nothing* — no milk, no butter, no food for their children. They lived in holes in the ground during their first winter in Massachusetts, and winters in Massachusetts are *atrocious*. The people that were able to bear that were *iron* — they were cruel to one another and to their bodies. Softer people could not have done it." She even gave them a brief history lesson about trial procedures in Lizzie Borden's day.

The 1990 revival of *Fall River Legend* was so successful that ABT performed it through the next three seasons, with Cynthia Gregory followed by Martine van Hamel, Alessandra Ferri, Carla Fracci, and Sylvie Guillem as the Accused.

Agnes had continued to rework her Schubert ballet, as she called it, using films of previous versions as a reference. She rearranged the music, reworked the lyrical portions, cut the broad comedy, and strengthened the principal roles. The core of the ballet was unchanged. ABT would finally present it, in 1992, as *The Other*.

"In my beginning is my end," wrote T. S. Eliot.* Agnes's preoccupations had not changed, but her perceptions had deepened. *The Other* is a companion piece to *Where the Wings Grow*, a dreamy remembrance of childhood summers at Merriewold. Both ballet and book celebrate the cycles of life, and both accept the inevitability of loss — but in *The Other*, Agnes's balletic valedictory, Death is an actual character.

The Other incorporates elements familiar throughout Agnes's work: the romantic triangle (the Maiden, the Lover, the Other),† the pastoral setting, the circular patterns. There are playful games in which adolescent boys in Tyrolean lederhosen show off for dirndled girls who sweetly run, skip, and dance, and there are ominous undertones, as in *Allegro*. There is an idealized Child, as in *Fall River Legend*, and a violent fight between the principal men, as in *Oklahoma!* But *The Other* has no macho

* "East Coker," *Four Quartets*.

† Danced by Amanda McKerrow, Victor Barbee, and Roger Van Fleteren.

cowboys or miners or loggers. The Lover is a tender, Byronic soul; Death is stronger, but also capable of tenderness. At one point he even kneels sorrowfully, almost apologetically, before the Maiden; as the Virgin comforted the Devil in *Three Virgins and a Devil,* the Maiden comforts Death.

Agnes envisioned the Death figure as "a bridegroom, the God Baldur, the symbol of resurrection and continuance."[2] He comes not as an enemy, but as a mysterious friend — blond, shining, all in white; in a bravura solo he spins, sweeps around the stage, bends, leaps, swivels, and spreads his arms wide to designate his domain. The Maiden dances with him, frightened but curious; at one point they face each other, arms outstretched to their sides, turning clenched fists up and down, their pulses synchronized. When she weakens, her Lover challenges Death, who conquers but does not kill him; it is the Maiden he wants. Death falls forward heavily three times, hitting the floor flat, with a thud of finality. Rising for the third time, he points meaningfully at the girl and exits. There follows a final, ineffably poignant pas de deux, danced to the rapturous "Du Bist die Ruh" (You Are My Peace). The Lover lifts the girl high, his arms fully extended above his head. As he starts to carry her off, Death reaches up swiftly and takes her away, still poised aloft.

At the technical rehearsal, Agnes, attentive to the myriad of details meant to create the illusion of effortlessness, crackled and snapped like a severed high-tension wire. She loved the ballet, but she saw its flaws. It was uneven; the contrasting moods seemed disjointed, and some of the movement paled against Schubert's sublime music. She disliked the sentimentality of the final image — the Lover alone, under a starry sky — but she was not able to improve upon it.

The Other premiered at the Kennedy Center in Washington, D.C., on April 3, 1992. The Washington reviews were superb ("If *The Other* had been made by an unknown choreographer, it would have made that unknown a star overnight"),[3] but New York critics were generally dismissive. Anna Kisselgoff said, "One admires Miss de Mille for continually revising her own work. Yet in stripping down what she may have considered an overblown idea, she has delivered a blown-up miniature."[4] Nevertheless, at eighty-six, after seventeen years in a wheelchair and with her mobility drastically limited, Agnes had created a ballet that many people found immensely moving.

In the spring of 1993, Agnes, looking like the splendid remnant of a grand army, accepted a special Antoinette Perry award commemorating the fiftieth anniversary of *Oklahoma!* (told she could speak only for a minute, she protested, "You can't say anything in one minute except 'Help,' or 'Fire!' And they're not even paying me for this!"). In June, ABT presented what would be its final gala tribute to Agnes, at the Metropolitan Opera House. The program consisted of *The Informer, Three Virgins and a Devil* (a new production), and *Rodeo.* When the curtain rose after the second intermission, the audience, expecting *Rodeo,* saw Agnes, resplendent in a gold gown, seated alone on the stage. In the warmth of the spotlight, she shed twenty years; her presence charged the hall and brought the audience to its feet, roaring. She put her finger to her lips for silence and then made a brief but fervent plea on behalf of ABT, which was once again facing extinction. "Our society is in bad shape," she concluded. "Ballet Theatre points to excellence — think what that word means! — and the magic without which we cannot live, without which we dare not live. And *beauty.*"

She kept busy throughout the summer — still curious, still learning, still productive. She was disappointed when publishers rejected a second volume of "portraits" (some of which were rejects from the first), but nevertheless began work on a new book, about early Hollywood. She was revising her fifty-year-old *Tally-Ho,* and planned to start rehearsals in the fall. She spent weekends at Merriewold when the logistics were manageable. In September, Anderson Ferrell asked her to critique the manuscript of his new novel. Her only comment was "Don't be afraid to be clear." Intellectually, Agnes was always clear.

In spite of her increasing frailty, it still seemed inconceivable that anything could still the force that was Agnes. She herself was prepared but not yet ready to accept "the alternative." Although she had put Death on the stage, she spoke of it only obliquely. But when she heard that a terminally ill young man had described his idea of an afterlife as a big Ziegfeld production number with music by Jerome Kern, perfect in every detail, she said, "Oh, I hope it's not like that! I don't want perfection! The *struggle* is everything!"[5]

Agnes's struggles in this world were ended by another stroke, sometime during the night of October 6, 1993. She had had a busy day and a festive dinner at the restaurant next door with Paul Moore. It was a belated celebration of her eighty-eighth birthday (Paul had been out of town on the day), and Agnes informed him that they would both dress up. Paul thought she seemed tired; her face was flushed, and her eyes swollen from an infection. Paul's wife was working in Europe, and he and Agnes compared their own first impressions of Europe, and spoke of their youthful love affairs there. "It was fun," Moore said. "We laughed a lot."[6]

Ivy helped Agnes to bed that night and discovered her body the next morning. Death had come suddenly but apparently not before Agnes recognized it and made an abortive attempt to summon help. Paul Moore heard the news on his car radio as he was driving to Merriewold to close up the house for the winter. Like everyone else who had known Agnes up close, he could not believe she was gone. "She was in some ways like a terrific wind," her son said. "Never still, til now."[7]

"Leaders may be venerated," Agnes wrote of Martha Graham; "they are seldom loved. Along with dominance comes jealousy and anger; and in the world of dance . . . these inflamed emotions predominate. . . . Time will erase the hideous fevers. . . . The quality of work is all that matters."[8] Of her own work she wrote, "The dances I had done had been sprightly, adroit, timely, diverting, but peripheral, unrooted."[9] In fact, she had a plethora of roots, stretching in many directions — to city and country; to classical, modern, and folk dancing; to burlesque and vaudeville; movies and theater; music; poetry; and all the visual arts, as well as history, sociology, politics, and even tennis.

It is easy to forget how revolutionary her dances, so familiar to us for so long, were when they first appeared. She created new ways of seeing and thinking about dance. She brought fresh air into ballet and irrevocably changed dance on the Broadway stage, setting a new standard and popularizing what had been elitist. Like Graham, she was a pioneer who believed fiercely in her own artistic vision and blazed her own trail to realize it. If she did not found a new religion, as Graham did, she was nevertheless a major force for dance in America in the twentieth century and influenced generations of choreographers that followed her. "She was a bearer of great thought and light for all of us to bask in," Tommy Tune said after her death. "*Oklahoma!* pushed the idea of what dance could be further than I could imagine it, beyond entertainment, into story telling, the revelation of character and dramatic impact."[10] In her Broadway work, Walter Kerr had written, she created the art of "that sudden, almost imperceptible, moth-like flutter of life that starts with the barest movement of the actors' bodies, flickers for a moment on the verge of definition, and then is — before you have caught the miracle in the act — deeply involved in stating some of the more touching truths of everybody's life."[11]

She believed in the qualities of the people she called the intrinsic Americans, who built this country — "very strong, down-to-earth, salty, humorous, sardonic . . . with a tremendous sense of the earth and humanity and neighborliness."[12] She put them on the stage "full out, with feeling," earlier, and better, than anyone else.

Agnes often lamented the ephemeral nature of dance — that it is written on air and in the muscle memories of the dancers. Other means of preservation exist, none of them totally satisfactory: video, film, written notes, interviews with the choreographer, and mechanical notation, which is meticulous and extremely time-consuming. Because her dances depend to a great extent on nuances that cannot be notated, Agnes resisted notation.* Some of her dances, in various stages of completion, are on film. ABT agreed to videotape her rehearsals from 1990, and provided a videocamera, but it was merely set up and turned on, to pick up whatever happened to be in front of it — most of which was fragmented, tedious, and repetitious. In 1992, the Rodgers and Hammerstein Organization finally acknowledged that "to do *Carousel* without the de Mille dances is like reading a great book with one of the main characters missing" and put those dances on video, with Agnes and Gemze de Lappe analyzing and explaining the movement.[13]

De Lappe and a handful of other dancers of three generations who

* The Dance Notation Bureau has notated *Rodeo, Fall River Legend,* and *Brigadoon.*

have danced in and helped stage Agnes's works do their best to keep them alive; they know the spirit as well as the style, steps, groupings, and timing. Done badly, her choreography can look corny and dated. Done properly, by first-rate dancers, it is affecting and timeless.

Like any artist, Agnes should be judged by her best work, most of which was on Broadway. But *Rodeo* is a recognized landmark in American ballet, popular all over the world for its vitality and humor. *Fall River Legend* is also an international success, and at least a dozen dramatic ballerinas have interpreted Lizzie in quite different ways.*

Described as "perhaps the best dancer ever to write and the best writer ever to dance,"[14] Agnes communicated her thoughts in words, her feelings in dance, and her wonderful sense of the ridiculous in both. But her greatest achievements were neither her choreography nor her writing, nor her ability to speak eloquently, in places of power, for all dancers; it was the totality of her spirit. Her small person contained a cornucopia of passions and gifts best described by the old-fashioned word that she applied to Martha Graham: nonesuch. Her achievements transcended her contradictions and enriched American culture.

Her ashes were interred beside Walter's at Merriwold, in the presence of family members — Jonathan and Rosemary, their sons, and niece Judith Donelan — and friends, among them Terry Orr, Anderson Ferrell, Zoe Caldwell, Robert Whitehead, and Paul Moore. A public memorial took place on February 8, 1994, at the St. James Theatre, where *Oklahoma!* had premiered (it would have pleased Agnes that the stagehands, against whose union she had so often railed, bent their rules to make the venue available). Mary Hunter Wolf, Terry Orr, Gemze de Lappe, James Mitchell, Anderson Ferrell, Jerome Robbins, and other friends, dancers, and colleagues reminisced about the Agneses they had known. Neurologist Fred Plum spoke of her as an inspiration to thousands of handicapped people. Morton Gould said, "Wherever she is now, she is arguing with Lucia." Isaac Stern recalled her exemplary discipline and her patriotism, in the best sense of the word ("she knew where people came from and what they brought with them, and she taught us the human history of the United States"), and played a Haydn adagio. Jona-

---

* Agnes's favorites were Nora Kaye, Sallie Wilson, and Virginia Johnson.

than spoke of their shared love of language, Zoe Caldwell read excerpts from Agnes's books, and ABT dancers performed portions of *Rodeo* and *The Other.*

The highlight of the afternoon was a film assembled for the occasion. On the screen, Agnes appeared throughout the seasons of her life, from Merriewold dance pageants to rehearsals conducted from a wheelchair. In a rare clip from *Rodeo,* an exuberant Agnes outdanced everyone, "always trying something a little beyond her, and whether she succeeds or fails she is as cocky as hell."[15] The Cowgirl — the essence of her creator — goes on celebrating life in all its absurdity and glory, lifting hearts, embodying hope . . . surviving.

Danceography

Recital/Concert Pieces

(costumes by Agnes de Mille except where otherwise noted)

Stagefright (Delibes); first presented at the Little Theatre, New York City, March 13, 1927.

Dance with a Boy on a Lawn (Chopin), *Rain* (Brahms), *Jenny Loved a Soldier* (old English tunes); first presented at Cornell University, Ithaca, New York; April 1927.

Ballet Class, first presented at the Republic Theater, New York City, January 22, 1928.

'49 (Guion), first presented at the Republic Theater, New York City, March 3, 1928.

Ouled Nail (Kurdish tunes), *May Day* [with Warren Leonard], *Tryout* (George Gershwin and Ray Henderson), *Civil War* (medley of patriotic songs), *Harvest* [later *Harvest Reel*] (Irish tunes arranged by Percy Grainger); first presented at the Martin Beck Theatre, New York City, February 17, 1929.

Julia Dances (sixteenth-century madrigal), first presented at MacDowell Club House, New York City, January 26, 1930.

Gigue (Bach), first presented at the Italian Historical Society, New York City, May 2, 1930.

The Parvenues [with Warren Leonard] (Waldteufel and Strauss), first presented at The Music Box Theatre, Los Angeles, July 16, 1930.

Armistice Day (Irwin), *Theme and Variations* (Haydn), *Burgomaster's Branle* [with Warren Leonard] (ancient Dutch airs, arr. by Roentgen); first performed at The Craig Theatre, New York City, February 1, 1931.

Scherzo (Beethoven), *Hymn* (Bach-Hess); first presented at The Arts Theatre Club, New York City, March 17, 1932.

Primitive Spell [later *Witch Spell*] (Stravinsky), *Mozart Minuet* (Mozart, costume by Andrée Howard); *Galliarde* [later *Incident with the Spanish Ambassador*] (Dowland, arr. by Norman Franklin), *Mountain White* (trad. songs, arr. by Louis Horst), *Dance of Death (Agincourt Song), I've Got a Right to Sing the Blues*; first performed at the Mercury Theatre, London, October 31, 1934.

The Ship (trad. sea chanteys), *Hornpipe* [later *Clipper Sailing*] (Scarlatti), *Georgia Cracker, The Harvesting* (folk tunes, arr. by Vaughan Williams), *Strip Tease* (Gershwin), *Dust* (midwestern farm song, arr. by Robert Mueller-Hartmann), *Boston*

Brahmin, Blues (Gershwin-Saunders), *Daybreak Express, Western Dance, Grotesque Heroique* (Prokofiev and Stravinsky), *Rehearsal: Symphonic Ballet* (Beethoven); first performed at the Mercury Theatre, London, January–February, 1937.

Minuet (Weber), *Allegro* (Scarlatti), *Rondo* (Norman Franklin and John Simons), *Waltz* (Lanner); first performed at the Mercury Theatre, London, March 8, 1937.

Elizabethan Suite, first performed at the Playhouse, Oxford, June 18, 1937.

Rodeo (cowboy songs, arr. Franklin-Guion), *Rehearsal: New York Dance Group* (Bliss-Kodaly); first performed at the Fortune Theatre, London, May 26, 1938.

Czech Festival: 1940 (Smetana), first performed at the YMHA, New York City, January 15, 1939.

Conversations Pleasant and Unpleasant (Scarlatti-Handel, arr. by Trude Rittman), *Hares on the Mountain* (Kentucky folk song); first performed in 1939.

Running Set (trad. folk tunes, arr. by Arthur Kleiner and Trude Rittman, costumes by Hugh Laing and Agnes de Mille), *Clipper Sailing* (trad. sea chanteys), *Hell on Wheels* (trad. folk tunes); first performed by American Actors Company in *American Legend,* New York City, May 1941.

Night Scene (Ravel), first performed at The Chicago Memorial Theatre, October 30, 1941.

Theater Choreography

With Warren Leonard: "Can Can" for *The Black Crook* (Offenbach); Lyric Theater, Hoboken, New Jersey, March 11, 1929.

With Warren Leonard: "Smokin' Reefers" for *Flying Colors,* 1932.

Nymph Errant (Porter); London, September 1933.

Oklahoma! (Rodgers and Hammerstein), 1943.

One Touch of Venus (Weill, Nash, and Perelman), 1943.

Bloomer Girl (Arlen and Harburg), 1944.

Carousel (Rodgers and Hammerstein), 1945.

Brigadoon (Loewe and Lerner), 1947.

Allegro (Rodgers and Hammerstein), 1947.

Gentlemen Prefer Blondes (Styne and Loos), 1949.

Paint Your Wagon (Loewe and Lerner), 1951.

The Girl in Pink Tights (Romberg and Robin), 1954.

Goldilocks (Anderson and Kerr), 1958.

Juno (Blitzstein, O'Casey, and Stein), 1959.

Kwamina (Adler and Arthur), 1961.

110 in the Shade (Jones, Schmidt, and Nash), 1961.

Come Summer (Baker and Holt), 1970.

Film Choreography

"Pavane," *Romeo and Juliet* (anon., arr. Norman Franklin), "Court Ballet" (Weelkes, arr. Louis Horst); 1935.

Oklahoma!, 1954.

Ballets

Obeah, Black Ritual (Milhaud). Decor by de Molas. Performed by Ballet Theatre, Center Theater, New York City, January 22, 1940.

Three Virgins and a Devil (Respighi). Scenario by Ramon Reed, costumes by Motley, scenery by Arne Lundberg. First presented by Ballet Theatre with Agnes de Mille, Annabelle Lyon, Lucia Chase, and Eugene Loring at the Majestic Theater, New York City, February 11, 1941 (an earlier version with different music was in the 1934 London revue *Why Not Tonight*).

Drums Sound in Hackensack (Cohen). Costumes by Joep Nicolas. First presented by Jooss Ballets with Ulla Soederbaum and Hans Zullig at Maxine Elliott's Theatre, New York City, October 2, 1941.

Rodeo (Copland). Scenery by Oliver Smith, costumes by Kermit Love. First presented by the Ballet Russe de Monte Carlo with Agnes de Mille, Frederic Franklin, and Casimir Kokich at the Metropolitan Opera House, New York City, October 16, 1942.

Tally-Ho (The Frail Quarry) (Gluck/Nordoff). Decor and costumes by Motley. First presented by Ballet Theatre with Janet Reed, Anton Dolin, and Hugh Laing at the Los Angeles Philharmonic Auditorium, February 25, 1944.

Fall River Legend (Gould). Costumes by Miles White, scenery by Oliver Smith. First presented by Ballet Theatre with Alicia Alonso, Diana Adams, Muriel Bentley, Peter Gladke, John Kriza, and Crandall Diehl at the Metropolitan Opera House, New York City, April 22, 1948.

The Harvest According (Thomson). Scenery and costumes by Lemuel Ayers. First presented by Ballet Theatre with Gemze de Lappe, Liane Plane, Ruth Ann Koesun, Kelly Brown, and Jenny Workman at the Metropolitan Opera House, New York City, October 1, 1952.

The Rib of Eve (Gould). Costumes by Irene Sharaff, scenery by Oliver Smith. First presented by Ballet Theatre with Nora Kaye, James Mitchell, and Barbara Lloyd at the Metropolitan Opera House, New York City, April 25, 1956.

Sebastian (Menotti). Ballet Theatre "Previews" production with Nora Kaye, Darrell Notara, John Kriza, and Lupe Serrano at the Phoenix Theatre, New York City, May 27, 1957.

The Bitter Weird (Loewe and Rittman). Costumes by Motley, scenery by John Graham, first presented by Royal Winnipeg Ballet with Richard Rutherford and Marilyn Young at the Manitoba Centennial Concert Hall, Winnipeg, March 9, 1962 (an earlier version, called *Ballade,* was performed by the Agnes de Mille Dance Theatre in 1953).

The Rehearsal (Gould). First presented by Royal Winnipeg Ballet with Wendy Barker and Richard Rutherford, narrated by Agnes de Mille at the Manitoba Centennial Concert Hall, Winnipeg, October 2, 1964.

The Wind in the Mountains (trad. folk tunes, arr. by Laurence Rosenthal). Costumes by Stanley Simmons, scenery by Oliver Smith. First presented by American Ballet Theatre at the New York State Theater, New York City, March 17, 1965.

The Four Marys (trad. folk tune, arr. by Trude Rittman). Costumes by Stanley Simmons, scenery by Oliver Smith, lighting by Jean Rosenthal. First presented by American Ballet Theatre with Carmen de Lavallade, Judith Jamison, Cleo

Quitman, and Glory Van Scott at the New York State Theater, New York City, March 23, 1965.

Golden Age (Pitot after Rossini, arr. by Laurence Rosenthal). Costumes by Stanley Simmons, scenery by William and Jean Eckart, lighting by Jennifer Tipton. First presented by the Harkness Ballet at Clowes Hall, Indianapolis with Elisabeth Carroll, Susan Whelan, Claudia Corday, and Richard Wagner, October 26, 1967.

A Rose for Miss Emily (Hovhaness). Costumes by Stanley Simmons, scenery by A. Christina Giannini. First presented by the North Carolina School of the Arts with Gemze de Lappe and David Evans in Winston-Salem, October 25, 1970. First performed by American Ballet Theatre with Sallie Wilson and Gayle Young at City Center, New York City, December 30, 1970.

Texas Fourth (Schmidt, plus trad. tunes, orchestrated by Hershy Kaye). Scenery by Oliver Smith, costumes by A. Christina Giannini, lighting by Nananne Porcher. First presented by the Agnes de Mille Heritage Dance Theatre at the North Carolina School of the Arts, Winston-Salem, April 1973. Presented by American Ballet Theatre with Dennis Nahat, William Carter, Rebecca Wright, Eric Nesbitt, George de la Pena, Buddy Balough, and Ruth Mayer in principal roles at the New York State Theater, New York City, July 8, 1976.

Summer (Schubert). Costumes by Agnes de Mille and E. Virginia Williams, lighting by Thomas Skelton. First presented by the Boston Ballet with Anamarie Sarazin, David Brown, Woytek Lowski, pianist David Baker, and singer David Arnold at the Music Hall, Boston, April 10, 1975.

A Bridegroom Called Death (Schubert). Costumes by Stanley Simmons, lighting by Thomas Skelton. Presented by the Joffrey Ballet with Denise Jackson, Gregory Huffman, and Burton Taylor at the 55th Street Theatre, New York City, November 1, 1978.

Inconsequentials (Schubert). Costumes by Santo Loquasto, lighting by Richard Moore. Presented by the Richmond Ballet with Maria Gisladottir and Jerry Schwender at the Mosque, Richmond, Virginia, October 25, 1981.

The Informer (Celtic songs, arr. by Marc Blitzstein, Martha Johnson, John Morris, Trude Rittman). Scenery and costumes by Santo Loquasto. Lighting by Jennifer Tipton. First presented by American Ballet Theatre with Victor Barbee,

Johan *[sic]* Renvall, and Kathleen Moore at the Shrine Auditorium, Los Angeles, March 15, 1988.

The Other (Schubert, to poems by Goethe). Costumes by Santo Loquasto, lighting by Jennifer Tipton. First presented by American Ballet Theatre with Amanda McKerrow, Victor Barbee, Roger Van Fleteren, singer Paul Rowe, and pianist William Wolfram at the Kennedy Center Opera House, Washington, D.C., April 3, 1992.

Television

Omnibus Programs:

"The Art of Ballet," 1956.

"The Art of Choreography," 1956.

"Lizzie Borden," 1957.

Bloomer Girl, 1956.

Gold Rush, 1958.

The Cherry Tree Carol (trad., arr. by Trude Rittman). Costumes by Motley. Performed by the North Carolina School of the Arts, 1973.

The Bitter Weird, 1964.

"Conversations About the Dance," 1980.

Source Notes

Agnes's reverence for history ensured that vast collections of relevant material were meticulously preserved and catalogued. In the notes that follow, most materials referred to may be found in the Agnes de Mille Papers in the Dance Collection at the New York Public Library (NYPL). That collection includes 249 letters from William de Mille to Anna de Mille; Walter Prude's early journals and poetry and his correspondence with Agnes during World War II; Agnes's diaries and writings from school days throughout her career; the manuscripts of six of her books, as well as those of some published articles and unpublished stories. There are more than 3,700 items of correspondence to and from other dancers, choreographers, and writers, and other personal and professional friends. There are also legal and financial documents, music scores, scenarios, playscripts, television scripts, drafts and final texts of speeches, and extensive choreographic notes on her ballets. Thirty-eight oversized scrapbooks contain articles, programs, posters and photos; these are roughly chronological, but a few consist of items dating from 1913 to 1944, and others contain anachronistic surprises, such as a newspaper account of Anna de Mille's 1902 wedding in a scrapbook labeled 1975–1980. In addition to all the printed material, there are a number of audio- and videotapes of interviews and rehearsals, kinescopes of Agnes's *Omnibus* and other television appearances, and films, their quality ranging from good to terrible, of many of her ballets and Broadway dances. A few additional kinescopes may be seen at The Museum of Television and Radio in New York City.

The Records of the Ballet Russe de Monte Carlo (Sergei Denham Collection), the American Ballet Theatre Records (1936–circa 1967), and the Carmelita Maracci Papers are also housed at the NYPL's Dance Collection.

The Sophia Smith Collection in the Smith College Archives in Northampton, Massachusetts, houses another substantial Agnes de Mille Collection; it deals primarily with Agnes's years in London, but also contains manuscripts of some articles and books, and scenarios for the *Carousel, Fall River Legend,* and *Oklahoma!* ballets.

Copies of some correspondence between Agnes de Mille and Rebecca West were supplied to me by The McFarlin Library, Special Collections, at the University of Tulsa.

Archives at The Kurt Weill Foundation for Music in New York City contain information on *One Touch of Venus.*

The Fred Zinneman Papers at the Margaret Herrick Library, Academy of Motion Picture Arts and Sciences, Beverly Hills, California, are a source of background information concerning the *Oklahoma!* movie.

Correspondence between Agnes and her literary agent is housed in the Archives of Harold Ober Associates at Princeton University, Princeton, New Jersey.

An unedited transcript of interviews conducted in 1986 for *Agnes: The Indomitable de Mille* was kindly made available to me by Judy Kinberg, who produced the show for public television's "Dance in America" series.

Some of the following citations lack page numbers because the primary sources were in personal scrapbooks, provided by clipping services that noted dates but not pages.

Introduction

[1] *Dance to the Piper,* p. 127.

[2] Oliver Smith to Agnes de Mille, December 8, 1959.

[3] *Washington Star-News,* September 9, 1974.

[4] Roy Newquist, *Showcase,* p. 100.

Chapter 1: Genes

[1] Sumiko Higashi, *Cecil B. De Mille, A Guide to References and Resources,* p. 33.

[2] Agnes de Mille, *Where the Wings Grow,* p. 54.

[3] According to his granddaughter, Henry George became the best-known serious American writer and the best-known American after Theodore Roosevelt and Mark Twain. "At the turn of the century [his Single Tax theory] was better known than Communism and George was more read than Marx." *Where the Wings Grow,* p. 50.

[4] Agnes de Mille, *Dance to the Piper,* p. 4.

[5] Anna George de Mille, *Henry George: Citizen of the World,* p. 190.

[6] Ibid., p. 194.

[7] *Where the Wings Grow,* p. 56.

[8] William de Mille to Anna de Mille, February 1902.

[9] William to Anna, July 15, 1902.

[10] William to Anna, September 1902.

[11] William to Anna, December 1902.

[12] William to Anna, November 1902.

[13] William to Anna, January 26, 1903.

[14] William to Anna, February 17, 1903.

[15] *Dance to the Piper,* p. 4.

[16] William to Anna, December 25 and December 30, 1904.

Chapter 2: Golden Days

[1] William de Mille to Anna de Mille, undated.

[2] William de Mille to Anna de Mille, undated.

[3] *Where the Wings Grow,* p. 283.

[4] Ibid., p. 44.

[5] The plays, written by William, often had serious themes, e.g., the suffragette movement or the Single Tax theory, in which William devoutly believed (*Where the Wings Grow,* p. 68).

[6] *Where the Wings Grow,* p. 45.

[7] Ibid., p. 46.

[8] Ibid., p. 23.

[9] Ibid., p. 29.

[10] Ibid., p. 32.

[11] Ibid., p. 20.

[12] Ibid., p. 36.

[13] William de Mille to Anna de Mille, summer 1910.

[14] William de Mille (from Washington, D.C., where he was trying out *The Woman*) to Anna de Mille, April 20, 1911.

[15] William de Mille to Anna de Mille, August 17, 1911.

[16] William de Mille to Anna de Mille, August 29, 1911.

[17] Sumiko Higashi, *Cecil B. De Mille, A Guide to References and Resources,* p. 60.

[18] *Dance to the Piper,* p. 6. Had William invested, he'd have wound up with a one-eighth interest in Paramount Pictures.

[19] William de Mille to Cecil B. DeMille, September 3, 1913.

[20] Kenneth Magowan, *Behind the Screen,* p. 267.

[21] William de Mille, *Hollywood Saga,* p. 58.

[22] Ibid., p. 61.

[23] William de Mille to Anna de Mille, October 2, 1914.

[24] William to Anna, October 11, 1914.

[25] William to Anna, October 13, 1914.

[26] William to Anna, October 17, 1914.

Chapter 3: The Kingdom of Shadows

[1] Agnes de Mille, Diary, July 1916.

[2] AdM, Diary, 1916.

[3] AdM, Diary, August 1916.

[4] Agnes de Mille, *Portrait Gallery,* p. 225.

[5] AdM, Diary, May 18, 1918.

[6] AdM, Diary, May 1918.

[7] AdM, 1915 Diary.

[8] William de Mille to Anna de Mille, September 24, 1914.

[9] *Dance to the Piper,* p. 32.

[10] Agnes de Mille to Ted Ritter, September 28, 1960.

[11] AdM, Diary, September 1915.

[12] Agnes de Mille to Carol Easton.

[13] *Where the Wings Grow,* p. 94.

[14] Mary Hunter Wolf to CE.

[15] Irene Selznick to CE.

[16] According to Louis Horst in *Dance Observer* (October–November 1934), she was seven.

[17] *Dance to the Piper,* p. 44.

[18] AdM Scrapbook.

[19] Agnes de Mille to Margaret de Mille, 1917.

[20] Beulah Marie Dix Flebbe to Agnes de Mille, September 29, 1959.

[21] *Dance to the Piper,* p. 63.

[22] *Los Angeles Examiner,* July 13, 1930.

[23] *Dance to the Piper,* p. 54.

[24] Ibid., p. 81.

[25] AdM Scrapbook.

[26] Mary Hunter Wolf to CE.

Chapter 4: Fault Lines

[1] "The White Dress," unpublished short story.

[2] Mary Hunter Wolf to Carol Easton.

[3] Agnes de Mille to CE.

[4] Agnes de Mille to CE.

[5] Irene Selznick to CE.

[6] Mary Hunter Wolf to CE.
[7] Agnes de Mille to CE.
[8] Mary Hunter Wolf to CE.
[9] William de Mille to Anna de Mille, July 1902.
[10] William de Mille to Anna de Mille, October 13, 1915.
[11] *Photoplay,* 1923 (quoted by Anne Edwards in *The DeMilles*).
[12] Phil A. Koury, *Yes, Mr. De Mille,* p. 312.
[13] Cecilia De Mille Presley to CE.
[14] "Goodnight, C.B.," Agnes de Mille, *Esquire,* January 1964.
[15] Adela Rogers St. John in *Photoplay,* December 1920.
[16] Mary Hunter Wolf to CE.
[17] Agnes de Mille to CE.
[18] "Pine Points," May 1922.
[19] *Dance to the Piper,* p. 88.

Chapter 5: Earthquake

[1] Agnes de Mille to Carol Easton.
[2] *Dance to the Piper,* p. 89.
[3] *Los Angeles Examiner,* July 14, 1930.
[4] *Theatre Arts,* November 1951.
[5] Agnes de Mille, "Games," *Good Housekeeping,* August 1957.
[6] AdM, 1916 Diary.
[7] Scrapbook: Friday Morning Club *Bulletin,* May 1925.
[8] Scrapbook: *California Grizzly,* March 20, 1925.
[9] Ibid.: *California Grizzly,* November 30, 1925.
[10] *Dance to the Piper,* p. 92.
[11] Agnes de Mille to Anna de Mille, December 5, 1925.
[12] *Dance to the Piper,* p. 94.
[13] "A Soul for Mary Jane," *Pasadena Star News,* May 4, 1926. She had help with the scenario, settings, and costumes, but the choreography was her own.
[14] AdM Scrapbook, 1913–44: *California Grizzly,* May 6, 1926.
[15] William de Mille to Anna de Mille, January 2, 1925.
[16] William de Mille to Anna de Mille, January 10, 1925.
[17] AdM, 1925 Journal.
[18] Agnes de Mille to CE.

Chapter 6: Alchemy

[1]*Dance to the Piper,* p. 103.

[2] "Agnes: The Indomitable de Mille," unedited transcript of public television documentary filmed in 1986.

[3] William de Mille to Anna de Mille, September 10, 1918.

[4] Wire from William to Anna, November 1924.

[5] William de Mille to Agnes de Mille, November 17, 1926.

[6] William to Agnes, September 23, 1926.

[7] AdM, 1926 Journal.

[8] Agnes de Mille to Carol Easton.

[9] *Where the Wings Grow,* p. 198.

[10] Ibid., p. 236.

[11] Agnes de Mille to CE.

[12] *Dance to the Piper,* p. 106.

[13] Ibid., p. 105.

[14] Agnes de Mille to Ruth Page, July 23, 1927.

[15] *Brooklyn Citizen,* January 20, 1927.

[16] Agnes de Mille to Ruth Page, July 23, 1927.

[17] *San Diego Union,* October 10, 1982.

[18] AdM Scrapbook.

[19] *Santa Fe New Mexican,* July 27, 1927.

Chapter 7: Entertainer

[1] *New York Herald-Tribune,* February 29, 1928.

[2] *Dance to the Piper,* p. 72.

[3] *New York Times,* March 4, 1928.

[4] Mary Hunter Wolf to Carol Easton.

[5] Ferdinand Davis to CE.

[6] Agnes de Mille to Ruth Page, July 23, 1927.

[7] Agnes de Mille to Anna de Mille, November 16, 1928.

[8] Agnes to Anna, undated.

[9] Anna to Agnes, all written in November 1928.

[10] John Butler to CE.

[11] *Dance to the Piper,* p. 146: "I almost always thought of her as a girlfriend—almost, but not quite always; one does not domesticate a prophetess."

[12] Agnes de Mille, *Martha,* p. xii.

[13] Ibid., p. 262.

[14] Agnes de Mille to Ted Ritter, September 29, 1960.

[15] Agnes de Mille to CE.

[16] Lee Freeson to CE.

[17] *Los Angeles Examiner,* July 17, 1930.

[18] John Martin, *America Dancing,* p. 270.

Chapter 8: Warren

[1] Agnes de Mille to Anna de Mille, September 18, 1930.

[2] Agnes de Mille to Carol Easton.

[3] Agnes de Mille to Anna de Mille, November 4, 1929.

[4] Anna to Agnes, undated.

[5] Doris Humphrey to Agnes de Mille, undated.

[6] *New York Herald-Tribune,* February 13, 1930.

[7] Anna de Mille to Agnes de Mille, April 1930.

[8] "Lorelei," unpublished manuscript.

Chapter 9: Aftershocks

[1] William de Mille to Agnes de Mille, November 3, 1929.

[2] William to Agnes, 1929.

[3] William to Agnes, January 18, 1928.

[4] William to Agnes, March 27, 1928.

[5] William to Agnes, March 21, 1928.

[6] William to Agnes, March 13, 1930.

[7] William to Agnes, April 24, 1930.

[8] *Dance to the Piper,* p. 137.

[9] *Los Angeles Examiner,* June 25, 1930.

[10] *The Stage,* June 28, 1930.

[11] Agnes de Mille to Carol Easton.

[12] Anna de Mille to Agnes de Mille, July 22, 1930.

[13] Warren Leonard to CE.

[14] Anna de Mille to Agnes and Margaret de Mille, August 11, 1930.

[15] Anna de Mille to Agnes, August 1, 1930.

[16] Agnes de Mille to Anna, August 10, 1930.

[17] Agnes de Mille to CE.

[18] *Where the Wings Grow,* p. 83.

[19] Agnes de Mille to CE.

[20] Anna de Mille (in L.A.) to Agnes, who is to reserve suites at New York's Hotel Pierre for Cecil and Constance: "Do not mention the name de Mille. Say it is for friends . . . the hotel will be grateful for guests and will probably throw a pound of tea in free. Jew them down . . . get the hotel man to show you the rooms and write the prices on hotel paper and send it to me." May 19, 1931.

[21] Agnes de Mille to CE.

[22] *Dance to the Piper,* p. 36.

[23] Agnes de Mille to CE.

[24] William de Mille to Agnes de Mille, March 7, 1928.

[25] Frances Beranger Triest to CE.

[26] *New York Herald-Tribune,* February 2, 1931.

[27] John Martin, *America Dancing,* pp. 265–270.

[28] *Architectural Digest,* December 1984.

[29] Margaret Lloyd, *Christian Science Monitor,* March 30, 1935.

[30] An Open Interview with Walter Terry at the 92nd Street Y, 1951.

[31] Dorothy Bird to CE.

[32] *Dance to the Piper,* p. 158.

Chapter 10: Sea Change

[1] Agnes de Mille to Carol Easton.

[2] *Dance to the Piper,* p. 163.

[3] Anna de Mille to Agnes de Mille, August 27, 1932.

[4] *New English Weekly,* January 6, 1933.

[5] *Christian Science Monitor,* December 31, 1932.

[6] *Dance to the Piper,* p. 158.

[7] *Speak to Me, Dance with Me,* p. 40.

[8] Brigitte Kelly to CE.

[9] Agnes de Mille to Anna de Mille, June 11, 1933.

[10] Frederic Franklin to CE.

[11] Arnold L. Haskell, *Balletomania,* p. 209.

[12] Agnes de Mille to Anna de Mille, June 9, 1933.

[13] William de Mille to Agnes de Mille, November 3, 1929.

[14] Agnes de Mille to CE.

[15] Agnes de Mille to CE.

[16] Warren Leonard to CE.

[17] *Speak to Me, Dance with Me,* p. 97.

[18] Agnes de Mille to a Mrs. Maitland Baldwin in Montreal, who had questioned remarks about homosexuals in *Dance to the Piper,* April 1, 1952.

Chapter 11: Ramon

[1] Mary Hunter Wolf to Carol Easton.

[2] Agnes de Mille to Anna de Mille, May 28, 1933.

[3] Agnes to Anna, May 29, 1933.

[4] Agnes to Anna, May 21, 1933.

[5] Agnes to Anna, September 5, 1933.

[6] Ibid.

[7] John Fearnley to CE.

[8] Agnes de Mille to Margaret de Mille Fineman, February 10, 1934.

[9] Anna de Mille to Agnes de Mille, September 5, 1933.

[10] Agnes de Mille to Anna de Mille, October 4, 1933.

[11] *Speak to Me, Dance with Me,* p. 216.

[12] Ibid., p. 247.

[13] Ibid., p. 277.

[14] *Dance to the Piper,* p. 210.

[15] Ibid., p. 170.

[16] *London Observer,* September 2, 1956.

[17] Therese Langfield Horner to CE.

[18] John Fearnley to CE.

[19] *Speak to Me, Dance with Me,* p. 230.

[20] Therese Langfield Horner to CE.

Chapter 12: Cecil and Cleopatra

[1] Cecil B. De Mille to Agnes de Mille, March 6, 1934.

[2] Cecil B. De Mille to Agnes de Mille, March 19, 1934.

[3] *Speak to Me, Dance with Me,* p. 258.

[4] Ibid., p. 260.

[5] Agnes de Mille to Warren Leonard, April 1934.

[6] Agnes de Mille to Anna de Mille, April 21, 1934.

[7] Judith Fineman Donelan to Carol Easton.

[8] Warren Leonard to CE.

[9] Philip Koury, *Yes, Mr. De Mille,* p. 239.

[10] Agnes de Mille to CE.

[11] Agnes de Mille to Anna de Mille, March 28, 1934.

[12] Agnes de Mille to Warren Leonard, April 1934.

[13] Agnes de Mille to Anna de Mille, April 21, 1934.

[14] Agnes de Mille to Warren Leonard, April 21, 1934.

[15] Ibid.

[16] Ibid.

[17] Ibid.

Chapter 13: "Something of a Portent"

[1] Agnes de Mille to Anna de Mille, August 13, 1934.

[2] *Dance to the Piper,* p. 64.

[3] *And Promenade Home,* p. 221.

[4] *Dance to the Piper,* p. 66.

[5] *And Promenade Home,* p. 225.

[6] Ibid., p. 224.

[7] Agnes de Mille to Ferdinand Davis, July 1, 1934.

[8] *Speak to Me, Dance with Me,* p. 302.

[9] Agnes de Mille to Ferdinand Davis, July 1, 1934. The original title, *Primitive Dance,* was changed in the United States, where Martha Graham's *Primitive Mysteries* had caused a sensation in 1931.

[10] Mary Hunter Wolf to Carol Easton.

[11] Agnes de Mille to Anna de Mille, November 6, 1934.

[12] Ibid.

[13] Ibid.

[14] *London Sunday Pictorial,* November 18, 1934.

[15] Agnes de Mille to Anna de Mille, November 27, 1934.

[16] *Speak to Me, Dance with Me,* p. 313.

[17] Warren Leonard to CE.

[18] Agnes de Mille to Warren Leonard, April 1934.

[19] *Speak to Me, Dance with Me,* p. 15.

[20] Warren Leonard to CE.

[21] *Dance to the Piper,* p. 216.

[22] Agnes de Mille to CE.

[23] *American Dancer,* March 1935.

[24] *New York Times,* February 10, 1935.

[25] Per *Dance Magazine,* November 1952, re John Martin's twenty-fifth anniversary as *New York Times* dance critic.

Chapter 14: Such Sweet Sorrow

[1] Warren Leonard to Carol Easton.

[2] *Dance to the Piper,* p. 227.

[3] Ibid., p. 230.

[4] *Portrait Gallery,* p. 58.

[5] Lee Freeson to CE.

[6] Maracci Papers, Dance Collection, NYPL.

[7] Barbara Parry to CE.

[8] *Los Angeles Times,* July 26, 1935.

[9] *Hollywood Citizen-News,* July 26, 1935.

[10] Agnes de Mille to Anna de Mille, August 15, 1935.

[11] Agnes to Anna, September 30, 1935.

[12] Anna de Mille to Agnes de Mille, undated.

[13] Agnes de Mille to Anna de Mille, October 7, 1935.

[14] Agnes de Mille to CE.

[15] Ramon Reed to Michael Hertz, January 14, 1936.

[16] *Dance to the Piper,* p. 231.

[17] Agnes de Mille to Anna de Mille, March 16, 1936.

[18] Ibid.

[19] *Daily Variety* and the *Hollywood Reporter,* July 16, 1936.

[20] Ramon Reed to Michael Hertz, March 26, 1936.

[21] *Speak to Me, Dance with Me,* p. 358.

[22] Agnes de Mille to CE.

[23] Agnes de Mille to Michael Hertz, March 12, 1937.

Chapter 15: Cobweb Love

[1] "Mrs. Obie," unpublished ms.

[2] Agnes de Mille to Michael Hertz, March 12, 1937.

[3] *London Daily Telegraph,* January 6, 1937.

[4] Agnes de Mille to Anna de Mille, April 27, 1937.

[5] Agnes to Anna, March 29, 1937.

[6] *London News Chronicle,* February 20, 1937.

[7] Maude Lloyd to Carol Easton.

[8] Agnes de Mille to Michael Hertz, March 12, 1937.

[9] Agnes de Mille to CE.

[10] Carlheinz Ostertag to CE.

[11] Therese Langfield Horner to CE.

[12] Quoted in a February 1978 letter from Warren Leonard to Agnes de Mille.

[13] William de Mille to Agnes de Mille, September 14, 1932.

[14] *Dance to the Piper,* p. 101.

[15] Jule Styne to CE.

[16] Agnes de Mille to CE.

[17] Anna de Mille to Agnes de Mille, January 5, 1934.

[18] Agnes de Mille to Anna de Mille, April 29, 1937.

Chapter 16: American Suite

[1] Agnes de Mille to Anna de Mille, July 15, 1937.

[2] Quoted in the *Journal of Stage Directors and Choreographers Foundation,* Fall 1989.

[3] *Portrait Gallery,* p. 100.

[4] Agnes de Mille to Michael Hertz, Fall 1937.

[5] Ibid.

[6] Agnes de Mille to Anna de Mille, August 21, 1934.

[7] Therese Langfield Horner to Carol Easton.

[8] Elisabeth Schooling to CE.

[9] Charlotte Bidmead to CE.

[10] Agnes de Mille to Anna de Mille, February 8, 1938.

[11] Agnes to Anna, February 3, 1938.

[12] Agnes to Anna, January 28, 1938.

[13] Agnes to Anna, April 5, 1938.

[14] *To a Young Dancer,* p. 131.

[15] "The Creative Mind," WGBH-FM Boston, no date.

[16] *To a Young Dancer,* p. 39.

[17] From Agnes's 1964 program notes for *Bitter Weird.*

[18] *Dance to the Piper,* p. 9.

[19] Notes for original *Rodeo.*

[20] Therese Langfield Horner to CE.

[21] Peggy van Praagh and Peter Brinson, *The Choreographic Art,* p. 311.

[22] Ferdinand Davis to CE.

[23] Agnes de Mille to Anna de Mille, June 9, 1938.

[24] Agnes de Mille to CE.

[25] Therese Langfield Horner to CE.

[26] Ruthanna Boris to CE.

[27] Dame Peggy van Praagh interviewed by Margaret Dale for Oral History Project of NYPL Dance Collection October–November 1978.

[28] Agnes de Mille to CE.

[29] Agnes de Mille to Margaret Storrs Grierson (director of Smith College Archives).

[30] Charlotte Bidmead to CE.

[31] *Dance to the Piper,* p. 245.

Chapter 17: Regrouping

[1] Richard Watts, *New York Herald-Tribune,* November 30, 1938.

[2] Agnes de Mille to Mary Ware Dennett, February 6, 1935.

[3] John Houseman, *Unfinished Business,* p. 50.

[4] Agnes de Mille to Carol Easton.

[5] Oliver Smith to CE.

[6] Sybil Shearer to CE.

[7] Agnes de Mille to CE.

[8] Agnes de Mille to CE.

[9] Sybil Shearer to CE.

[10] Joseph Anthony to CE.

[11] Sybil Shearer to CE.

[12] Eleanor Fairchild to CE.

[13] Ruthanna Boris to CE.

[14] Agnes de Mille to Mary Meyer Green, November 24, 1938.

[15] Agnes de Mille to Cecil B. De Mille, December 1938.

[16] Ruthanna Boris to CE.

[17] Sybil Shearer to CE.

Chapter 18: "A Really Fine Night-Club Show"

[1] *Dance to the Piper,* p. 253.

[2] Dick Cavett interview, 1981.

[3] *Dance to the Piper,* p. 252.

[4] *To a Young Dancer,* p. 80.

[5] *Dance to the Piper,* p. 257.

[6] Agnes de Mille to Carol Easton.

[7] *New York Times,* January 23, 1940.

[8] Sybil Shearer to CE.

[9] Cecil Smith, *Chicago Daily Tribune,* October 31, 1940.

[10] Agnes de Mille to CE.

[11] Joseph Anthony to CE.

[12] Ibid.

[13] Ibid.

[14] Agnes de Mille to CE.

[15] Agnes de Mille to CE.

[16] *Dance to the Piper,* p. 261.

[17] Sallie Wilson to CE.

[18] Walter Terry, *New York Herald-Tribune,* July 10, 1941.

[19] Lotte Goslar to CE.

[20] Walter Terry, "Floor Shows," *New York Herald-Tribune,* June 15, 1941.

Chapter 19: Walter

[1] *And Promenade Home,* p. 5.

[2] Sybil Shearer to Carol Easton.

[3] Judith Fineman Donelan to CE.

[4] *New York Herald-Tribune,* October 3, 1941: *Time,* October 20, 1941.

[5] Allyn Ann McLerie to CE.

[6] Bambi Linn to CE.

[7] Walter Prude journal.

[8] *And Promenade Home,* p. 14.

[9] Agnes de Mille to CE.

[10] *And Promenade Home,* p. 16.

Chapter 20: "Full Out, with Enthusiasm"

[1] From the scenario.

[2] From Agnes's program notes for the October 28, 1976, Joffrey Ballet production.

[3] Records of the Ballet Russe de Monte-Carlo Dance Collection, NYPL.

[4] Agnes de Mille speaking at the Dance Magazine Award ceremony, March 1, 1979.

[5] Oliver Smith to Carol Easton.
[6] Robert Pagent to CE.
[7] Frederic Franklin to CE.
[8] James Starbuck to CE.
[9] *Dance to the Piper,* p. 284.
[10] *Omnibus,* December 30, 1956, and *Dance to the Piper,* p. 285.
[11] Robert Pagent to CE.
[12] Robert Lindgren to CE.
[13] Lee Freeson to CE.
[14] *Dance to the Piper,* p. 297.
[15] Agnes de Mille to CE.
[16] Agnes de Mille to Aaron Copland, September 2, 1942.
[17] Agnes de Mille to Mikhail Baryshnikov, December 12, 1980.
[18] Morton Gould to CE.
[19] Agnes de Mille to Mary Meyer Green, August 5, 1942.
[20] Agnes de Mille to Mary Meyer Green, August 6, 1942.
[21] Agnes de Mille to Walter Prude, October 15, 1942.
[22] Claudia Cassidy in the *Chicago Tribune,* January 1943.
[23] Frederic Franklin to CE.
[24] *Dance to the Piper,* p. 305.
[25] *Dance Observer,* December 1942.
[26] John Martin, *New York Times,* November 1, 1942; Edwin Denby, *Modern Music,* November–December 1942; *New York Herald-Tribune,* October 17, 1942; *New York PM,* October 18, 1942; Irving Deakin in *Cue,* October 24, 1942; *Dance Observer,* November 1942.
[27] *San Francisco Chronicle,* November 23, 1942.
[28] Aaron Copland and Vivian Perlis, *Copland,* p. 281.
[29] Alexandra Danilova, *Choura: The Memoirs of Alexandra Danilova,* p. 141.
[30] *Dance to the Piper,* p. 321.
[31] Ibid.

Chapter 21: *Oklahoma!*

[1] From two versions of the scenario — one in NYPL notebook, folder III-2, labeled "Rodeo" but referring to Laurey and clearly for *Oklahoma!* and the other in Irving Deakin's *At the Ballet,* p. 135.

[2] John Martin, *New York Times,* May 1, 1943.

[3] *New York World-Telegram & Sun,* June 26, 1951 ("Beauty Is All Right, But Dancing Is First").

[4] Elaine Steinbeck to Carol Easton.

[5] Dorothy Rodgers to CE.

[6] Celeste Holm to CE.

[7] Bambi Linn to CE.

[8] Related by Dania Krupska.

[9] *Dance to the Piper,* p. 324.

[10] Jay Blackton to CE.

[11] Elaine Steinbeck to CE.

[12] Agnes de Mille to Anna de Mille, March 24, 1943.

[13] *New York Times,* April 1, 1943.

[14] Vincente Minnelli, *I Remember It Well,* p. 162.

[15] *New York Herald-Tribune,* May 2, 1943.

[16] Agnes de Mille to Robert Lawrence, *New York Herald-Tribune,* May 1943.

Chapter 22: The de Millennium

[1] Agnes de Mille to Walter Prude, March 23, 1943.

[2] Agnes de Mille to Mary Meyer Green, June 1943.

[3] Florence Powdermaker to Agnes de Mille, June 4, 1943.

[4] Anna de Mille to Agnes de Mille, June 13, 1943.

[5] Walter Prude to Paul Nordoff, June 27, 1943.

[6] *And Promenade Home,* p. 50.

[7] Walter Prude to Anna de Mille, July 7, 1943.

[8] *And Promenade Home,* p. 40.

[9] *Dance to the Piper,* p. 334.

[10] Ibid., p. 335.

[11] Sybil Shearer to Carol Easton.

[12] Dorothy Bird to CE.

[13] Agnes de Mille to Kurt Weill, July 22, 1943.

[14] Agnes de Mille to Kurt Weill, July 11, 1943.

[15] Sono Osato, *Distant Dances,* p. 209.

[16] Robert Pagent to CE.

[17] Agnes de Mille to Kurt Weill, July 11, 1943.

[18] Ibid.

[19] Maurice Abravanel to CE.
[20] Trude Rittman to CE.
[21] Maurice Abravanel to CE.
[22] Cheryl Crawford, *One Naked Individual,* p. 129.
[23] Sono Osato, *Distant Dances,* p. 214.
[24] *And Promenade Home,* p. 112.
[25] Elia Kazan, *Kazan: A Life,* p. 234.
[26] Sono Osato, *Distant Dances,* p. 217.
[27] Howard Barnes, *New York Herald-Tribune,* October 17, 1943.
[28] Edwin Denby, *New York Herald-Tribune,* October 24, 1943.
[29] Burton Rascoe, *New York World-Telegram,* October 8, 1943.
[30] John Martin, *New York Times,* November 14, 1943.

Chapter 23: Power

[1] Agnes de Mille to Anna de Mille, January 8, 1934.
[2] Agnes de Mille to Sergei Denham, May 1944, Ballet Russe Papers (NYPL).
[3] *Christian Science Monitor,* July 8, 1944.
[4] *Tally-Ho* scenario.
[5] Agnes de Mille to Mary Meyer Green, April 26, 1944.
[6] Agnes de Mille to Anna de Mille, February 15, 1944.
[7] John Martin, *New York Times,* April 16, 1944.
[8] John Martin, *New York Times,* May 28, 1944.
[9] Kitty Carlisle Hart to Carol Easton.
[10] Agnes de Mille to Mary Meyer Green, October 22, 1944.
[11] *And Promenade Home,* p. 194.
[12] Ibid., p. 196.
[13] James Mitchell to CE.
[14] Betty Low to CE.
[15] *New York News,* October 15, 1944.
[16] *Dance Observer,* August 1945.
[17] *The Nation,* October 21, 1944.
[18] *Philadelphia Inquirer,* September 17, 1944.
[19] *New York Herald-Tribune,* October 6, 1944.
[20] *Wall Street Journal,* October 7, 1944.
[21] *New York Herald-Tribune,* December 23, 1945.
[22] *And Promenade Home,* p. 202.

Chapter 24: Rodgers and Hammerstein and de Mille

[1] Walter Prude to Agnes de Mille, December 1943.

[2] Walter to Agnes, December 1943.

[3] Walter to Agnes, June 1944.

[4] Agnes to Walter, December 7, 1944.

[5] Walter to Agnes, June 10 and September 30, 1944.

[6] Walter to Agnes, June 10, 1944.

[7] Agnes to Walter, June 14, 1944.

[8] Agnes to Walter, October 29, 1944.

[9] Agnes to Walter, December 31, 1944.

[10] Walter to Agnes, October 11, 1944.

[11] Agnes to Walter, December 31, 1944.

[12] Agnes to Walter, January 24, 1945.

[13] Agnes de Mille to Carmelita Maracci, October 29, 1944.

[14] Agnes de Mille to Walter Prude, January 7, 1945.

[15] Agnes to Walter, March 1945.

[16] *Boston Herald,* March 22, 1943.

[17] Agnes de Mille to Carol Easton.

[18] Dorothy Rodgers to CE.

[19] Dorothy Rodgers to CE.

[20] Mary Rodgers to CE.

[21] Trude Rittman to CE.

[22] Agnes de Mille, *Carousel* instructional video, 1992.

[23] Agnes de Mille to Ted Ritter, September 29, 1960.

[24] *New York PM,* March 22, 1945.

[25] *Carousel* scenario.

[26] *The Stage* (London), June 15, 1950.

[27] Agnes de Mille to Walter Prude, April 3, 1945.

[28] Bambi Linn to CE.

[29] *Dance Magazine,* June 1945, p. 15.

[30] *New York Herald-Tribune,* October 17, 1943.

Chapter 25: Home

[1] Agnes de Mille to Anna de Mille, June 25, 1945.

[2] Agnes de Mille to Arthur Lyons, August 1945.

[3] Agnes de Mille to Anna de Mille, August 10, 1945.

[4] Brigitte Kelly to Carol Easton.
[5] Agnes de Mille to Walter Prude, December 31, 1944.
[6] Agnes de Mille to Anna de Mille, September 16, 1945.
[7] Walter Prude to Agnes de Mille, September 30, 1944.
[8] Agnes de Mille to Walter Prude, November 5, 1943.
[9] *And Promenade Home,* p. 213.
[10] Bambi Linn to CE.
[11] Agnes de Mille to Walter Prude, December 26, 1944.
[12] Bill Hayden to Walter Prude, undated, circa 1944.
[13] Agnes de Mille to Mary Meyer Green, November 27, 1945.
[14] Agnes de Mille to CE.
[15] Agnes de Mille to Cornelia Runyon, May 14, 1946.
[16] *And Promenade Home,* unedited ms.
[17] Glen Tetley to CE.
[18] Kirsten Valbor to CE.
[19] *New York Herald-Tribune,* October 28, 1946.

Chapter 26: *Brigadoon*

[1] Robert Lewis, *Slings and Arrows,* p. 168.
[2] James Mitchell to Carol Easton.
[3] Agnes de Mille to CE.
[4] Agnes de Mille to Therese Langfield Horner, October 22, 1962.
[5] *Dance to the Piper,* p. 311.
[6] James Mitchell to CE.
[7] Trude Rittman to CE.
[8] *Christian Science Monitor,* February 21, 1947.
[9] Choreographic notes, Agnes de Mille Papers, NYPL.
[10] *New York Herald-Tribune,* March 14, 1947.
[11] *Christian Science Monitor,* February 21, 1947.
[12] *Life,* July 21, 1947.
[13] *Saturday Review,* April 5, 1947.
[14] *New York Times,* March 22, 1947.
[15] Agnes de Mille to CE.
[16] Agnes de Mille to CE.
[17] Agnes de Mille to CE.
[18] Agnes de Mille to Warren Leonard, April 20, 1947.

Chapter 27: ***Allegro***

[1] Agnes de Mille to Carol Easton.

[2] *To a Young Dancer*, p. 141.

[3] Agnes de Mille to CE.

[4] Gloria Wills Landes to CE.

[5] Evelyn Taylor to CE.

[6] Rufus Smith to CE.

[7] James Mitchell to CE.

[8] Interview in *Toronto Daily Star*, January 24, 1968.

[9] Agnes de Mille to Walter Prude, March 24, 1945.

[10] Bill Bradley to CE.

[11] Gloria Wills Landes to CE.

[12] Agnes de Mille, *America Dances*, p. 191.

[13] *Theatre Arts*, November 1947, p. 13.

[14] *New York Times*, January 18, 1948.

[15] *Dance Magazine*, November 1947; *New Republic*, October 27, 1947.

[16] Hugh Fordin, *Getting to Know Him*, p. 256.

[17] *New York PM*, October 13, 1947.

[18] *Dallas News*, November 2, 1947.

[19] Richard Rodgers, *Musical Stages*, pp. 251–252.

[20] Agnes de Mille to CE.

Chapter 28: Lizzie Borden, C'est Moi

[1] Isaac Stern to Carol Easton.

[2] Mary Hunter Wolf to CE.

[3] Agnes de Mille to CE.

[4] Judith Fineman Donelan to CE.

[5] Oliver Smith to CE.

[6] Morton Gould to CE.

[7] Agnes de Mille to Rebecca West, 1969.

[8] Unpublished speech.

[9] Harold Taylor to CE.

[10] Kitty Carlisle Hart to CE.

[11] Dania Krupska to CE.

[12] Agnes de Mille to Walter Prude, November 26, 1944.

[13] Martin Feinstein to CE.

[14] Agnes de Mille Papers, NYPL.
[15] Program note.
[16] Agnes de Mille to Anna de Mille, August 7, 1930.
[17] Agnes to Anna, May 1931.
[18] *Lizzie Borden: A Dance of Death,* p. 158.
[19] Agnes de Mille to Walter Prude, December 7, 1944.
[20] Agnes to Walter, January 30, 1945.
[21] Muriel Bentley to Agnes de Mille, July 1946.
[22] Agnes de Mille to Oliver Smith, July 31, 1946.
[23] Morton Gould to CE.
[24] "Agnes: The Indomitable de Mille," unedited transcript of public television documentary filmed in 1986.
[25] *Lizzie Borden: A Dance of Death,* p. 137.
[26] Nora Kaye, "The Challenge of Lizzie Borden," *Sunday Times* (London), March 15, 1959.
[27] Scott Douglas to CE.
[28] Morton Gould to CE.
[29] *New York Times,* May 30, 1948.
[30] *Musical America,* February 1951.
[31] Interview with Lillie F. Rosen, *Dance Scope,* Fall/Winter 1976/1977, vol. 11, no. 1.

Chapter 29: *Gentlemen Prefer Blondes*
[1] Adelaide Bishop to Carol Easton.
[2] Kitty Carlisle Hart to CE.
[3] Olin Downes, *New York Times,* January 9, 1949.
[4] Clifford Simpson to Agnes de Mille, August 6, 1946.
[5] Carol Channing to CE.
[6] Bill Bradley to CE.
[7] Oliver Smith to CE.
[8] Honi Coles to CE.
[9] Jule Styne to CE.
[10] Interview with *Winnipeg Free Press,* 1964.
[11] Carol Channing to CE.
[12] Oliver Smith to CE.
[13] Jule Styne to CE.

[14] Walter Terry, *New York Herald-Tribune.*

[15] John Martin, *New York Times,* February 26, 1950.

Chapter 30: *Dance to the Piper*

[1] Arnold St. Subber to Carol Easton.

[2] Bella Lewitzky to CE.

[3] Related by Agnes de Mille to CE.

[4] Dania Krupska to CE.

[5] Glen Tetley to CE.

[6] Arnold St. Subber to CE.

[7] Agnes de Mille to CE.

[8] Agnes de Mille to CE.

[9] Agnes de Mille to Edward Weeks, January 24, 1966.

[10] *Dance to the Piper,* p. 3.

[11] Ibid., p. 101.

[12] Ibid., p. 68.

[13] Ibid., p. 68.

[14] Ibid., p. 14.

[15] Ibid., p. 43.

[16] Ibid., p. 75.

[17] Douglass Montgomery to Agnes de Mille, January 27, 1951.

[18] William de Mille to Agnes de Mille, July 8, 1951.

[19] Clara Beranger de Mille to Agnes de Mille, July 10, 1951.

[20] Judith Fineman Donelan to CE.

[21] Cecil B. De Mille to Agnes de Mille, July 7, 1951.

[22] Agnes de Mille to Cecil B. De Mille, September 5, 1951.

[23] Agnes de Mille to William de Mille, November 5, 1951.

[24] Agnes de Mille to CE.

[25] Craig Barton to Agnes de Mille, March 10, 1950.

[26] John Martin, *New York Times,* February 10, 1952.

Chapter 31: *Paint Your Wagon*

[1] Mavis Ray to Carol Easton.

[2] Ted Thurston to CE.

[3] *San Francisco Chronicle,* March 1, 1953.

[4] Loren Hightower to CE.

[5] *Theatre Arts,* November 1951.
[6] Mary Burr to CE.
[7] Daniel Mann to CE.
[8] Dania Krupska to CE.
[9] Ted Thurston to CE.
[10] Agnes de Mille to Walter Prude, March 21, 1943.
[11] Daniel Mann to CE.
[12] Daniel Mann to CE. In *Martha* (p. 118) Agnes referred to a theory that Martha Graham had learned from a voice teacher: "Everything fruitful and meaningful happens below the navel."
[13] Agnes de Mille to CE.
[14] Gemze de Lappe to CE.
[15] James Mitchell to CE.
[16] Dania Krupska to CE.
[17] *Time,* November 26, 1951.
[18] Ibid.
[19] Walter Kerr, *New York Herald-Tribune,* November 13, 1951.
[20] Walter Kerr, *New York Herald-Tribune,* November 25, 1951.
[21] Claudia Cassidy, *Chicago Tribune,* December 17, 1951.
[22] Agnes de Mille to Clara Beranger de Mille, November 1951.

Chapter 32: Harvest

[1] An Open Interview with Walter Terry at the 92nd Street Y, May 27, 1951.
[2] Jennifer Taylor Tuthill to Carol Easton.
[3] Jonathan Prude to CE.
[4] Agnes de Mille to Mabel Ludlum, May 6, 1952.
[5] Ibid.
[6] Agnes de Mille to Michael Hertz, August 6, 1952.
[7] Sergei Denham to Agnes de Mille, January 23, 1948.
[8] Agnes de Mille to Sergei Denham, September 22, 1949.
[9] Sergei Denham to Agnes de Mille, September 30, 1949.
[10] Mobile, Alabama, *Press-Register,* October 1951.
[11] John Martin, *New York Times,* April 28, 1951, and Rosalyn Krokover, *Musical Courier,* May 15, 1951.
[12] Douglas Watt, *The New Yorker,* May 5, 1951.
[13] Charles Payne, *American Ballet Theatre,* p. 354.

[14] Mary Burr to CE.
[15] Melissa Hayden to CE.
[16] Eliot Feld to CE.
[17] Original draft of an article for the *San Francisco Chronicle,* March 1, 1953.
[18] Ibid.
[19] Ruth Ann Koesun to CE.
[20] Maria Karnilova to CE.
[21] Isaac Stern to CE.
[22] Ruth Ann Koesun to CE.
[23] *Martha,* p. 412.
[24] Bambi Linn to CE.
[25] Bunty Kelly to CE.
[26] Paul Olson to CE.
[27] Frances Herridge, *New York Post,* October 2, 1952; Walter Terry, *New York Herald-Tribune,* October 3, 1952; Richard Woods, *Chicago Tribune,* October 25, 1952.
[28] Margaret Lloyd, *Christian Science Monitor,* December 2, 1952.

Chapter 33: Not *Swan Lake*

[1] Robert Sabin, *Musical America,* February 15, 1954.
[2] Agnes de Mille to Lucia Chase, October 27, 1952.
[3] Agnes de Mille to Carol Easton.
[4] Agnes de Mille to CE.
[5] Mortimer Becker to CE.
[6] Agnes de Mille to Catherine Drinker Bowen, May 1962.
[7] Loren Hightower to CE.
[8] Virginia Bosler to CE.
[9] George Jean Nathan, *New York Journal-American,* March 28, 1954.
[10] Jerome Chodorov to CE.
[11] Bill Ross to CE.
[12] Loren Hightower to CE.
[13] Loren Hightower to CE.
[14] Agnes de Mille, "The Valor of Teaching," *The Atlantic,* June 1955.
[15] Walter Kerr, *New York Herald-Tribune,* March 6, 1954.
[16] Speir Collins, *Augusta Chronicle,* October 29, 1953.

[17] Daniel Mann to CE.
[18] *And Promenade Home,* p. 188.
[19] An Open Interview with Walter Terry at the 92nd Street Y, May 27, 1951.
[20] Elmer Bernstein to CE.
[21] *And Promenade Home,* p. 182.
[22] *Newsweek,* April 12, 1965.
[23] James Mitchell to CE.
[24] *And Promenade Home,* pp. 179–180.

Chapter 34: Oklahoma in Hollywood

[1] Agnes de Mille to Rodgers and Hammerstein, March 20, 1954.
[2] Jay Blackton to Carol Easton.
[3] *Dance to the Piper,* p. 239.
[4] Richard Rodgers, *Musical Stages,* p. 285.
[5] John Fearnley to CE.
[6] Elmer Bernstein to CE.
[7] "Agnes: The Indomitable de Mille," unedited transcript of public television documentary filmed in 1986.
[8] Oliver Smith to CE.
[9] James Mitchell to CE.
[10] Bambi Linn to CE.
[11] Elmer Bernstein to CE.
[12] Loren Hightower to CE.
[13] Elmer Bernstein to CE.
[14] Spyros Skouras to Rodgers and Hammerstein, May 10, 1954.
[15] *Time,* October 24, 1955.
[16] *Saturday Review,* November 5, 1955.
[17] *Dance Magazine,* November 1955.
[18] Agnes de Mille to Irving Lazar, December 30, 1954.
[19] Agnes de Mille to Michael Hertz, March 20, 1956.
[20] Bambi Linn to CE.
[21] *Speak to Me, Dance with Me,* p. 383.
[22] Agnes de Mille to Barbara Powers, 1966.
[23] AdM, Choreographic notebook, c. 1954.
[24] AdM, Notes, undated.

Chapter 35: Evangelist for Dance

[1] Agnes de Mille to Oliver Smith, April 11, 1955.

[2] Agnes de Mille to Lucia Chase, January 25, 1955.

[3] Lucia Chase to Agnes de Mille, January 29, 1955.

[4] Frances Herridge, *New York Post,* April 26, 1956.

[5] Miles Kastendieck, *New York Journal-American,* April 26, 1956.

[6] Robert Coleman, *New York Daily Mirror,* April 27, 1956; John Martin, *New York Times,* April 26, 1956.

[7] Louis Biancolli, *New York World-Telegram & Sun,* April 26, 1956.

[8] Darrell Notara to Carol Easton.

[9] Gemze de Lappe to CE.

[10] Glen Tetley to CE.

[11] Robert Coleman, *New York Daily Mirror,* May 29, 1957.

[12] Agnes de Mille to CE.

[13] Enrique Martinez to CE.

[14] Agnes de Mille to CE.

[15] John Butler to CE.

[16] *New York Herald-Tribune,* January 6, 1957.

[17] Dance Magazine Award ceremony, February 19, 1957.

[18] *Omnibus,* March 8 and 24, 1957.

[19] Agnes de Mille to Joseph Welch, September 27, 1960.

[20] Joseph Welch to Agnes de Mille, April 8, 1957.

[21] Walter Terry, *New York Herald-Tribune,* April 7, 1957.

Chapter 36: Just Living

[1] *Sunday Times* (London), May 25, 1958.

[2] Carlheinz Ostertag to Carol Easton.

[3] Harold Taylor to CE.

[4] Marilyn Mercer interview, *New York Herald-Tribune,* November 20, 1958.

[5] "Agnes: The Indomitable de Mille," unedited transcript of public television documentary filmed in 1986.

[6] Jonathan Prude to CE.

[7] Agnes de Mille to Edward Weeks, April 21, 1952.

[8] Edward Weeks to Agnes de Mille, November 12, 1953.

[9] *And Promenade Home,* p. 242.

[10] Ibid., p. 190.
[11] Ibid., p. 191.
[12] Ibid., p. 182.
[13] *New York Herald-Tribune,* October 28, 1958.
[14] *New York Herald-Tribune,* October 12, 1958.
[15] Walter Kerr to CE.
[16] *Philadelphia Inquirer,* September 3, 1958.
[17] Walter Kerr to CE.
[18] Noël Coward, *Diaries,* p. 386.
[19] Leo Lerman, *Dance Magazine,* November 1958, pp. 16–17.
[20] Pat Stanley to CE.
[21] Agnes de Mille to CE.
[22] Joseph Stein to CE.
[23] Glen Tetley to CE.
[24] Agnes de Mille to CE.
[25] Mavis Ray to CE.
[26] Agnes de Mille to CE.
[27] José Ferrer to CE.
[28] Murray Schumach, *New York Times,* March 1, 1959.
[29] Glen Tetley to CE.
[30] Joseph Stein to CE.
[31] Lynn Austin to CE.
[32] Trude Rittman to CE.

Chapter 37: "Echoes and Extensions"

[1] Agnes de Mille to Brooks Atkinson, undated.
[2] Agnes de Mille to Louise Gilbert, undated.
[3] Agnes de Mille to Edward Weeks, May 25, 1959.
[4] *Lizzie Borden, A Dance of Death,* p. 228.
[5] "Graduate Comment" published by Wayne University, November 1960.
[6] Robert Schnitzer to Agnes de Mille, undated.
[7] Lucia Chase to Agnes de Mille, July 18, 1960.
[8] Lucia Chase to Agnes de Mille, August 30, 1960.
[9] *To a Young Dancer,* p. 102.
[10] Walter Kerr, *New York Herald-Tribune,* July 23, 1962.

[11] Agnes de Mille to Joan Campbell, December 1, 1959.
[12] Agnes de Mille to Ted Ritter, September 28, 1960.
[13] Rosamond Gilder, *New York Herald-Tribune,* April 26, 1964.
[14] *The Book of the Dance,* pp. 189–192.
[15] *And Promenade Home,* p. 178.
[16] Agnes de Mille to Jerome Robbins, October 24, 1945.
[17] Agnes de Mille to Jerome Robbins, December 2, 1963.
[18] Arthur Todd, *Dance Observer,* November 1963.
[19] Richard L. Coe, *Washington Post,* November 20, 1963.
[20] "Here Is America's Innocence," *New York Times,* September 30, 1973.
[21] Agnes de Mille to Fritz Loewe, November 28, 1961.
[22] Malcolm Lowry to Agnes de Mille, January 29, 1959.

Chapter 38: Fairy Godmother

[1] Agnes de Mille to Margaret Storrs Grierson, May 14, 1963.
[2] Agnes de Mille to Dorothy Hammerstein, undated.
[3] Agnes de Mille to Therese Langfield Horner, July 21, 1961.
[4] Gemze de Lappe to Carol Easton.
[5] John Morris to CE.
[6] Leo Lerman, *Dance Magazine,* December 1961.
[7] Arthur Todd, "The Dynamics of Musical Theatre," *Musical America,* December 1961.
[8] Elinor Hughes, *Boston Sunday Herald,* October 1, 1961.
[9] *Time,* November 3, 1961.
[10] Melvin Maddocks, *Christian Science Monitor,* September 28, 1961.
[11] Walter Terry, *New York Herald-Tribune,* January 7, 1962.
[12] Arnold Spohr to CE.
[13] Roy Newquist, *Showcase,* p. 100.
[14] Agnes de Mille to Therese Langfield Horner, October 22, 1962.
[15] Arnold Spohr to CE.
[16] Ken Winters, *Winnipeg Free Press,* March 10, 1962.
[17] James Clouser to CE.
[18] Arnold Spohr to CE.
[19] Jean Stapleton to CE.
[20] *New York State Exhibitor,* October 12, 1955.
[21] Agnes de Mille to Michael Kidd, July 8, 1980.

Chapter 39: Out of Step

[1] Arthur Todd, *Dance Observer,* May 1963.

[2] Harvey Schmidt to Carol Easton.

[3] N. Richard Nash to CE.

[4] Tom Jones to CE.

[5] Inga Swenson to CE.

[6] Lesley Ann Warren to CE.

[7] Agnes de Mille to Michael Hertz, September 25, 1963.

[8] N. Richard Nash to CE.

[9] Harvey Schmidt to CE.

[10] Tom Jones to CE.

[11] Bill Ross to CE.

[12] Joseph Anthony to CE.

[13] Agnes de Mille to CE.

[14] Tom Jones to CE.

[15] Harvey Schmidt to CE.

[16] N. Richard Nash to CE.

[17] Agnes de Mille to Mary Meyer Green, undated.

[18] William Goldenberg to CE.

[19] Agnes de Mille to Edward Weeks, November 15, 1963.

[20] "Agnes: The Indomitable de Mille," unedited transcript of public television documentary filmed in 1986.

[21] Jonathan Prude to CE.

[22] Therese Langfield Horner to CE.

[23] Agnes de Mille to Therese Langfield Horner, September 10, 1964.

[24] *Dance Magazine,* April 1965.

[25] Ted Thurston to CE.

[26] Agnes de Mille to Catherine Drinker Bowen, May 1962.

[27] Horton Foote to CE.

[28] Agnes de Mille to Agnes Meyer, March 7, 1961.

[29] Agnes de Mille to James Clouser, December 17, 1963.

[30] Agnes de Mille to Victor Bator, April 24, 1961.

[31] Richard Rodgers to Agnes de Mille, June 1962.

[32] Agnes de Mille to the De Mille Trust, Spring 1962.

[33] Agnes de Mille to Victor Bator, November 27, 1962.

[34] Agnes de Mille to Therese Langfield Horner, April 13, 1963.

[35] Walter Terry, *New York Herald-Tribune,* January 12, 1964.
[36] Agnes de Mille to Walter Terry, January 15, 1964.
[37] Agnes de Mille to Edward Weeks, January 14, 1964.
[38] Agnes de Mille to the *New York Herald-Tribune,* undated; an edited version was published March 15, 1964.
[39] James Clouser to CE.
[40] Agnes de Mille to Bella Lewitzky, October 9, 1964.
[41] Walter Terry, *New York Herald-Tribune,* October 30, 1965.

Chapter 40: Strip-Mining

[1] Gregory Peck to Carol Easton.
[2] *The Performing Arts:* Rockefeller Panel Report on the future of theater, dance, and music in America. McGraw-Hill, 1956.
[3] *Lizzie Borden, A Dance of Death,* p. 280.
[4] Agnes de Mille to Lucia Chase, September 14, 1964.
[5] Oliver Smith to CE.
[6] Ruth Ann Koesun to CE.
[7] Joseph Carew to CE.
[8] William A. Raidy, *Newark Star-Ledger,* March 18, 1965.
[9] Douglas Watt, *New York Daily News,* March 18, 1965.
[10] Carmen de Lavallade to CE.
[11] Glory Van Scott to CE.
[12] Sallie Wilson to CE.
[13] *Lizzie Borden, A Dance of Death,* p. 255.
[14] Scott Douglas to CE.
[15] "Russian Journals," *Dance Perspectives* 44, p. 56.

Chapter 41: "Bored Thou Never Wert"

[1] Jacob Javits, speech at Capezio Award Ceremony, February 28, 1966.
[2] Charlie Baker to Carol Easton.
[3] Douglas Watt, *New York News,* October 2, 1952.
[4] Agnes de Mille to Henry Andrews, October 28, 1968.
[5] Harold Taylor quoting Clive Barnes to Agnes de Mille, July 14, 1976.
[6] *New York Times,* October 31, 1965.
[7] *New York Times,* January 27, 1966.

[8] Brian MacDonald to CE.

[9] Brian MacDonald to CE.

[10] David Howard to CE.

[11] Clive Barnes, *New York Times,* November 9, 1967.

[12] Winthrop Sargeant, *The New Yorker,* November 25, 1967.

[13] April 15, 1967, at Kalamazoo, Michigan.

[14] Agnes de Mille to Joseph Welch, January 6, 1960.

[15] Agnes de Mille to Jane Ficke, May 20, 1968.

[16] Agnes de Mille to Henry Andrews, November 28, 1968.

[17] Reported by Agnes de Mille to Henry Andrews, October 28, 1968.

[18] *America Dances,* p. 135.

[19] *New York Herald-Tribune,* November 20, 1958.

[20] Agnes de Mille to Walter Kerr, June 3, 1960.

[21] Charley Baker to CE.

[22] James Mitchell to CE.

[23] Harold Taylor to CE.

[24] Isaac Stern to CE.

[25] Ed Dietz to CE.

[26] Isaac Stern to CE.

[27] Ed Dietz to CE.

[28] Isaac Stern to CE.

[29] Dania Krupska to CE.

Chapter 42: Indian Summer

[1] Reported by the Associated Press's William Glover in the *Baton Rouge Morning Advocate,* February 24, 1969.

[2] James Mitchell to Carol Easton.

[3] David Evans to CE.

[4] Clive Barnes, *New York Times,* March 19, 1969.

[5] Agnes de Mille to Philip Hanes, December 1969.

[6] John Butler to CE.

[7] Agnes de Mille to Philip Hanes, January 15, 1971.

[8] Joseph Gale, *Newark Evening News,* undated.

[9] *Speak to Me, Dance with Me,* p. 19.

[10] Ibid., p. 12.

[11] Ibid., p. 234.

[12] Clive Barnes, *New York Times,* July 4, 1971.

[13] Harold Taylor to CE.

[14] Bella Lewitzky to CE.

[15] Philip Hanes to CE.

[16] David Evans to CE.

[17] *Richmond News Leader,* October 3, 1973; John H. Harvey, *St. Paul Pioneer Press,* November 14, 1973.

[18] Albert Goldberg, *Los Angeles Times,* October 29, 1973.

[19] Hardin Goodman to Sheila Porter, November 13, 1973.

[20] Byron Belt, *Long Island Newsday,* November 5, 1974.

[21] Louis Pastore, *Dance Magazine,* December 1974.

[22] Clive Barnes, *New York Times,* November 17, 1974.

Chapter 43: Paying the Piper

[1] James H. Semans to Agnes de Mille, February 7, 1975.

[2] *Reprieve,* p. 167.

[3] Harold Taylor to Carol Easton.

[4] *New York Times,* July 4, 1976.

[5] *To a Young Dancer,* p. 27.

[6] *Reprieve,* p. 163.

[7] Ibid., p. 220.

[8] Ed Dietz to CE.

[9] Eda Gershgorn to CE.

[10] Agnes de Mille to Lisa Hewitt Harland, October 1973.

[11] Harold Taylor to CE.

[12] Kate Medina to CE.

[13] Agnes de Mille to CE.

[14] *Where the Wings Grow,* p. 126.

[15] Ibid., p. 198.

[16] Ibid., p. 266.

[17] Ibid., p. 20.

[18] Ibid., p. 198.

[19] Ibid., p. 100.

[20] Ibid., p. 281.

[21] Agnes de Mille to Clifford Curzon, June 1974.
[22] Sherry Traver Underwood to Agnes de Mille, December 1, 1976.
[23] Agnes de Mille to "Margaret's close friends."
[24] Michael Menzies to CE.
[25] Clive Barnes, *New York Times*, July 10, 1976.
[26] Anna Kisselgoff, *New York Times*, July 18, 1976.
[27] Agnes de Mille quoted by Deborah Jowett, *Chicago Tribune Magazine*, 1978.
[28] *Reprieve*, p. 63.
[29] Ibid., p. 155.
[30] Ibid., p. 191.
[31] Ibid., p. 190.
[32] Ibid., p. 226.
[33] Edward Weeks to Agnes de Mille, October 28, 1981.

Chapter 44: Phoenix

[1] Agnes de Mille to Carlheinz Ostertag, November 18, 1977.
[2] Clive Barnes, *New York Times*, November 11, 1977.
[3] Martin Bernheimer, *Los Angeles Times*, June 22, 1978.
[4] Agnes de Mille to Iris Fanger, April 5, 1981.
[5] Genevieve Oswald to Carol Easton.
[6] Agnes de Mille to CE.
[7] T. E. Kalem, *Time*, December 24, 1979.
[8] William Hammerstein to CE.
[9] Martin Berheimer, *Los Angeles Times*, May 4, 1979.
[10] Brendan Gill, *The New Yorker*, December 24, 1979.
[11] Josh Logan to Agnes de Mille, May 20, 1983.
[12] Mary Rodgers Guettel to CE.
[13] Robert Whitehead to CE.
[14] Ed Dietz to CE.
[15] Anderson Ferrell to CE.
[16] Agnes de Mille to Carlheinz Ostertag, June 13 and June 20, 1986.
[17] John Morris to CE.
[18] Dirk Lombard to CE.
[19] Terry Orr to CE.
[20] Victor Barbee to CE.

[21] Lynn Garafola, *Ballet Review,* Fall 1988, pp. 60–61.

[22] Michael Menzies to CE.

[23] *Reprieve,* p. 266.

[24] Anderson Ferrell to CE.

Chapter 45: Decrescendo

[1] Agnes de Mille to Carmelita Maracci, January 8, 1985.

[2] Agnes de Mille to Alfred Longueil, March 13, 1952.

[3] "Agnes: The Indomitable de Mille," unedited transcript of public television documentary filmed in 1986.

[4] *Reprieve,* p. 242.

[5] Agnes de Mille to Carol Easton.

[6] Martha Graham to Agnes de Mille, 1975, undated.

[7] Mary Meyer Green to CE.

[8] Agnes de Mille to CE.

[9] Agnes de Mille to Peter Blakeley, September 19, 1952.

[10] *Portrait Gallery,* p. 98, p. 147.

[11] Ibid., p. 185.

[12] Ibid., p. 290.

[13] *New York Times,* April 7, 1991.

[14] *Martha,* p. 161.

[15] Tobi Tobias, *Los Angeles Times Book Review,* September 23, 1991.

[16] Patricia Birch to CE.

[17] Martha Graham to CE, March 23, 1990.

[18] *Martha,* p. 385, p. 328.

[19] Ibid., p. 31.

[20] Ibid., p. 40.

[21] Ibid., p. 416.

[22] Ibid., p. 400.

[23] *The New Yorker,* October 14, 1991.

[24] Elizabeth Kendall, *New York Newsday,* September 22, 1991.

[25] Jo Takamine to CE.

[26] Anderson Ferrell to CE.

[27] Agnes de Mille to David Baker, undated.

[28] William Goldenberg to CE.

[29] Agnes de Mille to Lisa Hewitt Harland, December 7, 1974.

[30] Agnes de Mille to Therese Langfield Horner, August 23, 1956.
[31] Thomas Skelton to CE.
[32] *Martha,* p. 263.

Chapter 46: The Other

[1] Agnes de Mille to Rebecca West, September 8, 1977.
[2] Agnes de Mille to Marcia Haydee, March 6, 1979.
[3] Octavio Roca, *Washington Times,* April 5, 1992.
[4] Anna Kisselgoff, *New York Times,* June 8, 1992.
[5] Michael Menzies to Carol Easton.
[6] Paul Moore to CE.
[7] Jonathan Prude to CE, October 27, 1993.
[8] *Martha,* p. 327.
[9] *Reprieve,* p. 236.
[10] Tommy Tune, National Public Radio, October 7, 1993.
[11] Walter Kerr, *New York Herald-Tribune,* April 7, 1957.
[12] "Agnes: The Indomitable de Mille," unedited transcript of public television documentary filmed in 1986.
[13] Mary Rodgers, *Carousel* instructional video, 1992.
[14] Janice Berman, *New York Newsday,* August 29, 1991.
[15] From the scenario.

Selected Bibliography

Abbott, George. *Mister Abbott.* Random House, 1963.

Amberg, George. *Ballet in America.* Duell, Sloane and Pearce, 1949.

Anderson, Jack. *The One and Only: The Ballet Russe de Monte Carlo.* Dance Horizons, 1901.

Atkinson, Brooks. *Broadway.* Macmillan, 1970.

Balanchine, George. *Balanchine's New Complete Stories of the Great Ballets.* Doubleday, 1968.

Barnes, Clive. *Inside American Ballet Theatre.* Hawthorn Books, 1977.

Brady, Joan. *The Unmaking of a Dancer.* Harper and Row, 1982.

Bordman, Gerald. *American Musical Theatre.* Oxford University Press, 1978.

Chazin-Bennahum, Judith. *The Ballets of Antony Tudor.* Oxford University Press, 1994.

Cohen, Selma Jeanne, and A. J. Pischl. "The American Ballet Theatre: 1940–1960," *Dance Perspectives* 6, 1960.

Copland, Aaron, and Vivian Perlis. *Copland 1900 Through 1942.* St. Martin's/Marek, 1984.

Coward, Noël. *The Noël Coward Diaries.* Little, Brown, 1982.

Crawford, Cheryl. *One Naked Individual.* Bobbs-Merrill, 1977.

Croce, Arlene. *Going to the Dance.* Knopf, 1982.

Danilova, Alexandra. *Choura: The Memoirs of Alexandra Danilova.* Knopf, 1986.
Deakin, Irving. *At the Ballet.* Thomas Nelson and Sons, 1956.
de Mille, Agnes. *Dance to the Piper.* Atlantic–Little, Brown, 1952.
———. *And Promenade Home.* Atlantic–Little, Brown, 1958.
———. *To a Young Dancer.* Atlantic–Little, Brown, 1962.
———. *The Book of the Dance.* Golden Press, 1963.
———. *Lizzie Borden: A Dance of Death.* Atlantic–Little, Brown, 1968.
———. *Speak to Me, Dance with Me.* Atlantic–Little, Brown, 1973.
———. *Where the Wings Grow.* Random House, 1978.
———. *America Dances.* Obolensky/Macmillan, 1980.
———. *Reprieve.* Doubleday, 1981.
———. *Portrait Gallery.* Houghton Mifflin, 1990.
———. *Martha.* Random House, 1991.
de Mille, Anna. *Henry George, Citizen of the World.* University of North Carolina Press, 1950.
de Mille, William. *Hollywood Saga.* Dutton, 1939.
Denby, Edwin. *Dance Writings.* Knopf, 1986.
Edwards, Anne. *The DeMilles.* Abrams, 1988.
Eels, George. *The Life That Late He Led.* Putnam, 1967.

Engel, Lehman. *The American Musical Theatre.* Macmillan, 1967.
Ewen, David. *Richard Rodgers.* Henry Holt, 1957.
Fordin, Hugh. *Getting to Know Him, A Biography of Oscar Hammerstein II.* Ungar, 1977.
Fraser, John, and Eve Arnold. *Private View — Inside Baryshnikov's American Ballet Theatre.* Bantam, 1988.
Gottfried, Martin. *All His Jazz.* Bantam, 1990.
Green, Stanley. *The World of Musical Comedy.* Ziff-Davis, 1960.
———. *The Rodgers and Hammerstein Story.* John Day, 1963.
Gruen, John. *The Private World of Ballet.* Viking, 1975.
Guernsey, Otis L. ed. *Playwrights, Lyricists, Composers on Theater.* Dodd Mead, 1974.
Guthrie, Tyrone. *A Life in the Theater.* McGraw-Hill, 1959.
Hart, Kitty Carlisle. *Kitty, An Autobiography.* Doubleday, 1988.
Haskell, Arnold L. *Balletomania.* Simon and Schuster, 1934.
Herrmann, Dorothy. *S. J. Perelman, A Life.* Simon and Schuster, 1986.
Higashi, Sumiko. *Cecil B. De Mille, A Guide to References and Resources.* G. K. Hall, 1985.
Hurok, S. *Impresario.* Random House, 1946.
Karsavina, Tamara. *Theatre Street.* Knopf, 1986.
Jablonski, Edward. *Harold Arlen, Happy with the Blues.* Doubleday, 1961.
Jarman, Douglas. *Kurt Weill, An Illustrated Biography.* Indiana University Press, 1982.
Houseman, John. *Unfinished Business.* Applause Theatre Books, 1989.
Kazan, Elia. *Elia Kazan, A Life.* Knopf, 1988.
Koury, Phil A. *Yes, Mr. De Mille.* Putnam, 1959.
Langner, Lawrence. *The Magic Curtain.* Dutton, 1951.
Lees, Gene. *Inventing Champagne, The Worlds of Lerner and Loewe.* St. Martin's, 1990.
Lerner, Alan Jay. *The Musical Theatre, A Celebration.* McGraw-Hill, 1986.
Lewis, Robert. *Slings and Arrows.* Stein and Day, 1984.
Macgowan, Kenneth. *Behind the Screen.* Delacorte, 1965.
Mandel, Dorothy. *Uncommon Eloquence.* Arden Press (Denver), 1986.
Martin, John. *America Dancing.* (1936). Dance Horizons, 1968.
———. *John Martin's Book of the Dance.* Tudor Publishing, 1963.
Marx, Sam, and Jan Clayton. *Rodgers and Hart.* Putnam, 1976.

Mazo, Joseph H. *Dance Is a Contact Sport.* Saturday Review Press, 1974.
Minnelli, Vincente. *I Remember It Well.* Doubleday, 1974.
Mordden, Ethan. *The History of the American Musical Theater.* Grossman/Viking, 1976.
———. *Broadway Babies.* Oxford University Press, 1983.
———. *Rodgers and Hammerstein.* Abrams, 1992.
Newquist, Roy. *Showcase.* Morrow, 1966.
Osato, Sono. *Distant Dances.* Knopf, 1980.
Payne, Charles. *American Ballet Theatre.* Knopf, 1978.
Perlmutter, Donna. *Shadowplay: The Life of Antony Tudor.* Viking, 1991.
Rambert, Dame Marie. *Quicksilver.* St. Martin's, 1972.
Robinson, Harlow. *The Last Impresario: The Life, Times and Legacy of Sol Hurok.* Viking, 1994.
Rodgers, Richard. *Musical Stages: An Autobiography.* Random House, 1975.
Sanders, Ronald. *The Days Grow Short: The Life and Music of Kurt Weill.* Holt, Rinehart and Winston, 1980.
Schwartz, Charles. *Cole Porter, A Biography.* Dial Press, 1977.
Selznick, Irene Mayer. *Private View.* Knopf, 1983.
Siegel, Marcia D. *Watching the Dance Go By.* Houghton Mifflin, 1977.
———. *The Shapes of Change: Images of American Dance.* Houghton Mifflin, 1979.
Steinberg, Cobbett, ed. *The Dance Anthology.* New American Library, 1980.
Stevens, Franklin. *Dance As Life, A Season with American Ballet Theatre.* Harper & Row, 1976.
Taper, Bernard. *Balanchine.* Harper and Row, 1960.
Taylor, Deems. *Some Enchanted Evenings.* Harper, 1953.
Taylor, Theodore. *Jule Styne.* Random House, 1979.
Terry, Walter. *The Dance in America.* Harper and Row, 1971.
Toobin, Jerome. *Agitato: A Trek Through the Musical Jungle.* Viking, 1975.
van Praagh, Peggy, and Peter Brinson. *The Choreographic Art.* Knopf, 1963.
Vaughan, David. *Frederick Ashton and His Ballets.* Knopf, 1977.
Wallock, Leonard, ed. *New York: Culture Capital of the World.* Rizzoli, 1988.
Watson, Stephen. *Strange Bedfellows: The First American Advant-garde.* Abbeville Press, 1991.
Weeks, Edwin. *Writers and Friends.* Little, Brown, 1981.

Acknowledgments

In 1989, a mutual friend, Marguerite Courtney, introduced me to Agnes de Mille. She was then eighty-four years old and seriously incapacitated, but only from the neck down; her mental processes were acute, and the power of her personality was undimmed. She agreed to cooperate with this biography by providing introductions and access to people and material but stipulated, "I can't be involved. I'm sick of the subject of me, me, me." She then proceeded to become very much involved. She invited me to lunches, teas, and dinners, to her speaking engagements and to Merriewold, her lifelong country home. One of the world's great talkers, she never had a more attentive listener than I. As my interviews expanded to include old friends — and enemies — whom she had not seen for years, I was able to report back with communiqués and observations from those fronts.

I sat beside Agnes at performances of her ballets and, most helpful of all, at countless hours of rehearsals, where she was in her element, totally focused and clear. I witnessed her brilliance, rudeness, temper, and kindness, and a daily courage that was humbling to behold. Like the famous Escher etching of the hand that both draws and is drawn, I was simultaneously participant and observer. My task was to remain objective while empathizing enough to see Agnes and her worlds through her eyes, for it was her perceptions of events that motivated and propelled her.

This is a life, not a critical study; the interpretations are my own, and Agnes would certainly dispute some of them. Yet although she knew from my previous books that this would not be hagiography, she gave me unrestricted access to her papers and permission to quote from them (characteristically, she charged a token amount of money lest I take advantage of her, as she believed so many others had done), never asking for what I most dreaded and could not have granted: approval of what I would write. And by the time I had written the book, she was gone.

The kindness and generosity of a great many strangers, some of whom have become treasured friends, made this book a reality. Over a five-year period, eighty years' worth of dancers, choreographers, actors, singers, composers, lyricists, conductors, playwrights, directors, designers, producers, stage managers, technicians, editors, arts administrators, agents, lawyers, publicists, friends, relatives, and neighbors contributed details of Agnes's story. Some were cautious, some protective; some wanted to settle old scores, while others had faulty or selective memories. Most tried to tell the truth as they knew it, pleased to stir the embers of emotions engendered long ago by one of the most fascinating individuals they ever knew.

Thanks to those who responded to my queries in writing or over the telephone: Maurice Abravanel, Elaine Bauer, William Beresford, Dorothy Bird, Adelaide Bishop, Charles Blackwell, Randy Brooks, Andrea Cagan, Joseph Carew, Ted Chapin, James Clouser, Brenda Lewis Cooper, John Edsall, José Ferrer, Miriam Golden, William Hammerstein, Phillip Hanes, Melissa Hayden, Alan Hohvaness, Shirley Jones, Philip Langner, Vernon Lusby, N. Richard Nash, David Nillo, Gyula Pandi, Lianne Plane, Marc Platt, Janet Reed, Emile Renan, Kathleen Richardson, Jerome Robbins, Richard Rutherford, Mariane Oliphant Sanders, Mrs. C. B. Snyder, Arnold Spohr, Pat Stanley, Joe Stein, Joan Stone, Dr. Jokichi Takamine, Jennifer Taylor Tudhill, Lesley Ann Warren, Patricia Wilde, and Peter Zeissler.

I am grateful to the following people for meeting with me for formal interviews and informal chats: Joyce Aimée, Jeanne Armin, Barbara Perry Babbitt, Jean Bach, Charlie Baker, Mortimer Becker, Muriel Bentley, Harry Bernstein, Peggy Best, Charlotte Bidmead, Patricia Birch, Shibley Boyes, Gladys Celeste, Judith Chazin-Bennahum, George Church, George Collins of the Henry George Institute, Jean Dalrymple, Alexandra Danilova, Carmen de Lavallade, Andrea Downing, Martin Feinstein, Peggy Friedman, Jean Tachau Haas, Gisella Svetlik Hackett, Kitty Carlisle Hart, Jane Hermann, Louise Hickey, Geoffrey Holder, Celeste Holm, Martha Johnson, Brigitte Kelly, Bunty Kelly, Walter Kerr, Carol Kirkpatrick, John Kobal, Pearl Lang, Leo Lerman, Biff Liff, Maude

Lloyd, Annabelle Lyon, Isabel Mirrow, Joanna Morris, Gene Nelson, Bennett Oberstein, Donald Pippin, Jonathan Prude, Julius Robinson, Gene Ruggiero, Marlene Sanders, Elisabeth Schooling, Lotte Goslar Seehaus, Rosalind De Mille Shaffer, Vivian Smith, Jean Stapleton, James Starbuck, Roger Stevens, Britt Swenson, Mildred Traube, Frances Beranger Triest, Glory Van Scott, Julia Waddell, and Cecille and Herb Wasserman.

For participating in longer or multiple interviews, my thanks to Victor Barbee, Elmer Bernstein, Jay Blackstone, Ruthanna Boris, Bill Bradley, Merrill Brockway, David Brooks, Mary Burr, Philip Burton, John Butler, Zoe Caldwell, Jeannot Cerrone, Carol Channing, Jerome Chodorov, Denise Cogan, Honi Coles, David Cryer, Danny Daniels, Ferdinand Davis, Ed Dietz, Judith Donelan, Virginia Bosler Doris, Scott Douglas, Charles Dubin, David Evans, Eleanor Fairchild, John Fearnley, Eliot Feld, Anderson Ferrell, Horton Foote, Frederic Franklin, George Gaynes, John and Eda Gershgorn, William Goldenberg, Diana Gonzalez, Dr. George Gorham, Morton Gould, Mary Meyer Green, Paul Haakon, Loren Hightower, Jean Hoolouse, Tom Jones, Michael Kidd, Ruth Ann Koesun, Dania Krupska, Warren Leonard, Bella Lewitzky, Lillian Libman, Robert Lindgren, Dirk Lombard, Betty Low, Brian Macdonald, Daniel Mann, Enrique Martinez, Allyn Ann McLerie, Kate Medina, Michael Menzies, Kathleen Moore, Paul Moore, John Morris, Darrell Notara, Helena Obolensky, Paul Olson, Terry Orr, Carlheinz Ostertag, Genevieve Oswald, Robert Pagent, Gregory Peck, Dorothy Hill Pelet, Cassandra Phifer, Cecilia De Mille Presley, John Quinlan, Tommy Rall, Mavis Ray, Trude Rittman, Harlow Robinson, Mary Rodgers, Milton Rosenstock, Laurence Rosenthal, Bill Ross, Herbert Ross, Donald Saddler, Arnold Saint-Subber, Christine Sarry, Harvey Schmidt, Stanley Simmons, Tom Skelton, Oliver Smith, Rufus Smith, Elaine Steinbeck, Isaac Stern, Ilene Strickler, Jule Styne, Paul Sutherland, Inga Swenson, Tony Tanner, Evelyn Taylor, Harold Taylor, Glen Tetley, Ted Thurston, Kirsten Valbor, Steven Watson, Frank Westbrook, Edward Weston, Miles White, Robert Whitehead, Sallie Wilson, Dusty Worrall, and Fred Zinnemann.

I owe an enormous debt to those individuals who provided the use of precious photos and other memorabilia, or who offered meals, shelter, and much-needed encouragement when the task seemed overwhelming. They are Sybil Shearer, Joseph and Perry Anthony, Therese Horner, Gemze de Lappe, Bambi Linn, James Mitchell, Lee Freeson, James Jamieson, Louise Kerz, Gloria Wills Landes, Beryl Towbin, and Mary Hunter Wolf.

I also wish to thank Fredrica Friedman, for her editorial skill and enthusiasm; Barbara Palfy and Faith Hanson, whose meticulous fact-checking and sensitive copyediting spared me considerable embarrassment; Mike Hamilburg, agent and friend par excellence; and Amanda Vaill, Carl Rollyson, Will Bundy, Joni Miller, Patricia Doran, Frances Ring, Lesa Sawahata, Joanie Socola, Sam Berger, Flory Barnett, Jacquie Miller, and Pamela Marshall, all of whom know what they contributed, but not how indispensable they were. Also indispensable were the members of the Biographers Seminar at New York University and of its Los Angeles counterpart, known as the Biogroup; both are welcome support systems for anyone engaged in the peculiar profession of inhabiting other people's lives.

Finally, I am forever indebted to librarians and archivists at the Rambert Dance Company Archive in London, the Kurt Weill Foundation for Music in New York City, the Smith College Archives in Northampton, Massachusetts, and, above all, the Dance Collection at the New York Public Library for the Performing Arts. The Dance Collection is a researcher's heaven, thanks in large part to its curator, Madeleine M. Nichols, and her staff (especially Rita Waldron, who facilitated the daunting process of picture research); their knowledge and patience transcend any conceivable job description. One of the library's pages — a tall, courteous, self-possessed African-American in his early twenties — surprised me one day by asking, after unloading an umpteenth stack of files on the table in front of me, "Are you going to put my name in your book?" I said, "Would you like me to?" He shrugged. "It would be nice to show my kids." Not long after that, he was dead, a victim of violence on the street. His name was Derrick Damon.

In *Biography: The Craft and the Calling,* Agnes's friend Catherine Drinker Bowen wrote an appropriate coda for this book. Published in 1968, its sentiments are applicable in all but gender, which I have changed accordingly:

> To spend three years or five with a truly great woman, reading what she said and wrote, observing her as she errs, stumbles, falls and rises again; to watch her talent grow if she is an artist . . . this cannot but seize upon a writer, one might almost say transform her. When the book is done the author returns to the outer world, but actually she will not be the same again. . . . One has climbed a hill, looked out and over, and the valley of one's own condition will be forever greener.

Venice, Calif.
August 1995